Freelance travel writer **David Abram** was born and brought up in south Wales and the Mendip Hills of Somerset. His first foray into the Corsican mountains came in 1986, during the sabbatical year of a French degree, when he stumbled upon some waymarks and followed them blindly for two days until wild pigs polished off his supplies. Since then, as an anthropologist and author of the *Rough Guide to India*, he's walked extensively in the Himalayas, Europe and North America but still regards Corsica as a benchmark trekking destination.

Regular opportunities to indulge his passion for the island's food and mountains are provided by annual updating trips for the *Rough Guide to Corsica*, which he co-authored. David lives and works in Bristol.

Trekking in Corsica
First edition: 2002

Publisher
Trailblazer Publications
The Old Manse, Tower Rd, Hindhead, Surrey, GU26 6SU, UK
Fax (+44) 01428-607571
info@trailblazer-guides.com
www.trailblazer-guides.com

British Library Cataloguing in Publication Data
A catalogue record for this book is available from the British Library

ISBN 1-873756-63-1

Editor: John King
Series editor: Patricia Major
Layout: Anna Jacomb-Hood and Bryn Thomas
Maps: Jane Thomas (trail maps); Nick Hill (town plans and illustrations on p68 & p141)
Index: Jane Thomas

Warning: mountain walking can be dangerous
Please read the notes on when to go (p24) and on mountain safety (pp41-3). Every effort has been made by the author and publisher to ensure that the information contained herein is as accurate and up to date as possible. However, they are unable to accept responsibility for any inconvenience, loss or injury sustained by anyone as a result of the advice and information given in this guide.

Printed on chlorine-free paper from farmed forests by
Technographic Design & Print (☎ 01206-303323) Colchester, Essex, UK

TREKKING IN CORSICA

DAVID ABRAM

TRAILBLAZER PUBLICATIONS

Acknowledgements

Je voudrais remercier tout d'abord ceux qui m'ont soutenu et aidé au cours de ma grande marche entre mai et juillet 2001, notamment: Phillipe Gabrielli (proprieter du magasin Omnisports, à Corte); Christophe le Bûcheron, à Soccia; Paul Ceccaldi et Antoine Nesa, à Marignana; et Jean, patron du ferme-auberge L'Albadu, Corte. Un grand merci aussi aux gardiens des refuges PNRC, pour leurs renseignements et leur hospitalité; et enfin à mes compagnons de marche sur le GR – l'équipe Dijonais (où que vous soyez) et Ror Por.

In the UK, thanks to the Trailblazer team: John King for editing and generally tidying up the book; Jane Thomas for drawing so many route maps so beautifully and for the index; Nick Hill for the town plans, colour maps and bird illustrations, Anna Jacomb-Hood for keying in all the corrections and for layout; and last but by no means least, Bryn Thomas, who proposed this project in the first place and accepted its postponement with great generosity.

Thank you also to Tim Glasby for additional photos and climbing tips; Robert Ackroyd for helping to identify the flowers; and to VSJM for putting up with yet another a long absence from home (and the interminable yarns, slide shows and writing-induced grumpiness that ensued on my return).

A request

The author and publisher have tried to ensure that this guide is as accurate and up to date as possible. Nevertheless things change. If you notice any changes or omissions that should be included in the next edition of this book, please write to David Abram at Trailblazer (address on p2) or email him at david.abram@trailblazer-guides.com. A free copy of the next edition will be sent to persons making a significant contribution.

Updated information will shortly be available on the Internet at
www.trailblazer-guides.com

Cover photo: South face of Capu Ladroncellu, GR20

CONTENTS

INTRODUCTION

My journey over the mountains was very entertaining. I past (sic) *some immense ridges and vast woods. I was in great health and spirits, and fully able to enter into the ideas of the brave rude men whom I found in all quarters.*

James Boswell, *The Journal of a Tour to Corsica*, 1765

Mer et montagne

'Une montagne dans la mer' is how Corsica is often described, but 'a *range* of mountains in the sea' would be a more accurate tag. Rising to 2706m (8876ft) at its highest point (more than double the height of Ben Nevis) the island's interior comprises a vast jumble of snow-streaked peaks, wind-scoured granite ridges and deep valleys reminiscent of continental Europe at its most rugged. Imagine such a wilderness surrounded by a cobalt-blue sea and a string of shell-sand beaches, with views that on clear days extend to the distant Alps and Tuscany, and you'll understand why many regard Corsica's landscapes to be quite simply the most astounding in all the Mediterranean.

For trekkers, this trademark juxtaposition of 'mer et montagne' presents a mouthwatering prospect. Preserved by a century and a half of depopulation, the island – despite the annual deluge of 1.75 million visitors that streams across it – has largely escaped the kind of development that has blighted much of the Med. The rivers that crash through Corsica's old-growth pine, chestnut and holm oak woods remain crystal clear, the forests teeming with wild boar, and whole chunks of the shore still blissfully roadless. It's no exaggeration to say that in Corsica you can walk for weeks without ever encountering a truck or a highway. Moreover, even the most remote nooks and crannies may be reached along waymarked trails. Exploiting the network of ancient transhumant and mule paths that formerly connected valley systems, the routes, cleared and marked by the Parc Naturel Régional Corse (PNRC), are ingeniously conceived and a joy to follow from start to finish, taking in the very best of Corsica's diverse topography.

GR20 and other walking routes

Justifiably the most famous among the waymarked itineraries is the mighty GR20. Keeping close to the line of the watershed, the route, often claimed to be the toughest of its kind in Europe, wriggles via a series of dramatic ascents and descents through the heart of the Corsican mountains. Around 17,000 trekkers attempt it each summer, carrying full packs of gear and provisions, sleeping in or bivouacking near isolated mountain huts and washing in ice-cold stream water. The pay-off for such privations is a non-stop parade of amazing scenery encompassing ice-encrusted ridges, glacial lakes, huge moraines and grassy stream banks grazed by herds of wild horses. You'd also be unlucky not to catch sight of Europe's most elusive mammal, the *mouflon*, a rare mountain sheep that survives only on the high ridges of Corsica and neighbouring Sardinia.

At lower altitudes, a choice of other waymarked routes thread more sedate but no less rewarding paths across the island. Dotted with beautiful red-tiled stone villages, they wind through a rural hinterland little changed since medieval times. Almost every night halt is punctuated by a *gîte d'étape* or inexpensive hotel where you can bunk down in clean sheets and tuck into a carefully prepared four-course meal of local specialities. Corsicans are deservedly proud of their simple but delicious cuisine – based on fresh, home-grown produce, honey, wild herbs and chestnuts – and the restaurants of the interior are the best places to sample it. Every settlement, no matter how small, also boasts at least one café, on whose plane-shaded terrace you can kick-start the day with a coffee-and-croissant breakfast.

The island's uncompromising gradients may make for some strenuous trekking, but this is one place in the world where your trip into the hills really will feel like a holiday – not least of all because of the weather, which from May until October remains dependably warm, dry and sunny. And if all this weren't incentive enough, all the routes featured in Parts 4-8 finish within easy reach of the coast, ensuring you'll be able to rest up after your trek on some of the most idyllic beaches in the world.

Using the guide

The aim of this book is to help you get the most out of your trekking trip: to make the planning easier, avoid wasting time and energy once you're on the trail and interpret the country you'll walk through. It's split into four main sections. The first tells you everything you'll need to know before leaving home. Part 2 introduces Corsica itself, setting out background on the island's history, culture, society and wildlife, as well as giving advice on more down-to-earth matters such as making phone calls and booking accommodation. Featured in the third section are practical accounts of Corsica's main towns, at least one of which you're bound to have to pass through en route to or from the hills.

Parts 4-8 go on to describe the trekking routes themselves. The five we've chosen cover the most distinctive corners of the Corsican mountains, along with an especially beautiful stretch of coast in the far south. Each of the route descriptions begins with a general introduction outlining the trek's relative merits and challenges. From then on the account is broken down into stages, or *étapes*, sketching out the terrain you'll cross on any given day and giving practical information you might need along the way, notably where to eat, sleep and find water, and how to reach other parts of the island by public transport.

Trail maps Our sketch maps are designed to be used in conjunction with the large-scale topographical maps published by IGN (the Institut Géographique National) – not to replace them. However, they include detail you won't find on other maps, such as **walking times**, **accommodation (marked as a black square)**, **view points**, **water sources** and **complicated junctions**. Everywhere to stay within easy reach of the route is also marked, be it a hotel or un-staffed hut. Further details on each place can be found in the text.

Up or down? The trail is shown as a dotted line. Many of the trails are up or down. One arrow indicates a steep slope; two arrows indicate a very steep slope. Note that the arrow points towards the higher part of the trail. If, for example, you were walking from A (at 900m) to B (at 1100m) and the trail between the two were short and very steep, it would be shown thus: A - - - **>>** - - - B.

Routes and walking times The routes are described in the opposite directions to those outlined in the French Topoguides. This means you should encounter fewer people travelling the same way as you. The exception is the GR20, which is outlined according to the conventional north–south itinerary; trekking in this direction you'll face the more rugged and scenic north sides of the mountains instead of the sun-bleached southern flanks. There's no reason why you can't follow any of the routes in the opposite directions to the ones we describe but, if you do, bear in mind that the times given on the borders of the maps will not be representative. None of the stage timings listed in the guide includes rests, so you'll need to **add on another 20–30 per cent for breaks** over the course of any *étape*. Inevitably, you may find yourself covering distances more quickly or slowly than we did, but after a few days you'll gauge how different your pace is and be able to adjust the estimates accordingly.

The Moor's Head

Flown everywhere from refuge rooftops on the GR20 to the masts of fishing boats in Bastia harbour, Corsica's quirky flag features an emblem whose emotive resonance is as strong as its roots are obscure. The **Tête de Maure**, or 'Moor's Head' – a profile of a black boy sporting a white bandanna – is known to have been imported to the island by the kings of Aragon in the 13th century. The image, which in Spanish heraldry appears with the head scarf covering the eyes, probably symbolized the crusades against the North African occupiers of the Iberian peninsula. But quite why 'King' Theodore von Neuhof and, later, Pascal Paoli adopted it as an icon of Corsican independence is a subject of much speculation.

One theory is that the Moor's Head harks back to an old legend in which a local peasant youth travelled to Granada to liberate his lover from the clutches of the king of Andalucia after she'd been abducted from her village by pirates. Having somehow sprung her from slavery, he returned to the island with her, hotly pursued by a Moorish army led by General Mansour bin Ismail. Wreaking havoc on the journey between Porto and Aléria, the invaders were eventually met and routed by a Corsican force who promptly impaled the defeated general's head on a pike and paraded it in triumph around the island – whence, some maintain, the source 'Tête de Maure' image.

Whatever the emblem's origins, it has over the past three decades gained considerable potency as a symbol of nationalist defiance and identity. Hung as a backdrop at paramilitary press conferences, you'll see it outside municipal buildings, on hunting knives and wherever a French Tricouleur is raised.

PART 1: PLANNING YOUR TREK

This section is designed to help you plan your trek: to make travel arrangements, calculate how much the trip will cost, and decide when to go, which route to follow and what to take with you. It also sets out basic advice on mountain safety and what to do in emergencies.

Of course how you approach a trekking trip is ultimately a matter of personal choice and there's no replacement for hard-won experience in the hills. However, forewarned is forearmed, and time spent reading up and planning ahead will pay dividends. Decisions that may seem trivial from the comfort of your armchair at home – such as what kind of sleeping bag to take or whether you'll be staying in the village *gîte*, hotel or refuge – can take on great significance when you're miles from anywhere.

Independently or with a group?

Corsica's network of waymarked trails, *gîtes d'étape* and staffed refuges provides a trekking infrastructure that's second to none. With the help of this book, the use of a phone or Internet connection and a smattering of French it's perfectly possible to organize your entire trip yourself, from purchasing your plane ticket to reserving a dorm bed in a remote village.

If, on the other hand, time is tighter than your budget, you might prefer someone else to make all the arrangements on your behalf. **Organized tours** come in a variety of forms. Larger operators tend to offer a choice between **group tours**, where you join a guided party for the duration of the trip, and **self-guided itineraries**, where you walk at your own pace along a selected route using a written guide. In both cases transport, accommodation, meals and luggage transfer are standard. All you have to do is pay the bill, pack the equipment on the company's recommended gear list, walk and eat the hot meals dished up on your arrival at the end of each *étape*.

Apart from sparing you a lot of hassle, the best thing about being pampered on an organized tour is that it allows you to walk unencumbered by a heavy pack. This can make a huge difference to your overall experience of the trail, especially the GR20 where it may allow you to attain altitudes otherwise beyond your fitness level. However, the luxury of *sac allegé* (literally 'lightened bag') is an expensive one: on the GR your kit will have to be carried by jeep and mule up to the refuges, which explains why the cost of GR20 tours are higher than low-level treks. The other drawback with organized holidays, of course, is that you're tied to a fixed itinerary with little scope for digression, which can be frustrating. Depending on the people in your party, the group atmosphere can also get claustrophobic.

What you end up paying for your trek depends on a wide range of factors: the quality of the food and accommodation, the size of the group, duration of the walk, qualifications of the guide, and the time of year. The only way to ensure a company's product is right for you is to read through its brochure carefully. Make comparisons between as many operators as you can (see p13 for a list of all those currently working in Corsica) and scrutinize the itinerary breakdowns and small print.

TREKKING AGENCIES

The prices quoted by agencies for organized treks do not usually cover the flight, although larger operators are only to happy to arrange air tickets for you (slapping on a hefty mark-up in the process). Nor will the listed price include visa fees, insurance, the cost of drinks, phone calls or tips. Solo travellers should also watch out for so-called **single-person supplements**; these apply mostly to tours involving stays in hotels and can add as much as 25% on to the cost of your holiday.

In the UK and Ireland

- **Exodus** (☎ 020-8675 5550, 🖹 020-8673 0779, 💻 www.exodus.co.uk) , 9 Weir Road, London SW12 0LT. Eight-day trips offering guided day-walks from comfortable two-star hotels for £570; or a varied two-week itinerary that cherry-picks the highlights of the Mare a Mare Nord and GR20 for £800 (not including flights). The latter route is particularly well thought-out but involves some nights of rough-and-ready accommodation in refuges and under canvas.
- **Explore Worldwide** (☎ 01252-760000, 🖹 01252-760001, 💻 www.explore.co.uk), 1 Frederick St, Aldershot, Hants GU11 1LQ. Ota to Corte in eight days via the Niolu Valley, essentially along the Mare a Mare Nord, using various kinds of accommodation and with groups of 6-14 people costs from £715.
- **HF Holidays** (☎ 020-8905 9556, 💻 www.hfholidays.co.uk), Imperial House, Edgware Rd, London NW9 5AL. HF offers an eight-day package of round-trip hikes out of Porto, or a guided trek down the Tra Mare e Monti between Col de la Palmarella and Cargèse for £750/£550 with/without flight.
- **Sherpa Expeditions** (☎ 020-8577 2717, 🖹 020-8572 9788, 💻 www.sherpa-walking-holidays.co.uk), 131a Heston Rd, Hounslow TW5 0RF. Established trekking operator offering the Mare a Mare Nord from Sermano (near Corte) to Porto in eight days for £730 (self-guided), or the GR20 (accompanied) as far as Bavella for £780. Be warned, however, that you'll have to carry your gear, tent and a share of the group provisions for most of the route as Sherpa doesn't use local mule contractors, which makes this a less enticing deal than those offered by the Corsican competition (see opposite).
- **Colette Pearson Travel** (☎ 01-677 1029, 🖹 01-677 1390, 💻 cptravel@indigo.ei), 64 South William Street, Dublin 2. Ireland-based agents for Exodus (see above).

• **Maxwells Travel** (☎ 01-677 9479, 🖹 01-679 3948), D'Olier Chambers, 1 Hawkins St, Dublin 2. Agents for Explore Worldwide (see above).

In Corsica

• **A Muntagnola Quenza** (☎ 04.95.78.65.19, 🖳 www.a-muntagnola.com), 20122 Quenza, Haute-Corse. One-week self-guided trips out of Bavella and Propriano into the Alta Rocca region, combining sections of the GR20 and Mare a Mare Sud for around 500€. Run by one of Corsica's few fully-qualified high-mountain guides, Jean-Paul Quilici.

• **Camina Mondi** (☎ 04.95.61.77.36, 🖹 04.95.61.77.36, 🖳 www.caminamondi.com), Place de l'Église, 20220 Pigna, Haute-Corse. Nine treks of different lengths and levels, focussing on the north-west of the island. All the guides are local polyphony celebrities, so you get Corsican singing recitals each evening (check out their website for RealAudio samples). Prices from 442€ to 675€.

• **Compagnie des Guides et Accompagnateurs de Montagne** (☎ 04.95.48.05.22, 🖹 04.95.48.08.80), 20224 Calacuccia, Niolu, Haute-Corse. Worth contacting if you wish to book a mountain guide independently.

• **Couleur Corse** (☎ 04.95.10.52.83, 🖹 04.95.22.24.30, 🖳 www.couleur-corse.com), 7 Domaine de Loretto, 20000 Ajaccio, Corse-du-Sud. Week-long self-guided walks in the Alta Rocca (530€) or fully supported 14-day GR20 tours (1060€).

• **Objectif Nature** (☎ 04.95.32.54.54, 🖹 04.95.32.57.58, 🖳 www.ifrance.com/obj-nature/), 3 rue Notre Dame de Lourdes, 20200 Bastia. Seven days of the GR20 and various Mare a Mare options for around 500€.

• **Montagne Corse en Liberté** (☎ 04.95.20.53.14, 🖹 33.04.95.20.90.60, 🖳 www.montagne-corse.com), Le Rond Point, 2 ave de la Grande Armée, 20000 Ajaccio, Corse. Corsica's largest trekking operator has five options for the GR20 alone, ranging from seven-day self-guided trips of the north, central and southern sections to fully supported sac allegé tours of the entire route. With their lower-level walks you can also opt to be accompanied or left *en liberté*. Prices from 500€ to 1100€.

• **Vallecime** (☎ 04.95.48.69.33, 🖹 04.95.48.69.36, 🖳 www.vallecime.com), Poggio, 20212 Sermano, Corse. Once again, a choice of GR20 options and various transverse routes led by experienced mountaineers from the Niolu Valley. One of them, Jean-François Luciani, holds the speed record for the GR20 (37 hours) and does a special fell-running tour for the absurdly fit. Wherever possible they use local B&B accommodation and family restaurants rather than hotels, and bivouac in working *bergeries*. English spoken.

In Continental Europe

• **Austria Charisma** (☎ 01-585 3680, 🖹 01-585 3680 60, 🖳 abyss@tauchreisen.at), Hofmuhgasse 20, A-1060 Vienna. Agents for Exodus (see p12).

• **Belgium Boundless Adventures** (☎ 02-426 40 30, 🖹 02-426 03 60, 🖳 boundless.adventures@joker.be),Verdilaan 23/25, 1083 Brussels-Ganshoren. Agents for Exodus (see p12).

• **Denmark** **Topas** (☎ 33-116922, 🖹 33-116988, 💻 info@topas.dk), Frederiksborggade 50, 1360 Copenhagen. Agents for Exodus (see p12).
Inter-Travel (☎ 33-150077, 🖹 33-156018, 💻 inter-travel@inter-travel.dk), Frederiksholms Kanal 2, Copenhagen K, DK 1220. Agents for Explore Worldwide (see p12).

• **France** **Trekking in the Alps** (☎ 04.50.54.62.09, 🖹 04.50.54.63.29, 💻 www.trekkinginthealps.com), Chemin des Biolles, Vallorcine 74660, France. Alps-based outfit run by a British woman who offers two annual six- or seven-day trips to Corsica, both out of Calvi, costing 950€ (without flights).

• **Germany** **Explorer Fernreisen** (☎ 0211-99 49 02, 🖹 0211-38 22 88, 💻 marketing@explorer-fernreisen.com), Huttenstrasse 17, 40215 Dusseldorf. Agents for Exodus (see p12).

• **Netherlands** **SNP Reiswinkel** (☎ 024-3277000, 🖹 024-3277099, 💻 www.snp.nl), Bijleveldsingel 26, 6512 AT Nijmegen, Postbus 1270, 6501 BG Nijmegen. Agents for Exodus (see p12).
Adventure World (☎ 023-5382 954, 🖹 ☎ 023-5384 744, 💻 atc@euronet.nl), Muiderslotweg 112, Haarlem, 2026 AS. Agents for Explore Worldwide (see p12).

In the USA and Canada

• **Adventure Center** (☎ 1-800-228-8747, 💻 www.adventurecenter.com), 1311 63rd Street, Suite 200, Emeryville, CA 94608. Agents for Explore Worldwide (see p12).
• **Butterfield & Robinson** (☎ 1-800-678-1147, 💻 www.butterfield.com), 70 Bond Street, Toronto, Ontario M5B 1X3. The definitive upscale tour of Corsica combining selected treks with trips to the island's top sights, meals in Michelin-starred restaurants and nights in landmark hotels. Eight days for the princely sum of C$4200 (not including flights).
• **G.A.P Adventures** (☎ 1-800-465-5600, 🖹 416-260-1888, 💻 adventure@gap.ca), 19 Duncan Street, Suite 401, Toronto, Ontario M5H 3H1. Agents for Exodus (see p12).
• **Trek Holidays** (toll-free in Canada ☎ 1-888-456-3522, ☎ 780-439-9118, 🖹 780-433-1283, 💻 adventures@trekholidays.com), 8412 109th Street Edmonton TGG 1E2. Agents for Explore Worldwide (see p12).
• **World Expeditions** (☎ 1-800-567-2216, ☎ 613-241-4189, 💻 www.worldexpeditions.com, 78 George Street, Ottawa, Ontario K1N 5W1), George Street, Ottawa. Seven/eight-day self-guided treks around the Niolu and Spelunca valleys and Alta Rocca region in the far south from around C$600. Group tours include an eight-day Tra Mare e Monti itinerary from C$900 and the full GR20 for C$1620 (not including flights).

In Australasia

• **Adventure World** (☎ 09-524 5118, 🖹 09-520 6629, 💻 discover@adventure-world.co.nz), 101 Great South Road, PO Box 74008, Remeura, Auckland. Agents for Explore Worldwide (see p12).

• **Peregrine Adventures** (☎ 1300-854 444 for an agent in your state, or ☎ 03-9663 8611, 📠 03-9663 8618, 💻 sales@peregrine.net.au), 258 Lonsdale Street, Melbourne, Victoria 3000. Agents for Exodus (see p12).

Getting to Corsica

FROM THE UK AND IRELAND

Since the advent of charter and low-cost flights, the cheapest and fastest way to get to Corsica from the UK has been by air. Overland travel, involving two ferry crossings and a long rail or road journey via Paris, is a commendable option only for those wishing to take their time and see a bit of France en route.

By plane

Corsica is about 2½hrs flying time away from Britain, depending on which airport you use. The only direct flights are with **charter** airlines; services operate from around early April until mid-October (usually on Sundays). Most of their seats tend to be block-booked by package-holiday operators but you can often pick up unsold tickets through a travel agent, by contacting an operator direct, or – most conveniently of all – by telephoning Holiday Options (see box p16) which consolidates fares on all charter flights to the island. Tickets cost from around £250 in peak season down to £100 for last-minute deals. Basically, the later you leave booking a charter seat the cheaper it is likely to be, although this obviously means you might end up losing out on a ticket altogether. Charters fly out of regional airports (Manchester, Birmingham and Edinburgh) as well as London (Gatwick, Heathrow and Stansted).

To get to Corsica on a **scheduled flight** from the UK always involves at least one change of plane, either at Paris, Lyon or one of the ports on the Côte

Which airport in Corsica?

Corsica boasts four international airports and you can fly to any of them from the UK. The fare and point of departure will probably be your main priorities initially but it's also worth bearing in mind which trek you plan to do as this could also affect your choice of gateway.

For anyone intending to tackle the GR20, **Calvi** is the most convenient option; Calvi Sainte-Catherine airport lies so close to the trailhead at Calenzana that with a well-timed flight you can arrive and have the first étape under your belt by nightfall. Calvi is well connected to both Ajaccio and Bastia by rail but the journey from either takes half a day.

For the other treks covered in this book **Ajaccio** would have to be your first choice of arrival point. Full details of how to get from there to trailheads appear on pp95-6. Arrive at **Bastia-Poretta** or **Figari** airport (in the far south) and you'll either have a long bus or train ride ahead of you, or the choice of following your trek in the reverse direction from that described in this book.

TRAVELLING INDEPENDENTLY FROM UK AND IRELAND

The following summary should prove useful if you intend to make your own travel arrangements. Of all the contacts listed, Holiday Options is probably the single most useful for anyone wishing to fly to Corsica by charter. Travelling on a scheduled airline such as Air France or British Airways, you're invariably better off letting a travel agent make the booking.

Charter agents and tour companies in the UK

With the exception of Holiday Options, which specializes in 'flight-only' tickets to Corsica, the following are package tour companies and sell flight-only tickets only when they have a surplus. Few advertise the fact, however, and you'll have to ring each one close to your intended date of departure to dig up the best bargains.

- **Corsican Affair** (☎ 020-7385 8438), George House, 6-7 Humbolt Rd, London W6.
- **Corsican Places** (☎ 01424-460046, 🖳 www.corsica.co.uk), 16 Grand Parade, St Leonards on Sea, East Sussex TN37.
- **Holiday Options** (☎ 01444-244411, 🖳 www.holidayoptions.co.uk), Martlet Heights, 49 The Martlet, Burgess Hill, West Sussex RH15 9NJ.
- **Simply Corsica** (☎ 020-8995 9323), Kings House, Wood St, Kingston-upon-Thames, Surrey KT1 1SG.
- **VFB Holidays** (☎ 01242-240310), Normandy House, High St, Cheltenham, Glos GL50 3FB.
- **Voyages Ilena** (☎ 020-7924 4440, 📠 020-7924 4441), 7 Old Garden House, The Lanterns, Bridge Lane, London SW11.

Airlines in the UK and Ireland

- **Aer Lingus** (☎ 01-886 8888 or ☎ 021-432 7155, 🖳 www.aerlingus.ie) Daily flights to Paris from Dublin and Cork.
- **Air France** (☎ 0845 084 5111, 🖳 www.airfrance.fr) The widest choice of routes with the fastest connections through Nice and Marseille.
- **British Airways** (☎ 0345 222111, 🖳 www.british-airways.com) Indirect flights via Paris, Marseille or Nice from a range of regional airports in the UK, with the last leg on Air Littoral.
- **British Midland** (☎ 01332-854274; www.britishmidland.co.uk) Non-stop flights to Nice.
- **Buzz** (☎ 0870 240 7070, 🖳 www.buzzaway.com) Cheap single or return flights to Marseille at civilized times.
- **easyJet** (☎ 0870 600 0000, 🖳 www.easyjet.com) Bargain fares to Nice from Gatwick, Luton and Liverpool.
- **Go** (☎ 0870 607 6543 or ☎ 01279-666388, 🖳 www.goairways.co.uk) Nice from London Stansted or Bristol from £65 return.
- **Ryanair** (☎ 0870 156 9569, 🖳 www.ryanair.com) Daily flights to Genoa from Stansted from £39 return, and rock bottom fares from the Republic of Ireland to the UK.

d'Azur. With Air France you can fly to any of Corsica's four civilian airports from several airports in Britain, including London Heathrow, but fares tend to be top whack (from £200 to £400 return). Journey times are also considerably greater than with charter carriers as you have to wait for at least 2½ hours before picking up your connecting flight (which may even leave from a different airport if you fly through Paris). The best way to unravel the various permutations

Travel agents in mainland France

Any of the following can book you onto flights to Corsica from the Côte d'Azur, although they may ask you to fax a photocopy of your credit or debit card before going ahead with any transaction. Country code for France is +33.

- **Go Voyages** (☎ 01.53.40.44.29)
- **Nice Voyages** (☎ 04.93.13.36.86)
- **Nouvelles Frontières** (☎ 08.25.00.08.25)
- **Tropical Voyages** (☎ 04.93.55.02.02)
- **Connect Voyages** (☎ 01.42.44.14.00)

Airlines in mainland France

- **Air France** (☎ 08.20.82.08.20, www.airfrance.fr) Return fares to Corsica start at around £70 from Nice, or £120 from Paris.
- **Air Liberté** (☎ 08.03.80 .58.05, www.air-liberte.fr) Nice–Ajaccio from £120 return, or slightly more from Marseille.
- **Air Littoral** (☎ 08.03.83.48.34, www.air-littoral.fr) Flights to Bastia, Calvi and Ajaccio from both Marseille and Nice, from £120 return.
- **Compagnie Corse Mediterranée** (☎ 04.95.29.05.00, www.ccm-airlines.com) Three to six flights daily from Nice and Marseille to Ajaccio and Bastia for £90–£150 return depending on the season.

of flying schedules is to ask a travel agent. They'll take your dates of travel and work out the best options and fares.

Your third option, and potentially the cheapest if not the most convenient, is to travel to Marseille or Nice with one of the **low-cost airlines** (Buzz, Go or easyJet) and pick up onward transport from there. easyJet's fares to Nice (from Gatwick, Luton or Liverpool) can be as low as £20 one-way but may involve departing or arriving at an awkward time of day. Go also flies to Nice (from Bristol and Stansted) from £65 and Buzz has daily flights from Stansted to Marseille from around £60 return. To find the cheapest deals you have to spend time trawling these airlines' websites (which advertise cheaper tickets than you'll be offered over the phone); it helps if you can be flexible with your travel dates.

How much money you save in the long run, however, will depend primarily on the cost of your **onward ticket from the Côte d'Azur** to Corsica. Air France and three smaller domestic airlines (Air Littoral, Compagnie Corse Mediterranée and Air Liberté) fly these routes but their lowest fares start at around £80 return. Add this to the cost of your other ticket and it's unlikely you'll end up with a cheaper deal than that offered by the charter agents. Another problem is that domestic French flights are relatively difficult to book from the UK, especially if you travel to France with one of the British low-cost airlines, none of which has an agreement with its counterparts in Nice and Marseille. This means you have to purchase your tickets over the Internet, or by telephone from an agent in France (see box above); an exception is Air France, which has offices in the UK. When booking your flight, let the agent know if you're travelling as part of a couple or group as you may be entitled to a reduction.

From Ireland you can fly with Aer Lingus from Cork or Dublin to Paris from 102€, and from there pick up a connection to Corsica with Air France. The cheapest option, though, would be to book a cheap Ryanair flight to London, Manchester or Birmingham and hook up with a charter.

Finally, the **rock-bottom option** is to buy one of easyJet's bargain tickets to Nice or a Ryanair flight to Genoa and catch the ferry to Corsica (which in theory is possible for as little as £100 return all-in). However, to do this you'd have to be sure that a boat was leaving from the same city on the same day as you arrive (far from a certainty). Otherwise you could well find yourself having to blow your net savings on a hotel room or a train ticket to whichever port the next scheduled ferry sails from. Bear in mind, too, the advice below on reserving tickets as they can be in short supply from late May onwards. Timetables are posted on the ferry company websites listed in the box opposite; but be warned: locating ferries that link up with cheap flights bought on the Internet can require the patience and mental dexterity of a brain surgeon. You're better off giving their London agents a ring.

By train and ferry

With the wealth of cheap flights to Corsica on offer these days you'd need a good reason *not* to want to fly there. Travelling by land and sea takes considerably longer (more than ten times longer even if you time your connections well) and rarely saves you money. It is, however, a more environmentally-friendly way to reach the island and can be a lot of fun if you're not in a hurry.

Thanks to the Channel Tunnel, the first leg of the journey from London (Waterloo) to Paris can now be covered quickly and usually painlessly on **Eurostar** trains. Tickets for the three-hour trip cost as little as £79 return when you book at least 14 days in advance. The alternative, **Hoverspeed**'s rail link from Waterloo via the channel ports, takes seven hours longer and shaves a mere £20 off the Eurostar fare.

From Paris **SNCF**, the swish French national rail network, offers a choice of services down to the Côte d'Azur. The one to go for is the flagship **TGV** (train à grande vitesse) **Mediterranée**, which zips to Marseille in 3 hours 50 minutes. The cheapest fare is £42 and has to be booked at least two weeks in advance. The regular service, which takes 10½hrs to cover the route, costs the same so it's worth booking ahead to secure a seat on the TGV. Nice lies three hours beyond Marseille by rail but you might want to travel the extra so as to pick up the super-fast NGV hydrofoil to Corsica (which doesn't operate out of Marseille), thereby saving nine hours or more on the crossing time (see p19).

By taking Eurostar and the TGV, it's possible to reach Nice in only 10 hours from London (excluding the hour or so you'll need to change stations in Paris) for around £120. There is, however, a catch: to be eligible you have to book within 65 days of the date of your *return* journey. Nor are **rail passes** valid with these rock-bottom fares. But if you're travelling on another kind of rail ticket it may be worth investing in a pass if you're under 26 or over 60.

In the UK the best **booking agency** and source of advice on passes for all French rail services, including Eurostar, is the SNCF subsidiary **Rail Europe**

(☎ 0870 584 8848, 💻 www.raileurope.co.uk), at 179 Piccadilly, London W1. You can also make reservations directly with SNCF through their website (💻 www.sncf.com). Phone Eurostar (☎ 0870 518 6186), or go to 💻 www.eurostar.com for on-line booking and timetable information.

Ferries to Corsica Ferries run year-round from Marseille and Nice to Corsica, and from Toulon between April and September. You can also get to the island via Genoa during the summer (June–Sept). However, finding out exactly which port the various companies sail to, and on what days, can be extremely difficult via the Internet unless you already know roughly which day and from which port you intend to travel. Thankfully each of the ferry companies has an agent in the UK who can fathom the complexities of the various schedules on your behalf (see box below).

The fastest route is **via Nice**, from where **NGV** (navire à grande vitesse) speedboats sail to Calvi, Ile Rousse, Bastia and Ajaccio. This service only takes around 3½hrs as against 6–12 hours on the slow ferry and is no more expensive. It runs more or less daily from Nice (but not from Marseille or Toulon, which are only served by slow boats). Fares for foot passengers range from £20 to £30 one-way depending on the time of year; you also have to pay a £6.50 harbour tax on top of the ticket price for each leg of the journey.

Crossings **from Genoa** in Italy cost considerably less (around £20) but are also less frequent with two to four departures per week to Bastia in the summer.

Ferries from France and Italy to Corsica

Listed below are the ferry options from France and Italy to Corsica. For more precise timetable information go to the ferry companies' websites or contact their agents by phone. Tickets can be purchased online through ferry companies' websites or, for identical prices, through their agents (see below).

Corsica Ferries
From Nice to Bastia and Ile Rousse
www.corsicaferries.com
In Nice: ☎ 04.92.00.43.76
In Corsica: ☎ 04.95.32.95.95
In the UK: c/o Via Mare (☎ 020-7431 4560, 💻 www.viamare.com)

Moby Lines
From Genoa to Bastia
www.mobylines.com
In Genoa: ☎ 010 254 15 13
In Corsica: ☎ 04.95.34.84.94
In the UK: c/o Via Mare (☎ 0207-7431 4560, 💻 www.viamare.com)

SNCM Ferrytérranée
From Marseille to Ajaccio, Bastia, Ile Rousee, Porto-Vecchio and Propriano
From Nice to Ajaccio, Calvi, Bastia and Ile Rousse.
From Toulon to Ajaccio and Bastia
In Corsica: ☎ 04.95.29.66.99
In the UK: c/o Southern Ferries (☎ 020-7491 4968)

Whichever ferry you choose, **advance booking** is essential. Don't just turn up at the port expecting to get a ticket. Places are limited by the number of reclining chairs in economy class, and even the big boats can be fully booked from mid-May onwards.

Also worth taking into consideration before you buy your ticket is which trek you aim to do, as this might affect your choice of ferry. The slow boat to Propriano from Marseille, for example, would be the perfect option for anyone intending to walk the Mare a Mare Sud, but less than ideal for GR20 trekkers.

By bus and ferry

Gone are the days when long-haul buses were the way to travel cheaply around Europe. It's still possible to get from London to the Côte d'Azur by coach but it's hard to see why anyone should want to. At £100 return to Marseille or £110 to Nice, Eurolines' (☎ 08705 143219) once-weekly service, which leaves from Victoria Coach Station in London and takes around 24 hours, works out pricier than flying and not all that much cheaper than taking the Eurostar and TGV.

See box on p19 for ferry services to Corsica from Marseille.

FROM CONTINENTAL EUROPE

In addition to Air France, most European airlines – including Lufthansa, KLM and Scandinavian Airlines – can sell a through ticket to Corsica with a change of planes in Paris, Marseille or Nice. The cheapest fares will be available through your local travel agent, who will also be able to advise you about direct **charter** flights to Corsica. These operate from Germany, the Netherlands, Belgium, Sweden, Norway, Denmark and Switzerland between the end of March and mid-October, and offer the most cost-effective and convenient route to the island, with fares that are usually well below those offered by scheduled airlines.

Alternatively, book a cheap flight to Nice or Marseille and then jump on a connecting flight (with one of the carriers listed in the box on p17) or a ferry (see box on p19). Low-cost airlines flying to the Côte d'Azur from continental Europe include Virgin Express (💻 www.virginexpress.com; from Brussels) and easyJet (💻 www.easyjet.com; from Amsterdam. Depending on which country you're travelling from you might also consider heading to France to link up with one of the many charter flights that fly out of Paris Orly or regional airports such as Strasbourg, Lille, Metz and Lyon. Fares range from around 170€ to 260€ according to the season. Once again your travel agent will have access to these flights, run by charter companies such as Nouvelles Frontières and Ollandini Voyages.

Travelling overland from most of northern Europe, the quickest route to Corsica is usually via Bavaria to one of the north Italian ferry ports such as Genoa, La Spezia or Livorno (Leghorn), from where ferries depart regularly throughout the summer (April–Oct) – see box on p19. The only year-round sea link shuttles from Santa Teresa di Gallura in Sardinia to Bonifacio.

For **train** travellers, the website 🖳 http://mercurio.iet.unipi.it/misc/ timetabl.html has hotlinks to all of Europe's national rail companies, where you can access up-to-the-minute timetable information and fares for trans-continental routes.

FROM THE USA AND CANADA

There are no direct flights from either the USA or Canada to Corsica. You have to either pick up a connection in Paris, or fly down to Nice or Marseille and change planes there. Tickets to the latter two cities tend to cost around US$150 more than you'd pay to fly to the French capital but you'll save most of that on the cost of the onward leg from the Côte d'Azur.

Published **fares** for a return flight to Ajaccio during the trekking season are about US$500–750 from New York (via Paris), US$750–1000 from LA, and US$400–800 from Montreal. Good first stops for quotes in the US are STA (☎ 0800-777-0112, 🖳 www.statravel.com) and Council Travel (☎ 800-226-8624, 🖳 www.counciltravel.com); in Canada try Travel CUTS (☎ 800-667-2887, 🖳 www.travelcuts.com).

FROM AUSTRALIA AND NEW ZEALAND

Flying from Australasia, Paris will be the gateway as there are no direct flights to the Côte d'Azur. Any of the dozen or so long-haul airlines who fly to France will be able to add on the domestic leg to Corsica. Alternatively you could catch the TGV down to Nice or Marseille and take the ferry, which would allow you to see a bit more of France en route (see p18 for details).

Return **fares** during the summer shoulder and peak seasons (including the cost of the add-on to Ajaccio or Bastia) start at around A$3500 from Sydney, or NZ$3700 from Auckland. Budget-flight specialist STA Travel (🖳 www.statravel.com) has branches in Sydney (☎ 02-9212 1255) and Auckland (☎ 09-309 9995).

Visas

Citizens of all **EU countries**, **Norway**, the **USA**, **Canada**, **Australia** and **New Zealand** do not need a visa to enter France. Most other nationalities do.

Obtaining a visa from your nearest French consulate is fairly straightforward, but check their opening hours before turning up and allow plenty of time, especially in the summer. EU nationals who stay in France longer than 30 days are supposed to apply for a *carte de séjour*, a residency permit for which you need proof of earnings at least comparable with the French minimum wage (*le SMIG*). In practice, however, EU passports are no longer stamped so there is no proof of how long you've been in the country.

Budgeting

A trekking holiday in Corsica needn't make a big hole in your wallet, at least if you can resist the temptations of the island's *café terasses* and mountain cuisine. At lower altitudes even those on flexible budgets will probably have to keep tabs on their expenses but the higher you hike the cheaper life tends to get. Apart from a handful of ski stations where it's possible to splash out on four-course meals and draught beer, your only noteworthy expenses are likely to be provisions, which are sold at premium prices in the shops and refuges along the route. **For rates of exchange see p87**.

COSTS ON THE GR20

If you camp or bivouac outside refuges, stay out of cafés and restaurants altogether, re-stock only at road-level shops rather than at the *gardien*'s stores and cover the entire route in 10 days or less, the GR20 will be a very cheap trek indeed by European standards. With a modest daily food allowance of, say, 12€/£7.50/$15, plus camping/bivouac fees of 6.50€/£4/$8 per night, you could spend as little as 200€/£120/$240. Only a handful of diehards, however, get by on so little. You're more likely to have at least a couple of cooked meals along the way, maybe half a dozen drinks, a night or two inside a hut in bad weather and a celebratory splurge at Conca. Add in transport to and from the trailheads, a night or two in a hotel en route plus a few days' camping on the beach to round things off, and you'll be looking at a minimum 400€/£250/$500 spending money for the fortnight. Plenty of people, however, manage to get through double that – usually by taking time out at villages off the main route, ordering slap-up meals and sleeping in comfortable hotels.

COSTS ON THE LOW-LEVEL ROUTES

Passing through villages two or three times each day, low-level routes such as the Mare a Mares and the Tra Mare e Monti offer more opportunities to spend money than the *haute-route*. Your main expense will probably be accommodation, which for the most part means gîtes d'étape. With dorm beds priced at around 11.50€/£7/$14 per night, gîtes aren't all that expensive, especially if you cook for yourself in the hostel kitchen. However, the majority of people staying in a gîte tend to opt for half-board (*demi-pension*; about 25€/£16/$24) when it's available (in some cases you may even be obliged to take it; see p76). Then there are the cafés along the way, village *épiceries* crammed with tasty *charcuterie* and *fromage corse* and, of course, those lovely old hotels with their tempting sprung mattresses and hot showers.

Thus if you stick to half-board at gîtes d'étape, picnic lunches and don't go over-board *à la terasse* a five-day trek will set you back in the region of 200€/£130/$190. On a budget of 320€/£200/$300 or more you could stay in hotels and afford the odd restaurant meal.

Of course, it would be possible to follow the low-level routes and spend virtually nothing if you camped or bivouacked, shopped in local épiceries and cooked for yourself. But by doing so you'd be both breaking the law (it's illegal to camp in the Parc Naturel let alone light fires, see p78) and running the risk of upsetting local people, many of whom feel strongly that trekkers should pay their dues by patronizing local businesses. That said, if you stick to the woods and remote stretches of the path no-one is likely to bother you.

CALCULATING COSTS

How much your trip ends up costing will depend on numerous factors: which route you choose, how long it takes to finish, and where you eat and sleep. But there are also a host of other expenses that are worth taking into account when working out exactly how much cash you'll need. A chunk of them are likely to be incurred travelling through the gateway towns – Ajaccio, Bastia, Calvi and Porto-Vecchio – where money can disappear very quickly indeed. Hotels on the coast tend to be pricier, as does eating out; and you might also have bus tickets, stamps, camera film and medical bits and bobs to buy. The most reliable way to estimate a figure is to calculate how much money you think you'll need altogether, then add at least 50% on top of that, just to be on the safe side.

GETTING CASH

Places to change money are few and far between on Corsica's trekking routes so you'll need to carry enough cash to see you through. In all the major towns the high street banks offer bureau de change facilities where you can cash **travellers' cheques**, but transactions usually incur a commission fee of 5–7.5€. To avoid this, take cheques issued by Thomas Cook and cash them free at a branch of Société Générale.

Exchange rates tend to be better for travellers' cheques than for hard currency but you may not always be able to cash them when you need to, which is where plastic credit or debit **cards** come in handy. These days it's possible to withdraw money from ATMs (*distributeurs automatiques de billets*) at any bank or post office on the island using your normal pin number for a fee of 1.5% of whatever you take out. The downside, of course, is the worry of what you'd do if your card went missing: always take a second card as a back-up, keep some emergency cash in your passport or money belt, and write the telephone number of your bank or credit card company somewhere you'll be able to find it if anything does go wrong.

It's also worth knowing that many post offices in Corsica (which are more numerous than ATMs in the interior of the island) will give **cash advances** against a Visa or MasterCard.

When to go

The trekking season for the **GR20** gets underway as soon as the snow on the high passes melts, which it usually does by early June, and lasts until the return of icy conditions in late October or early November. In terms of both weather and trail congestion, **mid-June to mid-July** and **mid-September to mid-October** are best. At these times storms tend to be less frequent, visibility more consistently good and, most important of all, the route itself relatively uncongested.

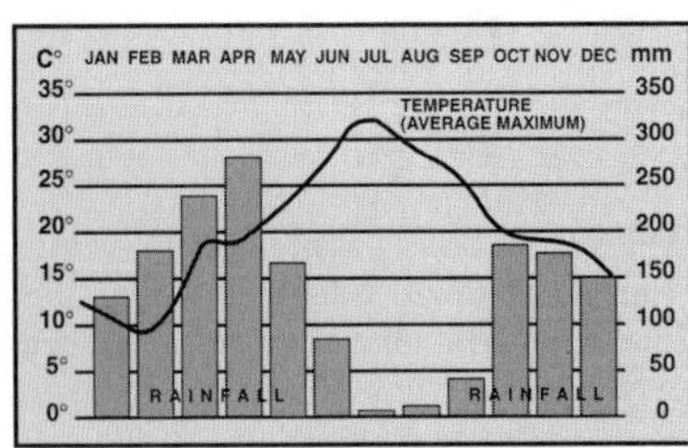

Temperature and rainfall

For the island's **other long-distance treks**, spring – when the weather is warm but not too hot and the wild flowers are most abundant – is the ideal season. However, from around the start of May until mid-June and between mid-September and mid-October, the gîtes d'étape on popular trails such as the Tra Mare e Monti and Mare a Mare Sud tend to be busy.

Spring and autumn are also the best periods for coastal walking: both the Littoral Sartènais and the Tra Mare e Monti can get unbearably hot and dusty in mid-summer, despite the on-shore breezes that blow in the afternoon, while the beaches are at their most packed.

Few trekkers come to Corsica in **winter** but with the right equipment and a bit of planning this can be a rewarding time to tackle the lower-altitude routes, which you'll have virtually to yourself. Nearly all gîtes d'étape close from November until the end of March but with advance warning most *gérants* will open a dormitory for you as long as you're happy to do your own cooking.

Route options

The waymarked trekking routes described in this book have all been devised so as to make the most of the outstanding landscapes they pass through. Each has its own distinct character, attributes and challenges. To find out which one is most likely to suit you, first browse the table opposite and the map on the inside back cover. Then flick through the chapter introductions where you'll find a concise overview of the route: what it's like, how long it takes to complete and the reasons why you might want to choose it.

❑ ROUTES AT A GLANCE

(see maps inside back cover)

GR20

● **Duration** 10–12 days **(see pp108-203)**
● **Pros** Magnificent high mountain scenery from start to finish; immaculate way-marking; well set-up refuges at convenient intervals
● **Cons** Many steep, long and strenuous gradients; you have to carry supplies and water; less dependable weather than at lower altitudes; frequent storms in August; congestion from mid-June to mid-September

Mare a Mare Nord

● **Duration** 4–5 days **(see pp204-34)**
● **Pros** Rugged valleys and great views of Corsica's highest peaks; crosses the island's most spectacular pine forest and the beautiful Niolu Valley; can be combined with a section of GR20 via Lac de Nino; descends the awesome Tavignano Gorge along an ancient paved mule path; ends at Corte, the island's only mountain town
● **Cons** None

Mare a Mare Nord Variant

● **Duration** 3–5 days **(see pp234-46)**
● **Pros** Can be combined with Mare a Mare Nord to create a superb 7 to 10-day round route, with fine views throughout; crosses the island's most extensive wilderness area and some impressive chestnut woods; dotted with villages
● **Cons** Food can be difficult to obtain along some sections and there's a shortage of accommodation; you have to plan well ahead and be relatively self-sufficient but the route is well worth the effort

Tra Mare e Monti

● **Duration** 7–10 days **(see pp247-71)**
● **Pros** Dramatically contrasting scenery, with some of the island's highest mountains and most impressive marine landscapes juxtaposed; passes through the Scandola nature reserve and remote, roadless fishing village of Girolata – two of Corsica's 'must sees'; good choice of accommodation and places to eat along most of the route so you don't have to carry much
● **Cons** Heat in summer; the route's popularity, which ensures busy trails and full gîtes in May, June and Sept; the last couple of stages are comparatively dull

Mare a Mare Sud

● **Duration** 4–5 days **(see pp272-99)**
● **Pros** Diverse scenery and lots of historic monuments, from Megalithic sites to Pisan chapels and Baroque churches; picturesque villages; miles of pristine deciduous forest, including stretches of rare ancient oak woodland; regular gîtes d'étape of a high-standard; plenty of places to swim from river banks; restaurants and cafés along most stretches of the route; starts and ends at impressive sea gulfs
● **Cons** Gîtes often booked up well in advance; last half of last stage is a dull plod

Littoral Sartènais

● **Duration** 2 days **(see pp300-10)**
● **Pros** Unspoilt coastal scenery, with turquoise bays, weird rock formations and gorgeous white-sand beaches punctuating the whole route; intense feeling of remoteness
● **Cons** Shortage of food, water and human settlement: you have to remain entirely self-sufficient on this route

Other options

Most trekkers follow a route from start to finish but there's no reason why you shouldn't cover only part, or else combine sections of routes to tailor-make your own itinerary. This can be a particularly worthwhile approach to the GR20 which, for all its spectacular scenery, keeps well away from the coast and mountain villages. The orange-waymarked trails that intersect it at various points – notably at Col de Verghio and Onda – allow you to explore lower, more populated valleys and coastal landscapes that are a world away from the high-mountain terrain of the watershed. Three suggestions are listed below. Splicing together some of Corsica's finest trekking étapes, they progress in the same direction as the route outlines in this guide.

• **Round trip from Calenzana via the GR20, Col de Verghio, Girolata and Galéria in 9–12 days** This route cherry-picks the most dramatic stretches of the GR20 and Tra Mare e Monti. Having followed the GR for six étapes, you swing west at Col de Verghio, descending through the magnificent Forêt d'Aïtone and Spelunca Gorge to Ota, and from there follow the coast northwards past Scandola and Girolata to Galéria. The final three stages follow the Tra Mare e Monti through Tuarelli and over the Bocca di Bonassa pass to Bonifatu. This combines Corsica's most acclaimed landscape with what must be the island's ultimate round-trip walk.

• **Calenzana to Corte, via the Tavignano Valley in 7–8 days** Instead of turning right at Col de Verghio after the first six étapes of the GR20, you can turn left and descend the Niolu Valley to Albertacce. From there another two unforgettable days take you over the Col de l'Arinella and down the awesome Tavignano Gorge via an ancient paved Genoan mule track to Corte, Corsica's old capital. A superb six-day extension to this route would be to follow the Mare a Mare Nord *Variant* from Vivario to Onda, drop west down the wild Cruzini Valley and then cross the mountains to Cargèse on the coast.

• **Round-trip from Marignana in 6–7 days** Marignana, at the head of the Spelunca Valley, is perhaps the most remote village in Corsica accessible by bus from Ajaccio. Leaving its welcoming gîte d'étape, you can walk over to Evisa and thence up the valley through the Forêt d'Aïtone to Col de Verghio. From there the easiest leg of the GR20 leads along the ridge-tops to serene Lac de

Variants (and _Variantes_ . . .)

Throughout this book you'll come across outlines of waymarked alternatives to the main routes called *Variants* or *Variantes* (the extra 'e' denotes a feminine noun: GR is short for *la Grande Randonnée*, whereas the other routes, *sentiers*, are nominally masculine). These may be liaison paths to villages, easier or more strenuous side options avoiding weather-prone obstacles, or just plain alternatives. In each case we sketch out their relative merits in boxed text or under a separate heading and provide route maps with trekking times and other useful information to help you navigate them.

Nino, the island's most picturesque high-altitude lake, beyond which you can follow the GR20 over the watershed to Petra Piana and Onda and pick up the Mare a Mare Nord Variant for the remaining three days back to Marignana. The area around Lac de Nino sees a fair amount of snow so this option is feasible between June and October only.

WAYMARKING

All Corsica's long-distance trekking routes have been painstakingly way-marked with blobs of coloured paint. Dabbed at regular intervals on tree trunks, rocks, buildings and lamp-posts, the *balisage* (or *flèchage*) allows you to follow the path without constantly having to refer to a map. Up in the mountains, where the route may otherwise not be clearly defined, the marks are a godsend, especially in bad weather. They come in four different colours, designating different types or grades of route:

Red and white

WRONG WAY

The distinctive red-and-white waymarks are the exclusive preserve of the GR20. They're more frequent and prominent than any other kind of marker and indicate only the principal route. A pair of parallel lines or spots means 'carry on'. If the lines have a stem beneath them, forming a 'flag', expect a turning ahead (in the direction of the flag). A red-and-white cross shows that you've gone the wrong way and should turn back. There are other variations but they are self-evident: a pair of lines which clearly bend left or right mean that you should follow the path around a corner, for example.

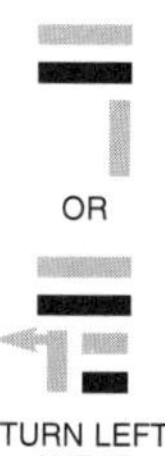

Yellow

Yellow paint marks show alternative (ie *Variante*) routes of the GR20, usually more challenging ones via summits or high ridges. They tend to be simple spots rather than lines.

Orange

Anyone following the Mare a Mare or Tra Mare e Monti trails will start seeing orange waymarks in their sleep after a couple of étapes. With a few exceptions (highlighted in the route descriptions) they are regular and reliable and difficult to lose.

Red or green

Single red or green marks (without white ones next to them) are to be found only on approaches to a few prominent 2500m+ peaks, such as Punta Minuta next to Monte Cinto.

Cairns

Little piles of rocks, or simply two or three rocks balanced together, are used to mark mountain ascent routes that get covered in snow (where paint waymarks would be useless for much of the year). The big drawback with them is that they often trace different routes of varying grades and can therefore lead you off-track onto steeper rock than you might be comfortable with.

What to take

It's hard to overstate the importance of getting your choice of kit right. If you don't you could well spend your entire trek regretting it. Little things – like an ill-fitting boot, a sleeping bag that's a bit too thin or a rucksack that rubs – can not only make life uncomfortable but could bring your holiday to a premature end. Of those who fail to finish the GR20, for example, the vast majority do so because of feet problems rather than lack of fitness – problems that could well have been avoided with a little advance preparation.

What you should take ultimately depends on the type of trek you intend to do: how high and far you hope to walk; the time of year; the kind of terrain you'll be crossing; how you sleep and where you eat along the route. The overriding principle to keep in mind, however, should be the **weight** of your rucksack: keep it as light as possible. Whichever route you choose you'll have to contend with some lengthy ascents and lugging a heavy pack uphill for hours can be a grind, especially in the heat. So before you set off, weigh everything you're taking. Men shouldn't carry much more than 15kg, or a quarter of their body weight; women will generally feel overburdened with more than 10–12kg. Take into account the weight of any water and food you'll be trekking with, and if the load is still too much think again about what you could live without.

There are all sorts of ways to keep the weight of a pack down to a minimum (Nicholas Crane famously chops the ends of his toothbrushes and drills holes in what's left, and only takes three socks which he wears in strict rotation). For most people, though, getting a full bag to a manageable weight will mean spending money. Light, strong, good-quality trekking equipment doesn't come cheap but once you're on the trail the investment will feel worthwhile.

FOOTWEAR AND FOOT CARE

Your top priority, whether tackling the GR20 or a lower-level route, should be your **boots**. These days, outdoor equipment stores stock a bewildering array of technical footwear, ranging from stiff plastic winter boots for use with crampons to ultra-lightweight trainer-style shoes that wouldn't look out of place on a tennis court.

Corsica's trails require something in between. For the **GR20** a good, solid, two- or three-season boot with plenty of ankle support and a durable Vibram-style sole is the ideal choice. Bear in mind you'll be walking over rough, sharp granite most of the time, and will have to negotiate patches of loose scree, smooth and wet rock, *névés* of snow or ice and the odd scramble up very steep slabs. So your footwear should be supportive without being too rigid, waterproof (with a sewn-in tongue) and have a sole that grips well even in wet conditions. Leather boots have for generations been regarded as unbeatable but these days synthetic 'breathable' fibres such as Gore-Tex, in combination with water-resistant Nubuck leather, keep your feet just as dry and cool in hot weather (an important consideration in Corsica).

At **lower altitudes** on routes such as the Mare a Mares and Tra Mare e Monti you can get away with a much lighter two-season shoe or boot, perhaps with Gore-Tex lining and mesh-and-leather uppers. Again, it should be waterproof and have a grippy, hard-wearing out-sole, but ankle support is less essential. So-called 'multi-purpose' footwear – hybrids between mountain boots and trainers – are increasingly popular and more than adequate most of the time in dry weather. However, in early spring and late autumn, when you're likely to encounter rain, you'd definitely be glad of something sturdier.

One definite advantage of these new versatile shoes is that they take a lot less **wearing in**. At the other extreme, stiff leather boots need at least a couple of weeks' use before they become supple. This inevitably involves some discomfort (until the leather molds to the shape of your foot) and should always be done gradually, *before* your trek. Leave the breaking in of new

Blisters – prevention and cure

Blisters are the bane of every trekker. Caused by friction between boot and foot, which produces a protective layer of liquid or pus to build up beneath the skin, they can completely ruin any long-distance walk. Bad ones sometimes take four or five days to heal – enough to curtail your trek.

As with most equipment-related problems, prevention is better than cure and you can do a lot to avoid getting blisters. Firstly, always wear your boots in well. Secondly, never walk with wet feet; if your socks get soaked in perspiration or water, take your boots off and dry them out each time you stop for a breather. The old wives' tale says to rub surgical spirit (alcohol) into your feet each evening for at least a week before you trek, to toughen them up. This will certainly harden the skin but it won't necessarily prevent blisters. In fact it can cause worse ones to form between the harder external layer and the softer skin beneath.

Never ignore discomfort. At the first sign of rubbing, either cover the affected area of the foot with zinc-oxide tape or plaster, or – best of all – apply a hydrocolloid blister pad such as Compeed. This acts like an additional layer of skin and once stuck on your foot should stay there for a couple of days. Although quite expensive they're extremely effective if you catch the blister early enough. Ordinary plasters can fold and run against your skin, actually causing blisters rather than preventing them.

The only way to deal with a blister once it's become unbearable is to burst it and to rest up. Use a hypodermic syringe (an essential component of your trekking medical kit – see p36 – which most pharmacists will give you for nothing) or, if you don't have one, a needle (which you can sterilize by burning its tip until it turns black). Allow the blister to dry out afterwards, then apply antiseptic and some kind of dressing.

The worst-case scenario would be if your blisters became infected, which happens when bacteria enter the wound. In this case a few days' rest with your feet up and repeated bathing with antiseptic might sort you out; if not, limp to the nearest doctor.

boots until you're on a long-distance route and you'll almost certainly suffer for it.

Finding the correct combination of **socks** for your boots is another way of avoiding blisters. Since the introduction of synthetic fibres that wick-out perspiration, man-made blends have tended to supersede pure wool and cotton as the benchmark materials. For Corsica a very thin inner layer together with one thicker technical outer sock (ideally with extra woven padding on the toes and heels) should suffice. The inner layer protects you from rubbing while the outer sock provides insulation.

Quality modern boots all have state-of-the-art padding and should be extremely comfortable from the outset but you can increase their shock-absorbability with **insoles** made of rubber-like materials such as Sorbothane. Good ones are expensive but they can be an invaluable aid for anyone who suffers from foot ache or knee problems.

During the summer trekking season there's too little snow on the GR20 to warrant **crampons**. However, you might be glad of a pair of **trekking poles** (see below) when crossing névés and short **gaiters** ('*stop-tout*' in French) are good for keeping ice, water and annoying pieces of grit out of your boots.

Finally, one item of footwear you'll be glad of in the evenings to give your feet a break from boots after a day's trekking, is a pair of flip-flops or **slippers**. Better still, invest in a pair of Teva-style **outdoor sandals**, which are very light, comfortable and have grippy soles. They'll also come in useful if you take time out on the beach.

RUCKSACK

As with boots, comfort is the key when choosing a rucksack. After you've found one that fits well, then and only then compare capacities and features. External frames are best avoided (internal ones tend not to stick into your back and are less rigid); pockets are always handy; and you might be glad of buckles and elastic webbing for roll mats, and easily accessible compartments for things like water bottles, maps and guide books. To accommodate the fluctuations in volume as you work through your food, an extendable lid is also a good idea.

Rucksacks come in all sizes, from slim climbing bags to bulky backpacks. For trekking in Corsica a medium-sized one will probably suit you best. Make sure the straps can be adjusted: when walking uphill it's better to take the weight on your shoulders; descending tends to be more comfortable if you loosen shoulder straps and tighten the waistband.

Finding out the most efficient way of **packing your sack** usually takes a day or two of experimentation but it always helps to store your things in plastic carrier bags or stuff sacks. These not only divide gear into more manageable sections but also prevent essentials such as down kit, clothing, books and maps getting damp. Remember, no rucksack will be 100% waterproof in a torrential downpour, despite what the manufacturer may imply in its blurb.

SLEEPING BAG AND MAT

Whether you bed down in gîtes d'étape, refuges, or on open mountainsides, a good sleeping bag is a must. Even in mid-summer, night temperatures in Corsica can be quite chilly at altitude.

When choosing a bag it's always a trade-off between weight and warmth. Ounce for ounce, **down** insulates best but loses its efficiency when damp and is difficult to dry out. Artificial fillings, on the other hand, don't lose their loft so dramatically when wet and are much cheaper, but are a lot less compressible; they're also a little bit heavier (typically 150g for a full-length 2+ season bag).

All things considered, the top choice for the GR20 would have to be a pricey goose-down sleeping bag offering two- to three-season comfort in temperatures of -5° to -10°C. For maximum flexibility you might consider fortifying it with a lightweight outer shell, or **bivouac sack**, made from a breathable, waterproof fabric such as Gore-Tex; this would allow you to sleep outside without the worry of the feathers getting damp. Bottom-of-the-range bivvy sacks tend to be waterproof enough but not all that breathable; this means your body heat will condense on cool nights to form a liquid layer inside the shell which can then soak into your sleeping bag – a nuisance if it's made of down.

In refuges and anywhere at lower attitudes, a lightweight summer sleeping bag should suffice. But if you're aiming to bivouac, consider taking an outer sack too. Some kind of **liner**, made from fleece fabric or a cotton or silk **sheet-sleeping bag**, might also be a good idea; apart from adding extra warmth if you need it they're ideal for clammy or hot summer weather down at sea level.

A **sleeping mat** is essential if you intend to camp or bivouac but would be a waste of space inside refuges or gîtes d'étape. Self-inflating Thermarest pads are ideal for sleeping in tents. However, they tend to pierce easily and are thus less suited to bivvying than foam mats; of the latter, the so-called Z-Rest is the most compact (it also unfolds and lies flat straightaway unlike its rolled counterparts).

TENT

With gîtes d'étape and refuges punctuating all the major trekking routes in Corsica, you can easily make do without a tent. A good sleeping bag should provide enough warmth, and on those rare nights when it rains you can always seek shelter inside a hut. That said, the privacy and security offered by a tent can be very welcome, especially on the GR20 where bivouackers tend to be corralled together into enclosures, and you'd also be glad of one if you spend time on the beach at any point. Of course, the extra kilos are a lot less onerous if you can split the tent between two or more people. For solo trekkers the benefit-weight equation comes down firmly against camping unless you have an ultra-light one-man tent that compacts well.

CLOTHING

Shorts and T-shirts, and maybe a sunhat and glasses, are generally all you'll need to wear while trekking in Corsica. Between May and October the weather is generally warm and dry and you'll work up a constant sweat even at altitude. To be equipped for the sudden changes of weather the island can be prone to, however, you'll also need some clothes for wet and cold conditions, and something snug for those fresh evenings in the hills.

Once again it pays to invest in purpose-made outdoor gear if you can. Cotton and wool will certainly do the job but hi-tech wicking textiles, which transfer moisture from the inside to the outside of the garment, will keep you much drier and more comfortable on the trail, while fleeces provide considerably more warmth for less weight than a woollen jumper.

The following tips apply only to the late spring–early autumn trekking season. If you're planning to tackle snow and ice at altitude during the winter in Corsica and aren't sure what kit you'll need, nor how to use it, consider signing up for a winter mountain-skills course or changing your plans.

Base layer

Cotton may be soft on the skin but it's no longer the most comfortable base layer to trek in. Once it gets wet it stays that way, which means you're soaked in perspiration most of the day. For Corsica, **T-shirts** made of light wicking fibres are the ideal thing to wear next to your skin. They literally dry in minutes, are ultra-light, warm and can be washed with little or no soap (which means you can get by with only two of them). Unfortunately they fray easily when caught in brambles and thus fare badly in the *maquis*; and they're expensive.

As far as **underwear** goes, women will do fine with three pairs of whatever they normally wear. Men, however, should bear in mind the potential horrors of 'crotch rash', an ailment that's nowhere near as amusing as it sounds if it strikes when you're hours away from the nearest hut. One of the most effective ways of preventing the rubbing that sets it off is to wear close-fitting lycra 'shorts-style' briefs instead of boxers (which can bunch up inside your shorts). Sports shops even sell them impregnated with an anti-microbial compound that kills the offending fungi or bacteria before they can take hold. You should also change your underwear daily and ensure that the tops of your legs get a chance to dry out periodically in hot weather. If you do develop a rash, hydrocortisone cream, available over the counter at most pharmacies, is the most effective treatment.

For the GR20 an additional **thermal base layer** will come in useful for anyone intending to bivouac or camp. A close-fitting suit of ultra-fine Polartec-type fleece material will keep you cosy at night, or you could go for an all-in-one outfit with a long zip up the front (these have the advantage of not riding up to leave a gap between your trousers and top).

Opposite: Approaching the forepeak of Monte Cinto – see p130. (Photo © David Abram).

Mid-layer

The job of a mid-layer is to provide insulation: to keep out the chill that quickly sets in if you sit around in a sweaty shirt on top of a hill and, in cold or wet weather, to generate a warm buffer between your inner garment and outer shell. **Fleece** long ago succeeded wool as the benchmark fabric because it's light, wind-resistant and fast drying. Nowadays, pricier fleeces also boast a degree of water-resistance (although this may reduce breathability). Other features you'll need in any mid-layer are a long body so your lower back won't be exposed when you stretch while scrambling or bending forwards. Large chest pockets for storing maps are another plus, and you may be glad of a long front zip so you can cool off more quickly after exercise. Finally, check out the weight of the fleece before you buy it: 500–600g will be ample for trekking in Corsica. Any heavier than that and you'll probably find it too warm.

As for **trousers**, a pair of running shorts or anything made of four-way-stretch fabric (such as Lycra) that gives complete freedom of movement is all you're likely to need during the day. If the weather turns chilly, track pants (jogging trousers) or some other kind of lightweight long trousers are a good idea. Outdoor shops stock a range of technical ones with natty features like micro-fleece lining, articulated knees, lower leg zippers (to make them easy to take on and off while wearing boots) and cargo pockets. But the most important thing is that they should be light and tough. When trekking at lower altitudes in Corsica, a pair of long trousers made of rip-stop fabric will prevent your legs getting badly scratched in the maquis.

Outer layer

You shouldn't scrimp on your **jacket**, especially if you're setting off on the GR20. At altitude, a good one can literally mean the difference between life and death.

These days, the only jackets worth bothering with are those made from the new generation of light-weight, waterproof and highly breathable fabrics such as Gore-Tex, Triplepoint Ceramic and Sympatex. Sometimes called 'shells', they're essentially just that. Worn over a mid-layer fleece, breathable outer layers keep out the wind, rain and snow while preventing the build-up of moisture that can form a life-threatening layer of ice in extreme cold, and even in moderate conditions will quickly drain away body heat.

The important criteria to consider when choosing a coat are its overall fit and comfort and the durability of the fabric (the heavier and stiffer it is, the longer it's likely to last). The pricier ones tend to have lots of knobs and bells you probably won't need, such as complicated zip configurations giving adjustable ventilation, velcro flaps and jazzy elastic drawcords. They also have a maze of different pockets; ones in the chest are easily accessible places to

---

Opposite Top: The Cinto massif in early spring. (Photo © Tim Glasby). **Bottom:** Ortu di u Piobbu refuge, with the ridge ascent to Monte Corona in the background – see p120. (Photo © David Abram).

store maps, though be warned that the more gear you stuff into them the less breathable your coat's expensive fabric will be.

Even on the GR20 the summer heat in Corsica can seem Saharan at times, making some kind of **sunhat** indispensable. Apart from stopping your face and neck from burning, it'll also prevent your head from overheating (sunstroke) and reduce the risk of heat-induced fatigue and dehydration.

After the sun disappears it can soon get surprisingly cool and you'll be glad of a **warm hat**, especially at night. An additional layer inside your hood will also come in very useful in windy weather, which is common on the high ridges of the watershed.

Pack a pair of thin thermal **gloves** if you intend to trek at altitude around the beginning or end of the season when the risk of cold snaps increases. In wet weather you'd be glad of ones with a waterproof and breathable outer layer and preferably some kind of grippy material lining the palms and fingers. Another feature that will make life that little bit more comfortable are elastic, close-fitting wrist bands; these ensure your gloves fit snugly inside the sleeves of your jacket.

COOKING GEAR

Every refuge and gîte d'étape should in principle have gas hobs but a portable stove allows you to cook up hot meals and boil water for tea wherever you are and whenever you want to. This can be a real advantage on the GR20, in particular, where queues for the gas rings are par for the course in peak season. On those occasions where you find yourself having to camp or bivouac in the middle of nowhere, it's also nice to be able to cook for yourself rather than make do with a cheerless cheese roll for an evening meal.

As ever, weight is the crucial factor when deciding **which kind of stove** to take. For ultimate efficiency and flexibility, MSR-style multi-fuel burners – which are feather-light, run on virtually every kind of inflammable liquid and operate reliably even in extreme cold – are unbeatable. They are, however, very expensive. Most people make do with some kind of cheaper cartridge-based stove system, where you screw a flame burner onto a small, pressurized gas container. The catch here, of course, is that you're not allowed to take compressed gas onto aircraft and thus have to rely on what's available locally – which in the case of Corsica means very little indeed. The only kind of cartridges routinely sold in village shops and supermarkets on the island are old-fashioned Bleuet Camping Gaz ones. These are very light and cheap (as are their burners) but don't work all that well in cold weather, nor when they're running low (which can take a frustratingly long time). A more convenient option would be some kind of stove fuelled by resealable cartridges. These are hard to get hold of in Corsica but you can buy adapters that convert standard Camping Gaz canisters into resealable units at any good outdoor equipment shop.

For Trangia owners, and anyone with a MSR-type stove, methylated spirits is the most readily available fuel in Corsica, where it's sold as *alcool à brûler* (Corsican housewives use it to clean windows).

Water

On a typical day's trekking in Corsica you should aim to carry a minimum of three litres of water and drink as much as you can before you set off. On the trail itself, top up whenever you pass a spring and remember the old axiom that 'little and often is better than lots in one go'.

As with most parts of the world, stream water should not be considered safe to drink unless you purify it first (with either chlorine-, silver-nitrate- or iodine-based tablets, or a filter). Animals drink from and defecate in streams up to source altitudes, while in summer thousands of trekkers on the GR20 wash and bathe in streams every day.

Although it's always a good idea to take some kind of water **purification tablets** as a back up, springs (safe to drink from without purifying the water) are numerous enough in Corsica for you not to need them. Throughout this book we highlight where the most convenient water sources are located and how much liquid you're likely to need to get by.

Wherever possible, avoid buying mineral water. Although the 1.5-litre bottles it comes in make good-sized containers, the empties create unnecessary refuse. Lightweight aluminium ones, such as those made by Swiss manufacturers Sigg, are a more environmentally-friendly and durable alternative, as are **Platypus Hoser**-type reservoirs. Made from durable plastic laminate that doesn't adversely flavour liquids, these come in a variety of shapes and sizes, from one to four litres, and can be stored in rucksack pockets or inside jackets. You drink from them by sucking on a hose that's normally attached to your shoulder strap, which not only saves you having to stop and remove your pack to drink but also frees up your hands and encourages you to consume more.

PHOTOGRAPHIC EQUIPMENT

Good-quality, compact 'point-and-press' cameras are light, tough and will provide a perfectly adequate record of your trip. But an SLR and a few lenses will give a lot more scope to be creative and capture some of the subtle light effects you experience in the mountains. On the other hand, a heavy camera and its peripherals will seem a burden if you don't get a lot of use out of them.

If you're serious enough about photography to consider an SLR is worth the additional kilo or two, take a powerful **zoom lens**, ideally 28–250mm; this will give maximum compositional flexibility for minimum weight. Smaller essentials to pack in your camera bag would be a **lens hood** for reducing glare and a **UV filter** for cutting through the high-altitude haze that envelops the Corsican mountains for much of the summer. A **polarizer** will do the same job and deepen the blue of skies. Take along a sturdy, well-padded **carrying case** that you can sling around your neck or attach to your pack; stash your camera in your rucksack and you'll probably find yourself less inclined to use it. Finally, for those essential self-timer shots, a small, lightweight **tripod** is very handy indeed; these days you can get tiny ones that perch on rocks. If you use one of these, don't forget to pack a **shutter release cable**.

Landscape colours and contours are at their richest in the early morning and late evening; snap away in the middle of the day and you'll find the results drained and flat-looking. And be aware of the havoc snow can play with your exposure meter. When photographing névés, it's always a good idea to bracket up a half or one stop.

Kodak and Fuji print **film**, and Fuji-Sensia slide film, are available everywhere, but professional-quality slide film (*pellicule diapositive*) is harder to come by. It's also much more expensive in Corsica than in the UK, Holland or USA, so stock up before you come.

MEDICAL KIT

The best kind of medical kit is the one you never use but even healthy, fit trekkers usually have to dip into theirs a couple of times to deal with the kind of everyday aches, pains and minor ailments thrown up by punishing routes such as the GR20. What follows is a list of basic bits and pieces you shouldn't trek without. Finally, don't forget to bring an adequate supply of any **prescription drugs** you might need while you're away.

- Hydrocolloid **blister pads**: always good to have even if you don't use them. In Corsican pharmacies they're known by their brand name, Compeed
- **Zinc-oxide tape** with strong adhesive: just the stuff for fixing dressings that might otherwise get rubbed off by the movement of your boots or clothes
- **Sterilized gauze**: soaks up blood and pus, and keeps wounds clean
- **Antiseptic cream** or spray: for preventing minor infections
- **Plasters**: ditto
- Anti-inflammatory, Ibroprufen-based **pain killers**, such as Nurofen: these effectively suppress the discomfort of sprains, bruises and toothache
- **Mosquito repellent**: DEET-based ones are the most effective but they're also considered by many to be harmful. Citronella is a natural alternative
- **Deep-heat spray** or balm: eases minor sprains and pulled muscles
- **Hydrocortisone cream**: for treating heat rash ('crotch rash')
- **Hypodermic needles**: for piercing blisters. Most pharmacists in Corsica will give you some for nothing if you explain you want them to '*percer des ampoules*'
- **High-factor sun cream**: simply essential, whichever trek you do
- **Knee support**: a good strong elastic support can greatly strengthen weak or injured knees, particularly on long descents
- **Nail scissors** or file: to prevent painful in-growing toenails
- **Spare pair of glasses** or contact lenses if you wear them

ODDS AND ENDS

Here's a checklist for those little things that are all too easily forgotten but which could well prove indispensable:

- **Compass** or GPS: no trip into the Corsican mountains should be undertaken without a compass or GPS but bear in mind that neither will get you out of a scrape if you don't know how to use it

- **Trekking poles**: up to half of your combined body and pack weight can be shifted from legs to arms with a properly adjusted pair of poles (long for descents and short for climbs); this can take a lot of the stress off your knees and generally increase your speed and efficiency over gradients
- **Body wallet**: the best place to stow away your passport, money, air ticket and other paper valuables; slip them inside a plastic bag first, to stop them being soaked through by perspiration
- **Penknife**: no self-respecting Frenchman takes to the hills without his trusty Opinel to slice baguettes, cheese and charcuterie; but Swiss Army or Leatherman multi-purpose knives, with corkscrews, bottle openers, scissors, files and all kinds of other useful tools, are much more versatile
- **Sunglasses**: ideally with some kind of strap to stop them falling off if you take a tumble
- **Head torch**: much better than a normal pocket lamp because it allows you the use of both hands. When buying one, compare how long batteries last and take along a spare set. The new generation of LED-diode lamps are far lighter and last far longer than standard ones, although the beam they produce is more diffuse.
- **Plastic map case**: useful for protecting guidebooks as well as maps; don't put it around your neck, where it will flap uncontrollably in the wind, but attach the cord to one of your zip pullers and store it inside a chest pocket
- Piece of **tent fabric** and **glue**: for emergency repairs if you're camping
- **Liquid soap** for washing clothes: most Corsican shops stock stuff called Génie, which works well but should never be used in streams; more biodegradable brands are available through large camping stores in northern Europe and the US (but not Corsica)
- **Puritabs**: chlorine-based tablets kill all water-borne bacteria and viruses, and are healthier over long periods than iodine solution. Silver-nitrate tablets (such as Micropur) taste better than either of these, but take a long time to work
- A long piece of **string** and some **clothes pegs** for drying washing
- **Gaiters**: especially useful in early summer for crossing melting névés
- **Mobile phone**: coverage is very patchy on high ground but a mobile could be useful to call the mountain rescue service (☎ 112); see p42
- Half-litre aluminium **bottle**: the ideal container for cooking oil. **Film canisters** are perfect for storing small quantities of salt, spices and stock powder or cubes.
- **Towel**: outdoor shops sell special low-bulk, highly absorbent ones specially designed for trekking
- **Swim suit**: handy for those tempting mountain streams, pools and Corsican beaches
- Spare pair of **bootlaces**
- **Toothpaste** but only as much as you'll need; squeeze the rest out to save weight
- **Snorkel and face mask**: you'll be glad you carried one if you end up on the beach as the seas around Corsica are unbelievably clear
- **Toilet paper**

RECOMMENDED READING

Background

At some stage of your trip you could well find yourself pinned down by bad weather or killing time waiting for a bus, in which case a good paperback will prove worth its weight. Unfortunately there are few Corsica-related titles still in circulation.

One explanation for this is the monolithic reputation of Dorothy Carrington's *Granite Island* (Penguin). Since it was first published (in French) in the 1960s, *Île de Granite* has been regarded as the definitive introduction to the island and its people. Part history, part travelogue, it roves engagingly over Corsica's past, with fascinating digressions into some of the more arcane facets of island life such as banditry, vendetta, religious brotherhoods and the occult. Although a touch dated now, it still deserves to be top of your reading list.

Dorothy Carrington subsequently wrote a string of erudite books on Corsica, including *Napoleon and his Parents on the Threshold of History* (Viking), the definitive work on the early years of France's future emperor. Anyone interested in matters more occult than historic might enjoy her most recent offering, *Dream Hunters of the Soul* (Phoenix), where she lifts the lid on the hidden worlds of Evil Eye healing, vampires, witchcraft and pagan sects.

James Boswell, posing here in Corsican dress, visited the island in 1765 and wrote a best-selling account of the trip, entitled *An Account of Corsica*.

The book that first defined the island in the minds of English readers, however, was written two centuries before Dorothy Carrington's. *An Account of Corsica* by James Boswell, a 25-year-old dilettante adventurer who would later become famous as Dr Samuel Johnson's biographer, is a quirky travelogue describing the author's quest to meet the rebel leader Pascal Paoli in 1765. Clutching a letter of introduction from no less than Jean-Jacques Rousseau, Boswell lands in Cap Corse from where he sets off on a journey across the island that will leave him enraptured by its mountains, forests and wild inhabitants. *An Account of Corsica* was a best seller in its day, playing a seminal part in Britain's later military alliance with the rebels against France. But it's very much a product of its times and non-specialist, modern-day readers tend to find Boswell's style and philosophical pretensions less than riveting.

General guidebooks

For those who intend to explore Corsica by road or rail as well as via its footpaths, two English-language guidebooks stand out. The *Rough Guide to Corsica* (by the same author as this book) includes dozens of walks and treks, plus a wealth of historical and cultural background. In addition to full coverage of places to stay and eat, you also get more than the usual level of contemporary references, which makes it an engaging read. Lonely Planet's *Corsica* covers much the same ground, albeit more thinly. Its strong points are lengthy sections on the GR20 and on diving, and consistently detailed restaurant reviews throughout (it was written by a team of French writers).

Specialist guidebooks

For technical advice on climbing the island's lesser-known peaks get hold of Robin Colomb's *Corsica Mountains*. Written more for rock climbers than trekkers, it covers the main routes and summits and plenty more besides, backed up with helpful line drawings.

Field guides

The most comprehensive guide to the region's flora is *Mediterranean Wild Flowers* by Grey-Wilson and Blamey (HarperCollins). Comprising 560 pages of species descriptions and wonderful colour illustrations, it includes most of the trees, shrubs and flowers you're likely to come across between sea level and 1000m. Apart from its comparatively high price, its only shortcoming is its weight, which makes it impractical for trekking. A lighter-weight, more modern alternative is *Wild Flowers of Southern Europe* by Davies and Gibbons (The Crowood Press), more than 200 pages shorter but still more than adequate as an identification aid. Well designed and concise, it uses photographs rather than paintings.

Bertel Brun's classic *Birds of Britain and Europe* (Hamlyn) covers most of the avian species you'll spot on the island but for a more Corsica-focused rundown, try to get hold of Jacquie Grozier's *A Birdwatching Guide to France South of the Loire* (Arlequin Press), which includes a site guide to Corsica's birding hot-spots. Few non-specialist bookstores stock it but you can order it direct from the publisher (☎ 01245-267441, 💻 www.arlequinpress.co.uk/birdwsg.htm). Although too cumbersome to serve as a field guide, the definitive *Birds of Corsica* (BOU), by local ornithologists Thibault and Bonnacorsi, is the academic's choice, placing the island's birdlife in the wider context of the Mediterranean region. It lists all 323 species ever recorded and contains a hefty bibliography.

Other commendable titles you're unlikely to want to trek with but which provide excellent reference sources are Burton, Arnold and Ovenden's *Field Guide to the Reptiles and Amphibians of Britain and Europe* (HarperCollins), great for identifying those scuttling creatures encountered on Corsica's trails, and Higgins and Riley's *Butterflies of Britain and Europe* (HarperCollins).

MAPS

The maps in this guide should be adequate for navigating the trails. But when exploring off-track areas, or for a fine-grain picture of outlying terrain, you might want to invest in a set of **IGN** (*Institut Géographique National*) **TOP25 Séries Bleue maps**. Published in distinctive blue covers, these range over the island in 19 overlapping maps at a scale of 1:25,000 (1cm=250m). Their level of detail and accuracy is of the highest standard and they're beautifully drawn, with 10m contour lines and helpful shading to emphasize the topography. Every footpath is clearly highlighted, along with refuges, gîtes d'étape, springs, different kinds of woodland, standing stones, caves and anything else that could possibly be of interest to trekkers. They're also GPS friendly. The catch is the

WHERE TO BUY MAPS OF CORSICA

IGN maps are less expensive in Corsica and mainland France than elsewhere (usually around £2 cheaper) but shops on the island may not always have the ones you want in stock (this is especially true of the TOP25s covering the GR20, which tend to sell out early in the season). The only way to be sure of obtaining the maps you want is to buy them in advance in your home country. Below is a list of specialist map shops from whom it is possible to purchase both the TOP25 and Michelin series. You can order by phone or over the Internet but, before parting with any money, compare prices and check the retailer's shipping costs and typical delivery times as these vary greatly.

In the UK

Maps By Mail (☎ 020-8339 4970, 🖳 www.mapsbymail.co.uk)
Maps Worldwide (☎ 01225-707004, 🖳 www.mapsworldwide.co.uk)
Stanfords (☎ 020-7836 1321, 🖳 www.stanfords.co.uk)
The Map Shop (☎ 0800 085 4080 or from abroad ☎ 44-1684-594 559, 🖳 www.themapshop.co.uk)

In Continental Europe

France: **Institut National Géographique (IGN)** (☎ 01.43.98.80.00, 🖳 www.ign.fr)
Germany: **Geocenter** (☎ 711-788 9340, 🖳 www.geokatalog.de)
Denmark: Nordisk Korthandel (☎ 3338 2638, 🖳 www.scanmaps.com)

In the US

Distant Lands (☎ 626-449-3220, 🖳 www.distantlands.com)
Maplink (☎ 805-692-6777, 🖳 www.maplink.com)
Omnimap (☎ 336-227-8300, 🖳 www.omnimap.com)

In Canada

World of Maps (☎ 613-724-6776, 🖳 www.worldofmaps.com)
World Wide Books and Maps (☎ 604-687-3320, 🖳 www.itmb.com)

In Australasia

Australia: Map Land (☎ 03-9670 4383, 🖳 www.mapland.com.au)
The Map Shop (☎ 08-8231 2033, 🖳 wwwmapshop.net.au)
New Zealand: Mapworld (☎ 03-374 5399, 🖳 www.mapworld.co.nz)

cost: at 9€ each (around £6) you'd need to spend 54€ (£36) for the full set of six covering the whole GR20, or up to 27€ (£18) for a short trek such as the Mare a Mare Sud. Map lovers, however, will consider this money well spent; if nothing else, TOP25s make great souvenirs.

The standard-issue map for motorists is the cheaper **yellow** 1:200,000 (1cm=2km) **Michelin No 90**, which covers the whole of Corsica on a single sheet. Again, it's clear, impeccably accurate and attractively styled. A neat feature of Michelin maps is the green shading which indicates roads offering outstanding scenery or views.

Mountain safety

When walking Corsica's waymarked trails it's easy to be lulled into a false sense of security. But accidents do happen, especially on exposed and remote stretches of the GR20. Nearly all are the result of inexperience, of underestimating potential dangers or being inadequately prepared for sudden deteriorations in the weather.

The key to avoiding trouble in the mountains is to **plan ahead**. Carefully assess the physical challenges of your chosen route and the impending weather conditions, and make sure you've enough warm, dry clothing, food and water to cope if things take an unexpected turn for the worse. It's also important to know your own limits: knee, ankle and foot injuries are particularly common over the first few days of a trek, before your body has fully acclimatized; and navigation is an altogether more difficult and serious business in poor visibility.

The majority of accidents happen when trekkers wander off the trail. Corsican waymarks, especially those along the GR, follow ingeniously simple routes than often mask the potentially treacherous nature of the terrain. Allow your concentration to lapse for a few minutes and you'll soon see how much steeper, more slippery and awkward the rock tends to become off the path. So if you lose the paint blobs, retrace your steps until you find them and start again rather than press on in the hope of re-joining the trail later. This is particularly important in fog or mist when you're scrambling over high ridge-tops.

Trekkers with experience of wilder, non-waymarked routes will find plenty of incentive to explore areas off the main paths. We've highlighted some of the most rewarding detours in our route guides but bear in mind that help is less likely to be at hand if you do venture off-trail and that you should thus redouble your safety precautions: keep a vigilant eye on the weather, take along a map and compass and make sure you don't go up anything you wouldn't feel happy descending afterwards. Also, take time to view your route in reverse as you progress, memorizing key landmarks in case you have to retrace your steps.

TREKKING ALONE

One of the golden rules of mountain safety is, 'never trek alone'. Without company you're considerably more vulnerable if anything should go wrong. Break a leg or ankle and you could have a very long wait or crawl to reach help. In practice, however, trekkers are rarely alone for long on Corsica's routes and many people do choose to walk solo. In this case, a few extra safety precautions are advisable. Firstly, always leave your name with a gardien if you leave the main path (eg, to climb a side peak or follow a rarely-frequented *Variant* route) and remember to let them know you've arrived safely afterwards. Secondly, wear bright clothing and carry a torch and a whistle for attracting attention if need be. The international **distress signal** in the mountains is to hold your arms above your head in a 'Y' shape; with a whistle, blow six short bursts at one-minute intervals. A mobile phone might also be a piece of precautionary kit worth considering.

In the event of accident or injury, **dehydration** is a serious risk. If you're immobilized and unable to reach help you probably won't be able to get to a water source either. It is therefore essential to carry extra water if you trek alone. On the GR20 solo walkers should also bear in mind where they are in relation to other people following the étape. Fall asleep on a rock somewhere off the main trail after lunch and you could easily find yourself detached from the main body of trekkers, which could mean a night without shelter if you injure yourself.

MOUNTAIN RESCUE

Corsica boasts a first-class, professional mountain rescue service operated by a special division of the police force (*gendarmerie*) based at Corte. Throughout the summer their red-and-white helicopters patrol the mountains, airlifting out injured trekkers and climbers. If you're ever in the unfortunate position of needing to summon their help, make sure you know as exactly as possible where you are (and can ideally quote map coordinates).

Staffed refuges all have radio links with the gendarmerie. Otherwise, the liaison routes outlined throughout the guide indicate the quickest way to a telephone.

When the chopper or rescue team appears, alert the crew by raising both your arms above your head. Try to get the victim on to open ground from where they may be most easily recovered.

Finally, bear in mind our advice on insurance (see p44). The gendarmerie

Emergency help

- **By phone** In the event of a serious accident, phone ☎ **17** (police) or ☎ **18** (fire brigade). If you're unable to get through to either of these numbers try the Peloton de Gendarmerie de Haute Montagne (PGHM) on ☎ 04.95.30.36.32 or ☎ 04.95.29.18.18
- **At a refuge** Emergency services may be summoned from any refuge.
- **By mobile phone** In principle, even in areas without coverage, you should be able to reach the emergency services by dialling ☎ **112**.

Lightning

The proximity of Corsica's mountains to the sea ensures a steady succession of violent electric storms in the summer. Lightning thus poses a very real risk to trekkers, especially those on the GR20. Over the past decade it has been the cause of more fatalities than anything else along the route.

The way to work out if a storm is heading in your direction is to count the gap between the 'flash' and the 'bang'. Light travels around one mile (1.6km) in five seconds, so if you hear the thunder ten seconds after you see the lightning, it means the storm is only two miles away. You should then check repeatedly to see if this gap is increasing or decreasing.

To avoid being struck:

- Avoid open water (streams and lakes)
- Jettison anything metal you may be carrying, such as carabiners or trekking poles
- Move off high, exposed ground as quickly as possible
- Do not shelter under solitary trees
- Avoid close contact with other trekkers; if you're in a group, spread out
- Avoid places where elements meet (such as stream banks, boulder edges and the bottom of trees)
- Never shelter under boulders (dry crevices in rocks are OK). Other relatively safe places to hide include shrubs, ground beneath trees of uniform height and dry trenches.
- Crouch with your feet together and your head tucked over your knees if possible.
- Remain vigilant for 30 minutes after the storm has passed.

don't always charge for their services but are entitled to do so (they will if they think you've been imprudent), in which case your rescue could set you back a huge amount of money.

WEATHER FORECASTS

The latest weather bulletins for the Corsican mountains are posted (in French) twice daily on ☎ 08.36.68.02.20 and on the Internet at 💻 www.meteofr/meteo net/. However, they tend to offer only a general picture of expected conditions over the interior massifs. The most reliable sources of localized weather information, particularly high in the mountains, are the refuge gardiens, who are familiar with conditions typical of the route you'll be covering.

Health and insurance

Citizens of all EU countries are entitled to free emergency medical care on production of an **E111 form**. In the UK these are available at most post offices; get one and fill it out before you leave home. An E111 won't, however, cover the cost of a routine doctor's consultation, nor of medicine or dental treatment (in principle you can claim a proportion of these expenses back from your home health service by sending off the receipts on your return).

More importantly, E111s don't cover mountain rescue, which can cost a small fortune in Corsica. For this reason some kind of private **insurance** cover is essential. Most companies will include trekking in their standard travel policies as long as it doesn't involve the use of ropes, but you should always check beforehand.

In addition to meeting medical and emergency expenses, typical travel policies also insure your equipment, money and air ticket against theft or damage and will make good costs incurred through loss of luggage or journey curtailment. However, the level of cover varies considerably between companies, which is why you should carefully read and compare benefits tables before you purchase any insurance.

PART 2: CORSICA

Background

HISTORICAL OUTLINE

Corsica has been continuously inhabited for at least 9000 years, since settlers first crossed the Tyrrhenian Sea from what we now know as the Tuscan coast. Based on hunter-gathering and simple forms of settled agriculture, their society, whose enigmatic standing stones and burial chambers still litter the Corsican *maquis*, was perennially under threat from more technologically advanced invaders. When these first Megalithic peoples were finally forced into the mountains by warlike settlers known as the Torréens, a pattern was established that would be repeated throughout Corsica's troubled history. Time and again, waves of conquerors have poured onto the flat east coast, sweeping aside its previous colonizers to seize the region's lucrative sea lanes. Yet their subjugation of the indigenous inhabitants was rarely absolute. Greeks, Romans, Vandals, Pisans, Genoans and most recently the British and French have all counted Corsica as theirs, but none successfully quashed the spirit of rebellion that has always defined the island psyche.

Prehistoric Corsica

Archaeologists are agreed that the first permanent settlers arrived in Corsica in the seventh millennium BC, probably from northern Italy, and that they lived as hunter-gatherers in walled-up rock shelters and caves. The oldest human remains so far discovered – a 9000-year-old skeleton of a woman known as the 'Dame de Bonifacio' (see p289) – dates from this period. Rudimentary agriculture and knowledge of animal husbandry arrived a thousand years later with other incomers, establishing a pattern of transhumant life that has survived in the mountains until the present day.

The first structures – dolmens and standing stones (menhirs) – were erected in the fourth millennium. Some were carved with faces, ribs and daggers, or with helmets that when viewed from behind were unmistakably phallic. Among the oldest figurative sculpture ever found in the western Mediterranean, they are thought to have been representations of enemy warriors rather than funerary stones.

The basis of this theory was the tempestuous arrival, shortly after the period when carved menhirs started to appear (around 1500BC), of a new society on the island. The **Torréeans**, named after the huge dry-stone towers (*torri*) they piled over the remains of the megalithic peoples they vanquished, are believed to have migrated from Asia Minor. They brought with them iron-working skills – hence the daggers and helmets – and an altogether more sophisticated ritual life.

Greeks and Romans

The patterns of settlement and stone building established by the Torréeans lasted until in-fighting between various sub-groups precipitated what seems to have been a large-scale migration across the straits to Sardinia, where another bumper crop of torri sprang up over succeeding centuries. In Corsica, meanwhile, the east coast saw the first arrival of the **Greeks**. Fleeing Persian persecution and attracted by the island's position within easy reach of the Italian and French coasts, the **Phocaeans**, based at an outpost they called Alalia (now Aléria), introduced viticulture and olive trees. They also instigated a prosperous trade in grain and in copper, lead and iron ore mined in Cap Corse. The colony's success, however, did not go unnoticed by the Phocaeans' rivals in the Mediterranean and within 30 years Alalia found itself overwhelmed first by the **Etruscans** and later by the **Carthaginians**, with the former colonizers pushed north-west to their new capital at Massiglia (now Marseille).

Hot on their heels was the **Roman** general Lucius Cornellius Scipio, who invaded in 259BC, renaming the settlement **Aléria**. A systematic programme of building and territorial expansion ensued, but it took another 40 years to subdue the Corsican tribes of the east, who had teamed up with the Carthaginians to fight the occupiers, and a full hundred years before the interior could be brought to heel.

Bolstered by thriving trade in luxury goods such as jewellery, ceramics, honey and clothes – and by the presence in the largest of the east coast's lagoons of a major naval base – Corsica's Pax Romanica endured for five centuries, during which time **Christianity** gained its first toe-hold on the island. Aléria's downfall was ushered in by the devastating fire of AD410 which laid waste to most of its civic buildings and much of its population.

Weakened by constant malaria epidemics, the dwindling Roman settlement that survived was further depleted by attacks from the **Vandals**, who occupied much of the island in the late fifth century. They, in turn, were ousted by a succession of regional powers: Byzantines, Ostrogoths and, in AD725, the Lombard kings from Italy. By this time, however, Corsica was beginning to reel from repeated incursions by **Saracen** raiders from the Barbary states of North Africa. What began as essentially a campaign of piracy, mounted to take slaves and plunder, gathered momentum until permanent settlements crept inland.

Saracen raid, ninth century
(Lithograph from *Histoire Illustrée de la Corse*, Galletti)

Papal rule

Meanwhile, a promise had been made in 754 by Pépin le Bref, king of the Franks, by which he agreed to hand over the island to the **Papacy** in exchange for help defeating his arch-enemies, the Lombards – a contract eventually honoured two decades later by King Charlemagne (781–810), Pépin's heir. But, despite mounting punitive missions to the Maghreb coast, the Papacy found it impossible to repulse the Saracen raids, which were draining the coastal settlements of their lifeblood and destroying the island's already lame economy.

Forced to take refuge in the interior, the islanders regrouped in the mountains as the Papacy in alliance with the Pisans and Genoese attempted to curb the Saracen onslaught. In their fortified *castelli*, the Corsicans gradually evolved their own system of loose feudal government, dominated by local overlords (*signori*) known as the **Cinarchesi** who, opposing or conciliating the Papacy, Pisa and Genoa as circumstances required, ruled their respective territories. Although elected chiefdoms initially, many were able to consolidate their power by taxing their subjects and establishing hereditary clans. Some of these dynasties, such as the Colonna d'Istrias and Della Roccas, continue to dominate the island's political life to this day.

Ruthlessly individualistic, jealous and unprincipled, the Cinarchesi dissipated their power by constant feuding; they failed to mount a unified challenge against either the Saracens or their Italian rulers. However, they were able to increasingly assert their authority as the Saracen threat subsided, beaten back by retributive attacks mounted from Pisa and Genoa.

Pisans and Genoans

By 1077 Pope Gregory VII had given up attempting to administer Corsica and its troublesome nobles and, in recognition of Pisa's support for the Papacy's war against the Saracens, dispatched the Pisan Bishop Landolph to whip the island's church into shape. Full administrative control was handed over 14 years later by Gregory's successor, Urban V.

The most eloquent and enduring symbols of **Pisan rule**, and of the ambitious ecclesiastical mission the Pisans mounted in Corsica in the eleventh and twelfth centuries, are the exquisite Romanesque **chapels** dotted all over the island. Made of immaculately dressed yellow granite, these churches were marvels of medieval mathematical precision. Unostentatious yet quietly impressive, they were built first on the ruins of the old Roman cities and later at major intersections of mule paths at the centre of traditional *pieves*, or parishes. One of the best preserved of them – the Chapel of Saint Jean Baptiste – still stands alongside the Mare a Mare Sud trekking route, on the fringes of Fozzano in the Alta Rocca region of south Corsica (see p276).

Pope Urban's decision to make Corsica a Pisan protectorate only served to intensify Genoan claims to the island. In 1133 the Papacy was finally forced to appease the two warring Italian superpowers, dividing the bishoprics between them. The fighting, however, continued unabated, with Genoa capturing Bonifacio in 1187 and Calvi in 1208 before decisively defeating the Pisan navy in the battle of Meloria in 1284.

Taking advantage of the ongoing struggle, the Corsican leader **Sinucello della Rocca** marshalled popular resentment against the increasingly rapacious local Cinarchesi *signori* and declared Corsica an autonomous principality, with himself as head. Through clever politicking he even mustered enough support to form a prototype national assembly, complete with its own rudimentary constitution, before the rout of the Pisan navy deprived him of his strongest ally. Stripped of his lands and betrayed by an illegitimate son, Sinucello was finally captured by the Genoans in his 90s and imprisoned on the mainland, where he died in 1306.

Only nine years earlier, Pope Bonifacio VIII had made a bold initiative to forestall Genoa's replacement of Pisa as Corsica's overlords by conferring sovereignty on the Spanish kings of **Aragon**. They, however, were unable to press their claim despite repeated attempts to do so in the 1330s. Their attacks were repulsed by the Genoans, whose own campaigns to break out of the coastal strongholds and extend power across the island were foiled by outbreaks of the Black Death.

The People's Revolt of 1358

With both Aragon and Genoa held at bay, a power vacuum formed in which the Cinarchesi warlords, whose influence had for decades been limited by Pisan domination and the unassailable supremacy of Sinucello della Rocca, were able once again to flex their feudal muscles, increasing taxes on the local population and making repeated calls to arms in pursuit of their territorial claims.

Popular indignation at such abuses of seigneurial power eventually erupted into a full-blown **people's revolt,** led in 1358 by **Sambocuccio d'Alando**. He and his army quickly seized control of the land north and east of the island's watershed – known as the Diqua dai Munti ('this side of the mountains') – driving the Cinarchesi signori from their castles and incorporating their ancestral lands into a region known henceforth as the Terra del Comune. Keen to consolidate these victories and form a buttress against any future Aragonese/Cinarchesi expansion, Sambocuccio invited the Genoans to send a governor for the province. Meanwhile, the wild south-west of the island, the Dila dai Munti ('beyond the mountains', also known as the Terra dai Signori), remained a Cinarchesi stronghold backed by the kings of Aragon.

The Terra del Comune regime instituted by Sambocuccio, which endured for nearly two hundred years, was an extraordinarily enlightened one for the times. Villages were governed democratically by *consulte*, assemblies made up of local people (some of them women), while agricultural land was owned and managed collectively.

Ensconced in their coastal fortresses, the trade-oriented Genoans were content to allow the Terra del Comune's rural population to rule itself. Over time, however, the visionary democratic system began to crumble as a new hereditary class of nobles – the so-called *caporali* – emerged and revived the old system of private land ownership. At around the same time the Aragonese-backed Cinarchesi started to mount vicious attacks on the Genoans' main strongholds, pitching the island into a period of great instability.

The most successful of the Cinarchesi warlords was the demonic **Vincentello d'Istria**, a lurid, charismatic figure with a wart on his face the size of a dislodged eyeball. Through exceptional military prowess and some inspired statesmanship he was able to extend his rule over nearly all the island and might have achieved total independence for Corsica had not his erstwhile supporters mounted a coup and handed him over to the Genoans for execution.

Unable to contain the mounting anarchy of the early fifteenth century, Genoa was compelled to transfer stewardship of Corsica to the **Office of St George**, a wealthy trade corporation with its own private army. It was the Office who erected the mighty citadels that still dominate many Corsican towns and strengthened coastal defences with a chain of watchtowers (see p301). Their forces managed to impose order, containing the perennial threat from the Cinarchesi warlords, whose repeated attempts to oust the Office eventually proved their downfall. By 1511 the last of them had been wiped out.

Sampiero Corso and the Genoan era

Meanwhile the struggle for power in Europe between Francis I of France and the Hapsburg Emperor Charles V was being continued by their sons, Henry II of France and Philip II of Spain. The Genoans – and involuntarily the Corsicans – were under alliance to the Hapsburgs and so Henry II despatched an expeditionary fleet against them to take Corsica and its key Genoan ports. Dominated by a large Turkish contingent under the infamous corsair Dragut, this naval force was led by a Corsican mercenary, **Sampiero Corso**, who had forged an illustrious reputation as a captain in the French army. Having quickly and easily taken Bastia, Ajaccio and Corte he mounted protracted sieges against the tougher nuts of Bonifacio and Calvi, which were bombarded by the Turkish galleons before being comprehensively pillaged.

Sampiero Corso

French rule, however, was short-lived. As part of the expedient and far-reaching Treaty of Cateau-Cambrésis of 1559, through which France allied itself with Genoa to fight the Austrian Hapsburgs, the Genoans were handed back the island. Furious at this betrayal, Sampiero responded by staging an insurrection of his own in 1564. He and his troops swiftly took control of the interior, but support for their cause began to wane following repeated failures to take the Genoan ports. He was finally ambushed and beheaded in 1567, not by his Italian arch-adversaries but by his former brothers-in-law, who claimed to be avenging the death of their sister (Sampiero had strangled her after she'd betrayed him to the Genoans and run off to France with his family fortune).

With the Cinarchesi defeated and the French neutralized, Genoan rule settled into a period of relative stability in the sixteenth century. The Italians tightened their economic grip on the island: punitive taxes, trade monopolies and artificially low grain prices were imposed on a disgruntled rural population. Nevertheless they gave Corsican agriculture a much-needed boost: vast forests of chestnut trees were planted to make good a shortfall in cereal on the continent, and extensive olive orchards and vineyards were established. The resulting prosperity, which gave rise over time to a new Corsican bourgeoisie, lasted for 170 years, until the educated, politicized class the boom had spawned turned on its Genoan rulers.

The wars of independence

The catalyst for the **uprising of 1729** was the refusal of villagers near Corte to pay taxes imposed in the wake of two failed harvests. Spurred on by their compatriots' example, other villages followed suit, leading to a formal declaration of national independence two years later. To help put down the rebellion, the Genoans petitioned their old allies, the Austrians. Hapsburg Emperor Charles VI of Austria agreed to send a force of 8000 troops in 1732, but the venture got off to a bad start when hundreds of them were massacred while trying to storm Calenzana (see p113). Having licked their wounds, the Genoan and Austrian commanders made a much better job of the other Balange strongholds, eventually pounding the rebels into a surrender.

The insurrection flared up again as soon as the fleet had left, but the Corsicans were depleted and hopelessly short of finance. Help, however, was at hand in a most peculiar form: **Théodore Von Neuhof**, a wealthy Westphalian dandy who had been a page in the French court, saw in Corsica a golden opportunity to realize his fantasy of becoming a reigning monarch. Having secured finance from Jewish and Greek merchants in Tunis, he landed at Aléria dressed as a Turkish Sultan with a retinue of Italians and Moors. Desperate to get their hands on his money and guns, the Corsican rebels agreed to the bizarre preconditions the adventurer made for his support and proclaimed him King Théodore I of Corsica. But after a few half-hearted sieges and ineffectual war games with the Genoans, it became clear the island's first king was far more suited to swanning around his make-believe court than ousting the Italian oppressors, and eight months later in November 1736 he was forced to make an ignominious departure from the east coast disguised as a priest.

The ensuing stalemate was broken two years later when, in response to a Genoan appeal for aid in 1738, the **French** sent troops to subdue the uprising. They killed more than a thousand patriots and many more were forced to flee before the French pulled out three years later. But the tide seemed to turn in the rebels' favour when the British, Austrians and Sardinians, seeking strategic advantage against the Genoan-French-Spanish axis in the War of Austrian Succession, dispatched a fleet to reinforce the Corsican general **Gian'Pietru Gaffori**. Hope that this support would prove decisive was dashed when the British signed a peace treaty with the French and withdrew, but the war of independence rumbled on. Gaffori proclaimed a national constitution in 1752, based on military rule with himself as de facto head of state. That same year he and his patriot army stormed the Genoan stronghold of Corte.

Pascal Paoli

Gaffori was assassinated by Genoan stooges the following year, but his death only strengthened the nationalists' hand. To replace him the *consulta* at Corte recalled from the continent the heir of one his most trusted generals, Giacinto Paoli, who had fled the island during the French onslaught. By the time he had become leader of the nation in 1755, **Pascal Paoli**, only 29 years old, was already steeped in the egalitarian political philosophies of Montesquieu and Rousseau. His plan was explicit from the start: to expel the Genoans and French by force of arms and install a lasting, autonomous, democratic government on the island.

The **Constitution** he subsequently devised was built on the island's existing model of representative democracy. According the vote to every man over the age of 25 and requiring that every parish send an elected deputy to a National Assembly based at Corte, it embodied the political tenets of the Enlightenment (sovereignty of the people, subordination of church to state, and the suppression of hereditary privileges) and was a pioneering experiment for its time. Rousseau praised Paoli's achievement in the strongest terms (he even considered coming to live in Corte) and the Americans were clearly inspired by Corsica's blueprint when they drafted their own Constitution 15 years later.

Pascal Paoli

Other trappings of state followed: a mint and printing press were established, along with schools and the island's first university, and an arms factory opened. Radical new laws were also passed to curb the appalling **vendettas** that had caused tens of thousands of deaths during the Genoan period.

A visionary and charismatic politician he may have been, but the man granted the honorific title 'U Babu di a Patria' (Father of the Nation) possessed a far from flawless military sense. Time and again during his 14-year generalship the forces under his command squandered opportunities to evict the Genoans from their six citadels. Weakened by the naval blockade, the patriot army was also grossly under-equipped to take on the French forces occupying the five main coastal towns.

The beginning of the end for Paoli's regime came in 1768, when the Genoans finally sold off their remaining claim to the island to the French, who promptly

The Battle of Ponte Nuovo

dispatched 9000 troops to bring the Corsicans to heel. Although outnumbered nearly two-to-one, Paoli's men held on by harrying their better-trained, better-equipped adversaries with guerrilla attacks. But when 15 more battalions were sent from the mainland, bolstering the invading force to 30,000, Paoli made the fatal error of committing his army to open combat. Drawn into a pitched battle at **Ponte Nuovo** on May 8, 1769, the Corsicans were massacred and their leader, who was not present at the final engagement, fled to England.

Fêted by London high society and granted a stipend of £12,000 a year, Paoli bided his time for two decades until the French monarchy was swept aside and the new revolutionary state announced an amnesty for political exiles. Seeing this as his cue, the former leader returned in a blaze of glory and was quickly installed as president. Corsica, however, had moved on. A whole new generation had grown up since Ponte Nuovo and its most promising members – among them a young Napoléon Bonaparte – had been creamed off into French military academies where any latent nationalism had been drummed out of them. Of the old guard that remained, few had any stomach for the fight envisaged by Paoli – a fight that was doomed from the start. On the very day he set foot on the island again the Corsican Assembly voted to become an integral part of the new French state.

Napoléon Bonaparte as a young officer

The Anglo-Corsican interlude

Nevertheless, Paoli still boasted many supporters on the island and when he finally fell out of favour with the French (over their ill-conceived invasion of neighbouring Sardinia) the resurgent Paolists, led by the Assembly, rallied to prevent his arrest. Fearing a civil war, families loyal to Paris – including the Bonapartes – fled, leaving their homes to the rampaging nationalist mobs.

Paoli and his ageing generals, meanwhile, knew they would be hopelessly outgunned when the inevitable French backlash came and moved quickly to secure the support of their old British allies, who sent a fleet under **Sir Gilbert Elliot** to bail them out in 1794. Spurred on by a young **Horatio Nelson**, the expeditionary force laid siege to the French garrisons at Bastia, Saint-Florent and, finally, Calvi (where Nelson lost the sight in his right eye). But the price for this intervention would be a high one. Rather than restoring Paoli as president, the British nominated Elliot as viceroy. The move provoked riots across Corsica, whereupon Paoli was forcibly exiled to London. When his humiliated soldiers started to join forces with the French to mount reprisals on the British, Sir Gilbert and his troops made a prudently swift exit.

The Napoleonic era and restoration of the French monarchy

In spite of this fleeting, expedient alliance, patriotic opposition to French rule continued unabated throughout the 1790s. However, the uprisings were given short shrift by Napoleon and his dictatorial generals, who mounted a succession of brutal crackdowns culiminating in the imposition of direct military rule in 1801.

Although Napoleon never enjoyed the unanimous respect of his fellow islanders, his demise 14 years later marked the end of an era for Corsica. Impoverished by centuries of rebellion and vendetta, its population began towards the beginning of the nineteenth century to set aside aspirations of independence and accept that its best chance of advancement lay in a future with France. Along with French citizenship came new opportunities. The expanding trade empire in Africa and South America needed administrators, and thousands of Corsicans would carve out lucrative careers as *pieds noirs* (literally 'black feet'; expatriates) in the colonies. Still more left their ancestral land to emigrate to the great cities of metropolitan France.

Back on the island itself, development gathered pace. A network of new roads and a railway line between Bastia and Ajaccio improved connections between sides of Corsica which had for centuries been separated by high mountains. More schools were founded and mines opened to generate work. Even the bloody tradition of vendetta, which had resisted Paoli's attempts to stamp it out, went into decline. None of this, however, could stem the flood of **emigration**. The island remained in essence a peripheral, deprived and irredeemably poor part of the country, and during the second half of the nineteenth century its population almost halved.

The impact of emigration on the traditional economy was devastating. Subsistence farming disappeared altogether, while in the mountains whole villages became deserted as their inhabitants gave up shepherding to seek wage labour elsewhere.

The early twentieth century

Considering its history of acrimonious opposition to French rule, the island responded with surprising commitment to the general mobilization of 1914. Grouped into their own regiments, Corsican soldiers quickly earned a reputation for the ferocity of their hand-to-hand fighting, epitomized by their use in combat of the *rustaghja* (a kind of billhook meat-chopper designed for *charcuterie)*. However, Corsican bravery on the battlefield was ill-suited to the brutal realities of machine-gun warfare. In all, around 20,000 islanders perished in the 1914–18 war – more per capita than from any other region of Europe.

If the effects of pre-war emigration had been dire, the loss of what amounted to an entire generation of men had catastrophic consequences for Corsica. With the economy in ruins, anyone who could do so sent their children to the continent where, if family contacts could not procure salaried jobs, they eked out a precarious living as pavement vendors or migrant labourers. Others slipped into the **underworld** and during the 1920s organized crime on the Côte d'Azur came to be dominated by Corsican gangsters.

For the first time, ordinary uneducated islanders started to become familiar with money. Even if they weren't living on the continent and earning much themselves, they would see what it could buy. One of the consequences of this shift from subsistence to a more cash-oriented economy was the emergence of a new kind of **banditry**. Forced to take to the maquis after committing a vendetta murder, the traditional Corsican *bandit d'honneur* (see p278) was a tragi-heroic figure; a victim of deeply-held honour codes who lived a life of poverty, dependent on the goodwill of his clansmen. During the 1920s, however, Corsican outlaws, taking their cue from the continental *milieu* (underworld), began to turn to racketeering and armed robbery. The resulting levels of violence and intimidation became so bad by 1931 that in November of that year the *gendarmerie* sent a special expeditionary force to wipe out the *bandits percepteurs* ('tax-collecting bandits'). The crackdown was successful, but the way in which traditional vendetta-style violence had slipped into naked extortion had set a dangerous precedent for the future.

Corsican Maquisards, 1943

World War II

Concerns over Corsica's endemic poverty and crime problems were swept suddenly aside by the outbreak of war in 1939. The Italian dictator Benito Mussolini had long before set his sights on Corsica, regarding the islanders as Italians in all but name, and took the opportunity to mount what he regarded as a 'Liberation'. The Corsicans, however, regarded the arrival of 80,000 Italian troops on their soil somewhat differently.

Penned up by the saturation force, they could do little to counter the occupation until the Free French command in Algiers, under the rival generals de Gaulle and Giraud, decided to set up a Resistance network on the island. This was achieved using a submarine, the ***Casabianca***, which made daring missions to the Corsican coast from North Africa to drop agents, radios, arms, munitions and money. In all, seven landings were completed between December 1942 and September 1943, when the 12,000-strong Resistance movement – known as the Maquis because its members spent most of the occupation hiding out in the bush – was finally called into action.

Maquisard, 1943
Note British sten gun and *Tête de Maure* symbol

The catalyst was the signing of the Italian armistice. Mussolini's fall and Germany's subsequent declaration of war on its former ally had neutralized the Italian troops stationed on the island. But it had also unleashed a much more sinister force of 10,000 Germans dug into a bridgehead near Bonifacio. As the Allies pressed northwards from Sicily in the autumn of 1943, Marshal Kesselring withdrew his Ninth Panzer Division via Sardinia and Corsica's east coast, covered by the German rearguard. Together with special operations battalions from North Africa the Maquis did their best to forestall the German retreat and there was fierce fighting around Levie and along the east coast. However, with the bulk of the allies' air forces tied up in Italy, Kesselring's general, Von Senger und Etterlin, was able to evacuate most of his division from Bastia to Leghorn (Livorno) without significant loss.

American bombing of Bastia
This catastrophic attack took place on the day after the city's liberation by Free French forces, September 1943.

Nonetheless, the departure of the Germans was hailed as a **Liberation** – the first of a metropolitan French *département* – and Général de Gaulle moved swiftly to claim credit for the victory (even though it had been masterminded by his arch-adversary, Giraud). Meanwhile the left-wing leaders of the Maquis seized control of the island's administration, much to the chagrin of the right-wing Général, who went to great lengths in the coming years to prevent the same thing from happening again when mainland France was liberated by the allies.

For the rest of the war Corsica served as an advance base for 'Operation Anvil', the invasion of southern France. American forces were stationed on the east coast and Bastia's Poretta airport became an important base from which allied planes flew missions into occupied Italy. Among the many airmen

Liberation
(Contemporary illustration, 1943)

who lost their lives while stationed there was the French novelist Antoine de St-Exupéry, who disappeared on a reconnaissance flight out of Bastia in 1944.

The post-war period

After 1945 thousands of demobilized Corsicans returned to find their homeland as poor as ever. The Americans had sprayed the eastern coastal plain with DDT to rid it of malarial mosquitos, but paid employment was still scarce and the rate of emigration continued to rise: port records from the 1960s show that there were 10,000 more departures than arrivals annually.

To reverse the effect of centuries of economic neglect, the French government launched a two-pronged regeneration programme aimed at reviving **agriculture** and **tourism** on the island. Fruit and wine-growing took off on the east coast and visitor numbers rose to more than half a million in the early 1970s, but few Corsicans felt any real benefit from the initiatives. On the contrary, de Gaulle seemed bent on penalizing the islanders, stripping away their long-standing tax exemptions and increasing duty on cigarettes, tobacco and public transport. The effect of such attempts to bring the Corsican economy in line with that of the mainland was a sharp downturn in the balance of payments and rampant inflation.

Repeated strikes by an increasingly militant workforce seemingly had no effect on de Gaulle, who enraged public opinion still further by announcing that the remote Balagne-Déserte area south-west of Calvi was to be used as a testing ground for atomic bombs. When peaceful public protests failed to reverse his decision, angry armed activists kidnapped a team of government surveyors and threatened to kill them if the Elysée Palace didn't back down. It did, though: at the last minute work on the project was suspended. The **Argentella episode**, as the controversy became known, was effectively the first time since the restoration of the monarchy that Corsicans had taken up arms against the French state. It was to prove a turning point in the island's history.

Nationalist violence and the FLNC

De Gaulle's short-sighted policies had stirred up considerable anti-French feeling, but it was under the presidency of Giscard d'Estaing that this resentment coalesced into a fully-fledged **armed struggle**. Its prologue was the arrival in Corsica of around 15,000 *pieds noirs* refugees, repatriated to the island following the Algerian war. Hot on the heels of the Argentella debacle, their appearance was seen as yet another example of the State using Corsica as a 'dumping ground'. When it emerged that some of the *pieds noirs* wine growers were adulterating their produce with sugar to bump up its alcohol content (thereby threatening the reputation of the island's *appellation contrôlée* vineyards) a group of radical nationalists decided to teach them and the Elysée Palace a lesson.

On August 21, 1975, a team of separatist commandos occupied the cellar of an offending grower in **Aléria** and a siege ensued in which two of the 1250-strong force of *gendarmes* dispatched by Paris to flush them out were shot dead. The gunmen eventually surrendered and were packed off to prison on the mainland but their action led to the creation soon after of the Fronte di Liberazione Nazionale di Corsica, or **FLNC**.

For the next four years the Front pursued its goal of total independence with bombing campaigns, assassinations and machine-gun attacks on State property, both in mainland France and on the island itself. Second homes became another popular target, as did drug dealers. Money for the Front's struggle was raised initially through racketeering, which over time became institutionalized as *impôt revolutionnaire,* or 'revolutionary tax'. Inevitably the system's potential for abuse proved too strong a temptation for Corsica's petty criminals, the so-called *petits truands*, who soon followed in the footsteps of their bandit forebears and began extorting money under the umbrella of FLNC legitimacy.

Attempts by successive French governments to crack down on the worrying levels of separatist-related crime on the island failed to have any impact. Less than a decade after Aléria, what had started out as an ideologically motivated campaign of violence directed primarily at the State had degenerated into a form of organized crime with its own momentum.

By the late 1980s fault lines had begun to appear in the heart of the movement. With the Mitterrand-Rocard administration adopting a more conciliatory approach to *le problème corse*, disagreement raged over how best to take the struggle forward. Personal rivalries within the Front also began to intensify, culminating in 1990 with the **division of the FLNC** (and its respective political wings) into two factions: the Canal-Habituel and Canal-Historique.

Far from resolving the old power struggles, the split came as a de facto declaration of war between opposing elements in the armed nationalist movement. A bloody feud erupted and by the mid-1990s Corsica seemed to have descended into the dark days of its vendetta-ridden past. Dozens of militants were gunned down or car bombed – 15 of them in the summer of 1995 alone.

In Paris, meanwhile, under the presidency of Jacques Chirac, Prime Minister Juppé's government was pursuing a double-handed policy, publicly claiming not to talk to terrorists while secretly meeting FLNC leaders. These clandestine negotiations bore dramatic fruit in 1996 when between 450 and 600 Canal-Historique militants, armed to the teeth with a terrifying array of modern weaponry, staged a nocturnal press conference (or *nuit bleue*) at **Tralonca** to announce a truce. But the publicity stunt backfired hopelessly on its participants. Confronted with this mass of balaclava-wearing gunmen – not to mention their awesome arsenal of AK-47s, Kalashnikovs, grenade launchers and anti-aircraft missiles – the French public was horrified. As a result, Juppé could neither be seen to be giving in to the Front's demands nor even fulfilling promises made covertly in the talks that preceded the show of force. A deadlock ensued that was broken in defiant style the following summer when the FLNC-Canal-Historique bombed Bordeaux's *mairie* (where Juppé had been mayor since 1995).

By far the most shocking recent FLNC atrocity was the murder in 1998 of Préfet **Claude Erignac**, the French State's most senior representative on the island; he was shot in the head while leaving the opera in Ajaccio with his wife. The murder provoked outrage in Corsica and a groundswell of opposition to the armed struggle among ordinary islanders. One of the telling statistics revealed by a public enquiry into the troubles that year was that Corsica accounted for around half of France's violent crime, despite having only 0.05% of its population.

Paris, however, left the moral high ground it briefly occupied in spectacular style when Erignac's hard-line successor, Préfet Bernard Bonnet, was arrested and imprisoned for having ordered police commandos to carry out an illegal arson attack on the business of an FLNC militant. The so-called **Affaire de la Paillote** (the beach-shack scandal) redrew the political map: soon after it thousands of indignant Corsicans marched through the streets of Ajaccio calling for greater autonomy.

Meanwhile, the war between paramilitary factions rumbled on. A compelling behind-the-scenes insight into the feud appeared in April 2000 with the publication of a book by two former leaders of the FLNC, Jean-Michel Rossi and François Santoni. In it the two exploded the culture of secrecy that had enshrouded the inner workings of the armed struggle since its inception, exposing the degree to which the FLNC had become corrupted by mafia-style organized crime. Rossi and Santoni must have known that by breaking the Front's cardinal code of silence, not to mention blowing the whistle on some very powerful players in the Corsican underworld, they were signing their own death warrants. Yet their eventual assassinations – Rossi's on an Ile Rousse café terrace in July 2000, and Santoni's at a family wedding a little over a year later – still deeply shocked the island.

Corsica today

Santoni's murder had the side effect of intensifying hawkish opposition to the peace negotiations which Prime Minister Lionel Jospin had reinitiated in the spring of 2000. The crux of these talks between Paris and the nationalists had been the so-called **Matignon Plan**, a wide-ranging portfolio of proposals offering increased autonomy for Corsica in return for an end to separatist violence. But the worsening situation on the island, plus the dramatic resignation of Jospin's Interior Minister over the PM's Corsica policies, had forced a climbdown by the Elysée Palace. Crucial parts of the initiative were withdrawn or diluted and by the winter of 2000–2001 the Gaullist opponents of Matignon were claiming the peace process was dead in its bed.

It was therefore with an immense sigh of relief that the island greeted news in December 2001 that a compromise had finally been forged between the government and a confederation of nationalist parties. Granting a radical degree of independence to the island, including executive powers for the Corsican Assembly, the Matignon agreement was hailed as a major breakthrough.

One of its key achievements was an implicit recognition of the sea change in popular attitudes to French rule that had take place in Corsica. At the start of the nationalist struggle in the early 1970s the movement's agenda was clear, its objectives, and methods deployed by the FLNC in pursuit of them, largely supported by the majority of the population. But since then many of the root causes of resentment – under-investment, the treatment of political prisoners and the status of the Corsican language – have been addressed. France now pours €1.07 billion (around £660 million) of subsidies each year into the island, which benefits from preferential tax laws and social security exemptions. Four international airports, eight maritime ports and a network of high-grade roads have also been built, and there have been two amnesties for paramilitary prisoners as well as the inauguration of a Corsican university at Corte.

Such concessions may not have entirely made good the damage done by years of government neglect, but they did render Corsicans far more sympathetic to the idea of being part of the Republic. A poll in 1998 revealed that 92% of islanders were in favour of remaining French. Even hardliners these days concede that full independence is no longer a realistic or desirable objective. Without huge financial support from the French State Corsica could simply not hope to survive economically.

At the same time, what the traumas of the past three decades seem to have reaffirmed above all else is that the island's problems cannot be resolved by money alone. Underpinning the armed struggle is a traditional Mediterranean culture dominated by clan affiliations and readiness to resort to violence as a means of solving disputes. No amount of cash is likely to eradicate such tendencies. On the contrary, the recent tourist boom and massive investment from Paris and Brussels seem only to have exposed just how deeply entrenched these old values remain. The vicious feud between FLNC factions may have been expressed in terms of nationalism, but it embodied precisely the same fault lines that have fractured Corsican society since medieval times, and probably long before.

GEOLOGY

Corsica is broadly composed of two contrasting types of rock: crystalline **granite** in the south, centre and west, and schist in the north-east. It cannot be coincidental that the ancient political divisions of the Diqua and Dila dai Munti (see p48) – not to mention the modern rivalry between the départements of Corse-du-Sud and Haute-Corse, and their respective capitals Ajaccio and Bastia – replicate this essential geological dichotomy, which has endowed Corsica with a distinctly dual nature.

The two kinds of rock were created by different processes. First to form was the **magmatic**, which emerged hot from the earth's crust and over time cooled to become granite (including rhyolite and gabbro), mica and quartz. Later, volcanic lava poured from the crater of what is now Monte Cinto, Corsica's highest mountain, to add dollops of multi-coloured alkaline granite – the source of Scandola's startling red porphyry and the green-tinged cliffs of the Spelunca Gorge.

While these crystalline rocks were being eroded into the convoluted mass they are today, newer sedimentary deposits were forming in the sea beside them. Compression, caused by heat and tectonic movement as the Alps were being formed in the Tertiary Period 30 million years ago, then compacted these deposits to form **metamorphic** schist, the dark-green, shiny, slate-like rock of the island's northern and eastern flanks.

It is thought that throughout this period the Sardo-Corsican land mass was still firmly attached to the continent. By matching up rock on Corsica's west coast with the granite of the Massif de l'Estérel in Provence, geologists have theorized it must at some point have broken away and rotated south and east through the Mediterranean towards Italy.

Successive submergings then sculpted this drifting land mass, eroding basins which over millennia became filled with further sedimentary deposits – the origin of the white chalk outcrops and plateaux of Saint-Florent and Bonifacio. Glaciation added the final touches: the U-shaped valleys of the Corsican interior, arêtes (sharp mountain ridges), cirques (giant bowl-shaped hollows at the head of valleys), moraines (colossal dumps of boulders) and suspended valleys that dominate the landscape along the GR20 were all formed by the movement of vast ice flows.

The retreat of the glaciers and massive fluctuation in sea levels as the earth passed through its various ice ages might also explain how animals first reached Corsica. It is believed that at some point in its distant geological past the island was lapped by a much lower sea and that some kind of land bridge must have existed with the Italian coast, across which the first mammals would have migrated.

TOPOGRAPHY

An extension of the southern Alps adrift in the Mediterranean, Corsica is essentially a mountain range marooned in the sea. Most of the island lies more than 320m above sea level, and half a dozen peaks rise to an altitude of more than 2300m, the highest of them Monte Cinto (2706m). These major summits are all grouped in the **north-west**, from where the mighty Corsican watershed wriggles in a south-easterly direction. Running off it is a twisting, herringbone mass of deep valleys that funnel countless streams and rivers down to the coast. Each of these 19 principal valley systems makes up a distinct micro-region, often with its own patterns of weather, flora and land use. Walking between them you'll get a strong sense of their contrasting characters as rock colours, forest constitutions and humidity levels change.

In the **west** the mountain spurs of the central range extend right into the sea in many places, creating a convoluted coastline of dramatic, fjord-like inlets separated by huge ridges. The most spectacular of these is the Golfe de Porto, where giant red porphyry cliffs soar vertically from the shoreline, rising to meet the nearby massif of Paglia Orba and its mantle of towering pinnacles. Strings of beautiful coves and shell-sand beaches also indent the west

Vital geo-statistics

- Corsica is 183km long from north to south (including the 40km finger-shaped peninsula of Cap Corse) and 85km wide at its broadest point.
- Its total surface area is 8682 square kilometres (roughly the same size as Crete, or just under half the size of Wales). Its nearest neighbour, Sardinia, 12km to the south, is nearly three times bigger.
- The island boasts nearly 1000km of coastline.
- Monte Cinto (2706m) is the highest mountain, with Monte Rotondo (2622m) second and Paglia Orba (2525m) third.
- At a little over 90km from source to mouth, the Tavignano River is Corsica's longest, although the Golo, which rises on Paglia Orba and drains into the sea on the east coast, flows faster.

coast, whose dramatic topography continues underwater as the land mass plunges to abysses of 800m or more.

The **eastern side** of the island, by contrast, comprises a more restrained, gently shelving alluvial plain, narrow in the north but widening towards its middle before being squeezed out by the encroaching hinterland. Striped with vineyards and fruit orchards, the fertile plain – broken by large lagoons (*étangs*) and expanses of reed-choked wetlands – provides Corsica's most productive agricultural land. Along its shore an immense, largely featureless beach extends in a straight line along virtually the whole bulging length of the island.

In the far **south** the mountains tumble into a broad wedge of undulating scrubland, dotted with outcrops of granite. A belt of white chalk crowns the tip of this south-western edge, where the former Genoan stronghold of Bonifacio clings to an overhanging lip of grooved cliffs, the shadowy profile of Sardinia clearly visible across the straits.

The watershed A watershed – *le partage des eaux* in French – is the dividing line between river systems. In Corsica's case it refers to the granite spine of the island, the central ridge down the sides of which water flows towards the different coasts. Forming a natural barrier between valley heads, the line of highest ground cleaves diagonally from the hinterland of Calvi in the north-west to Solenzara in the far south-east – the guiding principle of the GR20. The *partage des eaux* also forms the ancient frontier between the regions of Diqua and Dila dai Munti, the basis for the modern départemental division of the island.

Its name implies the presence of water, but the watershed – which remains above 1163m once clear of the coast and is crossed only three times by roads (at Col de Verghio, Vizzavona and Bocca di Verdi) – is actually bone-dry for most of its extent. Nowhere are you more aware of this fact than on the *haute-route* section of the GR20 between Pietra Piana and Monte d'Oro, where the path follows a parched, sharp-edged ridgeline from which the mountainside falls away steeply to the east coast on one side and the west coast on the other.

CLIMATE

Corsica enjoys a typical Mediterranean climate, with comparatively short, mild winters and long, hot, dry summers when average maximum **temperatures** hover around 27°C/80°F. During heat waves in July and August it is not uncommon for the island to roast at 35°C/95°F for days on end. However, temperatures drop considerably at **altitude** (typically 5°C/9°F for every 1000m/3000ft gained). Above the1000m mark the weather rarely gets unbearably hot, while at 1800m/6000ft or over night-time remains fresh even in mid-summer. Ascend above 2000m/6500ft and you'll be in the high mountains proper where weather conditions can change swiftly (see p43).

In spring (mid-March–May) and autumn (Oct–Nov) average maximum temperatures drop to a very pleasant 15–17°C/60–64°F at sea level, although these times of year can be prone to heavy rain. Corsica receives an impressive 800–900mm (30–35 inches) of **rainfall** annually (more than some parts of Ireland). Most of it, however, comes in dramatic downpours that rarely last longer than a couple of days. When it does rain, flooding is often a problem, especially in late autumn when dry river beds can suddenly be transformed into fast-flowing torrents full of upended trees and mud slicks (a good reason never to camp on one).

Freezing, snowy conditions prevail in the high mountains from January until mid-March, when the watershed and its adjacent peaks are at their whitest and most picturesque. But **frost** is a rarity down on the coast (Ajaccio gets around a dozen frosty mornings per year, and Bastia half that). Corsicans love to boast of being able to eat outdoors until Christmas – in which case old ladies will warn that '*Natale à u balcone, Pasqua à u fucone*' (Christmas on the verandah, Easter by the fire).

Dry and sunny the island may be for most of the year, but there are few days without **wind**, particularly on the coast. Depending on the direction they blow from, Corsican winds have different names and characters. When chilly and coming from the north, it might be the biting winter *traumutanda* or the summer *mistral*, the result of temperature disparities between the continent and Mediterranean which force currents of cooler air down the Rhône Valley. From the south-west, the *libecciu* often brings storms and rain, as does the *gregale* which blows off the Italian coast to the north-east. A heavy swell is usually stirred up by the *livante*, the strong east wind, while mist and fog are often the by-products of the warm, humid *sciroccu*, which blows in from North Africa. The windiest places in Corsica are Bonifacio, whose straits are notoriously perilous, and the extremities of Cap Corse in the north where some of the hillsides are completely bare.

Up in the mountains you'll notice the effects of **convection**, as differences in temperatures between the land and sea build up. During the day the granite island warms more quickly that its surrounding water mass, generating thermals that suck in humid air from the sea, which then condenses to form cloud in the afternoon. In the evenings, the same phenomenon occurs in reverse as the island cools down more quickly than the sea, creating cool offshore breezes.

FLORA AND FAUNA

Following Corsica's footpaths you'll be constantly struck by how extraordinarily unspoilt the island is. Overgrazing, indiscriminate hunting and, most recently, devastating fires have all taken their toll but, if anything, the landscape shows less evidence of human encroachment today than it would have a century or more ago, when the villages were more populated and the pressure on forests, rivers and mountain vegetation correspondingly greater. That this remains the case, in spite of some 1.75 million visitors pouring into Corsica each year, is a tribute to the immense efforts of the Parc Naturel Régional Corse (PNRC; see below) whose domain encompasses 38% of the island's surface as well as important marine reserves. Rigorous environmental laws have also kept polluters and developers at bay, as have the activities of nationalist paramilitaries, whose bombings of unsympathetic constructions and second homes have protected the coast from the kind of abuse sustained by other beautiful corners of the Mediterranean.

National parks and nature reserves

The job of protecting Corsica's rare species – including mouflon, osprey, red deer and bearded vulture – is the responsibility of the Parc Naturel Régional Corse (PNRC). Established in 1972, 'Le Parc', as it's usually referred to, encompasses 350,512 hectares of the island – 38% of Corsica's surface area. Conservation is just part of the work carried out by its 100-strong workforce, who are also charged with maintaining the 1500km network of waymarked paths. One of the premises behind the PNRC's creation of this impressive trekking infrastructure was the regeneration of the interior's flagging economy, and considerable resources have been deployed over the past three decades to renovate *bergeries*, restore remote chapels, support local artisans and generally preserve the traditional ways of life and occupations in the mountains.

Aside from its many refuges the PNRC's principal interface with the public is its **information offices** around the island, which offer advice and printed material on trekking-related matters. The best equipped of these is in Ajaccio (see p92) but you'll find others in Corte (see p231) and Porto (see p251). For a full rundown of the PNRC and its activities check out its website 💻 www.parc-naturel-corse.com.

Corsica also boasts a string of smaller **coastal nature reserves** run by the Conservatoire de l'Espace Littoral et des Rivages Lacustres (Organization for the Conservation of Coastal and Lake Areas; 'Le Littoral' for short). Since its inauguration in 1975 this government-funded body has purchased around 15% of the island's shoreline and lagoons. A few of the reserves, notably the Littoral Sartènais featured on pp300-310, have been opened up to the public by coastal paths. Plans to add more of these are also in the pipeline.

As a trekker, the most conspicuous reminder that you're walking through a nature reserve or park will be the signboards that regularly punctuate waymarked routes. Some indicate onward or liaison paths with villages; others are there to reinforce the **restrictions on camping and bivouacking** imposed in all protected areas. At notable beauty spots such as Lac de Nino and Lavu di Creno, *gardiens* are employed to ensure no-one infringes the law, which also requires you to take litter out in your pack and refrain from lighting fires. For more on minimum impact trekking see the box on p79.

Arguably the greatest threat to Corsica's pristine state today are plans currently being thrashed out between Paris, the island's politicians and militant nationalists over how far the powers of regional government should be increased. Environmentalists argue that if Corsica is granted the degree of autonomy its leaders are demanding, tough French environmental legislation might be overridden by the financial interests of unscrupulous local speculators, hastening the spread of concrete along the coast.

For the time being, however, Corsica remains exceptionally green and wild, and there's no better way of getting to grips with its wealth of flora and fauna than on foot. The island's network of trails winds through all three of its distinct **habitats**. From sea level the rich, quintessentially **Mediterranean Zone** – with palms, eucalyptus, oleander, wild cacti, olive and citrus trees standing out against the fragrant maquis scrub – extends to around 1000m. Above that, lush canopies of sweet chestnut give way to the slender pine, beech and spruce trees of the **Mountain Zone**. Rock and stream beds scattered with bushes of odorous alder and hardy flowering shrubs characterize the **Alpine Zone** above 2000m, an altitude attained only by the GR20.

The maquis

Whichever trekking route you choose, you're certain to encounter the infamous Corsican maquis, whose dense green carpet of spiny, aromatic scrub dominates the coastal zone below 1000m. The bane of walkers, it can form impenetrable walls of thorns and rough foliage that grow to a height of more than two metres if left unchecked. The maquis – from the Corsican *macchjhe* – also gives off a magnificently pungent aroma which you'll notice as soon as you set foot on the island, and probably never forget. Napoléon famously claimed he could smell it while imprisoned on Elba.

The heady fragrance derives from a mixture of plants. Most distinctive among them are members of the **cistus** (*cistre*) family, identifiable by their striking, wrinkled pink or white flower petals, which are shed each evening and their sticky resinous stems and leaves. This is the source of myrrh; Corsican shepherds used to collect it from the beards of their goats. Juniper (*genévrier*), lavender (*lavendre*), rosemary (*romarin*), myrtle (*myrte*), strawberry trees (or arbutus; *arbousier* in French), mastic (*mastique*), broom (*gênet*) bearing bright yellow flowers, and tree heather (*bruyère*) also add their perfumes to the great olfactory melting pot.

The subject of innumerable myths and legends, the maquis traditionally provided a rich source of sustenance for the islanders, yielding fire wood, fruit and medicinal herbs, and giving cover to wild boar and other game. The Corsican Resistance in WWII, who depended on the scrub for their survival, also named itself Le Maquis, and after the island's Liberation in 1943 the term *maquisard* was taken up as a moniker by Resistance fighters on the French mainland.

Flowers

Around 2500 different species of flowering plants are to be found in Corsica, 8% of them endemic to the island and its neighbour Sardinia. Which flowers you come across while trekking will depend on the altitude, soil, time of year and humidity but spring is the best period if you want to experience the amazing floral diversity at its peak. From early April until mid-June, the verges, meadows and woodlands, few of which have ever seen a drop of pesticide or fertilizer, are filled with wild flowers, and the maquis is at its most aromatic.

Our photographic field guide below identifies some of the flowers you're most likely to encounter on the footpaths described in this book. For a more comprehensive checklist seek out one of the specialist books featured on p39.

Cinquefoil
Potentilla

Hottentot fig
Carpobrutus edulis

Prickly pear
(Indian/Barbary fig)

Broom
Sarothamnus scoparius

Yellow horned sea poppy
Glaucium flavum

Rock rose
Cistus saviaefolius

Helichrysum

Horse vetch
Hippocripis comosa

Star of Bethlehem
Ornithogalus

Corsican meadow thistle

Devil's bit
Succia pratensis

Water lotus

Fox glove
Digitalis

French lavender
Lavandula stoechas

Tassle hyacinth
Muscari comosum

Spotted orchid

Wild garlic
Allium triquentum

Gentian
Gentiana lutea

Cyclamen

Pink cistus, source of ladanum gum myrrh

Peony

Pink saxifrage

Knapweed
Centaurea pullata

Granny's Bonnet
Aquilegia alpina

Speedwell
Veronica

Saxifrage

Periwinkle
Vinca

Rampian
Phyteuma

Thrift
Armeria maritima

Corsican hellebore

Cacti

The **Indian fig**, or **prickly pear** cactus, which grows in banks on roadsides and wasteland, was originally imported to Corsica from Mexico, although locals will tell you the Saracens brought it with them (whence its French name, *figue de Barbarie*). The pale red and orange fruit it throws out is fiendishly hard to pick (try and you'll probably end up with fingertips full of tiny needles) but Corsican villagers traditionally gathered them to make jam.

Another foreign import that thrives in the wild throughout the Mediterranean is the **Agave**, or 'century plant' (see opposite), a giant, Jurassic-looking cactus whose huge flowers sway on 4–6m-high stems. You'll see them sprouting from parched, south-facing slopes at sea level all over the island.

Trees

At sea level the trees best adapted to withstand the hot sun and parched, sandy soil of the shoreline are **pines** such as the Aleppo (*pin d'Alep*) and umbrella or stone pine (*pin parasol*), both of which grow in profusion behind the beaches of southern Corsica. **Eucalyptus** (*eucalypte*), originally introduced to help drain stagnant bodies of water and combat malaria, also do well on the coastal belt, notably around Porto, where some have reached awesome sizes.

More definitively Mediterranean, however, is the **olive** tree (*olivier*), which was first brought to Corsica by the ancient Greeks and has thrived ever since. You'll see swaths of them around Calenzana and around the villages of the Alta Rocca in the far south, which have witnessed a revival of oil production over the past decade. Equally ubiquitous are the slender-topped **cypress** (*cyprès*) sprouting from family tombs and graveyards on the margins of towns and villages.

Two species of **oak** (*chêne*) are indigenous to Corsica, the most distinctive of them cork oak, whose bark has for centuries been stripped to provide corks for wine bottles. The bare, red-brown trunks exposed afterwards are still a typical feature of the landscape around Porto-Vecchio, although the industry has all but died out in other parts of the island. With its spiny leaves and gnarled branches, evergreen **holm oak** (*chêne vert*) was never exploited commercially but it has been badly hit by fire in Corsica and few extensive woods of it remain. In remote corners of the west coast you'll also come across the rare kermes oak (*chêne kermès*) which forms bushes of small, holly-like leaves.

At higher altitudes the flaky red bark and huge 15cm cones of the **maritime pine** (*pin maritime*) litter the trails winding through forests exposed to coastal weather. Ospédale, on the Mare a Mare Sud, is renowned for these spectacular trees, which grow to an age of around 150. When they die off the rotten trunks and branches become encrusted in fungus, often falling across footpaths.

The same is true of the poor old **sweet chestnut** (*châtaignier*), which in times past was integral to the rural economy but has since suffered from terminal neglect. In the fifteenth and sixteenth centuries the Genoans planted whole

---

Opposite Top: Mexican Agave aka 'century plant'. **Bottom:** Morilles – the tastiest mushrooms in the Corsican forests. (Photos © David Abram).

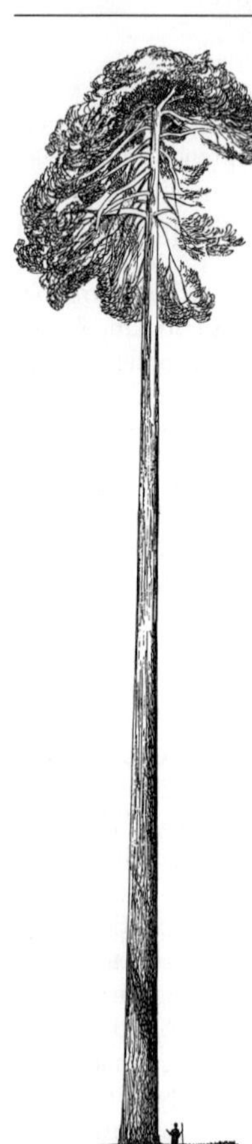

Laricio pine
(From *Journal of a Landscape Painter in Corsica*, Edward Lear)

forests of them to provide flour for export. These days, however, very few nuts are collected and milled; the vast majority are eaten by semi-wild pigs who fatten on them before they are slaughtered in late November (one of the reasons why traditional Corsican sausages are so famously tasty). Aside from the region of Castagniccia, near Bastia – which is carpeted by one vast, unbroken sweet chestnut forest but not crossed by any long-distance footpaths – the places you'll see large numbers of chestnut trees are remote villages in central and western Corsica such as Marignana, Renno and Guagno on the Mare a Mare Nord and its *Variant*.

The most Corsican of Corsica's trees, however, has to be the lofty **Laricio pine** (*pin laricio*), see the box on p216. These giants of the island's sub-alpine forests typically live for between 800 and 1000 years. Often sporting characteristic flat tops, the older specimens shed smaller (8–10cm) cones than those of the maritime pine and soar to a height of 50m. Their flexible, strong wood and great height made them highly prized by the Genoans, who gutted whole forests for ship masts and building timber during their rule. The most famous surviving Laricios are to be found in the Forêt d'Aïtone (penetrated by the Mare a Mare Nord) but you'll also cross forests of them on the GR20, notably around Vizzavona and while approaching Bocca di Verdi. The latter location also boasts the island's most impressive **fir** trees (*sapin*): until a few years back the stalwart Sapin de Marmaro, just below the plateau de Gialgone (see p174), was 56m tall and reputedly the tallest tree in Europe until the top was lopped off by lightning.

Among the few trees adapted to the stark, extreme conditions of the alpine zone are **beeches** (*hêtres*), more often than not contorted into ghoulish shapes by the wind. The high ridges south of Bocca di Verdi, above the Refuge d'Usciolu on the GR20, are renowned for these. Also on the GR20 look out for the beautiful woods of **silver birch** (*bouleaux blanc*) that line the stream beds around the Refuge d'Ortu di u Piobbu. The sap that dribbles from their eye-shaped bark knots used to be collected for use as a natural antiseptic; it also attracts ferocious red ants, so beware if you sit beneath one.

Birds

In common with many southern European countries, the local obsession with firearms has wrought havoc with the island's avian population, which seems to be regarded as fair game for target practice in the winter hunting season. Corsica may as a result offer a smaller number of birds than you'd expect for somewhere as wild but its diverse landscapes means a correspondingly broad spectrum of species is present. Some are rare enough to attract the attention of serious enthusiasts. But if you're not one of these, chances are you're unlikely to recognize a Corsican nuthatch, Sardinian warbler or Alpine accentor when you see one – all the more reason to sharpen up your bird-spotting knowledge before you come. The best way to do this is to get hold of one of the field guides recommended on p39; more committed birders might also surf the Web for the latest trip reports, which pinpoint the most promising spots for sighting specific species.

At the start of your trek, heading through the coastal maquis, **warblers** will continually flit across the path, sounding alarm calls from the tops of swaying bushes. Dozens of species live on the island, but the stars have to be the Marmara's warbler, which favours patches of low maquis, and the Sardinian and Dartford warblers, very rare in northern Europe but quite common in Corsica where they prefer high scrub. Listen out, too, for the distinctively explosive 'cheti-ti' cry of the buff-coloured Cetti warbler, another rare resident.

In the spring, overhead wires are where you're most likely to sight the viridescent **bee-eater**, the most colourful of Corsica's migrants. With its turquoise and emerald wings and red-brown breast, this exotic visitor presents a striking spectacle, especially when flashing in flocks across grassy meadows and around riverbanks.

At the shoreline, birdlife is less prolific than on comparable coasts in Britain and Ireland, with no large seabird colonies and surprisingly few gulls. However, exposed, rocky coasts such as those of the magnificent Scandola Nature Reserve (which features on the Tra Mare e Monti trail; see p262) are home to a small number of exciting species. Limited to a few small pockets in the islands of the western Mediterranean, the **Andouin's gull** is the rarest of these, recognizable by its slender wings and red-and-black striped beak. You'll almost certainly see it if you take one of the boat trips out into the Golfe de Porto, along with the **osprey**, or fish eagle, which builds enormous nests of twigs atop isolated rock pinnacles. There are thought to be only 10 pairs of this splendid bird of prey left in Corsica, but your chances of spotting one are good if you trek around the west coast where they dive to seize fish with their impressive talons. The Scandola region also harbours a thriving population of **Mediterranean shearwaters**, which skim at high speed across the waves.

The extensive interior **forests** are home to several endemics, the most famous of which is the **Corsican nuthatch**. Unique to the island, this tiny blue-grey bird was only identified as a separate species in 1883 by a British ornithologist (whence its misleading Latin name – *Sitta whiteheadi*). It's more often heard than seen – only an estimated 2000 nesting pairs survive – but in the forests of Aïtone, Asco and Ospédale you'd be unlucky not to glimpse one scurrying up a tree trunk.

Above the treeline the bird you'll get closest to will be the garrulous **yellow-billed chough**, which has carved a career for itself scrounging picnic

GOLDEN EAGLE

scraps along the GR20. The ridge section at the head of the Restonica Valley, above the Capitellu and Melu lakes, is one of the many places where this normally shy bird will hop right up to you pecking for crumbs. Its much larger cousin, the **raven**, scours the same slopes but from a safer height, its gruff croak echoing off the granite cliffs.

Golden eagles rarely deign to descend to path level, preferring to ride the thermals high above the rocky ridges of the watershed. But they are a common-enough sight along the GR20 where they prey on smaller birds, rabbits and mice. Their distinguishing features are their dark-brown colour and the gold flecks that tinge the fronts of their head and wings, which broaden noticeably towards the tips. In flight the tail is long, wide and square-ended. It's easy to distinguish from the smaller **Bonnelli's eagle**, whose undersides are greyish white with a prominent black band running along the rear of the wings and over the tail.

BONELLI'S EAGLE

The bird of prey every trekker wants to sight at least once in Corsica is the elusive **bearded vulture** or **lammergeier**. Their numbers have been reduced to only a handful of nesting pairs by centuries of persecution by shepherds, who mistakenly believed they took young lambs (whence the name which comes from the German, 'lamb-taker'). In fact, this majestic vulture, which boasts a wingspan of nearly three metres, survives off carrion left by hawks and eagles. Its nickname in French, *le casseur d'os*, derives from its habit of dropping bones to expose the nourishing marrow inside them. Lac de Nino on the GR20 is the place you're most likely to witness this extraordinary phenomenon; more background on Corsica's bearded vultures appears in the box on p141.

Finally, confirmed ornithologists should keep their binoculars handy in case one of the much smaller rarities of the island's mountains puts in a fleeting appearance. To sight the elusive **wallcreeper**, **snow finch** or **Alpine accentor** – the undisputed stars of the high-altitude zone – you'll need to hang around above 1900m for a few days and have a good deal of luck as they survive here only in perilously small numbers.

Reptiles

From spring until late autumn, Corsican trails teem with **lizards**, although differentiating between the half a dozen or so species (and numerous subspecies) that inhabit the island can be tricky. The easiest to identify are the ubiquitous **Tyrrhenian wall lizards**, which sport two broad green dorsal stripes on their mottled brown backs. At higher altitudes you might also spot a **Bedriaga's wall lizard**, which lives between 600m and 2000m, usually on stones or rocks overhanging water. Their tails, bright blue in the case of juvenile males, can be half as long again as their bodies. Come across one with a blue throat and orange underbelly, on the other hand, and you can congratulate yourself on having seen the much rarer **Dalmatian algyroides**, which hangs out in shady wall crevices or under boulders during the hottest times of day. Splayed-toed **geckos** are far more common and often pop up inside houses where they cling to walls and ceilings waiting for flies and spiders.

Perhaps the most striking member of Corsica's lizard family, however, is the **fire salamander**. Although not particularly rare, this slow-moving, slimy yellow-and-black creature is elusive, emerging from its hiding places only during wet weather, when it can often be seen skulking along the footpaths in search of baby frogs and newts. Traditionally collected for food, salamanders are also kept as pets and their numbers are thus declining in the wild.

Collectors, along with stray dogs and bush fires, have also been the principal scourge of the friendly **Hermann's tortoise**, which lumbers along the back roads and trekking trails of the coastal plain and lower-lying valleys in pursuit of its favourite foods: dandelion leaves and maquis berries. It's the only surviving species of tortoise still wild on the island.

Neither of the two kinds of **snake** resident in Corsica is poisonous but you should think twice before getting close as one of them, the **whip snake**, will take probably take a swipe at you if you do. Known on the continent as *la coléreuse* ('the bad tempered one'), it will hiss loudly and bite if threatened. The sub-species of whip snake most often encountered amid dry maquis tends to be shiny black with yellow-green markings and a lighter, yellow-brown underbelly. **Grass snakes** are paler in colour and altogether less aggressive, although they'll secrete a nasty smelling odour from glands in the neck if picked up.

Mammals

Considering the great passion with which they continue to be hunted, it is a testament to the resilience and adaptability of the **wild boar** that so many – roughly 30,000 – still inhabit Corsica's dense forests. Distinguished from their semi-domesticated pig counterparts by their stocky stature and glossy black coasts, the famously fierce *sanglier* subsists on acorns, chestnuts and wild fruit, which it supplements with juicy roots. The closest you're likely to get to one are the excavations they make in search of these, which cause considerable damage to ground cover in deciduous woodland. Constant pressure from humans has made boar highly secretive and you should count yourself fortunate if you see one, especially a full-grown male with tusks. These days they tend to be hunted in a most cowardly fashion: dogs are dispatched into the woods to flush the boar out onto a road where the camouflaged hunters wait with their rifles cocked. An estimated 10,000 are shot each year, making *la chasse au sanglier* by far Corsica's most popular sport.

The island's own indigenous species of **deer**, *Cervus elaphus corsicanus*, is far less numerous. The smallest of Europe's red deer, it disappeared completely in the 1960s and would have remained absent had not a last-ditch PNRC breeding programme, which reintroduced animals from neighbouring Sardinia, revived the population. From high-fenced enclosures in the Alta Rocca region near Quenza (passed by the Mare a Mare Sud footpath; see p286) a dozen or more young adults are released into the wild each year. Most are thought to fall victim to illegal hunting.

The only other mammalian subspecies believed to be unique to the island is the **Corsican doormouse** (*loir* in French). No-one knows for sure just how many of these shy, cute little creatures remain in the humid beech forests of the interior but they're often mistaken for squirrels due to their size (35cm) and the bushiness of their tails. Once again, hunting has been the cause of the animals' demise; men from the upper Taravo Valley (on the GR20), where they are most numerous, shoot them for their oily meat, prized both for its taste and its curative properties.

Yet another mammal hunted close to extinction, but which is now rigorously protected, is the **mouflon**, a reclusive sheep that inhabits remote mountain crags along the watershed. Corsica is one of its last strongholds. Only around 600 individuals survive in pockets high amid the central peaks, where you might be lucky enough to glimpse a flock grazing at sunrise or sunset. For more background on the mouflon, and tips on where to look for them see the boxes on p134 and p193.

ECONOMY

From the wealth of luxury cars, designer outfits and super-bikes on the streets of Bastia and Ajaccio you could easily get the impression Corsica was booming. The islanders' love of ostentation, however, masks some harsh economic realities. For starters, **per capita income** languishes at three-quarters of the French average. **Unemployment** may be virtually nonexistent in the summer but in winter it rises to 6% – a figure that does not take into account the thousands who migrate to the continent in search of work at the end of the season.

Tourism and related service industries are by far the largest employers, accounting for 10–12% of gross domestic product (GDP). Nationalists, however, have consistently resisted attempts by the French government to promote tourism as the answer to all Corsica's economic woes, pointing to the fact that jobs in the sector tend to be poorly paid and seasonal.

Many Corsicans would like instead to see a revival of the island's **agriculture**, which currently earns only a paltry 1–2% of GDP. But with the paucity of cultivable land and poor profit margins, farming looks unlikely to take off in any big way. Most Corsicans living off the land today are only able to do so with

Population pointers

- The native population of Corsica currently stands at around 260,000, but swells to three-quarters of a million in the summer.
- The 1884 high of 276,000 was reduced, following the two world wars and a century of emigration, to 170,000 by the mid-1950s.
- An estimated 800,000 Corsicans live on the continent, most of them in Paris, Marseille, Nice and the Bouches du Rhône region.
- Around 22,000 of the current population (just over 8%) is made up of immigrants, more than half of them Moroccan and Tunisian guest workers.
- 108,000 people (roughly 40% of the total population) live in Bastia and Ajaccio. By 2025 it is expected that two-thirds of the islanders will live on the coast. The interior, meanwhile, continues to empty; 15,000 people left their home villages in the last quarter of the twentieth century. If you exclude the coastal belt, the island has an overall population density of just 10 inhabitants per square kilometre, comparable with some regions of the Sahara.
- Corsica has a rapidly ageing population, with one-quarter of its inhabitants over the age of 60; that figure is expected to rise to one-third by 2030.

the help of huge **subsidies**. Until 1999 the island enjoyed EU Objective 1 status, which entitled it to massive handouts from Brussels. Combined with the equally vast sums being poured in by Paris, these made Corsica for years the most subsidized region in the EU.

Another telling statistic is that over one-third of all those employed on the island work for the government or local councils. Add to this the tax and social security exemptions enjoyed by Corsica, not to mention the heavily subsidized transport links with the continent on which its economy rests, and you'll understand why only a few extremists these days consider total independence from France a realistic option.

If the island had any raw materials to export or if its manufacturing base were stronger the economic picture might be rosier. But **industry** remains only marginally more profitable than farming, generating 7% of GDP. Of the 1500 or so establishments registered, just under half are sole traders and only 1% employ more than 50 people.

PEOPLE, SOCIETY AND CONDUCT

Corsican culture remains as archetypally Mediterranean as its climate. Superficially more Italian than French, the islanders' style is ritzy by the standards of northern Europe. When it comes to cars and motorbikes size definitely matters and in the towns, designer labels, lap dogs and wrap-around shades are manifestly de rigueur.

Such overt demonstrations of affluence serve to reaffirm both the individual's status and that of his or her family. The **family** still forms the backbone of the island's society. When introduced for the first time, Corsicans don't ask each other where they're from but say '*de qui* vous êtes?', literally '*whose* are you?'.

And the answer will have considerable resonance, situating the speaker within a clear network of clan allegiances.

The economic and cultural revolutions of the post-war period have done little to erode the pervasiveness of **clanism**, which continues to permeate most aspects of life. To get on – to secure better jobs, favourable planning decisions or smooth business affairs – it's not what you know that counts in Corsica so much as who you're related to. Every family at some point will have to call on the patronage of a highly-placed relative, who in turn can depend on that family for his (they'll almost always be a man) political support in the future.

Suspicion of outsiders is also integral to the island mindset and Corsicans are often accused of being cool with visitors. It's certainly true that down on the coast, where decades of mass tourism have visibly jaded many of those in the service sector, people can seem taciturn and, all too often, just plain impolite. But engage people with respect and you'll soon find the surface frostiness lift, especially in the villages of the interior where traditions of hospitality are still strongly upheld. Of course barriers are more easily broken down if you speak French but even without it you'll be surprised by how garrulous Corsicans can be.

Women

Gender roles in Corsica are not all that different from the prevailing norms across the water in Italy – or for that matter in most Catholic Mediterranean countries – but attitudes to women, in particular, are still quite conservative compared with northern Europe.

Corsican women are expected to look glamorous in public and to avoid bringing shame on their families through their relations with the opposite sex. After marriage a woman's role as mother and homemaker confers on her enormous prestige and respect but outside family life her influence tends to be limited. The proportion of women occupying political posts and top jobs in local government still lags well behind mainland France, despite the ever-growing female contribution to the island's economy.

The roots of Corsica's gender conservatism date back to traditional society when the treatment of women was frequently the cause of vendettas. Only a century ago the mere removal of a woman's headscarf on the church steps after Mass by a man outside her kin was enough to unleash a bloody feud. Adultery or even the suggestion of sex outside marriage could also have the direst of consequences: *vinditta* sometimes broke out if a girl so much as went for a walk with a sweetheart without the permission of her father. If a feud did erupt, however, it was often women who fanned the flames of vengeance by singing impassioned funerary dirges, known as *voceri*, over the corpses of dead relatives. Processing around the body in darkness, the female kinsfolk of the deceased would tear at their faces and hair as expressions of grief, urging the men seated outside to exact retribution and restore clan honour.

Women have tended to maintain a very low profile in the nationalist movement, though more recently widows of paramilitaries and others killed in factional violence have taken to the streets to voice their opposition to the troubles. Set up in 1996, the organization **Manifest pour la Vie** (Demonstrate for Life) has campaigned to great effect against the rule of terror in Corsica, despite constant intimidation and death threats.

Possible gaffes

When mixing with local people, even members of the younger generation, bear in mind that cultural differences do exist – albeit small ones – and that you might have to modify your behaviour in some situations. Above all **never discuss Corsican politics**. Even innocent questions about the troubles run the risk of causing offence; express an opinion and you could well find yourself at the wrong end of a gun barrel. Remember that some of the people you'll meet in mountain villages and refuges may have been, or still are, connected in some way to a paramilitary movement – either directly or indirectly through their family.

Minor **gaffes** that are unlikely to provoke a hostile reaction but which will do little to endear you to your hosts include: walking shirtless into a bar, restaurant, *gîte d'étape* or church (and most other public places except the beach); camping wild on the outskirts of villages without permission (see p78); entering family tombs; and complaining about prices. In fact, complaining about anything can be tricky. If you feel compelled to express dissatisfaction at any point, be sure do it without appearing confrontational.

Also, don't assume it's OK to use **toilets** in a bar if you haven't ordered at least a coffee for the sake of form. The main reason there are so few public loos in Corsica is that, contrary to attitudes in most of northern Europe, locals tend to regard the offering of such facilities as a service rather than a duty to visitors.

There are a few less obvious *faux pas* to be aware of, most of them associated with the so-called **Evil Eye** or *occhju*. Many Corsicans – and not merely members of the older generation – believe that what might be termed 'bad luck' elsewhere, such as health problems and things going wrong generally, derives from malevolent spells. These are cast unintentionally by individuals who are jealous of you in some way, whether they know it or not. Corsicans will perceive jealously in a range of remarks that in northern Europe would be construed as mere politeness: complimenting someone's appearance or that of a pet, saying a baby is beautiful or merely smiling at someone you don't know. Do so and you could well find yourself the object of a defensive gesture known as *les cornes* ('the horns'), made by clenching the fist and pointing the index and little finger downwards.

If *les cornes* fails to ward off the Eye, or if a spell has been cast without your knowledge, a run of bad luck will ensue that can only be stopped by visiting a spell breaker, or *signatori* (literally 'sign-maker'). These are traditional healers who make the sign of the cross and intone secret prayers over a bowl of water containing three drops of oil (possibly with a lock of the victim's hair underneath it).

LANGUAGE

French is Corsica's lingua franca – the first language of the overwhelming majority of islanders and the primary medium for government, law, business and the press. The locals, especially those in the interior, tend to speak with a thick, Italian-like accent but only a relatively small number remain fluent in **Corsican**, which was methodically suppressed by successive French administrations.

Considerable debate surrounds the status of Corsican, whose close resemblance to Tuscan many claim makes it a dialect. Nevertheless, an official language it is, with a symbolic value that seems to grow in inverse proportion to the number of people who speak it. Revival of the Corsican tongue has always been one of the top priorities of the nationalist movement, which has succeeded in reintroducing it as an optional subject in schools and as the main medium of instruction at the University of Corte.

As a visitor you'll hear the distinctive rhythms and intonations of Corsican in villages along the trekking routes. However, polite attempts by outsiders to speak the language may not be greeted with the encouraging response you might expect. Many locals are understandably defensive about their native tongue and may interpret phrasebook-inspired renditions of it from foreigners as patronizing, as if the speaker doesn't expect them to be fluent in French. That said, only the dourest of nationalists will be offended by you saying *tiran-graze* (thank you) at the end of a meal or when you leave a *gîte* or *refuge*.

After French, **Italian** is the most widely understood language, both because of the huge numbers of tourists from across the Tyrrhenian Sea and because of its affinity with Corsican. Nearly everyone, young and old, understands it even if they can't speak it fluently. The same, however, doesn't apply to **English**, which you won't be able to rely on outside the tourist offices.

Practical information for the visitor

ACCOMMODATION

Corsica is chock-full of places to stay and, in common with continental France, most offer good value for money. This is especially true of shoulder- and off-season periods (mid-September to mid-June), when hotels reduce tariffs in line with the drop in demand; the opposite applies in peak season (mid-June to mid-September) which typically sees accommodation rates double or triple across the island. That said, rates generally vary less in the interior than on the coast, and gîtes d'étape and refuges keep their prices constant throughout the year.

Whenever you come it makes sense to **book ahead**, particularly if you plan to spend a night or two in any of the gateway towns, where rooms can be hard to find at short notice. When you reserve it's also worth checking the establishment's half-board (*demi-pension*) policy and rates. Half-board may be obligatory (*obligatoire*) during peak periods, even in gîtes d'étape (but never in refuges, whose beds are allocated on a first-come-first-served basis).

Throughout this guide we list places to stay in all price brackets in the towns, villages and along the trekking routes outlined, from comfortable starred hotels in Bastia and Ajaccio to rough refuges high in the hills. In addition to a rundown of each establishment's credentials and contact details, you'll find a cross-section of prices giving an indication of how costs may vary at different times of year. Bear in mind that these rates are only a guideline and that they're prone to change. (The introduction of the euro looks set to have an impact on prices over the next few years pushing up the cost of hotel beds, and much else besides).

Reservations may be made by phone or letter (or by fax or email if the relevant details are provided in this guide). Some hotels might ask for a credit card advance as a deposit (*une caution*), which they'll keep if you fail to honour the booking but in practice most places will hold a room or bed for you if you reconfirm a few days in advance.

Hotels

The overall standard of hotels in Corsica is impressive and you'll get a whole lot more for your money than, say, in Britain or Ireland. Choice is widest in the coastal resorts and main towns, though demand frequently outstrips supply in places like Ajaccio, Bastia and Porto-Vecchio, especially at the bottom end of the market. Up in the villages of the interior, hotels are more of a rarity and tend to be quite traditional in style, with open fires, stone walls and stuffed trophies on the walls; they're also a notch cheaper than their coastal counterparts.

If your budget can stretch to such luxury, a hotel room is a great place to recover from the relative deprivations of life on the trail. In Corsica they're always impeccably clean and most have windows opening onto little balconies and views. Relaxing on your crisp cotton sheets after a steaming hot shower, the snoring and stuffiness of nights in gîtes d'étape or refuge dorms will soon feel a world away.

With the majority of places charging around 40€ per double, such comfort need not seriously dent your finances, either. In fact, if you're happy to share with one or more people (most hotels will install an extra bed or two for a minimal supplement) the cost of a hotel bed can often drop to around the same as one in a hostel or gîte.

When making a reservation, at least in more modest hotels, you'll probably be offered the choice of a room with or without a wash basin (*lavabo*), shower (*douches*) and toilet (*WC*, pronounced 'dooble-vay-say'). Rooms without a bathroom are generally described as '*chambres avec douche-WC à l'étage*' (ie 'rooms with shower and toilet on the landing'). More hotel terminology appears in the list of useful words and phrases on pp312-15.

An extra than can bump up your bill is **breakfast** as it may not be included in the room rate: if it isn't, count on anything between 4€ and 5.50€, or else head for a café (where it will cost around the same).

It's nearly always possible these days to settle up with a credit card but if this is your only means of paying make sure the hotel will accept your card when you check in. Finally, bear in mind that most places in Corsica, particularly those in the resorts and hills, open only during the summer. Wherever possible we've listed the opening period but it's always advisable to phone ahead, especially if you're around at the start or end of the season, as precise dates can fluctuate with demand.

Gîtes d'étape

Gîtes d'étape are the French equivalent of hostels. Set up specifically for trekkers, they aim to provide clean, comfortable and affordable accommodation at key points along major long-distance routes. Corsica's gîtes vary greatly in size. The more modest of them may only hold a dozen or so dorm beds; others could have four or five times that number, along with a choice of larger and more private double and family rooms. Nearly all, however, enjoy prime locations amid peaceful, quiet surroundings on the edges of villages.

The *nuitée* (nightly) rate charged by gîtes d'étape, typically around 11€, includes a dormitory bed and the use of self-catering facilities if there are any. Increasingly, however, *gérants* are imposing obligatory half-board rates of around 26€, meaning you can't stay at their gîte unless you opt for breakfast and evening meal. For those who can afford it this is invariably a much better deal than you could expect by eating elsewhere. The food is generally copious and efforts are made to provide local specialities (although rarely vegetarian alternatives). Mealtimes tend also to be enjoyable occasions, fuelled by unlimited jugs of wine. A lot, of course, depends on the personality of the couple who run the establishment and how much of a sense of vocation they bring to their work but all in all gîtes d'étape offer exceptional value for money.

Their one real catch is the communal dormitories, or more specifically the attendant risk of nocturnal noise; if you think you may be kept awake by snoring, come armed with a supply of ear plugs.

Advance reservation is not technically necessary for gîtes d'étape, but given the paucity of alternative accommodation in most villages it's well worth making the effort to book ahead. Gîtes on popular routes such as the Mare a Mare Sud and the Tra Mare e Monti may be fully reserved months before the start of the spring and autumn peak trekking seasons.

Chambres d'hôte

Bed and breakfast accommodation, or *chambres d'hôte* as its French equivalent is known, has only recently started to catch on in Corsica. But the few places that have sprung up along the trekking routes tend to be of a high standard. Prices are equivalent to those of small, simple hotels – roughly 30–35€ per double room or 40–50€ per head for half-board – but here you can expect warmer, more personal hospitality and a more authentic taste of village life. The food is invariably excellent, drawing on local ingredients and showcasing traditional dishes of the area.

Refuges

Corsica has a total of 16 mountain refuges, all on or near the GR20. Most were established in the 1980s by the PNRC to service the island's famous *haute route*, since when a handful of additional privately run huts have sprung up to soak up the overspill.

Whether humble converted shepherds' shelters or spacious, state-of-the-art glass and aluminium structures, refuges offer very basic bunk-bed accommodation, along with simple self-catering facilities, cold-water showers and water sources. The dorms tend to be dingy, cramped and stuffy when packed with people and gear, which they are most of the time in the summer while the GR is fully open. How well you sleep will depend on the extent to which you can block out the smell of sweaty boots, snoring, the rustle of rip-stop Pertex and pre-dawn head-torch eruptions. If this sounds like your idea of hell consider bringing a tent or a thick-enough sleeping bag to bivouac in the specially demarcated areas outside, which often have a few dry-stone wind shelters to sleep beside.

The real appeal of refuges lies less in their dubious comforts than their locations, which are invariably superb. Hours away from the nearest road and at altitudes above 1300m, most enjoy wonderful views. If you trek the GR20 you'll doubtless while away lazy afternoons on the deep wooden decks that front the huts, or sprawled on the grass slopes surrounding them.

During the **summer** Corsican refuges are staffed by gardiens who collect the *nuitée* fees from trekkers on behalf of the PNRC and generally keep the huts clean and tidy. They don't receive wages but instead are allowed to sell provisions and cooked food with stocks replenished by regular mule trips down to road level. These little businesses mean it's possible nowadays to trek the GR20 without having to make time-consuming re-provisioning detours to villages, although you'll pay for the privilege as the prices of supplies in most refuges are extraordinarily high.

From October until late May Corsican refuges are not staffed but their dormitories, kitchens and dining areas remain unlocked for use by **winter** trekkers. Don't, however, count on there being supplies of gas if you turn up off season. It's more common to find a fire's worth of wood, which you can burn in the fireplace or wood-burner and then replace for the next visitors.

A night inside a hut typically **costs** around 8.50€ per head, or just under half that if you sleep outside. Note that in most cases campers and bivouackers don't have the right to use the refuge kitchen (more rudimentary external facilities are provided instead). This doesn't apply in bad weather, when anyone can – at the discretion of the gardien – bed down inside wherever there's room.

The money raised from the nightly charge goes towards the maintenance of the refuges and the PNRC helicopter which is used to remove rubbish as well as provide a valuable search and rescue service. Beds are allocated on a first-come-first-served basis.

Camping

Corsica has a huge number of campsites (*terrains de camping*, or *campings* for short) but few of them are in the mountains. Chances are if you erect a tent it'll be in front of one of the refuges on the GR20 (see above). Along the other major routes, camping facilities are even scarcer. Gérants sometimes offer space in the back garden of their gîtes d'étape but don't bank on it (if they do this guidebook will tell you).

Camping wild (*camping sauvage*) is strictly forbidden throughout the Parc Naturel (which means across the entire GR20) and along the Littoral Sartènais. However, provided you pitch well away from houses, don't light fires and don't leave any kind of mess behind – in other words as long as you respect the minimum-impact trekking pointers outlined on p79 – no-one is likely to prevent you, at least not in out-of-the-way corners of the island. Closer to villages, ask in the bar or shop if anyone knows of a suitable place to '*dresser une tente*' for a night. Sometimes polite approaches like this lead to offers to set up on local football pitches or in family orchards, although to do so without permission would be asking for trouble.

Bivouacking

Bivouacking is most definitely not permitted along the GR20, or for that matter anywhere inside the Parc Naturel, except in places set aside expressly for the purpose (in which case they'll be marked as an 'Aire de Bivouac'). Elsewhere you're unlikely to experience much resistance. Corsicans seem better disposed towards sleeping *à la belle étoile* than under canvas, probably because they frequently do it themselves while hunting. At the same time, you should pick your spot judiciously, keeping well away from villages; and once again, follow the minimum-impact trekking guidelines on p79.

Minimum impact trekking: dos and don'ts

With 17,000 or more people pouring along just the GR20 each summer, the potential impact of trekking on Corsica's natural landscape is considerable. The onus is therefore on every visitor to help preserve the island's natural environment as far as possible. There are a number of ways you can do this without making any great personal sacrifices:

Don't leave litter

Everything you take with you on Corsica's trails should either be eaten or packed out and disposed of in the nearest village, where you'll always be able to find a municipal Wheely-Bin. This includes orange peel, which takes around six months to decompose. On the GR20 the refuges are all equipped with trash bins (emptied at great effort and expense by helicopter) which you're welcome to use.

Don't light fires

Never be tempted to burn your rubbish, or anything else, or to make fires if you camp wild. Each year upwards of 15,000 hectares of forest and maquis go up in smoke in Corsica (see p200). Some of the fires are started by careless trekkers.

Don't pick flowers

However tempting it may be, leave the flora completely intact for others to enjoy.

Don't pollute water sources

If there's a latrine available, use it. Never defecate within 20 metres of a water source.

When washing yourself or your clothes with detergents, don't pollute streams or lakes. Carry the water at least 20 metres from its source before pouring it away.

Dispose of toilet paper hygienically

In the summer months you rarely need waymarks thanks to the lines of discarded toilet paper that litter Corsica's footpaths. This is a particularly unpleasant problem with low-level routes such as the Tra Mare e Monti and Mare a Mare Sud but you'll also have to endure the tissue trail along the more accessible stretches of the GR20. The best way to deal with your used toilet paper is not to bury it, but stick it in a plastic bag for hygienic disposal when you reach a refuge or village.

Never defecate in the rocks, where your faeces will attract flies and create a health hazard. If you get taken short, dig a hole in woodland soil at least 20m away from any path or stream and cover it up well afterwards.

Apart from the obvious weight advantage of trekking without a tent, the main incentive to bivvy is that you can bed down wherever you choose and thus break the *étapes* into ideal lengths for your pace and itinerary. The downsides are the risk of getting soaked by a nocturnal storm, being woken by pigs or wild boar in the middle of the night and having to wash in freezing streams (or not at all).

Some advice on the kind of gear you'll need if you want to bivouac in Corsica appears on p31. Where appropriate good places to bivvy are shown on the route maps.

LOCAL TRANSPORT

Except for trains, public transport in Corsica is privately operated, which means few skeleton services, few routes to really out-of-the-way places and a sharp drop in departure frequencies outside the tourist season. Nevertheless, getting to and from the trailheads of the trekking paths described in this book is feasible throughout the year with a little advance planning (the exception being the Littoral Sartènais, which is unreachable by bus even in mid-summer).

Featured throughout our route chapters are details of transport services that will get you to the beginnings and ends of the treks. We also list train, bus and taxi information for the villages along the way, in case you need to break your trek or wish to start at that particular stage. However, bus information, in particular, should always be double-checked as timings tend to fluctuate according to the month, and sometimes from year to year. The best way to do this is to phone the operating company direct, or ask at the nearest bar or shop (where timetables are usually displayed); Corsica's tourist offices also keep transport timetables, although be warned that they may misread them.

Trains

Crossing the watershed between Ajaccio and Bastia via Corte, with a branch line peeling north-west to Calvi, Corsica's heavily subsidized train line – the Chemin de Fer de la Corse, or CFC – provides a year-round link between the island's major towns. Although somewhat slower and more rattly than the buses, the Micheline diesels offer a memorable way to travel. In fact, during the summer the line becomes a tourist attraction in its own right; of the 800,000 or so people who use it each year, more than half are visitors.

Unlike in mainland France, **fares** do not vary according to the day of the week or time of year. You pay for your ticket in advance at the station and present it to the conductor (*contrôleur*) during the journey. Special luggage areas provide ample space for rucksacks. It's also possible to store gear at the stations (ask at the ticket hatch for the *consigne*) but you have to pay between 4.50€ and 5.30€ (per working day or part thereof) for the privilege, and are pinned to the opening and closing hours of the station (which should always be checked before leaving your luggage).

The line has two separate **timetables** (*horaires*) for summer and winter, changing in late September and late June; the exact dates vary from year to year. The main difference between them is an increased number of services on Sundays and public holidays during the summer. On the Bastia–Corte–Vizzavona–Ajaccio line at least four trains operate Monday to Saturday, with two on Sundays. Only one or two, however, run daily from the junction at Ponte-Leccia to Calvi.

To check departure times you can phone the tourist office in Ajaccio, Bastia or Calvi; the staff all speak English. Better still, if your French is up to it, ring the CFC direct on ☎ 04.95.23.11.03.

Background information on Corsica's quirky narrow-gauge train line appears in the box on p162.

Buses

Getting hold of dependable information can be complicated when it comes to buses. With the exception of Ajaccio, no town has a bona fide bus station, while each route is served by a different company with its own seasons and headquarters. To compound the problem, tourist offices rarely have up-to-date timetables and when they do they often misread them. The only sure-fire way to check timings is to contact the bus company yourself. In Ajaccio you can do this in person at the *terminal routière* (bus station), where each company has its own counter. If these aren't staffed, ask at the information desk, which keeps a folder with the full set of current timetables.

The buses vary enormously, ranging from huge luxury coaches (as on the Ajaccio–Bastia route) to small 12-seater minibuses. While some are laid on with visitors in mind, others form essential lifelines to remote villages, carrying post and provisions as well as people.

Apart from the fragmentary nature of the island's network, the other problem you might fall foul of is that the buses may not be large enough. This is especially true during early and late season, when some companies cut costs by deploying smaller vehicles. For example, outside peak season the firm which operates the route up the west coast from Ajaccio to Porto via Cargèse (the starting point for the Mare a Mare Centre and Tra Mare e Monti trails) only runs a cramped minibus, with the result that trekkers routinely find themselves stranded without transport in the capital because the bus is full. The only solution to this is to book at least an hour ahead of the scheduled departure time.

Tickets are sold in advance at the bus station in the capital but elsewhere you have to pay the driver when you get on the bus. Note, too, that in larger towns where the company may operate through a travel agency (as is the case with the bigger firms) you can sometimes **leave your rucksack** at the agency free of charge until the bus departs.

Taxis

One reason why key tourist destinations such as Calvi Airport and Calenzana (starting point of the GR20) are so poorly served by buses is the influence of the local taxi drivers. Their powerful lobby also keeps fares comparatively high, and once outside the large towns you can expect some hefty meter charges if you catch a cab to or from a trekking route.

Unfortunately taxis are in many instances the only way (apart from hitching) to reach some villages or *stations de ski*, which is why this guide lists the contact details of registered drivers who serve places on or within reach of the main routes. If you do call out a cab, especially for a long drive, make sure you get a quoted fare over the phone in advance.

Hitching

No self-respecting Corsican would be seen dead hitching, but with a rucksack – and even better, a set of trekking poles – your chances of getting a lift are pretty good. As in most parts of the world, success rates seem to improve as you penetrate the mountains. From late June onwards a steady flow of tourist traffic ensures a dependable supply of potential lifts in all but the remotest areas.

You'll find cars much more likely to stop if you pick your spot well: stand on straight stretches of road with plenty of space to pull over on the hard shoulder (roadsides just past roundabouts are usually safe bets). And avoid busy highways and intersections; it's obviously harder for drivers to stop when they're in fast moving, bunched traffic.

Attacks on hitchers are unheard of in Corsica, but getting into a stranger's car inevitably brings with it a degree of risk, and it's always worth checking the driver out first. Never be afraid to refuse a lift if you feel unsure about it for any reason.

FOOD

One of the chief advantages of trekking routes as well conceived as those in Corsica is that you don't have to make do with tinned or dehydrated food. On the contrary: with the exception of the GR20 the footpaths all pass at regular intervals through villages, which means expresso-coffee-and-croissant breakfasts, as much crusty French bread, local cheese, charcuterie and fresh fruit as you can be bothered to carry and plenty of opportunities to re-provision.

In addition to the usual selection of packaged food, vegetables and staples, local *épiceries* stock a good choice of regional specialities that make ideal trekking fodder. Look out for *canastrelli*, thick calorific biscuits traditionally made from chestnut flour and olive oil. They come in a range of flavours – *anis* (aniseed), *noix* (walnut), *raisin* and *miel* (honey) – but our vote goes to *vin blanc* (white wine), which is the most consistently delicious.

Corsica is also deservedly renowned for its cured meats, or **charcuterie**, whose intense flavours derive from the fact that most pigs on the island roam free, feeding on windfall chestnuts and forest roots. As well as familiar, Parma-style smoked ham (*prisuttu*) you'll come across three main kinds of hard *saucisson* (sausage) hanging in Corsican grocery shops: *coppa* (shoulder), *figatellu* (liver) and, the most prized of all, *lonzu* (lean fillet). Quality charcuterie doesn't come cheap – expect to pay anything from 8€ to 15€ for saucisson from a reputed source – but its strong taste means you have to slice it thinly, which makes it last a long time. Above all, charcuterie provides an excellent, easily portable source of protein.

The same is true of Corsica's notoriously strong **cheese**, the most pungent and expensive of which is make from full-fat ewe's milk collected at altitude. A range of different strength *fromages corses* is offered at village épiceries and supermarkets, but for the real McCoy you'll have to shop at bergeries up in the hills, where shepherds sell direct from their cool stone cellars.

Cheese and charcuterie both feature prominently on the menus of the village **gîtes d'étape** punctuating the low-level routes, where trekkers can enjoy slap-up meals of home-made Corsican cuisine for around 13€ per head (including wine). Evening meals and breakfast are bundled with the cost of your bed into half-board deals at all but a handful of gîtes. Standards of cooking vary from place to place, but are consistently high considering what you pay, and the portions are rarely less than generous.

Up on the **GR20**, of course, it's a different story. Once away from the few points where the route dips down to road level, bubbling lasagnas and chestnut-flour flans steeped in maquis-scented honey become the stuff of dreams. GR trekkers have to rely on their own supplies, topped up periodically with the basic provisions sold from refuges (typically over-priced saucisson, Corsican cheese, noodles, pasta and biscuits, canned beer, wine and soft drinks). In addition, gardiens these days are augmenting their meagre incomes by dishing up hot stews and other simple cooked dishes; in fact, some are so keen to push these that they've stopped selling supplies altogether.

Restaurants

While sitting down to supper in a gîte d'étape may be a convenient and inexpensive way to assuage those monster trekking appetites, you'll be missing out if you don't eat in a restaurant (or *auberge* as they sometimes call themselves) once in a while. In common with mainland France, *la restauration* is regarded as a *métier* – a vocation – and it's rare to be served a duff meal in Corsica, especially in the hills where most restaurants are well-established, family-run places with an exigent local clientele as well as passing tourist trade to cater for.

All but the very poshest restaurants generally offer a range of ***menus fixes***. With these, you select one dish from the limited choice listed for each course, among which is invariably a *plat du jour* (chef's special or dish of the day). There's usually a cheap and cheerful budget menu for around 10€ and a *menu corse* offering a spread of local specialities for upwards of 17€. The most expensive menus will probably include especially-good charcuterie and cheese, fresh fish such as river trout, game or wild boar delicacies, and a home-made dessert.

It generally works out more expensive to eat à la carte (where you select individual dishes from a full-length menu) but in principal you get what you pay for, with access to the full range of house specialities. Note that the French word for menu is '*carte*'; ask for '*le menu*' and you'll be shown or told about the *menu fixe*.

Pizzas are enormously popular in Corsica and generally the most affordable way to eat out. Baked in wood-fired ovens (look for a sign outside the pizzeria saying '*Au Feu de Bois*'), a pizza typically costs between 8€ and 11€, depending on the toppings, which allows you to order a side salad or maybe a dessert and coffee, with a small *pichet* of wine, for less than 15€.

A lighter budget option would be to order from the long list of salads offered by most places, which cost around the same as pizzas and are usually large enough to make a meal in themselves. However, they tend to be unexciting: fresh vegetables on the island are mostly imported and tasteless, bulked out in salads with tinned sweetcorn or tuna, and smothered in mass-produced mayonnaise. Only in quality restaurants and at family places in the mountains are you likely to be served fresh, organically-grown leaves and vegetables from kitchen gardens.

Vegetarian food

Vegetarian dishes seem finally to be filtering onto menus in Corsica but the pace of change is even slower than in mainland France and most of the time non-meat-eaters have to make do with cold starters, run-of-the-mill salads and Neapolitan pizzas or pasta. Gîtes d'étape do not generally offer alternatives to their set menus, although it's always worth asking when you book. You should also scour the menus of Corsican speciality places for dishes based on chestnut flour, pasta and eggs, many of which are essentially vegetarian and can easily be prepared replacing their meat ingredients with *brocciu* (pronounced 'broodge'; soft ewe's cheese) or roasted vegetables. One delicious, and typically Corsican, vegetarian dish to look out for is stuffed aubergine (*aubergine à la bonifacienne*), a speciality of Bonifacio that pops up on a lot of menus in the south of the island.

The phrase you'll need to say to the waiter is: '*Je suis végétarien/ne. Est-ce qu'il y a des plats sans viande ou poisson?*' ('I'm vegetarian; do you have any dishes without meat or fish?').

DRINK

Nothing will sap your trekking legs quite so thoroughly as alcohol but it's all too easy to ignore the consequences at the end of a day's walking when the wine and chestnut beer start to flow. In Corsica, alcoholic drinks are routinely consumed before eating (as *apéritifs*), to accompany the different courses and to finish off meals (as *digestifs*). They're also served without food at cafés, where a significant proportion of the island's middle-aged male population pass their lives sipping *pastis* (also known by its various brand names such as Pernod and Ricard) – a dry, clear spirit heavily flavoured with aniseed that turns milky yellow when mixed with water or ice. The other classic Corsican appetizer is a fortified wine called **Cap Corse** (its brand name), whose distinctive bitter-sweet taste derives from a blend of sugar-rich muscatelle grapes and quinine. Now produced in a range of flavours, it was originally drunk as an anti-malaria prophylactic – the Corsican equivalent of British-India's gin and tonic. Ask for '*un Cap*' and you'll be well in with the locals.

More palatable to the uninitiated are the lager-style beers sold even in remote refuges up on the GR20. Arguably the most distinguished of them is Corsica's own brew, Pietra, made from chestnut flour. Although a notch pricier than 1664 and Stella Artois, it's darker, crisper and stronger than the competition. The same company has also brought out a delicious (and even more expensive) *weissbier* called Colomba, sold in bottles in most village bars.

The reputation of **Corsican wine**, which you'll see on sale everywhere, took a knock in the 1970s after it was revealed that some of the large-scale *pieds-noirs* producers on the east coast were illegally adulterating their cheap *vins de pays* to bump up alcohol content (a scandal that eventually provoked an armed siege, see p57). Over the past decade or so, however, the industry has recovered and now turns out some outstandingly good reds (*rouges*), whites

Corsican cuisine

It's commonplace on the island to say that while French food celebrates the genius of the chef, Corsican food celebrates the genius of God. Based on simple, natural ingredients, *la cuisine corse* relies substantially on freshness and quality for its flavours rather than fussy sauces and convoluted cooking techniques.

A prime example is the Corsican-style omelette, which is made with little more than mint (ideally picked at altitude) and that other quintessential component of Corsican cooking, **brocciu**. Produced in bergeries high up in the mountains of the interior, this mild, soft ewe's cheese is regarded as far superior to its continental cousin, *brousse*, and is used to add flavour and creamy texture to a variety of dishes, including desserts. **Soups** are another popular starter, whether based on beans or a peppery fish stock, the latter served with chunky croutons smothered in mustard-enriched mayonnaise.

Before the arrival of the main dish it's customary to serve side plates of ***fritella*** (griddle-fried fritters) or ***beignets*** (savoury donuts) made with chestnut flour and knobs of melted brocciu. But the traditional focal point of any major Corsican meal is a meat dish of some kind. During the winter hunting season, freshly shot **wild boar** will frequently dominate the table of Sunday lunches in the villages, served as fillets with roast potatoes, in a rich lasagna or in stews (*tianu di cingale*), flavoured with fresh maquis herbs such as rosemary, tarragon, sage, fennel and wild thyme. Roasted suckling kid (*cabrettu*) and lamb (*agnellu*) are other popular bases for stews, while veal (*veau*) is more classically prepared with olives. All manner of meat and game – including tripe, blackbird and even hedgehog – might end up rolled together and baked as ***stifatu***, which is served with a sprinkling of strong, hard ewe's cheese.

To round things off on an appropriately heavy note, *the* most Corsican of desserts is ***fiadone***, a flan made from chestnut flour, brocciu, eggs and maquis honey. You'll sometimes be served it flambéed in aromatic *eau de vie* liqueur.

(*blancs*) and rosés. The chalky-soil region of Patrimonio, in the north near Bastia, and the sea-facing slopes below Sartène in the far south-west, harbour the most celebrated *domaines*, but vineyards around Ajaccio, Calvi and Porto-Vecchio also enjoy Appellation d'Origine Contrôlée (AOC) status. In addition, Cap Corse, the 40km-long finger-thin promontory extending northwards from Bastia, is famous for its pale-amber **muscat**, a sweet dessert wine with a delicate floral aroma which Corsicans serve as an apéritif or with strong ewe's cheese.

Resembling quality Tuscan chiantis, the best Corsican reds are robust and dark. With the exception of muscat, the whites are far more delicate, with hints of apple and hazelnut that make the perfect accompaniment for the oysters gathered on the lagoons of the east coast (which Napoléon famously had shipped to him while in exile on nearby Elba). Names to look out for in the supermarket or on wine lists include: Domaine de Toraccio, Comte Péraldi and Clos d'Alzeto.

In restaurants you'll be offered a selection of bottled AOC wine from around the island, as well as less pricey house wines. These usually come in small jugs, or *pichets* – ask for 'un quart' (a quarter litre) or 'un demi' (a half litre) – and tend to be undistinguished vins de pays. In reputable auberges and some gîtes d'étape, however, the *patron* or *patronne* may pride themselves on their own local supply of AOC-standard wine which they'll serve at house rates.

No full-scale Corsican meal is considered complete without a small glass of spirit to round things off. The one you're most likely to be offered on the house is ***eau de vie***, a clear rocket-fuel liquid distilled from grape skins. For obvious reasons it's served in tiny quantities, and also used to flambé desserts, to which it imparts a delicate liquorice flavour. Liqueurs are also very popular on the island, especially ***vin de myrthe,*** whose taste comes from aromatic myrtle berries gathered from the maquis. The best of it seems to be made at home by people's grandmothers, but you can buy inferior stuff in fancy bottles at most souvenir shops.

BILLS AND TIPPING

Bills will all include sales tax (IVA) but not necessarily service charges unless you see '*service compris*' (or just '*s.c.*') printed at the bottom. '*Service non compris*' means you're expected to add the discretionary 15% yourself.

ELECTRICITY

Electricity is 220V out of double, round-pin wall sockets. European appliances should work with just a plug-in adaptor; North American ones will need this plus a step-down transformer.

HOLIDAYS, FESTIVALS AND OPENING HOURS

Traditional festivals, pegged to the religious calendar, are still celebrated with enthusiasm and, in some cases, great solemnity in Corsica. The island also boasts a string of more frivolous modern cultural events, introduced to inject a bit of life into quiet times of year or as focal points of the summer tourist season.

Neither these nor the conventional French public holidays have much impact on life in the interior villages, where shops, bars and restaurants keep to their normal opening hours. For most businesses these are 8am–noon and 2–6pm, Monday to Friday. Village épiceries tend to stay closed for most of the afternoon but open from 4.30pm until 7.30pm (or later in summer); bakeries open at the crack of dawn and keep working through the lunch hour until around 2.30pm, but generally close soon after that. Nearly everywhere closes on Sunday and most shops open for only half a day on Saturday.

On the GR20 it can be difficult to remember what day it is, let alone the date, so the festivals and holidays listed below will probably appear as distant irrelevancies if you're up on the haute route. The list includes only Corsica's main events; for a fuller rundown with precise dates, contact a tourist office on the island or browse one of the information websites listed on p89.

- **Good Friday – U Catenacciu** Sartène, in southern Corsica, hosts this famous nocturnal procession, when rows of Ku-Klux-Klan-lookalike hooded penitents imitate Christ's walk to Golgotha. There's a 12-year waiting list to be the Grand Pénitent, who gets to carry a heavy wooden cross through the candle-lit streets with chains wrapped around his ankles. Similar rituals are performed by religious brotherhoods on Easter weekend across the island.
- **June 2 – La Fête de Saint Erasme** The island's fishermen celebrate their patron saint's day with a special mass and firework displays at ports and harbours throughout Corsica.
- **Third week of June – Calvi Jazz** A world-class line-up of musicians perform on a stage set below Calvi's picturesque citadel, and then jam the night through at the quayside bars.
- **First and second week of July – Festivoce, Calvi** A festival dedicated to *a cappella* singing from around the world, with Corsican polyphonic groups contributing to the international line-up.
- **September 8–10 – Santa di u Niolu, Casamoccioli** Corsica's oldest established singing event revolves around an arcane choral joust between singers who trade improvised insults across a crowded bar up in the Niolu Valley. For more on this, see p225.
- **September 14–18 – Rencontres de Chants Polyphoniques, Calvi** The island's premier polyphonic festival showcases the finest exponents of a singing tradition unique to the island (more background on which appears on p225).
- **Last week of October – Festiventu, Calvi** The end of the tourist season and return of the autumnal winds is celebrated with a colourful kite festival on one of Corsica's most spectacular beaches.

MONEY

On 28 February 2002, the euro superseded the old Franc Français as France's sole legal tender. Euro **coins** come in eight different denominations – 2€, 1€, 50c, 20c, 10c, 5c, 2c, 1c. There are a total of seven euro **notes**, all in different colours and sizes, denominated in 500€, 200€, 100€, 50€, 20€, 10€ and 5€.

❑ Rates of exchange

	Euro
Aus$1	€0.60
Can$1	€0.72
NZ$1	€0.50
UK£1	€1.62
US$1	€1.14

For up-to-the-minute rates of exchange check the Internet: **www.oanda.com /convert/classic**

POST, TELEPHONE AND EMAIL

Post

Distinguished by their yellow-and-blue livery, Corsica's **post offices** are smart and reliable, despite being the repeated target of nationalist bomb and machine-gun attacks. **Stamps** (*timbres*) can be bought at all branches, as well as over the counter at tobacconists (look for the red '*tabac*' signs on most high streets) and at postcard shops. Letters up to 20g cost 50 cents for countries within the EU, or 60 cents for Australia and the US. Parcels of up to 500kg cost between 3€ and 5.32€, depending on the rate, or 6.40–11€ for countries out of the EU.

Telephones

Just about everywhere that sells stamps also sells cards (*télécartes*) for **public telephone** booths (*cabines*). These come in two sizes, costing around 7.50/15€ for 50/120 units respectively. To make a call using one, insert it chip-end first into the phone and wait a few seconds until the LCD display registers the number of unused units remaining. You can then dial. For telephone numbers in Corsica or anywhere in mainland France the ringing tones are long beeps. If the line's engaged you'll hear short beeps instead. Should your card run out midway through a call you can replace it by pressing the green button on the console. When the message '*retirez votre carte*' comes up, pull out the used card and wait until you see the words '*nouvelle télécarte*' before inserting the new one.

Coin-operated phone boxes are these days few and far between, although you do occasionally come across them in bars. It's therefore a good idea to buy as many *télécartes* as you think you'll need at the start of your trek as they can be hard to get hold of in more remote villages.

Public phone boxes should all receive **incoming calls**. Look for the cabine's number printed at the head of the instruction panel on the wall in front of you. Tell the person who is to ring you back all ten digits (or only nine, minus the first zero from +04, if they're abroad) and remind them to add the international code plus the code for France (+33).

Mobile phones (*portables*) are of limited use in the mountains, where coverage is very patchy, but function reliably enough in the major towns and most villages.

Email

Email and **Internet** access is hard to come by. The few bona-fide Internet cafés we unearthed on the island are listed in the relevant accounts. If you're desperate to get on-line, you could always ask the manager of any hotel you happen to be staying in to help you out.

THINGS TO BUY

Food and drink are the obvious things to take home from Corsica as presents. In the main towns you'll find little boutiques selling artisanally-made charcuterie, cheese, honey, maquis herbs and biscuits (canastrelli). They also stock a range of quality wines – including muscat, which makes a great souvenir as it's unique to the island – and will package anything you buy in fancy paper and ribbons if you explain it's '*un cadeau*' (a present). The same applies to bakeries, which all prepare their own Corsican speciality cakes and tarts.

Supermarkets may feel like less authentic places to shop but the larger ones have substantial Corsican produce sections and much lower prices than the 'Produits Corses' boutiques. Most also have racks of Corsican polyphony CDs, which can make good presents (see the box on p225 for some suggestions).

SECURITY

Corsica may suffer one of the worst rates of violent crime in Europe but the island remains an extremely safe place for tourists. Nationalist attacks are always tightly targeted and never affect visitors; aside from the ubiquitous political graffiti and occasional bombed-out building you'll be completely unaware that le problème corse even exists.

Theft is very rare indeed. Up in the closely-knit communities of the interior it's virtually non-existent. Trekkers routinely leave their packs outside bars, shops and gîtes without so much as a second thought. If anyone did steal from a visitor they'd probably soon find themselves staring down the barrel of a hunting rifle. Muggings and sexually-motivated violence against tourists are also unheard of, even in the two main towns, although you should take the same precautions you would anywhere when walking around late at night.

The one way you might be drawn into a violent encounter with a local person is if you insult someone. Corsicans are quick to react when they perceive they, their family or their political opinions have been slighted. For advice on conduct and possible gaffes see p73.

❑ **Corsica-related Websites**

In spite of the overall sluggish way with which Corsicans have responded to the Internet revolution, the Web these days supports a mass of information about the island. Anyone intending to attempt the big GR might also wish to surf some of the many homepages containing illustrated accounts of recent GR20 treks; (stick 'GR20' in your search engine and see what it comes back with).

http://perso.wanadoc.fr/euromail/cormed01.heml Corsica dedicated portal boasting more than 600 links – the most exhaustive gateway currently on the Net

www.corsica-isula.com Another general site with a wealth of info on every conceivable subject, including mountain trekking (www.corsica-isula/mountains)

www.parc-naturel-corse.com A full rundown of PNRC's projects and background on the park itself (French only)

www.corsematin.com The latest articles from the island's top selling daily (French only)

www.napoleon.org Richly-illustrated site devoted to Ajaccio's most illustrious son

www.liberation.fr/corse/archives.html For serious students of contemporary Corsican politics, this site collates some of the most penetrating articles on the island's troubles published over the past decade in the left-of-centre/liberal French daily, *Libération* (French only)

www.cjb.unige.ch/fdc Hugely-detailed map of Corsican flora, compiled by Geneva's Conservatoire & Jardins Botaniques (French only)

http://perso.wandoo.fr/d.aubin/cpa.htm One for history buffs: a massive collection of old postcards (1900–1940) covering most rural locations and Corsican topics

http://membres.tripod.fr/polog2marco Occult, mystical and prehistoric Corsica exposed by an obsessive local trekker; French only, but with lots of pictures

PART 3: GATEWAY TOWNS

Ajaccio/Aiacciu

Ajaccio, capital of Corse-du-Sud and seat of the regional government, is the island's largest town and its principal transport hub. Set against a grandiose backdrop of hills and distant snow peaks, its old port and eighteenth-century core of red-tiled tenements, where Napoléon Bonaparte was born and raised, are hemmed in by ugly suburbs of tower blocks that sprawl around the northern shore of a spectacular bay. Palm-lined promenades, rows of swish terrace cafés, and the notoriously glitzy dressing of its inhabitants lend to the town a strongly French-Riviera feel – a world away from the mountains visible across the gulf.

Napoléon and Ajaccio

Ajaccio's most illustrious son, Napoléon Bonaparte, may be regarded as the archetypal Frenchman but he started life as a staunchly nationalistic Corsican. The son of rebel leader Pascal Paoli's right-hand man, he was born only three months after the crushing defeat of Ponte Nuovo in 1769 when Paoli's army was routed by the French. Thereafter, the Bonapartes were quick to reconcile their political differences with the new overlords and prospered, with young Napoléon gaining a scholarship at a military academy on the continent.

By the time Paoli had rallied sufficiently to mount a second, British-backed attempt to overthrow the French 25 years later, Napoléon's family had become part of the gallicized Revolutionary élite in Ajaccio, making them a prime target for patriot ire. When rebel forces stormed through the town, the Bonapartes' Ajaccio home was among the first to be looted and the family was forced into exile. It is said that the young Napoléon never forgave his countrymen the insult. Apart from a brief visit in 1799 when his fleet was forced into Ajaccio by inclement weather on its victorious return from Egypt, he never came back.

As emperor, Napoléon became vehemently anti-Corsican, suspending the island's Constitution and ruthlessly suppressing any signs of nascent nationalism. He even gallicized his name (from the more Italian-sounding Napoleone). Ajacciens responded by disowning him. When the emperor announced his abdication in 1814 they celebrated by cheering in the streets and pitching a statue of him into the gulf.

These days it's a very different story. France's great leader and his memory have been enthusiastically rehabilitated by the town. Statues of him (wearing Roman togas and laurel leaves) now preside over the three main squares. The town's principal thoroughfare is called cours Napoléon, and there are a couple of small museums dedicated to the Boney cult. But the old animosity, however, still resurfaces from time to time: a few years back, the equestrian statue of Napoléon in place de la République was painted bright yellow.

Ajaccio, 1870 (from *Journal of a Landscape Painter*, Edward Lear)

In short, Ajaccio is somewhere guaranteed to make you feel frumpy in hiking boots but, as the location of Corsica's busiest airport and railhead, it's hard to avoid. It also suffers from a chronic shortage of hotel beds so plan your visit to avoid spending the night here, or far enough ahead to be sure of a room.

WHAT TO SEE

Conventional sights are thin on the ground in Ajaccio. Most people kill time with a leisurely amble around the fishing harbour and the grid of narrow streets packed behind the citadel where, sooner or later, you'll come across Napoléon's birthplace, on place Letizia. The **Maison Bonaparte** today houses a small museum (May–Sept Mon 2–6pm, Tues–Fri 9am–noon and 2–6pm; Sat 9–11.45am and 2–6pm, Sun 9am–noon; Oct–April Mon 2–6pm, Tues–Sat 10am–noon and 2–5pm, Sun 10am–noon; closed Sun pm and Mon am; admission 3.30€) containing less Napoléonic memorabilia than you might expect, most of the family's possessions having been pillaged by rampaging Paolists.

A more engaging selection of Boney trophies and relics is displayed at the **Salon Napoléonien**, in a grand hall above the entrance of the Hôtel de Ville on place Foch (June 15–Sept 15 Mon–Sat 9–11am and 2–5.45pm; Sept 16–June 14 Mon–Fri 9–11am and 2–5pm; admission 1.52€). The prize exhibits here are a replica of the emperor's death mask and a fragment of his coffin.

Napoléon's armies systematically looted the art collections of the European capitals they passed through and many of the period's finest treasures ended up in Ajaccio, where they were acquired by the emperor's uncle, Cardinal Fesch.

Those not sold off by later generations are preserved in the excellent **Musée Fesch** (July–Aug Mon 1.30–6pm, Tues–Thurs 9–6.30, Fri and Sat 10.30am–12.15pm, Sun 10.30am–6pm; April–June and Sept Mon 1–5.15pm, Tues–Sun 9.15am–12.15 and 2.15–5.15pm; Oct–Mar same hours, but closed Mon; 5.40€), rue Cardinal Fesch, in the centre of town. Among the superb array of mainly sixteenth and seventeenth-century masterpieces is an early Botticelli, 'Virgin and Child', and Titian's famous 'Man with a Glove'.

Across the museum's courtyard stands the **Chapelle Impériale**, where members of the Bonaparte family, including Napoléon's mother and uncle, are buried (same hours; admission 1.52€). If you're short of time skip this and head for the wonderful town library, the **Bibliothèque Municipale** (Mon–Fri 8am–noon; admission free), in the museum's north wing. The huge collection of leather-bound antique books stacked to its ceiling were mostly confiscated from fleeing aristos during the French Revolution. You can't touch the tomes, but this is also an atmospheric place to browse the local newspapers and magazines.

Of the two **beaches** within easy walking distance of the town centre, plage St François, below the citadel, is the least clean and appealing. You're better off plodding 20 minutes south-west down the promenade to a second, nameless beach backed by a row of shops, where the water is much clearer and the sand more salubrious.

ORIENTATION AND SERVICES

Ajaccio's Campo del Oro Airport (☎ 04.95.23.56.56) lies 8km south-west of the centre, around the bay. In the arrivals hall you'll find the usual gamut of car rental counters and an ATM. Taxis wait at the rank outside, or you could jump on one of the half-hourly buses that shuttle into town (7.60€).

The airport bus route passes the train station, just east of the centre, before dropping you at the imposing new *terminal routière* (bus station), which doubles as a *gare maritime* (ferry port). Both the train and bus stations have *consignes* (left-luggage offices), but their opening hours vary according to final arrival and departure times, so check when you deposit your gear.

Across the road from the terminal routière is place du Marché (market square) where you'll find Ajaccio's **tourist office** (☎ 04.95.51.53.03; Sept–June Mon–Fri 8am–6pm, Sat 8am–5pm; July and Aug Mon–Sat 8am–6pm, Sun 9am–1pm). The rest of the town's useful services and businesses are dotted along or around the main street, cours Napoléon, which runs the length of the centre. This is where you'll find the **post office**, **banks** (with ATMs) and **pharmacies**, as well as Ajaccio's only **outdoor equipment** shop, Luciani Sports.

For the latest information on Corsica's long-distance trekking routes, visit the **Parc Naturel's information office** at 2 rue Sergent Casalonga, just off cours Napoléon (☎ 04.95.51.79.10, 💻 www.parc-naturel-corse.com). They should have both Topoguides for the island and a range of IGN maps. If not, try the Maison de la Presse, five minutes' walk south-east on place Foch.

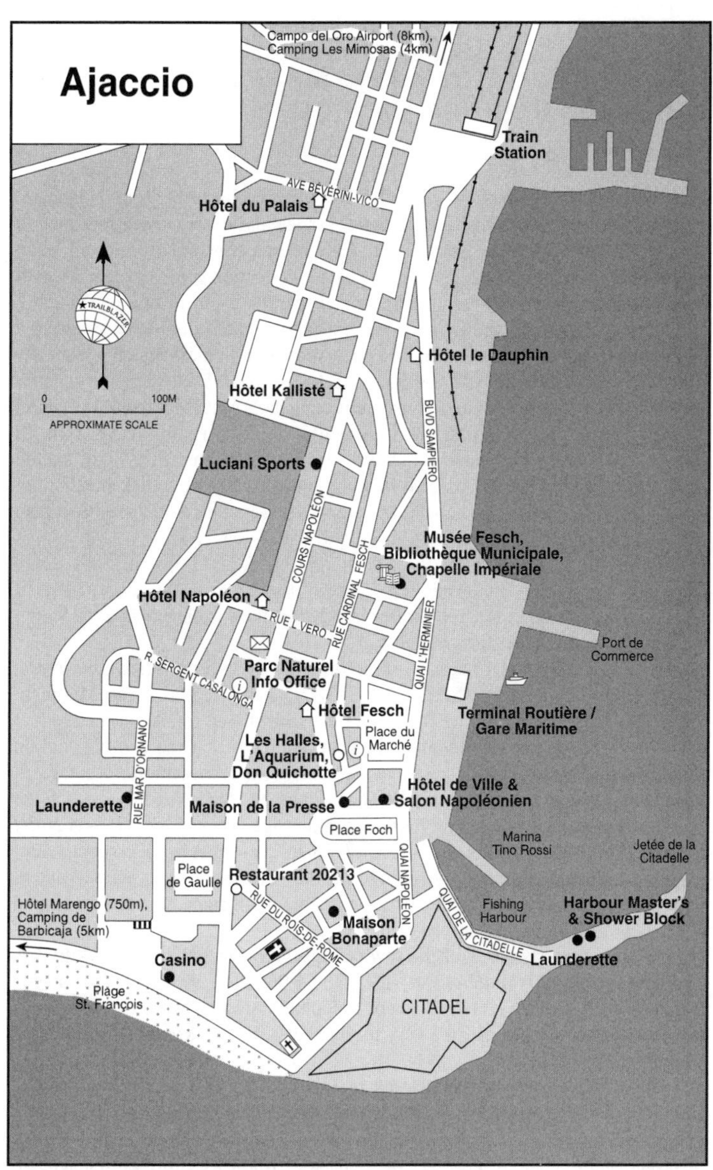
Ajaccio
Campo del Oro Airport (8km), Camping Les Mimosas (4km)
Train Station
AVE BÉVERINI-VICO
Hôtel du Palais
TRAILBLAZER
0
100M
APPROXIMATE SCALE
Hôtel le Dauphin
Hôtel Kallisté
BLVD SAMPIERO
Luciani Sports
COURS NAPOLÉON
RUE CARDINAL FESCH
Musée Fesch, Bibliothèque Municipale, Chapelle Impériale
Hôtel Napoléon
RUE L VERO
QUAI L'HERMINIER
Port de Commerce
R. SERGENT CASALONGA
Parc Naturel Info Office
Hôtel Fesch
Terminal Routière / Gare Maritime
Place du Marché
Les Halles, L'Aquarium, Don Quichotte
RUE MAR D'ORNANO
Hôtel de Ville & Salon Napoléonien
Launderette
Maison de la Presse
Place Foch
Marina Tino Rossi
Jetée de la Citadelle
QUAI NAPOLÉON
Place de Gaulle
Restaurant 20213
Hôtel Marengo (750m), Camping de Barbicaja (5km)
RUE DU ROIS-DE-ROME
Maison Bonaparte
QUAI DE LA CITADELLE
Fishing Harbour
Harbour Master's & Shower Block
Launderette
Casino
Plage St. François
CITADEL

There are two self-service **launderettes** in the centre: one on rue du Maréchal Ornano just off place de Gaulle (place Diamant); the other, on the jetée de la Citadelle, on the south side of the Marina Tino *capitainerie* Office, is a useful shower and toilet block where you can scrub up for 3€.

WHERE TO STAY

It's hard to overstate just how difficult it can be to find a hotel room in Ajaccio, especially at weekends. Pressure for beds is especially intense at the bottom end of the market, following what seems to have been a conspiracy in recent years to close down the town's cheaper hotels. A good solution is to get together with fellow trekkers and hunt for a triple or four-person room in one of the more upscale places, which can often be less expensive than a double or single in a budget hotel. All of the following are open year-round unless stated otherwise.

Hôtel Le Dauphin (☎ 04.95.21.12.94, 🖹 04.95.21.88.69), on blvd Sampiero, is a dependable and convenient budget choice. Prices start at around 39.50€ for a sparsely furnished en suite double, rising to 48.60€ in July–August. They also have a handful of cheaper rooms (32€; with shared showers and toilets) in an adjacent building, but you'll have to ask specifically for one of these as they try to fill the others first. The tariffs include breakfast, served on the pavement terrace of the slightly seedy bar.

As a fallback, try ***Hôtel du Palais*** (☎ 04.95.22.73.68), just off cours Napoléon at 5 ave Bévérini-Vico, where rooms cost 41.20–50.30€, or 45.70–56.40€ en suite. Recently refurbished, this place is clean and good value, and well placed for the train station.

In a similar bracket, though a 20-minute trudge south-west from the centre, is ***Hôtel Marengo*** (☎ 04.95.21.43.66, 🖹 04.95.21.51.26), at 2 rue Marengo. Rates here range from 38€ to 44€ for rooms with shared toilets on the landing to 42.60–55€ en suite. Although somewhat hemmed in at the end of a cul de sac, it's near the seafront and more peaceful than the competition.

If you want to be more in the thick of things on cours Napoléon, much the best option – in fact altogether the nicest mid-range hotel in Ajaccio – is ***Hôtel Kallisté*** (☎ 04.95.51.34.45, 🖹 04.95.21.79.00). The rooms in this recently renovated eighteenth-century building are on the small side but well appointed, with en suite bathrooms, comfy beds and cable TV. Prices go from 38.10€ to 64€ (including breakfast, served in the room).

Moving upmarket, one of the few central three-star hotels that usually has vacancies is ***Hôtel Napoléon*** (☎ 04 95 51 54 00, 🖹 04 95 21 80 40), on rue Lorenzo Vero. Rooms start at 63€ for a double, rising to 82€ in peak season, and they install extra beds for a very reasonable 17€. Breakfast (6.80€ extra) is a sumptuous buffet.

The other established three-star in this area is ***Hôtel Fesch*** (☎ 04.95 51.62.62, 🖹 04.95.21.83.36, 💻 www.hotel-fesch.com), on rue Cardinal Fesch, which became briefly famous in 1980 when the hotel was occupied by a gang of armed nationalists. Fitted out with chestnut-wood furniture and sheepskin rugs, the en suite rooms are all air-conditioned and have satellite TV. Tariffs range from 49.50€ to 69.40€ for a double, depending on the time of year and grade of room.

Ajaccio has two **campsites**, neither of them convenient for anyone without a car. Just under 5km west of town, on route des Iles Sanguinaires, ***Camping de Barbicaja*** (☎ 04.95.52.01.17; open May–Sept) is the easiest to reach by public transport. Jump on bus No 5 from place de Gaulle. ***Camping Les Mimosas*** (☎ 04.95.20.99.85; open April–Oct) gets marginally less crowded, but lies well off the beaten track on the northern outskirts of town. Catch a No 4 bus from place de Gaulle or cours Napoléon to the 'Brasilia' stop, and walk north to the big roundabout at the bottom of the hill. After crossing the intersection, head up the lane on its far side and turn left at the signpost, passing a tennis club soon after on your right. The site is another 1km uphill from there. Better still, take a cab for around 12€.

WHERE TO EAT

Ajaccio may suffer a dearth of hotels, but it isn't short of places to eat. Purely in terms of location, the row of identikit tourist restaurants lining quai de la Citadelle are hard to beat. The seafood tends to be mediocre but the views of the fishing boats and the gulf are compensation enough. Stick to pizza and a *pichet* of house red and you'll not go far wrong.

For anything more adventurous, take your pick from one of the open-air restaurants crammed into rue des Halles, the alley behind the covered market just off place du Marché. ***Restaurant Les Halles*** is a pre-war stalwart that does an excellent-value 11.40€ set menu of traditional Corsican *canelloni* with *brocciu*. ***L'Aquarium***, two doors down, is strong on fish from the gulf with menus from 14€ to 32€. At the opposite end of the street, the ***Don Quichotte*** specializes in T-bone steaks, washed down with better than average local AOC wines. *Menus fixes* range from 14€ to 27€.

If you're splashing out, ***Restaurant 20213*** at 2 rue du Roi-des-Rome is a safe choice. Decked out with traditional farming implements (and an old Vespa for some reason), it serves top-notch Corsican cuisine: Bastelica *charcuterie*, pungent ewes' cheese from the Niolu Valley, chestnut-flour desserts from Castagniccia and wine from Partimonio, Ajaccio and Sartène. Menus fixes are 16€ and 28€.

GETTING TO THE TRAILHEADS FROM AJACCIO

Calvi, jumping off place for Calenzana and the start of the **GR20**, is a 4½ to 5-hour train ride north across the island. Two services per day leave Ajaccio station to link up with a through service at Ponte Leccia junction. En route the Micheline passes via Vizzavona, near the foot of Monte d'Oro (see p160), from where you can pick up the GR20 at its midway point. Vivario and Corte, a short way further up the line, are both way stages on the **Mare a Mare Nord *Variant*** (see p234-46).

The other trails described in this book can only be reached by road. The various bus companies working out of Ajaccio have counters at the terminal routière, which open about half an hour before the bus is due to leave; this is where you should buy tickets and inquire about departure times. Don't rely on the tourist office for travel information.

For Cargèse on the west coast, starting point for the **Mare a Mare Nord** and **Tra Mare e Monti** routes, catch SAIB's Porto service (☎ 04.95.22.41.99 or 04.95.21.02.07). This leaves twice daily in July and August, and once or twice daily from Mondays to Saturdays the rest of the year; there is no bus on Sundays from September to June. Apart from peak season the company only lays on a small minibus so it is essential to book in advance, preferably the day before departure. At the very least, get there about 45 minutes before departure.

The trailhead for the **Mare a Mare Sud** is most easily approached on Eurocorse Voyage's (☎ 04.95.21.06.30) twice daily service to Propriano. If you've done all your shopping and don't need to venture into Propriano, ask to be dropped off at the Elf station 2km east, which will save you a long walk back along the main road.

Bastia

Bastia, capital of Haute-Corse, is smaller than Ajaccio but an altogether more authentically Corsican town. Looking east across the Tyrrhenian Sea to the coast of Tuscany, it feels closer to Italy in every way, and decidedly un-French. The industrial estates sprawling south to Poretta airport and the gritty suburbs stacked up the surrounding hillsides remind you that this is primarily a working town. Despite recent efforts to spruce up the citadel and make the centre more visitor friendly, tourism remains peripheral. That said, Bastia is arguably the island's most atmospheric urban point of arrival or departure. If you're passing through try to make time for at least a stroll around the old harbour district and citadel.

WHAT TO SEE

Enfolded by a horseshoe of crumbling Genoan tenements, Bastia's **Vieux Port** is easily the town's most picturesque quarter. Its defining landmark is the spectacular Baroque facade of the **Church of Saint Jean-Baptiste**, whose giant belfries loom above an extraordinary jumble of schist tile rooftops – a scene little changed since Nelson attempted to blow it to pieces in 1794.

Down at water level, cafés and restaurants hug the harbour, overlooking a forest of yacht and fishing boat masts. This is a particularly enjoyable place to

Opposite: Doorway, Ota, Tra Mare e Monti route – see p248. (Photo © David Abram).

FRANCHI A.

Bastia, 1870 (from *Journal of a Landscape Painter*, Edward Lear)

come for breakfast – when the sun rising over the Tyrrhenian Sea casts a rich light over the quayside terraces – and for sunset, when the sky is filled with flocks of screeching swifts.

The tranquillity of the Vieux Port, however, masks the fact that the *quartier* has long been a hotbed of nationalist politics. In 1998 it witnessed one of Corsica's most vicious terrorist attacks, when a car bomb exploded in broad daylight, killing one prominent militant and severely injuring another. As a result, your view of the marina will be obscured at regular intervals by armoured CRS patrols.

The police presence is less noticeable up the hill in the Citadel district, or Terra Nova, a warren of alleys and squares enclosed by its original honey-coloured Genoan ramparts. The main building of interest here is the **Palais des Gouverneurs**, which served as a prison before it was bombarded by Nelson during the British siege. It took another pounding in 1943 when the Americans mistakenly blitzed Bastia the day after it had been liberated, but was beautifully restored to its original state in the 1990s. Nowadays the palace accommodates the town's **Musée Ethnographique**, which was closed at the time of writing but should be open by the summer of 2002. Charting the history of Corsica from prehistoric times to the post-war period, the exhibition is less impressive

Opposite Top: Paglia Orba from the summit ridge of Monte Rotondo (see p153).
Bottom: Approaching the Bocca Palmenti, GR20 (see p166). Note red-and-white GR20 waymarks painted on rocks. (Photos © David Abram).

than the building itself, tours of which invariably end up in the dungeons, last used to imprison Resistance fighters in WWII.

ORIENTATION AND SERVICES

Bastia is fairly compact and you shouldn't have to take a taxi anywhere, even from **Poretta Airport**, 16km south. A **shuttle bus** (7.60€) connects with most flights, approaching the centre via the old quarter of Terra Nova or through the tunnel beneath the citadel. Either way you end up at the train station after a brief stop on place St Nicholas, the town's heart and most obvious reference point. The ferry dock – or Nouveau Port – lies just off its north-east corner, while the train station stands 10 minutes' walk west down ave Pietri and ave Sébastiani. Bastia's main shopping streets, blvd Paoli and rue Campinchi, are just west of place St Nicholas.

At the north end of place St Nicholas is the **tourist office** (☎ 04.95 31.81.34; June–15 Sept daily 8am–8pm; 16 Sept–May Mon–Sat 8am–6pm, Sun and holidays 9am–1pm) useful primarily for information about bus departures – which, in the absence of a proper bus station, can be a tricky business (see Getting to the trailheads on p101). The post office, which has an ATM, is three minutes' walk along ave Pietri.

Most other useful services – including the launderette, five minutes' walk north of place St Nicholas, near the entrance to the North Ferry Terminal – are at this end of town. Left-luggage facilities are available at the South Ferry Terminal and at the train station.

En route south from place St Nicholas to the old quarter of Bastia – the Vieux Port and citadel district, Terra Nova – you'll pass a string of bookshops that all stock FFRP Topoguides and IGN maps. Best of the bunch is L'Ile aux Livres on rue Campinchi, which also has a good range of flora and fauna field guides.

WHERE TO STAY

Camping is not easy without your own transport. The only site within walking distance, ***Les Sables Rouges*** (☎ 04.95.33.00.65) lies 5km south of town. It's close to a beach but cramped, shabby and insecure.

Hotels are a notch pricier here than elsewhere on the island and, once again, there's a shortage of budget rooms. Unless otherwise stated, the following are open year-round.

In the centre of town one budget place stands out. ***Hôtel Central*** (☎ 04.95 31.71.12, 📠 04.95.31.82.40, 💻 www.centralhotel.fr), south of place St Nicholas at 3 rue Miot, is a cozy, well-run little hotel close to the shops and main square. A room costs from 30.40/38€ low/high season for shared toilets to 53.20/63.60€ fully en suite and air-conditioned. Breakfast (optional) is served in a small dining room.

Central Bastia's other economy option is very popular and hard to get into without advance reservation. Close to the Nouveau Port, ***Hôtel Riviera*** (☎ 04

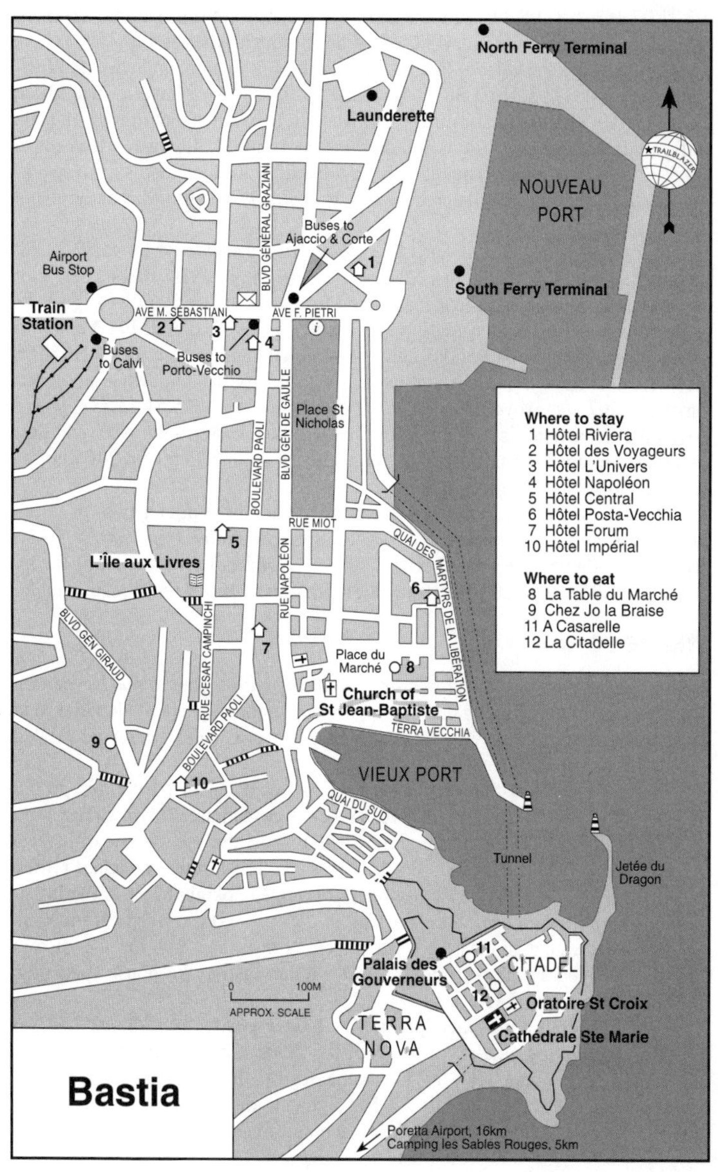
North Ferry Terminal
Launderette
NOUVEAU PORT
Buses to Ajaccio & Corte
Airport Bus Stop
South Ferry Terminal
Train Station
AVE M. SEBASTIANI
AVE F. PIETRI
BLVD GÉNÉRAL GRAZIANI
Buses to Calvi
Buses to Porto-Vecchio
Place St Nicholas
BOULEVARD PAOLI
BLVD GÉN DE GAULLE
RUE MIOT
L'Île aux Livres
QUAI DES MARTYRS DE LA LIBÉRATION
RUE NAPOLÉON
BLVD GEN GIRAUD
RUE CESAR CAMPINCHI
Place du Marché
Church of St Jean-Baptiste
TERRA VECCHIA
BOULEVARD PAOLI
VIEUX PORT
QUAI DU SUD
Tunnel
Jetée du Dragon
Palais des Gouverneurs
CITADEL
Oratoire St Croix
Cathédrale Ste Marie
0 100M
APPROX. SCALE
TERRA NOVA
Bastia
Poretta Airport, 16km
Camping les Sables Rouges, 5km
Where to stay
1 Hôtel Riviera
2 Hôtel des Voyageurs
3 Hôtel L'Univers
4 Hôtel Napoléon
5 Hôtel Central
6 Hôtel Posta-Vecchia
7 Hôtel Forum
10 Hôtel Impérial
Where to eat
8 La Table du Marché
9 Chez Jo la Braise
11 A Casarelle
12 La Citadelle

95.31.07.16, 🖷 04.95.34.17.39), which was recently refurbished, has 20 or so well aired en suite rooms for 48.60–58€ depending on the season.

Another budget place that's recently had a major upgrade is ***Hôtel L'Univers*** (☎ 04.95.31.03.38, 🖷 04.95.31.19.91), 3 ave Maréchal-Sébastiani near the train station. Its rooms are furnished to two-star standard with en suite bathrooms and air-con. Rates for doubles go from 53.20€ in low season to 68.50€ in high summer. They also have a handful of older rooms at rock-bottom rates, although you'll have to ask specifically for these as they're not advertised.

In a similar bracket, the venerable ***Hôtel Posta Vecchia*** (☎ 04.95.32.32.38, 🖷 04.95.32.14.05), on quai des Martyrs near the Vieux Port, offers a range of rooms from 38€ to 60€ in low season and from 48€ to 70€ in July–August. Its waterfront location is marginally more inspiring than that of ***Hôtel Napoléon*** (☎ 04.95.31.60.30, 🖷 04.95.31.77.83), 43–45 blvd Paoli, whose rooms cost 55€ to 99€. Most have a minibar and cable TV to justify the somewhat ambitious tariffs. ***Hôtel des Voyageurs*** (☎ 04.95.34.90.80, 🖷 04.95.51.53.33), 9 ave Maréchal-Sébastiani, is brighter, more modern, and close to the Nouveau Port and train station. The majority of its rooms go for around 75.50–96.20€, though a few are discounted in low season.

If all these are full, you might have to try one of the pricier two- or three-star hotels at the bottom of blvd Paoli. Rates at ***Hôtel Impérial*** (☎ 04.95 31.06.94, 🖷 04.95.34.13.76), 2 blvd Paoli, and ***Hôtel Forum*** (☎ 04.9531.02.53, 🖷 04.95.31.06.60), at 20 blvd Paoli, start at around 70€ for an en suite double.

WHERE TO EAT

Eating out in Bastia is a real pleasure. Kick off with a chilled *muscat* or Cap Corse at one of the relaxing cafés lining the west side of place St Nicholas, and from there make your way over to the Vieux Port or Citadel, which are riddled with snug little restaurants and pizzerias.

For a slightly off-the-wall experience of local cuisine, try ***Chez Jo La Braise*** (☎ 04.95.31.36.97), 7 blvd Hyacinte-de-Montreal/blvd Général de Gaulle. This is a local institution, renowned as much for the repartie of its garrulous *patron* (who claims to be a half-Russian-half-Chuwawa-Indian retired boxer from the Côte d'Azur) as for its wholesome cooking. Most of the ingredients – notably the charcuterie and chestnut flour – come straight from Mme La Braise's village in nearby Castagniccia. Prices are low for the district (around 17€ for the works); don't leave without tasting the house speciality, *banana flambé 'à la Jo'*.

A more serious atmosphere prevails at ***A Casarelle*** (☎ 04.95.32.02.32), at 6 rue Ste Croix in the citadel, whose chef has made it his mission to revive the old-fashioned cooking style of his home region, Balagne (the area around Calenzana at the start of the GR20). His signature dish, *storzzapretti*, is a mixture of soft ewes' cheese (brocciu), spinach and fresh maquis herbs baked in a rich tomato pesto. The set menu (19.80€) is only available at lunch time; in the evenings, count on around 26€ à la carte.

Just up the alley from A Casarelle on rue du Dragon is Bastia's swishest restaurant, ***La Citadelle*** (☎ 04.95.31.44.70; closed Sunday). You won't get much change out of 30€ per head but the food – an innovative blend of Corsican and French *haute cuisine* served in a beautifully restored vaulted dining room – is superlative.

More down to earth local food, such as traditional Corsican charcuterie, cheeses, pastries, herbs and wine, are the stock in trade of the daily **market**, held on place du Marché behind the Vieux Port. Bustling with shoppers from the surrounding quartiers, this is a lively spot to crowd-watch over a coffee. The east side of the square also has an excellent little restaurant, ***La Table du Marché*** (☎ 04.95.31.64.25; closed Sunday) that's particularly popular at lunch. Seafood is the thing to go for here: try their succulent *moules marinières* (9€), or check out the *plats du jour* board for the best-value fish dish of the day, washed down with a bottle of cold AOC Patrimonio white.

GETTING TO THE TRAILHEADS FROM BASTIA

You can reach Calvi, springboard for the **GR20** at Calenzana, by train or by bus. Both follow more or less the same route but the bus is cheaper and quicker. Operated by Les Beaux Voyages (☎ 04.95.65.11.35), it leaves from outside the train station twice daily. Departure times are best checked at the tourist office (see p98).

Calvi is also served by two trains per day, via Ponte-Leccia junction. The latter is where you have to change trains to reach Corte (on the **Mare a Mare Nord**), Vivario (on the **Mare a Mare Nord *Variant***) and Vizzavona (halfway point of the **GR20**). Current timetables are displayed in the station and at the tourist office.

For **Ajaccio**, departure point for services to Propriano for the **Mare a Mare Sud** and to Cargèse (trailhead for the **Mare a Mare Nord** and **Tra Mare e Monti**), you also have a choice of train or bus. Even though it's a lot slower, most people choose the former – the line through the mountains, crossing the watershed below Monte d'Oro, is among the most spectacular in Europe. Two to four services cover the route each day, taking 3 hours 40 minutes. The Ajaccio bus, run by Eurocorse Voyages (☎ 04.95.21.06.30), leaves from a small square opposite the tourist office and only takes three hours.

Buses to **Porto-Vecchio** (with Rapides Bleues; ☎ 04.95.31.03.79), jumping off place for the **Mare a Mare Sud** (if you intend to follow it in the opposite direction to the one described in this guide), depart from opposite the post office on ave Maréchal Sébastiani.

Calvi

There can be few towns in the world as inherently beautiful as Calvi that are so thoroughly eclipsed by their setting. Its squat citadel and yacht-filled harbour, where the Côte d'Azur jet-set drop anchor in August, are poised at the head of a magnificent turquoise bay and encircled by a gigantic backdrop of snow-streaked mountains. In good weather the grey escarpments seem magnified and it can be a surreal experience to sit on the quayside with a pastis in your hand staring up at the *névés* splashed across the north face of Monte Cinto, knowing that you'll be crossing them in a couple of days' time.

For those heading off on the big GR, or down the coast on the Tra Mare e Monti, the town's sophisticated pleasures only serve to sharpen anticipation of the trail ahead. Most hikers can't resist the call of the hills for long, heading inland as soon as they've stocked up with cash and other essentials not available in Calenzana. If you've already been trekking, Calvi is a place to ease aching feet with a well-earned break on the beach.

WHAT TO SEE

Packed onto a high bluff above the harbour, Calvi's ochre-walled **citadel**, erected in the fifteenth century by the Genoans, is the best place to get your bearings. Its entrance is just above place Christophe Colomb at the top of blvd Wilson, from where a cobbled alley winds up to an enclosed square, dominated by the **Cathedral of Saint Jean Baptiste** and the former Governors' Palace, now a military barracks.

Heading uphill along rue Colomb you'll eventually emerge at a ruined house which local legend asserts was the birthplace of **Christopher Columbus.** Shreds of tenuous evidence have been unearthed to support the connection but scholars remain unconvinced. Calvi, meanwhile, is milking the supposed link for all it's worth, renaming streets and squares, sticking up plaques and featuring an image of the discoverer of the New World in its tourist brochures.

With such inspiring views from the nearby ramparts it's hard to see why the hype is necessary. Calvi's natural attributes have exerted a powerful-enough pull on visitors for years, as demonstrated by the citadel's most famous café-restaurant, **Chez Tao**. Opened in the 1930s by a couple of Russian émigrés, one of whom was in the group who murdered Rasputin, it quickly established a reputation among the international jet-set. Three generations on it's owned by the same family and continues to attract film and rock stars, whose signed photos hang on the walls.

Chez Tao's view over the marina is legendary but for panoramas of the town and bay head for the **Chapelle de Notre Dame de la Serra**, perched on a ridge high above Calvi. You can walk there, starting from Hôtel La Villa; fol-

Calvi, 1870 (from *Journal of a Landscape Painter*, Edward Lear)

low the lane steeply uphill until you see a path forking to the left into the *maquis*. Set amid a pile of pink granite boulders that have sheltered a shrine since at least the 1400s, the present chapel dates from the nineteenth century.

From the south side of the marina Calvi's spectacular white-sand **beach** curves for more than 4km around the bay. The further from town you walk, the quieter and cleaner it becomes, though during the high season, crowds of campers from the sites hidden in the huge pine forest behind the beach can fill its entire length.

An alternative to lazing on the sand is to take one of the **boat trips f**rom the marina. At 42–50€ they're not cheap but offer a great way to see the magnificent coast to the south, including the famous red cliffs of the Scandola Nature Reserve (see p262). Before heading home most boats pull in for an hour at Girolata or Porto (hence the different ticket prices), from where you can pick up the Tra Mare e Monti trekking route. Tickets and timetables are available from the booths dotted along Quai Landry (see map).

ORIENTATION AND SERVICES

Calvi basically comprises one main street, blvd Wilson, which runs from the train station (☎04.95.65.00.61) to the foot of the citadel. Below its sloping walls, a tangle of narrow stepped lanes, little squares and winding alleys tumble down to quai Landry and the marina, where swish cafés and restaurants open onto a mass of gleaming white luxury pleasure boats. Ferries and hydrofoils from the continent dock at the far northern end of the harbour.

Buses from Bastia and Galéria pull into the small square near the train station, known locally as La Porteuse d'Eau because of the statue of a woman carrying water at its centre. Ste Catherine Airport (☎ 04.95.65.88.88), 8km south-west of the centre, is a far less convenient and welcoming point of arrival. The cab drivers' mafia has ensured that there's no bus service into town; you'll have to catch a taxi for a stiff 12.20–15.20€ depending on the time of day. As the airport is effectively on the way to Calenzana, many trekkers bypass Calvi completely. Taxis charge 23€ for the trip so it pays to group together with other hikers. You could try to hitch but you may have to walk a fair way and wait around (see Getting to Calenza from Calvi, p107).

The **tourist office** (☎ 04.95.65.16.67, 💻 www.calvitravel.com; June 15–Sept daily 9am–7pm, Oct–June 14 Mon–Fri 9am–noon and 2–5.30pm, Sat 9am–noon) is just above quai Landry. Bus times can be checked there, or better still at the travel agent on La Porteuse d'Eau.

Most of Calvi's other essential services are on blvd Wilson. The **post office** has an **ATM**, as do the big **banks** further up the road. You'll also find a bureau de change on La Porteuse d'Eau. FFRP Topoguides and IGN maps are available at several **bookshops**, including Halle de la Presse, at the top of blvd Wilson.

There's a small **supermarket** on rue Clémenceau but it's far pricier and offers a more limited choice than the huge Super U (June–Sept Mon–Sat 8am–8pm, Sun 8am–1pm; Oct–May Mon–Sat 8.30am–12.30pm and 3–7.30pm), 10 minutes' walk down ave de la République from **La Porteuse d'Eau.**

Cars may be rented from the usual range of companies at the airport, or from the Hertz office (☎ 04.95.65.06.64) on La Porteuse d'Eau. Europcar (☎ 04 95.65.10.35) has a counter on the west side of ave de la République, near the BVJ Corsotel, while Avis (☎ 04.95.65.06.74) works from a cabin in the car park next to the marina. For mountain bikes (18.20€ per day) and scooters (38€ per day), try **Location Ambrosini** (☎ 04.95.65.02.13) on rue Villa-Antoine. Deposits are charged by credit card.

Calvi's only launderette stands at the top of the car park next to Super U.

WHERE TO STAY

Visitors on a low budget are well catered for in Calvi, largely thanks to ***BVJ Corsotel*** (☎ 04.95.65.14.15, 📠 04.95.65.33.72; open April–Oct), 43 ave de la République, an enormous 133-bed hostel opposite the train station. Rates are fixed year-round at 22€ per bed in single-sex dormitories, with attached bathrooms. A filling breakfast is included in the price, making this an attractive deal in high season when tariffs soar everywhere else.

Occupying a prime position on one of the hills overlooking Calvi, the grandly-named ***Relais International de la Jeunesse 'U Carabellu'*** (☎ 04.95 65.14.16, 📠 04.95.80.65.33; open May–October) would be a great fallback were it not more than 4km (two of them uphill) from the centre. Head down ave de la République for 2km, where a signboard indicates the way to the right. Half-

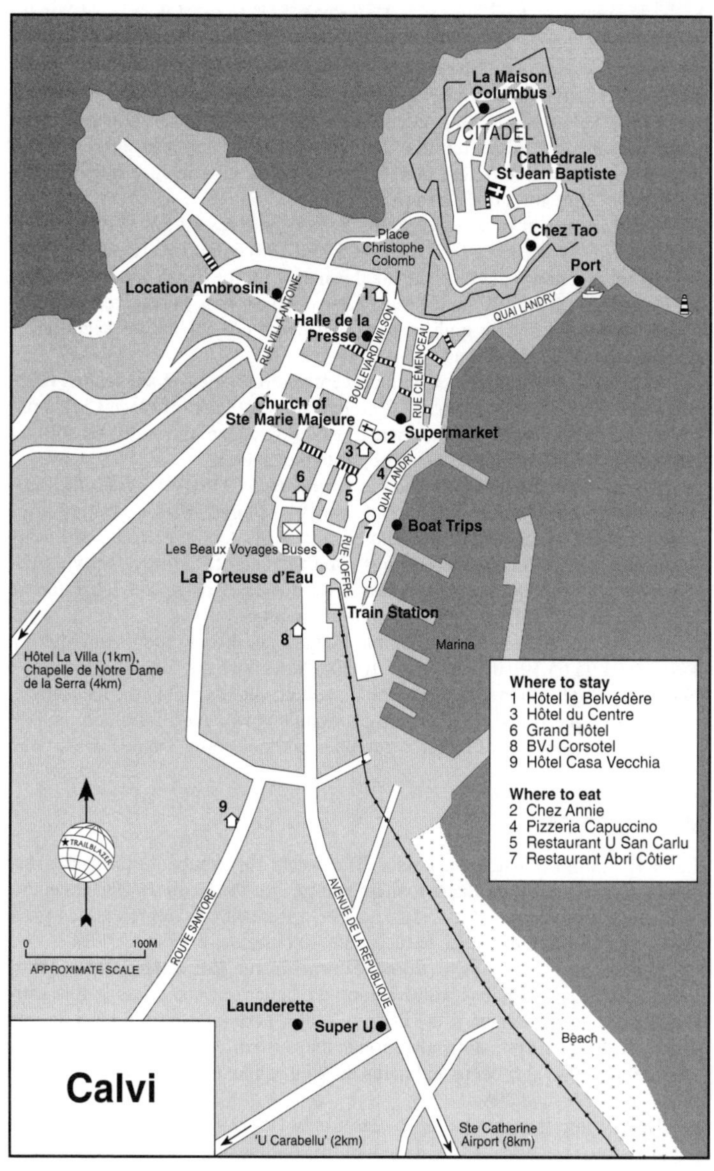
La Maison
Columbus
CITADEL
Cathédrale
St Jean Baptiste
Chez Tao
Port
Place
Christophe
Colomb
QUAI LANDRY
Location Ambrosini
RUE VILLA-ANTOINE
Halle de la
Presse
BOULEVARD WILSON
RUE CLEMENCEAU
Church of
Ste Marie Majeure
Supermarket
QUAI LANDRY
Boat Trips
Les Beaux Voyages Buses
RUE JOFFRE
La Porteuse d'Eau
Train Station
Marina
Hôtel La Villa (1km),
Chapelle de Notre Dame
de la Serra (4km)
Where to stay
1 Hôtel le Belvédère
3 Hôtel du Centre
6 Grand Hôtel
8 BVJ Corsotel
9 Hôtel Casa Vecchia
Where to eat
2 Chez Annie
4 Pizzeria Capuccino
5 Restaurant U San Carlu
7 Restaurant Abri Côtier
TRAILBLAZER
0
100M
APPROXIMATE SCALE
ROUTE SANTORE
AVENUE DE LA RÉPUBLIQUE
Launderette
Super U
Beach
Calvi
'U Carabellu' (2km)
Ste Catherine
Airport (8km)

board is obligatory but amazing value at 23€ per head and the views over the gulf from the terrace are superb.

If the hostels are full the next best budget option is ***Hôtel du Centre*** (☎ 04 95.65.02.01; open June–Sept), tucked away at 12 rue Alsace-Lorraine, near the Church of Sainte-Marie-Majeure. Most rooms in this converted gendarmerie share showers and toilets but the facilities are well maintained. Prices start at 28.80€ in high season, rising to 45€ for a large en suite in July and August – unbeatable value for a double room in Calvi.

A little way out of town on route Santore, the relaxing mid-range ***Hôtel Casa Vecchia*** (☎ 04.95.65.09.33, 🖷 04.95.65.37.93) comprises 10 pleasant bungalows set in a pretty garden. The hotel is handy for the beach and well secluded. Rates range from 30€ for the most basic double rooms (with exterior toilets) in low season, to 55€ in high season. Half-board (74.50–98.80€ per head) is obligatory in July and August.

In a similar price bracket is the recently-refurbished ***Hôtel le Belvédère*** (☎ 04.95.65.26.95, 🖷 04.95.65.33.20; open all year), just off place Christophe Colomb at the top of town. Rates here (40–67.80€ depending on the season) are restrained considering the location opposite the citadel.

A good place to splash out is the ***Grand Hôtel*** (☎ 04.95.65.05.74, 🖷 04 95.65.25.18; open April–Oct), at the bottom of blvd Wilson. Dating from Calvi's heyday at the turn of the 20th century, it has lots of period charm, with huge rooms and old fashioned fittings. Don't be put off by the slightly dowdy reception area. Rates start at around 60€ for a double, rising to 87.40€ for the larger rooms in peak season: good value for money.

Finally, for those on very flexible budgets the luxury four-star ***Hôtel La Villa*** (☎ 04.95.65.10.10, 🖷 04.95.65.10.50), 2km out of the centre on chemin de Notre-Dame-de-la-Serra, has to be the first choice. It's arguably the most attractive hotel on the island, with superb panoramic views over Calvi and the bay, best enjoyed from one of its three gorgeous outdoor pools. Double rooms start at 155€.

WHERE TO EAT

Calvi is crammed with restaurants. The wealth of competition ensures fair prices except along quai Landry where you pay for the location. One exception is ***Pizzeria Capuccino*** (☎ 04.95.65.11.19), a refreshingly unpretentious place serving delicious home-made pasta, salads and pizzas for 8.60–12.40€.

Overlooking the quayside from the corner of rue Joffre, ***Abri Côtier*** (☎ 04 95.65.12.76) offers the best value among the larger seafood joints in this strip. Grilled fish from the gulf is the thing to go for here (consult the plats du jour board for the chef's recommendation) but they also offer fresh salads livened up with delicious local brocciu and herbs, as well as inexpensive pizzas. Their set menus cost 22€ and 29€.

Deeper into the old quarter, ***U San Carlu*** (☎ 04.95.65.92.20), just off rue Clémenceau, is another of the town's old favourites, with no less than five set menus (15.70–23.30€) and a vast choice of à la carte dishes. The terrace, in a courtyard overhung with trees and flowering shrubs, is especially pleasant in the evening.

For relatively inexpensive Corsican specialities to take away, try ***Chez Annie*** at No 5 on the same road. All kinds of pastries, ewes' cheese, charcuterie and chestnut-flour flans and biscuits are sold here, as well as a good selection of quality local AOC wines.

GETTING TO CALENZANA FROM CALVI

The village of Calenzana, 15km south of Calvi, marks the start of both the **GR20** and **Tra Mare e Monti** routes. Unfortunately, despite the huge numbers of hikers passing through between May and October, getting there cheaply can be difficult – a fact attributable to the pressure brought to bear on the council by local taxi drivers.

Calenzana is reachable by bus but the timetable is erratic. From mid-September until the end of June the service is essentially a school run, pegged to holiday dates; check times with the tourist office or at the travel agent on La Porteuse d'Eau. During the summer months, however, the service operates twice daily, with regular departures at around 2pm and 7pm. For more information contact Les Beaux Voyages (☎ 04.95.65.15.02).

If you miss the bus your only options are to take a taxi (from La Porteuse d'Eau or the airport), walk, or hitch. That said, it is notoriously difficult to catch a lift, though your chances will improve considerably once you're off the main N197 onto the Calenzana road. From there it's a 10km plod across the plains and up the hill to the village – a grim prospect if you're weighed down with provisions and intending to make a dawn start the following day.

Thanks to its regular year-round train service, Calvi is well connected to Bastia, Corte (springboard for the **Mare a Mare Nord**) and all points south along the line to Ajaccio, including Vizzavona where you can join the **GR20,** and Vivario where the train line intersects the **Mare a Mare Nord *Variant***. For the other routes described in this book you'll have to pick up onward transport from Ajaccio.

PART 4: GR20

Overview

Among European trekkers, Corsica's *Grande Randonnée* – the GR20 – enjoys near-mythical status. It's the long-distance *haute route* every mountain enthusiast from Biarritz to Berlin aims to complete at least once in their lifetime. Around 17,000 succumb to its allure each year. Barely half, however, manage all 16 stages between Calenzana in the north and Conca in the south, a total distance of around 170km. The first three days alone, which involve a relentless series of ascents and descents of over 1250m, claim a drop-out rate rivalling that of the French Foreign Legion.

Physical challenges aside, the essence of the 'big GR's' appeal lies in the fact that, perhaps more than any other comparable walk in Europe, it takes you to places normally only accessible with ropes. Wriggling along the island's jagged watershed, it links ancient transhumant paths between valleys with a series of astonishing ridge-top traverses from where the full beauty of the Corsican interior is revealed in all its granitic glory. That these high, exposed sections over bare rock are rarely more taxing than an easy scramble is testament largely to the ingenuity of one man, the alpinist Michel Fabrikant, who devised the GR20 in the 1970s.

These days, under the stewardship of Corsica's Parc Naturel Regional (PNRC), Fabrikant's red-and-white waymarked route is as well set up as it was conceived. Between each of its *étapes* stand staffed *refuges* offering basic shelter, water, toilets, washing facilities and bivouac areas. Most also stock essential food supplies, and helicopters are on hand to remove rubbish left behind.

Trekkers used to wilder mountain routes where you have to rely on your own maps, compass skills and equipment, may find this level of infrastructure (not to mention the volume of pedestrian traffic in summer) somewhat intrusive. But the regular waymarking and accommodation does allow you to trek with a lighter pack – a godsend given the 19,000m or so of total altitude gain and loss on the route. Wander away from the marks and you'll quickly appreciate how helpful they are, especially in bad weather.

Any foray into mountains at this altitude has to be undertaken with a certain degree of caution, but don't be intimidated by the GR20's reputation. The severity of the route definitely tends to be exaggerated (not least by the Corsicans themselves, few of whom ever actually attempt it). The main reason for this reputation, ironically enough, is the very infrastructure that renders it so safe. Being without technical obstacles, the GR20 – which can be neatly slotted into a two-week holiday with time to spare for a break on the beach at the end

– attracts a large number of trekkers for whom it is the first real taste of high mountain terrain. Ill-prepared for the physical effort involved and carrying far too much kit, many fall by the wayside. Others tackle the route as if it were some kind of competition or army assault course to be completed as quickly as possible; they too like to talk up the trail's rigours.

The reality is that if you're moderately well equipped, keep your eye on the weather and are up to walking six to seven hours a day over steep gradients, the GR – or '*Jay-Er*' as it's referred to in French – should pose no insurmountable problems. In fact it is hard to think of another long-distance route in Europe where such untainted wilderness is so easily accessible.

WHEN TO TREK

The text in this guide applies uniquely to the summer months, from early June until late October. During the **winter**, when its waymarks become buried under snow and ice, the GR20 is transformed into an extreme alpine route requiring crampons, ropes, ice-axes and, above all, the necessary level of expertise to survive and navigate in sub-zero conditions. It is only practicable for non-specialist trekkers after the spring snow melt. Large *névés* still cloak the approaches to some of the higher passes well into July, but by then safe routes across them are well trodden and easy to follow.

The main climatic problems in **high summer** are the **heat**, which can be intense, particularly at lower altitudes (the last stage to Conca is notorious for claiming sunstroke victims) and electrical **storms.** Lightning poses a constant threat from mid-July until early September and is most common around mid-August, when a pre-dawn start is advisable so as to reach the end of the étape before the clouds bubble up around midday.

Apart from the weather the key factor when planning your GR20 expedition is the **crowds**. At the beginning of the season, just after the refuges open in June, and from mid-September until the first dusting of snow in late October, numbers are manageable. Camping space around the huts during these periods is adequate and the atmosphere along the trail relaxed. Once summer is in full swing, however, the GR20 becomes inundated. The past three or four seasons (since a French hit comedy film, *Les Randonneurs*, brought the route to the attention of a mass public) have seen the refuges swarming with trekkers. In addition to overburdening the very rudimentary facilities they offer, such congestion seriously detracts from the locations' natural beauty. The PNRC recently announced plans to revamp several huts to accommodate the upsurge in popularity but this is only likely to attract still greater numbers and will do little to alleviate congestion at notable bottle-neck sections – all the more reason to avoid July and August if at all possible.

ACCOMMODATION

One important decision to make before leaving home is how you intend to sleep along the route. There are several options. The first is to bed down in a **refuge**.

Although varying in size, all the huts punctuating the GR20 are fitted out with very basic bunk beds, costing around 8.50€ per person per night. They're warm, dry and secure; a two-season sleeping bag is all you'll need to keep you cosy during the summer months. The fee also gives you access to a fully-equipped, gas-fuelled kitchen, and sometimes to a separate shower and toilet block. Apart from the fact they tend to fill up by mid-afternoon, the downside of refuges is the constant nocturnal noise.

However, unless you sleep like a log you should consider carrying some kind of shelter of your own. If you're walking with partners, a **tent**, split down so as to share out the weight, is the simplest solution. All the refuges have camping areas served with running water and rudimentary washing facilities. The 6€ camping fee also includes use of an external gas stove, or the refuge's kitchen.

If you're trekking solo, the way to avoid lugging a heavy tent is to take a **bivouac** sack. With a good two- to three-season sleeping bag, an outer cover of some kind should be enough to keep out the cold and, depending on its design, light rain. For more advice on bivvy and sleeping bag combinations, see p31.

Gîte d'étape and **hotel** accommodation of varying standards is available at five points along the GR20. Anyone intending to pamper themselves with a night on a comfy mattress should reserve ahead as demand outstrips supply for much of the season.

EATING AND DRINKING

Time was when everything you ate or drank on the GR (other than spring or stream water) had to be carried in your backpack, and when re-provisioning meant carefully planned food drops or long detours off the trail to villages. These days, however, the *gardiens* of most refuges offer trekkers a selection of essential supplies: typically *charcuterie*, local cheese, tinned fish, pâté, pasta, noodles, condensed milk, chocolate and biscuits. Some also do a roaring trade in luxuries such as fresh bread, wine, beer and soft drinks, while others cook up hot soup, omelettes or coffee. Keeping these little businesses stocked at peak season means near-daily trips down to road level with a mule or two, which explains the sky-high prices of food in refuges. Rely on the gardiens' supplies and you'll rip through your money very quickly indeed.

You can re-stock more cheaply at Asco, Castel di Verghio, Vizzavona and Bavella, where the trail crosses tarmac. These hamlets, and *stations de ski*, also have small **restaurants**, which we review in the relevant sections.

MONEY

At none of the refuges or villages along the GR20 will you find an ATM, so take enough cash to get you through. Only at those places where the path dips down to road level (namely Asco Stagnu, Castel di Verghio, Vizzavona, Bergeries d'E Capanelle, Bocca di Verdi and Conca) are debit or credit cards accepted. It's worth noting, however, that some hoteliers may agree to a cash-back bill – ie, add an amount on top of what you owe them which is then paid to you as cash.

If you need to visit a bank to change or withdraw money while on the GR20, Corte (an easy hour-long train ride north from Vizzavona) is likely to be the nearest place to do it.

SAFETY AND EQUIPMENT

General advice on mountain safety and trekking equipment appears on pp28-43. However, it's worth reiterating the importance of being adequately prepared for **sudden and extreme changes in weather**, which can strike at any time on the GR20. In the late 1990s, seven trekkers perished in a snowstorm while descending from the Cinto Massif in early July, one of them a matter of minutes from the *station de ski* at Asco. Mist, high winds, rain, hail, sleet or snow can descend with little warning, radically transforming the state of the trail in an instant.

The golden rule if you get caught out by bad weather is to **never lose sight of the waymarks** unless you're absolutely confident of finding them again. Apart from the obvious fact that they present the quickest and most dependable route to safety, the red-and-white paint splashes offer your best chance of rescue should you fall into real difficulty.

If in any doubt about the weather ask the advice of the gardien before setting out. They will have the latest *méteo* report and can alert you to possible danger spots along the étape where flooding or lightning have struck in the past. While on the trail, always remain alert to what the weather is doing and bear in mind the dangers of crossing high, exposed ridges in storms (see p43 for advice on what to do in lightning strikes). When unsure, always go for the safest option.

Network coverage for **mobile phones** is very patchy along the GR20 so don't rely on yours for anything more important than booking a hotel bed.

TREKKING STYLES AND ROUTE OPTIONS

One of the curious things about the GR is that seemingly everyone – whether they're doing the route in five days or sixteen, with or without a tent, from the north or the south, alone or in a group – thinks their style is the way to go. Ultimately, of course, the best way is the way which most suits *you* and it pays to find out what that is early on.

To a large extent fitness will determine how much you can take on each day. Don't overstretch yourself. If your schedule means you have to double up days, ensure you combine easy, short ones rather than long étapes involving tough climbs. Above all, try not to be swept along by others walking at a faster pace than you're comfortable with, merely to arrive at Conca a day or two ahead of time.

One thing lots of trekkers regret after they've finished the route is that they didn't attempt one or more of the hugely rewarding **side trips**. Some of these, notably the waymarked trails up the big summits flanking the GR, take you into truly awesome landscapes that are a step up in every sense from what you experience along the main path. Bear in mind that some optional routings, such as the

Variante over Monte Renoso, are far more inspiring than their lower-level equivalents (which were originally envisaged only as poor-weather alternatives).

The majority of those who complete all 16 stages do so in 10 to 12 days. Do it any quicker and you'd have to be doubling or tripling up lengthy étapes. Take any longer and you'll have plenty of time for detours and for lazing around on the high spots. It's amazing how many people race off at dawn to arrive at the refuge by lunchtime when they could be enjoying sublime scenery up on the trail.

Also worth considering are itineraries that tie together sections of the GR20 with the other long-distance routes outlined in this book. Two of these – the Mare a Mare Nord (and its *variant*) and the Tra Mare e Monti – intersect the GR, giving access to radically different coastal or valley scenery and villages. Following them, even if only for a few stages, will give you a far more rounded picture of the island than you'd get from just the GR20. Suggestions for such **combination routes** are featured on pp26-7.

With less time, say around one week, you might opt to cover certain **sections of the GR20**. From Calenzana, Castel di Verghio is easily reachable in five days. With six to seven days you could press on to Corte via the Mare a Mare Nord (see pp204-46). This would take you through the most rugged and toughest stretches of the GR20 route, where the landscape is at its most spectacular. Alternatively, pick up the trail at Vizzavona, from where you can cover the more restrained (and correspondingly easier) southern section to Conca in six days.

NORTH OR SOUTH?

Many trekkers follow the Grande Randonnée from south to north, ie, in the reverse direction to that described in this book. The advantage is that you begin with the least strenuous étapes and build up to the more gruelling ones. On the other hand, walking northwards will present you with the more subdued, sun-blasted south faces of the massifs rather than the eternal snows and darker crags of their northern slopes. The waymarking is equally dependable in both directions. Ultimately you might end up following the trail from south to north just because your flight landed at Figari Airport, from where Conca is far more accessible than Calenzana. To avoid confusion, stage timings on our maps are given only from north to south.

The route

CALENZANA

Calenzana, the largest village in the Balagne region, has been a major centre of olive production since the time of the Romans. Set against the awesome backdrop of Monte Grossu's massive north-facing cliffs, its nucleus of old granite houses, grouped around the grand Baroque belfry and facade of the Church of Saint Blaise, preside over a swathe of gnarled trees that tumble downhill to meet the coastal *maquis* behind the Golfe de Calvi. It's an archetypal Mediterranean hill village, with twisting lanes that open onto a square where you can join the old boys in their blue overalls sipping strong coffee in the shade of plane trees.

But beneath Calenzana's sleepy feel, broken only by the steady stream of trekkers that plod through to begin the **GR20** and **Tra Mare e Monti** trails, lurks a decidedly dubious underbelly. Among Corsicans the village is infamous as a taproot for organized crime on the Côte d'Azur, the so-called *Milieu*. It is often asserted that its prosperity, which has endured generations of emigration and economic decline, derives from gangsterism in Marseille, a short ferry hop across the water. This might merely be jealous slander but few would deny that Calenzana remains discernibly better off than its neighbours. Come here in August and you'll notice a disproportionate number of luxury German cars sporting '13' (Marseille) number plates.

After a nose around the church, whose ornate, gloomy interior is dominated by an early eighteenth-century altar and very gory tabernacle, there's not much to do other than fortify yourself for the trials ahead.

The Battle of Calenzana

A small plaque on the south-west wall of Calenzana's church bell tower reminds customers in the Café Le Royal that beneath their feet around 500 Austrian mercenaries are buried, casualties of a bloody battle that took place here on February 2, 1732.

The foreigners formed part of a force of 8000 dispatched by Emperor Charles VI to bail out his Genoan allies, who had been struggling to quell an uprising on the island since the previous year. But the Corsicans, marshalled by the legendary Général Ceccaldi, were far better prepared and more highly motivated than the opposition. Rather than laying siege to Calenzana, where the rebels had dug in, the 600 attackers streamed headlong through the village, only to be met with fierce resistance from the locals. Boiling oil was poured over them from the upper storeys of narrow alleyways, and beehives and flaming branches were thrown from rooftops. As the mercenaries fled, bulls whose hides had been set on fire were released, allowing the defenders, aided by women and young boys armed with farm implements, to pick them off at will.

The attempt to flush out the rebels had been a total debacle: only 100 of the mercenaries survived. Doria, shocked at the ferocity of the Corsicans' close-quarter combat, never repeated the mistake. After licking his wounds, he marched with heavy artillery on the bastions of nearby Algajola and Saint-Florent and successfully routed the rebels' defences using old-fashioned cannonades. Some concessions were made by the Genoans in the ensuing treaty, but the islanders would have to wait another two decades before tasting true independence from Italian rule.

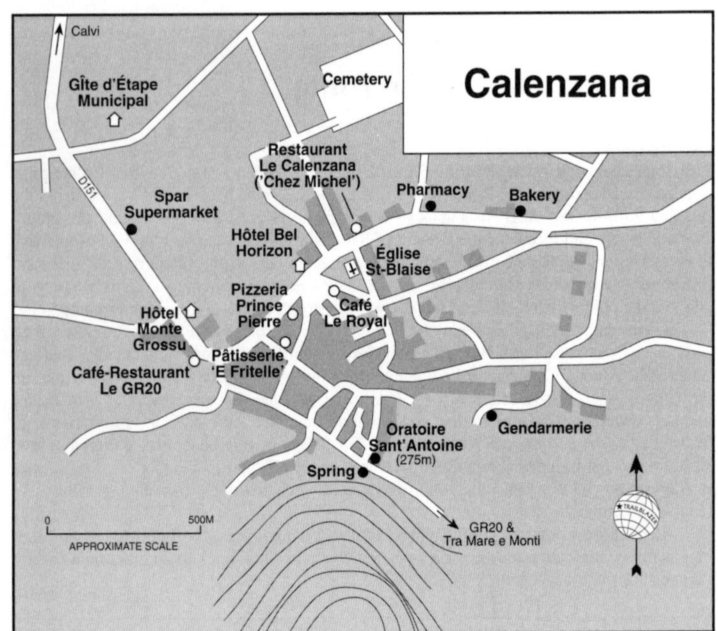

Orientation and services

Advice on how to get to Calenzana by **public transport from Calvi** appears on p107. A taxi here will set you back around 20€ one-way. Heading in the other direction, from Calenzana, call Taxis Biancardini on ☎ 04.95.62.77.80 or ☎ 06.08.16.53.65.

Anyone who didn't stock up with supplies before leaving the coast can do so at the large Spar **supermarket** on the main Calvi road. Fresh bread and pastries are sold there and at the small **bakery**, five minutes' walk east of the square.

Where to stay

In peak season, Calenzana struggles to cope with the influx of trekkers, in spite of the fact its ***Gîte d'étape Municipal*** (☎ 04.95 62.77.13; open May–Sept) was recently upgraded and enlarged. Situated just below the village proper, a stone's throw off the main road, this is where most people heading off on the GR20 hole up. Its four-berth dorms, ranged around a gravel-chipping courtyard, have en suite bathrooms and cost 13€ per head.

Bivouackers are charged 5.30€ for a pitch under the trees in the garden, plus 3.80€ per tent, for which you also get the use of an impressive power shower and toilet block. Self-catering facilities are limited to a tiny kitchen equipped with a single electric hob and some pans – a move obviously designed to encourage you to eat in one of the restaurants up in the village. For the same reason, breakfast is not available here (see p115).

Two hotels up in the village centre offer more comfortable alternatives. Neither is particularly swish but their rates are low compared with Calvi. ***Hôtel Monte Grossu*** (☎ 04.95.62.70.15, 🖹 04.95.62 83.21; open May–Sept) stands to the left of the main street, a short way beyond the

Spar, and has 10 simple, clean double rooms (all with en suite showers but toilets *à l'étage*). Rates range from 38€ to 42€ depending on the month.

Opposite the square, ***Hôtel Bel Horizon*** (☎/📠 04.95.62.71.72; open May–Sept) is in much the same mould, with rates from 30.50€ to 45.60€.

Where to eat

There's only one restaurant worthy of note in Calenzana. Situated opposite the main facade of the church, ***Le Calenzana 'Chez Michel'*** (open daily March–Dec, but closed Mon in Jan–Feb) offers staunchly traditional, delicious Corsican mountain cuisine and wood-baked pizzas. If you're not expecting to be within range of a decent meal for a while, splash out on one of the set menus (15€ and 16.70€). These kick off with a rustic *soupe corse* (complete with the bones) or *terrine de figatellu* (fragrant liver-sausage pâté), followed by wild-boar spaghetti, pan-fried veal with broad beans, or the restaurant's signature dish, tender suckling lamb and wheat-rolled roast potatoes.

Although marginally cheaper, neither of its competitors down the road, ***Pizzeria Prince Pierre*** and ***Café-Restaurant Le GR20***, offers comparable value for money, nor the same degree of hospitality. You may, however, be tempted by ***Café le Royal*** set breakfasts, served on a terrace behind the church. Since the *gîte* was forced by the municipality to stop serving breakfasts (in order to *faire travailler les cafés*), something of a price war has broken out in the village. A string of places now open at 6am to catch the dawn trekking exodus; the Royal is the friendliest and best situated.

On your way up the hill towards the trailhead, another place to carb up is the stark ***Pâtisserie E Fritelle***, on a lane called U Chiasu, which runs to the right off the main street just after the bend (if you're approaching the centre via the Calvi road). Open from 6am, it's renowned for its hot Corsican doughnuts (*beignets*) and Calenzana's own speciality biscuits, *cuggielli*, made with appropriately calorific chestnut flour. Ask for a bag hot out of the oven.

GR20 STAGE ONE: CALENZANA→ REFUGE D'ORTU DI U PIOBBU [MAP 1, p117]

Overview

Leading you from the coastal olive belt around Calenzana to the windy heights of the watershed, the first day of the GR20 is an unremittingly tough slog involving a net altitude gain of 1245m (think of Ben Nevis and then some). Weighed down with two or three days' provisions and three litres of water (there's no dependable source along the route once out of sight of Calenzana), most trekkers find it a gruelling introduction to the joys of Corsican trekking. You'll certainly make life a lot easier for yourself by getting an early start, which will enable you to cover the first major climb in cool shadow.

The stage's highlights are a succession of extraordinary panoramas revealed from the passes. Encompassing a large chunk of the Balagne coast, these grow steadily more impressive as you climb, culminating in your first glimpse of the Cinto massif and Paglia Orba, which flag the onward route.

Because of the length and overall difficulty of the next (second) étape, this is not a leg of the GR20 to double up unless you are already fit and comfortable with the altitude. Anyone arriving early in the afternoon at the Refuge d'Ortu di u Piobbu would do better to consider the ascent of Monte Corona (see box on p120) as an extension.

A *Variante* route to the refuge runs along the Tra Mare e Monti trail to Bonifatu and thence up the Melaghia Valley (see p118). Keeping to easy gradients for most of the way it has little to recommend it other than as a safe bad-weather approach to the main trail. Basically, if the first étape seems too much for you in favourable conditions you should probably think twice about attempting the GR20 at all.

Route guide

PNRC signboards dotted along the road from the gîte and around Calenzana's square point the way to the GR20/Tra Mare e Monti **trailhead** at the top of the village.

The official start is marked by a tiny chapel, the **Oratoire Sant'Antoine** (275m), opposite a gushing spring of the same name where you can fill up your water bottle. Beyond it a paved mule track squeezes between old retaining walls to start a steady climb through a mix of Laricio pines, ferns and maquis dotted with lightning-charred chestnut trees.

A stately old pine, roughly 45 minutes up the trail, heralds your arrival at a second spring, the **Funtana di Ortivinti**, which stands to the left of the trail a short way before it splits; this is the last dependable source of drinking water before Ortu di u Piobbu. At the **junction** (550m), the orange waymarks of the Tra Mare e Monti/GR 20 *Variante* run west (to the right). The main GR20, meanwhile, presses south (left) uphill through spiny maquis to cross a shoulder pass, the **Bocca di u Ravalente** (616m), from where you can see up the whole Figarella Valley to the Cirque de Bonifatu.

Once over the spur a steady traverse sweeps around the eastern flank of the valley to a distinctive rock outcrop, the **promontoire d'Arghioa** (820m). Take a break here to steel yourself for the hard, zigzagging ascent of more than 400 metres through scruffy heather and pines to the **Bocca a u Saltu** pass (1250m). Affording grandiose views across the wild Frintogna Valley to the summit of Monte Grossu, this pass forms the GR's gateway to the high mountains and is a great spot from which to admire the panorama of the Balagne coast (clearest from atop the outcrop immediately north-north-west of the pass itself; see Map 1, opposite).

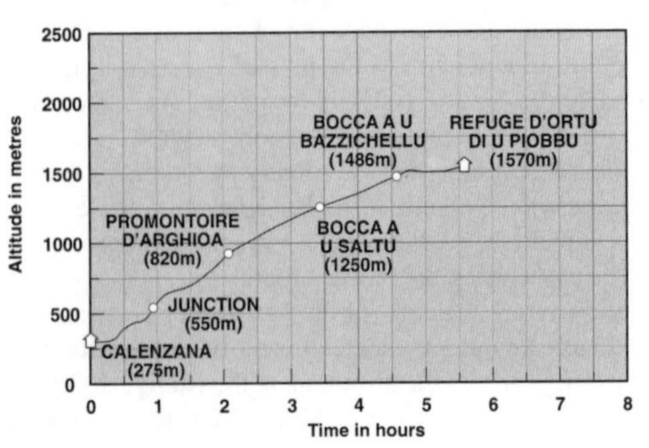

The Bocca a u Saltu also heralds a marked transition in the trail. After a short,

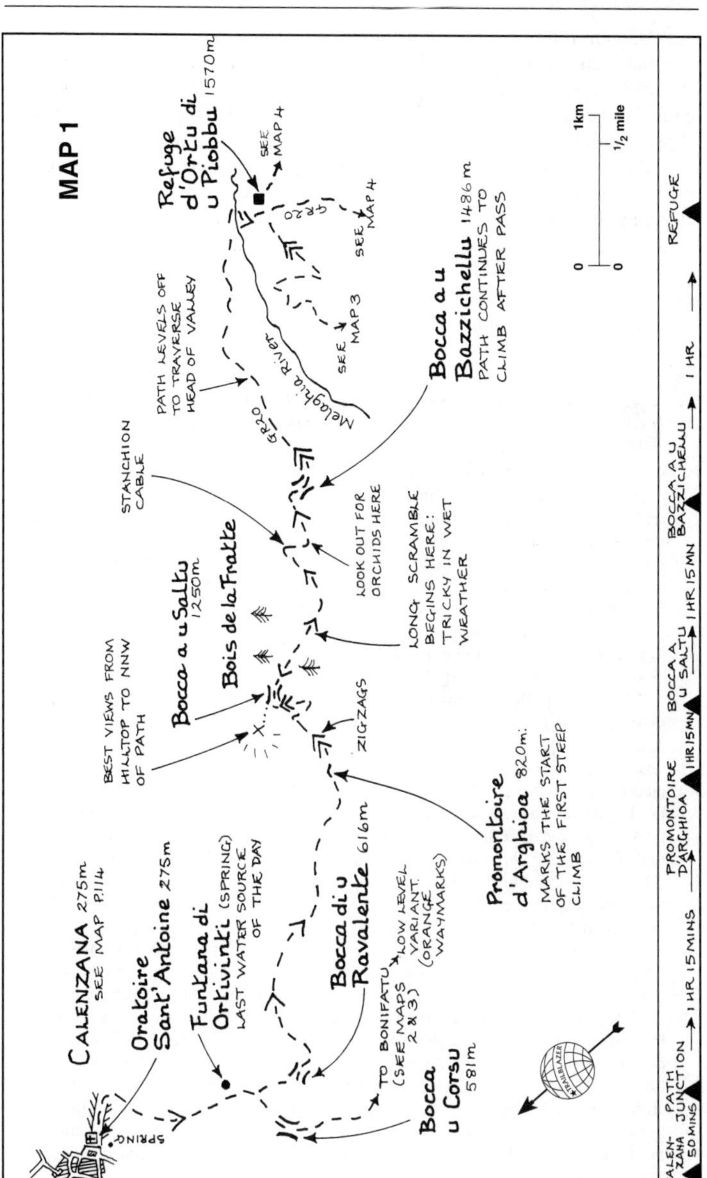
MAP 1
CALENZANA 275m
SEE MAP P.114
Oratoire Sant'Antoine 275m
Funtana di Ortivinti (SPRING)
LAST WATER SOURCE OF THE DAY
SPRING
Bocca u Corsu 581m
TO BONIFATU (SEE MAPS 2 & 3)
LOW LEVEL VARIANT (ORANGE WAYMARKS)
Bocca di u Ravalente 616m
Promontoire d'Arghjoa 820m:
MARKS THE START OF THE FIRST STEEP CLIMB
ZIG-ZAGS
BEST VIEWS FROM HILLTOP TO NNW OF PATH
Bocca a u Saltu 1250m
Bois de la Tratte
LONG SCRAMBLE BEGINS HERE: TRICKY IN WET WEATHER
LOOK OUT FOR ORCHIDS HERE
STANCHION CABLE
Bocca a u Bazzichellu 1486m
PATH CONTINUES TO CLIMB AFTER PASS
GR20
PATH LEVELS OFF TO TRAVERSE HEAD OF VALLEY
Melaghia River
SEE MAP 3
SEE MAP 4
GR20
Refuge d'Ortu di u Piobbu 1570m
SEE MAP 4
TRAILBLAZER
0
1km
0
1/2 mile
CALEN-ZANA
50 MINS
PATH JUNCTION
1 HR 15 MINS
PROMONTOIRE D'ARGHJOA
1HR 15 MN
BOCCA A U SALTU
1 HR 15 MN
BOCCA A U BAZZICHELLU
1 HR
REFUGE

easy descent through a beautiful Laricio pine forest (Le Bois de la Fratte) the waymarks thread steeply uphill though a messy mass of exposed granite that should be approached with caution, especially in wet weather. A **stanchion cable** has been fixed to one of the trickier pitches. Although a welcome help in slippery conditions it can prove a bottleneck in peak season.

Above it, more enjoyable scrambling across rocks dotted with spotted orchids and helebore brings you eventually to the second major pass of the étape, the **Bocca a u Bazzichellu** (1486m). The col is more rounded and wooded than the previous one but has less imposing views; you'll probably want to get straight on with the climb through the pine forest above it. Once clear of the trees, a wonderful panorama opens up to the south across the Melaghia Valley to Monte Cinto and Paglia Orba on the horizon.

Low-level *Variante*: Calenzana → Bonifatu → Ortu di u Piobbu [Map 2, opposite; map 3, p121]

The low-level *Variante* section of the GR20 between Calenzana and Ortu di u Piobbu, which follows the Tra Mare e Monti trail south to Bonifatu and then cuts back in a north-easterly direction to scale the Melaghia Valley, is only worth taking in especially poor weather, if driving rain or snow render the principal route impassable. Although less strenuous it's a comparatively dull option, keeping for much of the time to monotonous forestry tracks. During the summer this *Variante* also exposes you to a greater risk of heat stroke as its first half is almost devoid of tree cover.

See opposite for a route map of the leg between Calenzana and Bonifatu on the Tra Mare e Monti trail; the remaining section, from Bonifatu to the refuge, is covered in a separate map on p121.

From the **path junction** above Calenzana the *Variante*, indicated with orange waymarks, peels right (west) and after crossing the **Bocca u Corsu** pass (581m) descends sharply through dense, scratchy maquis to the Sambuccu stream. Here it levels off, following the contours of the hillside, and then climbs slightly to reach a clearly-defined **forestry track** which runs gently downhill for roughly 3km to meet the **Figarella River**. Under a large outcrop of weirdly-eroded orange granite, the path crosses the river via a motorable bridge, veers east along the true left bank for one kilometre and then cuts steeply uphill in a series of tight zigzags to join the road (D251). A left turn here will take you past the Maison Forestière to **Bonifatu** where the excellent ***Auberge de la Forêt*** (see p268) offers restaurant meals and gîte d'étape accommodation.

The *piste* resumes beyond the *auberge* at the far side of the coach park and barrier, winding for 1.5km alongside the river before coming to an abrupt end after around 30 minutes. At the junction where a signboard marks the meeting point with the GR20's *Variante* from Carrozzu bear left to cross the river and follow the **yellow waymarks** along a rough piste as it cuts beneath a series of cliffs and then climbs steadily through maritime pine and oak forest to ford the stream a second time. After another sequence of broad zigzags the track comes to a third and final crossing of the Melaghia, beyond which it turns into a steeper line that cuts straight up the the valley via a succession of tight switchbacks. Having emerged from the trees you veer sharply to the right (south-west) and follow the path up an open ridge to the refuge, visible above.

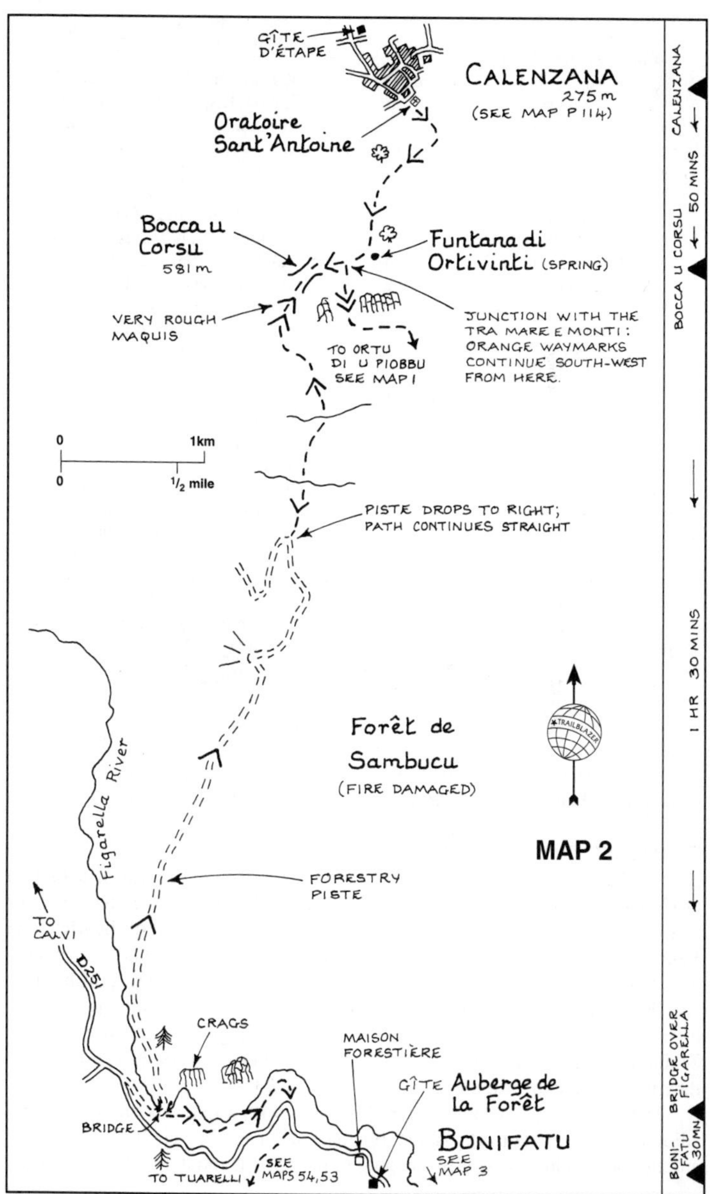

GÎTE D'ÉTAPE
CALENZANA
275 m
(SEE MAP P 114)
Oratoire Sant'Antoine
Bocca u Corsu
581 m
Funtana di Ortivinti (SPRING)
VERY ROUGH MAQUIS
JUNCTION WITH THE TRA MARE E MONTI: ORANGE WAYMARKS CONTINUE SOUTH-WEST FROM HERE.
TO ORTU DI U PIOBBU SEE MAP 1
0 1km
0 1/2 mile
PISTE DROPS TO RIGHT; PATH CONTINUES STRAIGHT
Forêt de Sambucu
(FIRE DAMAGED)
TRAILBLAZER
MAP 2
Figarella River
FORESTRY PISTE
TO CALVI
D251
CRAGS
MAISON FORESTIÈRE
GÎTE
Auberge de la Forêt
BRIDGE
BONIFATU
SEE MAP 3
TO TUARELLI
SEE MAPS 54, 53
CALENZANA
50 MINS
BOCCA U CORSU
1 HR 30 MINS
BRIDGE OVER FIGARELLA
BONI-FATU
30 MN

Monte Corona

Anyone not totally wiped out by the climb from Calenzana should consider this superb extension from Ortu di u Piobbu. Reachable in a round-trip of 2½ hours, the summit of Monte Corona (2144m) ranks among Corsica's most spectacular viewpoints, giving uninterrupted vistas of the north face of the Cinto massif as well as the rest of the interior watershed and north-west coast – well worth the labour to reach it.

The route, indicated with yellow waymarks, begins behind the refuge, skirting the side of the birch wood. Rough, loose and dusty at the outset, it zigzags steeply through the trees towards the windswept **Bocca Tartagine** (1852m). This impressive pass formed a major transhumant gateway in past centuries. Shepherds used to drive their animals across it en route between the Melaghia Valley and the Giunssani region to the east. These days the only animals you're likely to come across here are shy *mouflons* (*muvra*) scouring the scree above the col (for more on this reclusive and very rare animal, see p134).

From the pass, turn right and follow the line of the ridge steeply uphill through a dense carpet of scratchy, malodorous alder. **Cairns** sketch a rough zigzagging route through the rocks but you can also pick up the odd stretch of path across the bank of vegetation (being careful not to stray to the right into the alder scrub). This section can be frustratingly hard going in places, but after 45 minutes you emerge on the scree which covers most of the summit. A clearly discernable path leads to the top, marked by a large cairn and stone hollow, from where a truly extraordinary view extends all the way from Cap Corse in the north-east to Paglia Orba in the south-west. From the south flank of the summit you overlook the snow-flecked bulk of Monte Cinto, rising from the arid Asco Valley.

The descent by the same route is rapid (scree down the first bit and rock-hop much of the more difficult lower slope to the Bocca Tartagine).

With the last significant ascent of the day behind you, the traverse that follows, contouring around the headwaters of the Melaghia River, is a real joy. After crossing a stream the path rounds a boulder-strewn spur and ascends for one last push to the plateau on which Refuge d'Ortu di u Piobbu is situated.

Refuge d'Ortu di u Piobbu

Nestled below the summit of Monte Corona, the Refuge d'Ortu di u Piobbu (1570m) is one of the most attractively sited on the GR20. A perfect spot for sunset, the refuge sits on the site of an old *bergerie* at the head of the Melaghia Valley, looking west over ranks of receding ridges towards the coast. Arriving here from sea level in fine weather you'll be struck by the clarity of the light and shimmering silver birch wood that spills down the stream gully nearby. The high-mountain ambience is accentuated by prayer flags fluttering from a cairn behind the hut; the flags were erected by the gardiens and some Nepali friends they met on an expedition to climb Mansulu in 2000.

The refuge itself accommodates 30 people, with a spacious dining area and adjoining stove room. Dry-stone bivouac and camping shelters are dotted around the building. If you're sleeping in the open without a tent, expect to be

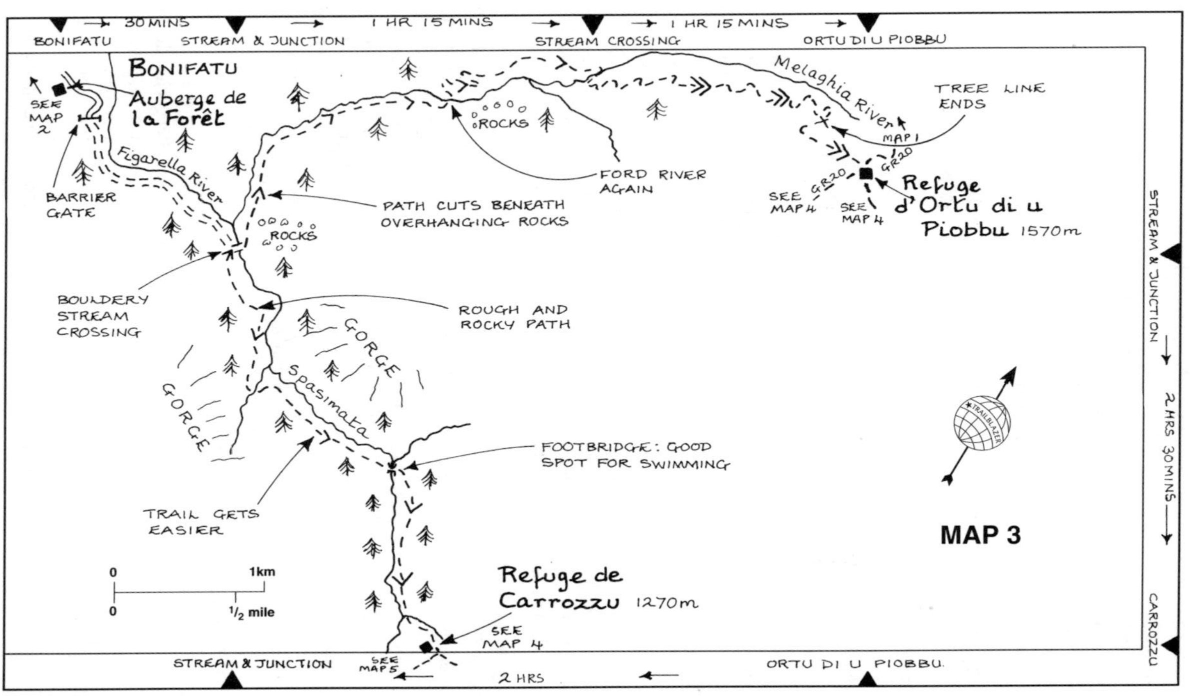
BONIFATU
30 MINS
STREAM & JUNCTION
1 HR 15 MINS
STREAM CROSSING
1 HR 15 MINS
ORTU DI U PIOBBU
STREAM & JUNCTION
2 HRS 30 MINS
CARROZZU
ORTU DI U PIOBBU
2 HRS
STREAM & JUNCTION
MAP 3
TRAILBLAZER
Bonifatu
Auberge de la Forêt
SEE MAP 2
BARRIER GATE
Figarella River
BOULDERY STREAM CROSSING
ROCKS
PATH CUTS BENEATH OVERHANGING ROCKS
FORD RIVER AGAIN
Melaghia River
TREE LINE ENDS
MAP 1
GR20
SEE MAP 4
Refuge d'Ortu di u Piobbu 1570m
ROUGH AND ROCKY PATH
GORGE
Spasimata
GORGE
TRAIL GETS EASIER
FOOTBRIDGE: GOOD SPOT FOR SWIMMING
Refuge de Carrozzu 1270m
SEE MAP 4
SEE MAP 5
0
1km
1/2 mile

hassled by cattle during the night. Note, too, that this mountainside can get especially chilly in the small hours as the warm westerly from the sea dies off and cooler air currents drift down from Monte Corona; so bed down in one of the round, tall-walled shelters rather than semi-circular wind-breaks if you can.

Hot drinks and cooked food, such as soupe corse and omelettes, are available here, in addition to the usual range of basic supplies when the refuge is staffed (from June until mid-September).

GR20 STAGE TWO: ORTU DI U PIOBBU → CARROZZU [MAP 4, OPPOSITE]

Overview

After an easy initial climb and short descent through forest, stage two of the GR20 gets stuck into to a hefty ascent, followed by a long ridge traverse and, to wrap things up, a very sharp drop. Taking you above 2000m for the first time it also features one of the most memorable sections of the walk, the traverse of Capu Ladroncellu's desolate south face. In the course of the day you'll be exposed to some testing terrain as the GR winds up slippery rock slabs, through tight corridors, past wind-eroded breaches overlooking dizzying drops, and down stretches of precipitous, loose shale.

Once again, **water** is in short supply and, given the length and steepness of some gradients on this étape, you'll need to carry plenty of it – at least three litres in warm weather. There are two springs along the route but they're too near the beginning to be of real use. Don't be tempted to scrimp on liquid to save weight. The toughest portions of the étape towards the end of day are south-facing and thus subject to the full force of the afternoon sun.

Route guide

From Ortu di u Piobbu the path winds south past the spring and into birch woods to begin a short, sharp climb that soon levels off. Following the contours of the hillside it crests a spur at 1627m and descends steeply down the drier, southern side of the ridge, where Laricio pines now predominate.

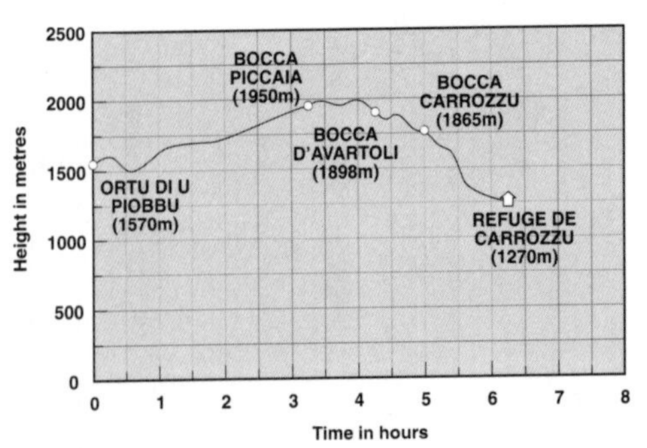

Shortly before fording a perennial stream you pass the picturesque **Bergeries de la Mandriaccia**, where there's a **spring.**

A low, bouldery pass after a second stream crossing heralds

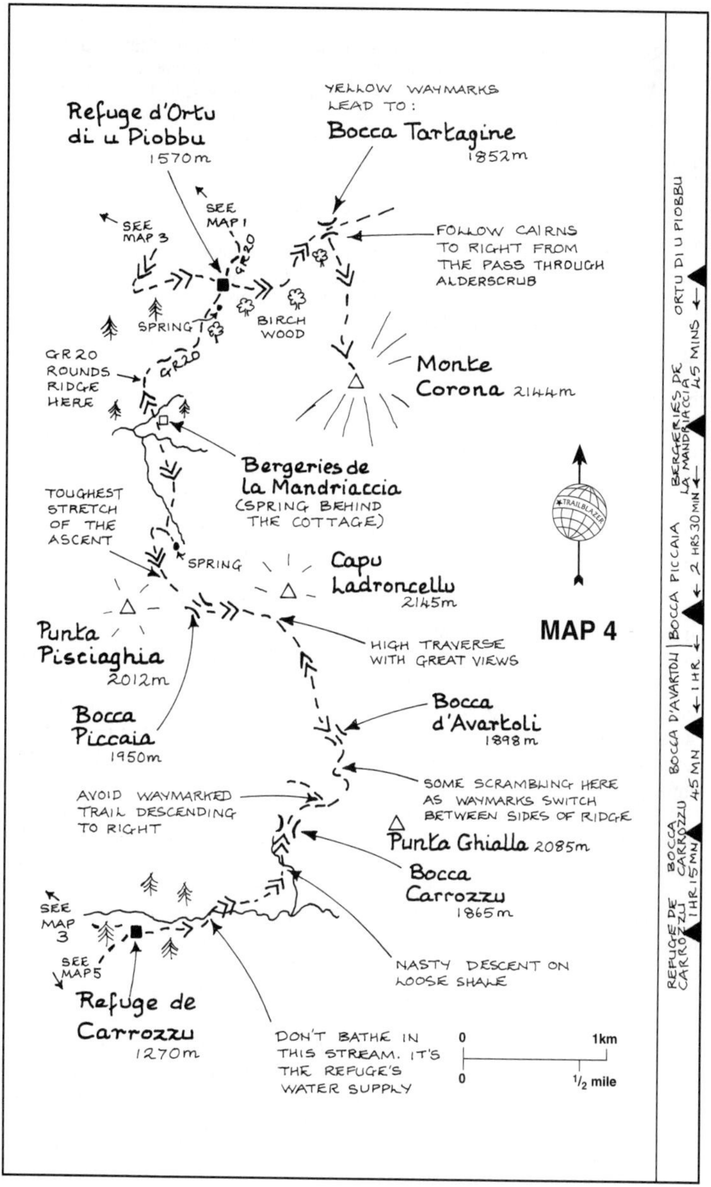

YELLOW WAYMARKS LEAD TO:
Bocca Tartagine
1852m
Refuge d'Ortu di u Piobbu
1570m
SEE MAP 1
SEE MAP 3
GR20
FOLLOW CAIRNS TO RIGHT FROM THE PASS THROUGH ALDERSCRUB
SPRING
BIRCH WOOD
GR 20 ROUNDS RIDGE HERE
Monte Corona 2144m
Bergeries de la Mandriaccia
(SPRING BEHIND THE COTTAGE)
TOUGHEST STRETCH OF THE ASCENT
SPRING
Capu Ladroncellu
2145m
Punta Pisciaghia
2012m
MAP 4
HIGH TRAVERSE WITH GREAT VIEWS
Bocca Piccaia
1950m
Bocca d'Avartoli
1898m
SOME SCRAMBLING HERE AS WAYMARKS SWITCH BETWEEN SIDES OF RIDGE
AVOID WAYMARKED TRAIL DESCENDING TO RIGHT
Punta Ghialla 2085m
Bocca Carrozzu
1865m
SEE MAP 3
SEE MAP 5
NASTY DESCENT ON LOOSE SHALE
Refuge de Carrozzu
1270m
DON'T BATHE IN THIS STREAM. IT'S THE REFUGE'S WATER SUPPLY
0 1km
0 ½ mile

ORTU DI U PIOBBU
← 45 MINS →
BERGERIES DE LA MANDRIACCIA
← 2 HRS 30 MIN →
BOCCA PICCAIA
← 1 HR →
BOCCA D'AVARTOLI
45 MN
BOCCA CARROZZU
1 HR 15 MN
REFUGE DE CARROZZU

Low-level *Variante*: Ortu di u Piobbu→ Carrozzu **[Map 3, p121]**
It's possible to bypass the GR20's second étape by dropping down the thickly forested Melaghia Valley from Ortu di u Piobbu to the river bridge just east of Bonifatu, and from there heading up the Spasimata Valley to rejoin the main path at Carrozzu. Taking around five hours, this low-level *Variante* is a much easier option than the conventional route, but misses out on some of the GR's most impressive landscapes. Trekkers tend to use it only when **bad weather** shrouds the high path, pressing on to Carrozzu rather than waiting at Ortu di u Piobbu for the clouds to lift.

The first section of the route, which is outlined in reverse in the box on p268, is waymarked in yellow and easy to follow throughout. Allow 2 hours to reach the path junction near Bonifatu and 2½ hours for the zigzagging ascent to the Carrozzu refuge through some of the island's loveliest Laricio pine and holm oak forest.

the day's hardest climb, which strikes south up a tributary valley of the Melaghia. Interspersed by patches of alder and arbutus bushes, huge, smooth-backed rocks carry the route steeply uphill, with impressive pinnacles and crags towering above. Around mid-way through the ascent, arrows show the way off the main path to a small **spring**. The steepest stretch, however, is still to come. There's precious little let-up in the gradient until you near the pass, a clearly defined niche in the ridge between Punta Pisciaghia (to the right) and Capu Ladroncellu (to the left).

By the time you reach the **Bocca Piccaia** (1950m) you're well and truly initiated into both the travails and payoffs of the GR. The long slog up the stream valley is rewarded with a view that comes as a spectacular surprise (if you didn't make it up Monte Corona). Plunging near vertically below you, the bare south wall of the Ladroncellu valley faces a vast sweep of eroded granite mountains, riddled with pinnacles, rock towers and vast cliffs. On the horizon, the serrated summits of Monte Cinto, Paglia Orba and Capu Tafonatu complete an unforgettable vista.

The views intensify as you press on from the pass, following the line of the ridge left (east) to an altitude of 2020m where the route levels off to begin the famous traverse of Capu Ladroncellu. For the next half-hour or so you keep to a more or less even gradient of around 150m below the summit, crossing scree and clumps of blue-grey rock. Make the most of the views here as in a short while you'll need to concentrate on a protracted, and at times tricky, descent over loose shale, which begins beyond a prominent overhang.

Bending southwards along the curve of the *cirque*, the path, after an initially sheer drop, negotiates a succession of steep, and in places awkward, scrambles on its gradual descent to the **Bocca d'Avartoli** pass (1898m), a rugged, knife-edge ridge separating Capu Ladroncellu from Punta Ghialla to the south. The next 45 minutes or so involve more short ups and downs, with the waymarks winding from one side of the ridge to the other via a sequence of impressive gaps. It's important to keep your eye on the paint blobs throughout this stretch as several (unmarked) minor paths peel off the GR20; lose your concentration and you could find yourself heading steeply down the wrong valley.

At the final gap, known as the **Bocca Carrozzu** (Bocca Inuminata; 1865m), the path suddenly plunges due south down a rugged, steep couloir that gets baking hot on summer afternoons. Dusty and loose underfoot, the descent, which takes around 80 minutes, is unrelentingly tough on the knees. With the refuge visible far below, it takes you through more alder bushes and, further down, silver birch woods before crossing the stream twice and easing off on its approach to Carrozzu.

Refuge de Carrozzu

Flanked by a Herculean pair of orange granite crags that peak at nearly 2000 metres, the Refuge de Carrozzu occupies an idyllic spot in the heart of the Cirque de Bonifatu. The hut's wooden deck, looking west over the treetops to the distant sea, is a great place to enjoy the sunset and socialize over a beer.

Sadly, Carrozzu has become a victim of its own success over the past few seasons. Its enviable location, proximity to the roadhead at Bonifatu and strategic position between two of the route's toughest étapes ensures it's invariably swamped at the height of the summer. The toilet facilities, in particular, strain to cope with the onslaught, making this a less than pleasant place to be towards the end of the year.

Sanitation aside, the refuge is well set up, with gushing cold showers, shaded camping-bivouac space, external gas hobs, and interior accommodation for 30 trekkers, as well as a fully-equipped kitchen. The gardien and his team provide a good selection of cooked food, including delicious soup served with chestnut-flour bread, and drink. Prices, it has to be said, are top whack but the location may well tempt you to splash out.

The one real gripe with Carrozzu has to be that, in order to maximize profits from the menu, its gardiens do not stock supplies; you'll have to wait until Asco Stagnu to reprovision.

GR20 STAGE THREE: CARROZZU → ASCO STAGNU

[MAP 5, p127]

Overview

More superb scenery lies in store on day three of the GR20. The crux of the étape is the long ascent of the Spasimata Valley to Bocca di a Muvrella, from where you get a magnificent close-up view of the Cinto Massif's north face. Far below, the ski station of Asco Stagnu, dwarfed by the surrounding mountains, sweetens the steep descent with the prospect of a cold beer and a hot meal.

Committed trekkers with supplies in hand may opt to forgo the hedonistic pleasures of the station to follow the rugged Muvrella ridge up the Tighjettu Valley – Michel Fabrikant's original GR20 route – which will put them in prime position for an early start on the infamous Cirque de la Solitude the following day.

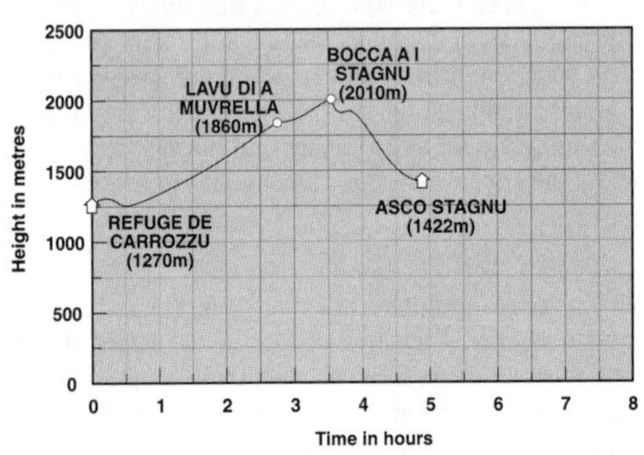

Although a relatively short stage, this is one that's hard to extend without bivouacking illegally (unless you've got the stamina and provisions to press on to the Refuge de Tighjettu on the far side of the cirque). Once beyond the lower reaches of the Spasimata Valley, it's also devoid of drinking water.

Finally, bear in mind that the ski station is the most convenient springboard for the ascent of Monte Cinto. Spend an additional night at road level and you'll be able to scale the island's highest peak for a vivid taste of high mountain terrain.

Route guide

A short but sharp 10-minute descent from the Refuge de Carrozzu gets the third day underway. It brings you to what must be the most photographed feature of the GR: a 35m suspension bridge, **la passarelle suspendue de Spasimata**, which spans the stream against an impressive backdrop of escarpments.

The climb starts as soon as you're across it, as the waymarks guide you through a narrow river gorge via a succession of huge, water-worn **slabs**. Presenting no difficulty in dry conditions, these can be treacherous in wet weather, hence the stanchion cables to help you up the steepest of them. The first sight of the Spasimata slabs tends to be the point at which anyone who found the first two days of the route too much turns around and heads for Bonifatu.

With the pass still high above the valley can feel like a test of resolve, but within an hour or so you're clear of the shadowy gorge and (weather permitting) contouring in bright sunlight across the open mountainside through patches of alder scrub.

A steep squeeze through a couloir followed by another climb to the top of a huge round-topped outcrop, three hours into the walk, brings your first glimpse of the beautiful **Lavu di a Muvrella** (1860m), a tiny lake at the bottom of a suspended glacial shelf. Frozen throughout the winter, it doesn't support any aquatic life; nor is it safe to drink. Moreover, bivouacking and camping are strictly forbidden at this exquisite spot which, warmed by morning sunshine and with fine views all the way down to Calvi, makes a good place to break before the final haul to the pass.

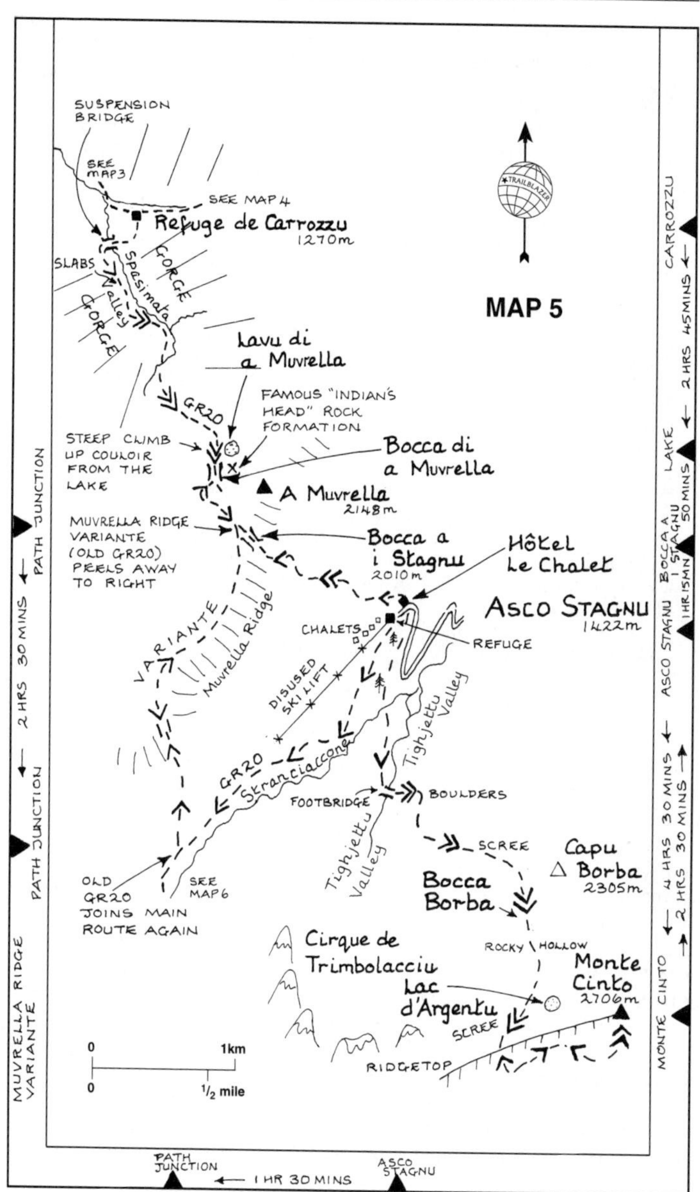
MAP 5
TRAILBLAZER
SUSPENSION BRIDGE
SEE MAP3
SEE MAP 4
Refuge de Carrozzu
1270m
SLABS
Spasimata
GORGE
Valley
GORGE
Lavu di a Muvrella
GR20
FAMOUS "INDIAN'S HEAD" ROCK FORMATION
STEEP CLIMB UP COULOIR FROM THE LAKE
Bocca di a Muvrella
A Muvrella
2148m
MUVRELLA RIDGE VARIANTE (OLD GR20) PEELS AWAY TO RIGHT
Bocca a i Stagnu
2010m
Hôtel Le Chalet
Asco Stagnu
1422m
CHALETS
REFUGE
VARIANTE
Muvrella Ridge
DISUSED SKI LIFT
Tighjettu Valley
GR20
Stranciaccone
FOOTBRIDGE
BOULDERS
SCREE
Capu Borba
2305m
Bocca Borba
Tighjettu Valley
OLD GR20 JOINS MAIN ROUTE AGAIN
SEE MAP6
ROCKY HOLLOW
Cirque de Trimbolacciu
Lac d'Argentu
Monte Cinto
2706m
SCREE
RIDGETOP
0
1km
0
1/2 mile
PATH JUNCTION
← 2 HRS 30 MINS
PATH JUNCTION
MUVRELLA RIDGE VARIANTE
CARROZZU
← 2 HRS 45MINS
← LAKE
50 MINS
BOCCA A I STAGNU
1 HR15MN
ASCO STAGNU
← 4 HRS 30 MINS
2 HRS 30 MINS →
MONTE CINTO
PATH JUNCTION
← 1 HR 30 MINS
ASCO STAGNU

Variante: Muvrella ridge to the Ancien Refuge d'Altore

[Map 5, p127; Map 6, p133]

The GR20 forks shortly before reaching the Bocca di a Stagnu, with a *Variante* path peeling south along the Muvrella Ridge towards the Ancien Refuge d'Altore. Until the mid-1980s, when the refuge was mysteriously destroyed by fire, this formed the main GR20 route as envisaged by Michel Fabrikant. However, pressure from the failing ski station, which desperately needed summer business, combined with the destruction of the refuge and the obvious logistical problems of a route that otherwise didn't touch a roadhead between Calenzana and Col de Verghio, eventually forced the PNRC into re-routing the GR to the valley floor.

The old waymarks have faded but the original route is still easy to follow. Apart from the dramatic views it affords over the Filosorma Valley, the main incentive to choose the old path is that it bypasses Asco Stagnu (no bad thing if you're reluctant to return to 'civilization'), bringing you out at the head of the valley below the Bocca Tumasginesca, gateway to the Cirque de la Solitude. It is thus the preferred route for anyone aiming to double up étapes between Carrozzu and the Refuge de Tighjettu.

To deter people from bivouacking at the old refuge the PNRC has concreted over the old spring so you'd have to be well stocked with **water** to overnight there and then press on over the cirque the following day. Unless you melt snow off the névé leading to the pass or make a detour to fill your bottles from the river, the next dependable source of water would be the Refuge de Tighjettu. This is a very long way from the previous one (Carrozzu/Spasimata) if you've walked along the Muvrella ridge.

Bank on between two and two-and-a-half hours for the *Variante* between Bocca di a Stagnu and the junction with the main GR route.

From the lake you also get a good view of one of the GR20's most distinctive rock formations, a huge eminence overhanging the pass that looks uncannily like a sculpted head of a Native American Indian, complete with feather headdress.

The path threading through the boulder-choked gully below it holds patches of snow and ice well into the summer, which adds a bit of interest to the steep approach to the **Bocca di a Muvrella**. Standing at the border of the island's Balagne and Filosorma regions, the pass reveals another stupendous view that takes in the entire central chain and red-granite cliffs of the west coast. Once over it the red-and-white waymarks plunge steeply to the right through a mass of broken rock before switching direction to begin a steadily ascending traverse to the second pass of the day, the **Bocca a i Stagnu** (2010m).

With an early enough start from Carrozzu you should be able to get here before clouds obscure the top of Monte Cinto; this is the most impressive view of Corisca's highest peak you'll get from the GR20 and few trekkers are in a hurry to put it behind them. Hopping down a precipitous jigsaw of creviced boulders, the 500-metre descent to Asco, whose rooftops, car park

Félix Von Cube

The relative accessibility of Corsica's mountains compared with the Alps or the Pyrenées means that few climbing reputations have been forged here over the years. One name, however, is closely associated with early exploration of the island's major peaks. Félix Von Cube, an Austrian doctor, first travelled to Corsica in 1899 and opened up a series of new routes around the Cinto massif. Three years later he returned with a group of friends to map and explore Monte Cinto more thoroughly and it was then that his team fixed the route that subsequently became the standard approach from the Asco side (described below). Von Cube's final visit was in 1904 when he became the first man to scale Capu Tafonatu, the famous pierced peak next to Paglia Orba.

His achievements (honoured by the re-naming after him of a peak overlooking the Cirque de la Solitude) are all the more impressive when you consider the kind of clothing and rudimentary equipment mountaineers had to contend with at the beginning of the 20th century. A couple of delightful old photos displayed in the bar of Hôtel Le Chalet at Asco Stagnu perfectly capture the mood of the times, when beards, pipes and suits were still de rigueur. One wonders what Von Cube and his cronies would have made of the ski station, which has so radically disfigured the area they used as a base for their groundbreaking forays onto Monte Cinto in 1902.

and helipad you can make out way below, is none too enticing. Allow at least 1¼ hours and stop regularly if your knees start feeling the strain. You'll need them to be in top shape for the next stage, which includes the GR20's steepest ascent and descent.

ASCO STAGNU

The former winter sports station at Asco Stagnu, or Haut' Asco as it's otherwise known, presents a bleak spectacle, its incongruous chalets and rusty ski lifts surrounded by scarred, deforested slopes. But for GR20 trekkers, the hotel, gîte d'étape and refuge here – not to mention the restaurant and bar – provide a welcome excuse to pause and recover from the exertions of the previous days. The complex also boasts a tempting terrace which, if you can ignore the dusty car park next to it, affords an inspiring view of the Cinto massif. After a hot shower and a couple of beers, the lure of the snow fields seduces many people into loosening their itineraries and slotting in the ascent the following day.

Orientation and services

Arriving from the Muvrella Ridge, bear left at the bottom of the pine forest for Hôtel Le Chalet or right, on the route indicated by the waymarks for the PNRC refuge. Below the latter you'll find a small Portacabin that houses Asco's **shop** (open all day and most of the evening; if it's closed ask the gardienne of the refuge to unlock it), which stocks the best range of trekking supplies between Calenzana and Vizzavona. Prices are lower than at the refuges.

There's no ATM here but the manager of Le Chalet will advance **cash** against a Visa or Mastercard if you've patronized the bar or restaurant.

The complex has two public **telephones**: one (which takes only coins) in the corner of the bar and a France Telecom booth (cards only) below the refuge. Anyone wishing to leave the GR20 here will have to phone for a **taxi** from Corte (see p231) and should expect to pay around 80€ for the luxury as there's no public transport to Asco.

Monte Cinto **[Map 5, p127]**

The ascent of Monte Cinto is the icing on the GR20 cake. Peaking at 2706m, Corsica's highest summit provides an unrivalled viewpoint over the route and its environs. The experience of standing on the peak with the entire central range spread below you will shift your perspective of the island's mountains; it also takes you through scenery quite unlike anything you'll encounter elsewhere.

The standard route from Asco Stagnu, although approaching the massif via its colder, harsher and more rugged north face, presents no technical obstacles. It's essentially a long, hard slog requiring a small pack and plenty of stamina. That said, the ascent shouldn't be taken lightly. In the course of the seven-hour round trip you notch up more than 2500 metres of altitude change, most of it over very steep rock, boulders and precipitous, loose scree. This is certainly one trek where you'll be glad of a pair of walking poles. The only thing to really worry about is the weather, which is notoriously fickle above 2000m. Clouds carrying sleet and snow can sweep in at any time of year and with very little warning, transforming your hike into a full-on battle with the elements. Just how dangerous Cinto's micro-climate can be was brought home in 1996 when, after being overtaken by a freak blizzard in early July, seven people died on the mountain in a single day. Check the forecast the night before (see p43) and remain vigilant throughout. If the weather looks like turning nasty it's always better to get off the mountain as quickly as you can rather than press on in the hope that conditions will improve. *(cont'd opposite)*

Hitching, however, is fairly reliable if you wait until afternoon when the daytrippers start to head home. Alternatively, ask at the hotel if any of the staff are driving into town that day.

Where to stay and eat

Asco Stagnu's institutional refuge overlooks the complex from the edge of the tree line. Rates are standard and the facilities spartan but adequate. The one compensation for its grim aspect are the blissfully hot showers. You can also cook in a fully-equipped kitchen. Sheltered bivouac and camping sites are dotted among the fir trees next to the building, although many have been spoiled by people shitting in the bushes beside them.

Turds also litter the unfinished rooms on the ground floor of the hulking concrete complex opposite the hotel, where construction work ceased a few years back when the owners ran out of money; if you're bivvying and the weather looks unpromising try one of the rooms on the upper storey, which were clean when we passed through.

By comparison the dorm beds in ***Gîte d'étape GR20***, part of ***Hôtel Le Chalet*** (☎/📠 04.95.47.81.08; open May–Sept), are luxurious. Rates here (6€ per bed or 25€ for half-board) are rock-bottom (lower, in fact, than at the PNRC's refuge). In the hotel proper, double rooms with shower and a small balcony cost 38€, or 45.60€ with an en suite toilet (30.40/36.50€ per head half-board).

Le Chalet's **restaurant**, off the left of the foyer as you enter the hotel, does a roaring trade. Most people eat here as part of a half-board deal but you'll do a lot better by spending a little more to eat à la carte (the half-board portions are on the small side). This will allow you to order their steak-frites, which (somewhat undeservingly it has to be said) enjoy near legendary status on the GR20. Count on around 20€ for a three-course meal, or 15€ for the *menu fixe*.

❑ Monte Cinto (cont'd)

The trail starts on the opposite side of the car park from **Hôtel Le Chalet** (look for the 'Monte Cinto' sign daubed on a boulder). Marked with red paint blobs (the orange waymarks at the beginning lead the way to the Punta Minuta, one of Cinto's sister summits), it follows a descending traverse past the old Austrian Alpine Club hut where Félix Von Cube used to hole up (see the box on p129) and through old-growth Laricio pine forest to the Stranciaccone stream. Once across the stepping stones here, you follow the true left bank of the Tighjettu uphill to a small **foot-bridge**, with the magnificent Cirque de Trimbolacciu and its crown of 2500metre peaks rising to the south. Beyond the *passarelle* the ascent proper gets underway as the route, dotted with red waymarks and small cairns, zigzags steeply up slabby rock and then bends south and eastwards to enter a spectacular side ravine. From a small shoulder at roughly 2100m you can look across to the Tour Penchée ('Leaning Tower'), the most distinctive among many amazing rock formations on the opposite flank of the ravine, standing out against gigantic red-brown cliffs.

Gradually the route progresses towards a large scree field which you traverse to reach the lip of an open depression beneath a saddle pass called **Bocca Borba** (2207m). A hollow under a big boulder here has been encircled by stones to create a shelter that makes a good place to pause. Once past this point, the way ahead over the Borba cwm is less clearly defined, splintering into a web of cairned routes that fans out across the enormous scree slopes below the summit. Keep heading south-east along any of them and you'll eventually hit **Lac d'Argentu**, a beautiful little lake that remains frozen well into the summer. Around it huge névés spread up the mountain; this is the snow visible on the far horizon from Calvi. Look out too for the weird, day-glo yellow lichen coating some of the shadier buttresses below Cinto's forepeak.

From the lake, you press on steeply uphill in a south-south-westerly direction across a couple of large névés and an increasingly sheer scree slope towards the **ridge**. This is the crux of the ascent, although the ridge itself, a flat saddle from which you can get your first sight of the Niolu Valley and mountains to the south, is something of a false summit. You've still a good 45 minutes ahead as the way-marks lead you first along the line of the crest towards the forepeak and then south off the ridge to start the last strenuous scramble to the top, up steep terraced slabs and grooves.

If you've been lucky with the weather the view from the top should be astounding. On very clear, windy days it's even possible to see the Alps and the French Riviera.

Allow 4½ hours for the ascent and 2½ hours for the descent (not including rest time).

GR20 STAGE FOUR: ASCO STAGNU → REFUGE DE TIGHJETTU → BERGERIES DE VALLONE [MAP 6, p133]

Overview

If one stage could be said to define the GR20 it would have to be this one. The passes on the fourth étape may not be the highest but the terrain they enclose – namely the infamous Cirque de la Solitude – tends to linger in the memory more vividly than any other on the route. The main reason is a series of sheer stepped

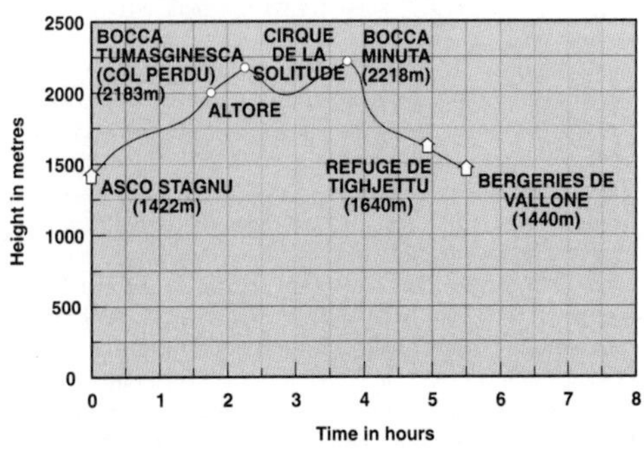

pitches, negotiated by means of fixed chains and a metal ladder, which take you across the head of a steeply concave valley.

Although undeniably strenuous, the scrambling is no more difficult than that experienced on some sections of the previous three days. In fact, with the fissured profile of Paglia Orba looming above you, this has to be one of the most intensely enjoyable legs of the whole GR20. Yet for some reason the cirque's reputation endures, a fact that probably accounts more than the actual terrain for the people-jams that form here. At the height of the summer trekkers comfortable and quick on steep, exposed rock will find themselves held up unless they get to the cirque early in the day before the queues form. Those of more nervous disposition should take solace in the fact that very few people fail to complete this section (not least because to avoid it you'd have to make a huge detour by road to Corte and another to Col de Verghio. If you do get the jitters in the cirque you'll be that much more proud of yourself once it's behind you.

By comparison, the rest of the étape – comprising one long, gradual ascent (the last bit of it across a névé) and a somewhat steeper descent through a huge boulder field – is easy going. Starting out from Asco Stagnu, it's not unusual for trekkers to press on to the Refuge de Ciottulu a i Mori after a leisurely lunch at the Bergeries de Vallone, one of the nicest pit-stops on the GR.

Route guide

The red-and-white waymarks lead out of Asco Stagnu along the line of the ski lift initially, bearing left towards the pine woods above you. As you progress up the valley the imposing profile of the Cirque de Trimbolacciu's peaks rise to the south through gaps in the trees.

The path emerges from under the pines to open, grazed ground carpeted in juniper, with clumps of crocuses and the odd orchid dotting the grassier patches. The route then makes a sweeping ascent of the valley's north side, nearing the stream towards the top.

A short, steeper section up a gravelly path brings you to the site of the **Ancien Refuge d'Altore**, which burned down in 1982. Its scant remains are scattered on a balcony below the first of the day's challenges, the 30-minute climb to **Bocca Tumasginesca** (also called Col Perdu; 2183m). This sheltered,

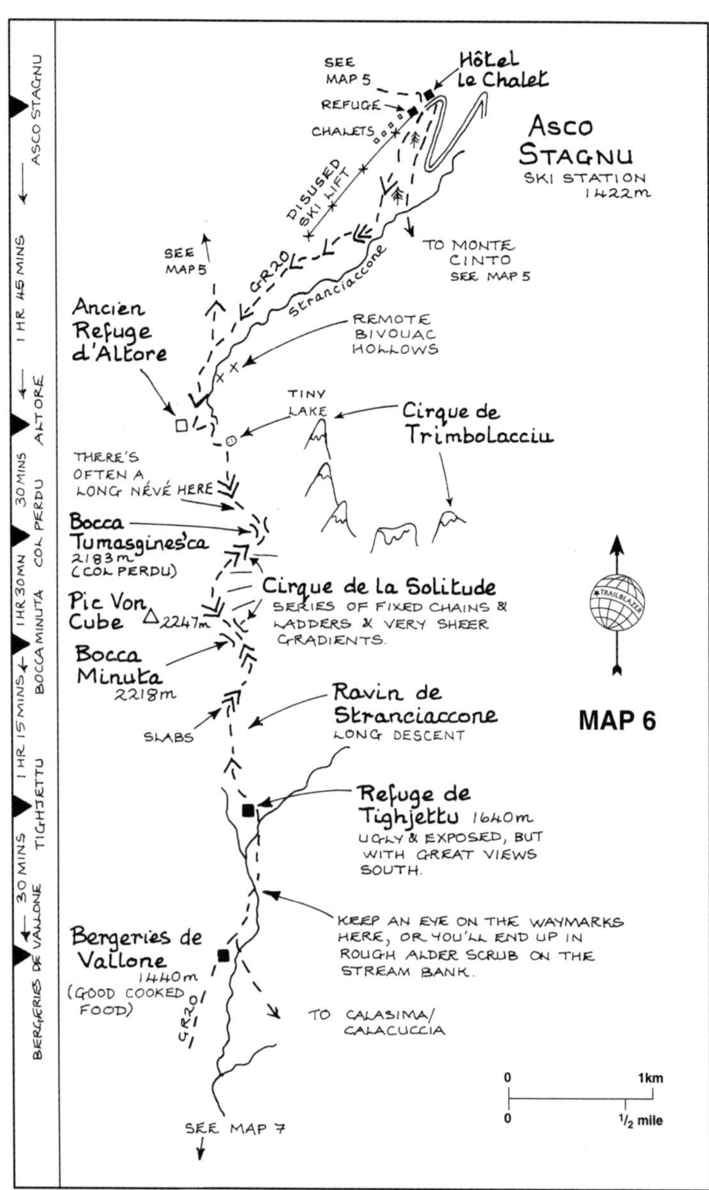
ASCO STAGNU
1 HR 45 MINS
ALTORE
30 MINS
COL PERDU
1 HR 30 MN
BOCCA MINUTA
1 HR 15 MINS
TIGHJETTU
30 MINS
BERGERIES DE VALLONE
SEE MAP 5
Hôtel le Chalet
REFUGE
CHALETS
DISUSED SKI LIFT
Asco Stagnu
SKI STATION
1422m
SEE MAP 5
GR20
Stranciaccone
TO MONTE CINTO
SEE MAP 5
Ancien Refuge d'Altore
REMOTE BIVOUAC HOLLOWS
TINY LAKE
Cirque de Trimbolacciu
THERE'S OFTEN A LONG NÉVÉ HERE
Bocca Tumasgines'ca
2183m
(COL PERDU)
Cirque de la Solitude
SERIES OF FIXED CHAINS & LADDERS & VERY SHEER GRADIENTS.
Pic Von Cube
2247m
Bocca Minuta
2218m
Ravin de Stranciaccone
LONG DESCENT
SLABS
MAP 6
TRAILBLAZER
Refuge de Tighjettu 1640m
UGLY & EXPOSED, BUT WITH GREAT VIEWS SOUTH.
KEEP AN EYE ON THE WAYMARKS HERE, OR YOU'LL END UP IN ROUGH ALDER SCRUB ON THE STREAM BANK.
Bergeries de Vallone
1440m
(GOOD COOKED FOOD)
GR20
TO CALASIMA/ CALACUCCIA
0
1km
0
1/2 mile
SEE MAP 7

Muvra

Hear rocks clattering from the cliffs above you and chances are if it's not a GR20 trekker it'll be a muvra. Corsica's elusive, short-fleeced sheep – mouflon in French – may be the symbol of the island's mountains but it's a far less sure-footed creature than the chamois and its other goat cousins on the continent. This is because it was originally a grassland animal, descended from domestic sheep thought to have been imported from the Middle East by early Neolithic peoples and forced by centuries of hunting, fires and competition from other animals to seek refuge in the mountains.

Males, distinguished by their long coiled horns and white facial markings, weigh up to 50kg. Females typically weigh 30kg and have stumpier, straighter horns. Only a vestigial population of around 600 survives, mostly in the higher reaches of Filosorma, Fango, Asco and Bavella.

During the winter – five months after the summer rut – the *muvrini* flee the snow to secluded, south-facing valleys that hold warmth throughout the year, where females give birth to their lambs. As the snow line recedes, they creep back up the mountainsides, spending the hottest months at the highest altitudes feeding on arbutus (stawberry trees) and alder.

On the GR20 you're most likely to catch a glimpse of a muvra on: Monte Corona (at the end of stage one); on the Muvrella ridge (*muvrella* means baby muvra) above Asco; at the head of the Asco valley and in the Cirque de la Solitude; around Paglia Orba; on the upper slopes of Monte Alcudina in the south; and on the Alpine section through the Bavella needles. First light and dusk, when the animals are most active, are the best times for muvra spotting.

north-facing slope often holds snow until well into the season. Towards the top of it you may be lucky enough to catch a glimpse of the Alps on the far horizon.

Most minds, however, tend to be on what's ahead at this point. From the lip of the pass the ground falls away almost vertically into the upper Filosorma Valley, bounded by the imposing profile of Paglia Orba and its surrounding mantle of rock towers.

To cross the **Cirque de la Solitude** to reach the Bocca Minuta, the niche visible on the opposite side, you have to descend 200 metres and clamber all the way back up again. In dry conditions proficient rock climbers will have little need of the chains whose clanking reverberates around the ravine, but these are essential aids when the granite is wet and slippery. Keep a close eye on the waymarks throughout and avoid dislodging loose rock onto people climbing below you.

With a clear run you can be across the cirque in 90 minutes or less. Once at the **Bocca Minuta** (2218m), a radically different landscape is revealed to the south. Visible on the horizon for the first time are the mountains of the central Corsican watershed, which you'll be crossing in the days ahead. The descent from the pass to the rocky **Ravin de Stranciaccone**, across a mixture of broken boulders and giant lichen-covered slabs, is straightforward though hot work in the afternoon; it's south-facing and almost entirely shadeless.

Refuge de Tighjettu and Bergeries de Vallone

Surrounded by a vast mass of green-tinged rock, **Refuge de Tighjettu** is perched atop a desolate spur between Stranciaccone and Stagni ravines, looking south across the Vallée de Vallone and the ridgetops of Niolu to Monte Rotondo in the distance. Built of wood, it's an angular modern construction with beds for 45 trekkers. The bivouac area is directly below the main building.

The size, popularity and overall ugliness of Tighjettu encourage many trekkers to continue down the valley for another half-hour to the more congenial **Bergeries de Vallone**, where a shepherd and his family have set up a small café offering hot meals, snacks, drinks and basic accommodation. A couple of old canvas tents provide sheltered beds (3.50€); you can also bivouac or camp here for 3.50€ (including the use of a flush-toilet). The food, served on their lovely wooden deck or rear terrace, is authentic and delicious (particularly the home-made charcuterie and Niolin ewe's cheese); the prices are reasonable too considering how far supplies have to be brought. If your budget can stretch to it go for the full 15.50€ four-course menu, which might include wild-boar stew or an omelette made with fresh mint and *brocciu*, rounded off with melt-in-the-mouth *fiadone*.

GR20 STAGE FIVE: BERGERIES DE VALLONE → CIOTTULU A I MORI [MAP 7, p137]

Overview

Sweeping around the base of Paglia Orba and over the Bocca di Fuciale pass into the Golo Valley, this relatively short, undemanding stage is easily doubled up. By doing so, however, you miss out on the chance of climbing Paglia Orba, Corsica's third-highest peak.

Route guide

Beyond the Bergeries de Vallone, the path rises gently to begin with and then follows a fairly level gradient south through pine forest. Having dropped downhill to cross the **Ravin de Paglia Orba** it then winds around another two wooded shoulders before swinging definitively south-west up the Foggiale Valley.

The route forks as it approaches the **Foggiale** stream; one (unmarked) branch heads left towards a cluster of bivouac circles on the bank. The other, the GR20, strikes uphill towards the col, steepening considerably as it leaves the forest and takes to the bare rock. As you ascend, with the waymarks cutting across a succession of seasonal streams, the Niolu Valley, dominated by the

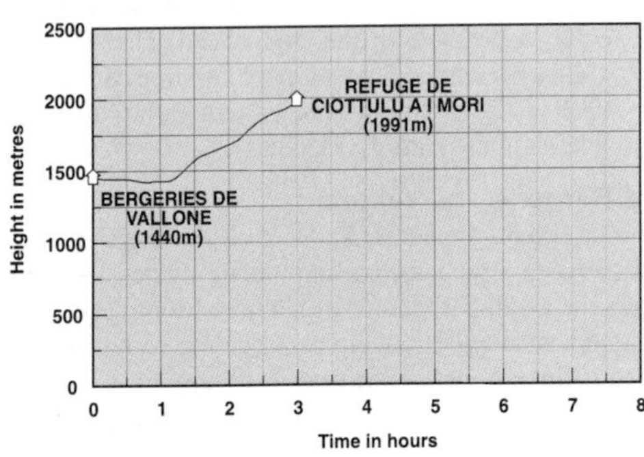

Calacuccia barrage, unfolds behind you.

The **Bocca di Foggiale** (1962m) is a bleak, windswept saddle covered in deep-red scree on whose upper slopes you might catch sight of grazing mouflons. To reach the refuge, the waymarks cut uphill to the right and then descend through a channel flanked by juniper and broom scrub. If you're planning to bypass Ciottulu a i Mori and press on to Castel di Verghio, follow the unmarked trail west from the pass which drops straight down the line of the

Paglia Orba and Capu Tafonatu **[Map 7, p137]**

Of the big three peaks over 2500m passed by the GR20, Paglia Orba (2525m), Corsica's distinctive shark's-tooth-shaped mountain, is the most readily accessible. You can get to the summit and back from the refuge in an easy half-day. With Monte Cinto only a sheep's cough across the valley and the sea close by, the views from it are as magnificent as you'd expect. However, the ascent – while technically straightforward, requiring neither ropes nor rock climbing skills – involves some highly exposed, tricky scrambling so you most definitely need a good head for heights. This is even more true for **Capu Tafonatu** (2335m), the extraordinary 'pierced peak' next to Paglia Orba, to which you can make a short but compelling detour en route. Think twice about attempting either in wet weather, or if you've found any of the ascents described so far in this book unnerving.

The approach to Paglia Orba, indicated by a PNRC signboard, starts from immediately behind Refuge de Ciottulu a i Mori. It begins with a leisurely ascent across boulders and scree to a pass called the **Col des Maures**, where you turn left if you wish to attempt Capu Tafonatu. Cairns mark the route up the peak whose characteristic arched hole Corsican mythology claims was made by the Devil in a fury. The stones trace the path south-west along a narrow ledge that snakes around the base of the peak. On arriving at a seam of white rock you have to make a vertigo-inducing climb around a large projection. Beyond it the route drops down and picks up another ledge which you follow most of the way to the giant arch. Allow two hours for the round trip to Capu Tafonatu from Col Des Maures.

The route up **Paglia Orba** turns right from just below the col, at the point where the Capu Tafonatu path veers left. Threading around a couple of low cliffs and gullies by means of eroded slabs and boulders, it's simple enough to begin with but grows steeper and more challenging when you penetrate a couloir crammed with fallen chunks of rock. *(cont'd opposite)*

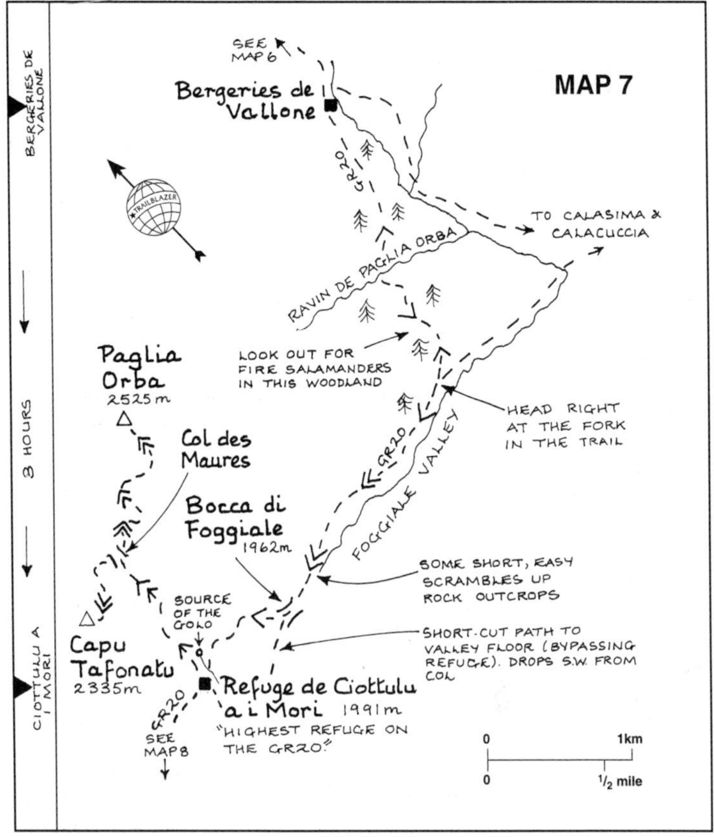

❑ Paglia Orba and Capu Tafonatu (cont'd)

With the arch of Capu Tafonatu visible for the first time behind you, the cairns lead to the right of the cleave, then squeeze through a niche above it, and from there around an exposed ledge that will have vertigo sufferers rooted to the spot. Jutting into a void, it overhangs the vast north face of the mountain above the Fango Valley.

On reaching a secondary peak on the east side of the massif soon after, the route drops through a breach to the **Combe des Chèvres** ('Goats' Combe'), a sheltered dip often lined with névés, from where a well-defined path strikes uphill to the ridgetop and summit.

Count on reaching the top in a little under two hours, with one hour for the descent.

Golo basin to river level; this cuts out an unnecessarily long, sweeping traverse, saving you a good hour or so.

Refuge de Ciottulu a i Mori

Along with Petra Piana and Usciolu, Ciottulu a i Mori (literally 'Hole of the Moors') ranks among the hot contenders for the title of 'most spectacularly-sited refuge' on the GR20. Clinging to the south flank of mighty Paglia Orba at an altitude of 1991m, it's certainly the highest mountain hut on the island. From its terrace you get a matchless view over the Golo basin, flanked by red-granite ridges that taper away to a jagged horizon dominated by the pyramidal Punta Artica.

The refuge is small, with beds for 26 people, and offers scant shelter for bivouackers; you'll be grateful for a snug sleeping bag or a tent if you're overnighting outside. Very little in the way of supplies is available here, and meals are not prepared by the gardien.

GR20 STAGE SIX: CIOTTULU A I MORI → CASTEL DI VERGHIO [MAP 8, OPPOSITE]

Overview

Stage six of the GR20 is a leisurely half-day's amble down the Golo Valley, offering plenty of potential for R&R along the way. Many trekkers combine it with the previous étape from Vallone or continue from Castel di Verghio to Manganu, but if you take your time you can linger around some of the gorgeous rock pools that line the river, blissing out to the clank of cowbells and the scent of pine resin from the giant Laricios.

Route guide

The stage starts with a sweeping traverse of the west flank of the Golo Basin. After dropping gently to a ridge that overlooks the Forêt d'Aïtone to the west, the well-worn path plunges down to join the river just south of the disused **Bergeries de Tula**. Note that if you're in a hurry you can cut out this section by following the cattle track due south down the line of the basin from in front of the refuge.

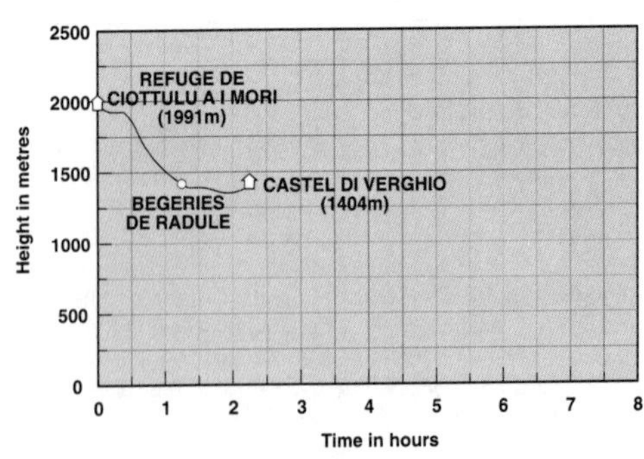

Once at river level the path keeps to an even course; this is one of the few lengths

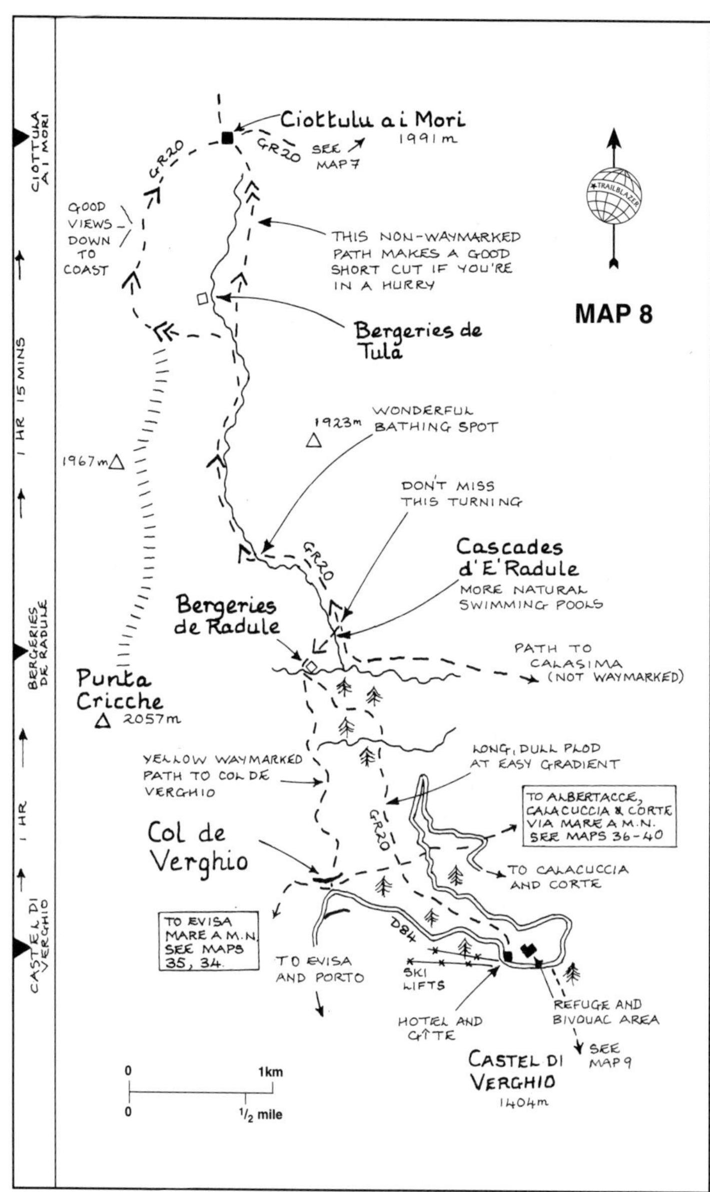

CIOTTULU A I MORI
1 HR 15 MINS
BERGERIES DE RADULE
1 HR
CASTEL DI VERGHIO
Ciottulu a i Mori
1991m
GR20
SEE MAP 7
GOOD VIEWS DOWN TO COAST
THIS NON-WAYMARKED PATH MAKES A GOOD SHORT CUT IF YOU'RE IN A HURRY
MAP 8
Bergeries de Tula
1923m
WONDERFUL BATHING SPOT
1967m
DON'T MISS THIS TURNING
Cascades d'E'Radule
MORE NATURAL SWIMMING POOLS
Bergeries de Radule
PATH TO CALASIMA (NOT WAYMARKED)
Punta Cricche
2057m
YELLOW WAYMARKED PATH TO COL DE VERGHIO
LONG, DULL PLOD AT EASY GRADIENT
TO ALBERTACCE, CALACUCCIA & CORTE VIA MARE A M.N. SEE MAPS 36-40
Col de Verghio
TO CALACUCCIA AND CORTE
TO EVISA MARE A M.N. SEE MAPS 35, 34.
D84
TO EVISA AND PORTO
SKI LIFTS
HOTEL AND GÎTE
REFUGE AND BIVOUAC AREA
SEE MAP 9
CASTEL DI VERGHIO
1404m
0
1km
0
1/2 mile

of the GR where you don't have to watch your footing. On reaching a bend in the valley overhung by large outcrop, the path switches to the left bank of the river and zigzags downhill through stands of pines via an old paved transhumant path to a well-known bathing spot that attracts day-trippers off the main road.

Once you've crossed the river a second time at the **Cascades d'E'Radule** – another lovely place to swim – the next landmark is the **Bergeries de Radule**, a picturesque cluster of dry-stone shepherds' huts around 1½ hours from the refuge. This marks the midway point of the étape. From here on you'll be walking more or less continually on springy trails through pine forest. The unfamiliar swoosh of motor traffic on the D84 heralds your arrival at Castel di Verghio, although you still have what can feel like an endless plod through the forest to get there.

CASTEL DI VERGHIO

Originally the GR20 bypassed Castel di Verghio, the ski station below the Col de Verghio. Like the station at Asco Stagnu this one has suffered from the warming of Corsica's climate over the past decade or so. A few years back, however, the owner decided to splash some red-and-white paint around and 'redirect' the GR through the hotel. His detour has since been rubber-stamped by the PNRC, offering a comfortable alternative to Ciottulu a i Mori and Manganu.

Resembling an early 1970s Eastern-bloc ski resort, the hotel, which sits on a spur above the Niolu Valley overlooking Paglia Orba and Monte Cinto, has gîte d'étape and refuge accommodation, camping space and a bar-restaurant as well as rooms. Poorly maintained by Corsican standards, it's an ugly blot on the landscape that gets mixed reviews, but many trekkers welcome the respite it offers from refuge life.

Orientation and services

Verghio lies on a seasonal **bus** route connecting it with Porto in the west and Corte, via Calacuccia and Albertacce, in the other direction. The service, run by Autocars Mordiconi (☎ 04.95.48.00.04), operates daily between mid-July and the end of September. Other than the bus or hitching, the only way to get to or from the ski station is by **taxi**: Michel Salviani (☎ 06.97.46.04.88 or mobile ☎ 06.03 49.15.24) from Calacuccia will drop you in Corte, the nearest railhead (see p231), for around 76€.

Where to stay and eat

The cheapest beds at ***Castel di Verghio*** (☎ 04.95.48.00.01; open May–mid-Oct) are in the **refuge**, a separate block next to the main building with grotty dorms (8.50€ per bed) and dirty bathrooms. In good weather, you'd be better off bivouacking or camping in the adjacent field (5€), though if you do be sure to shut the gate firmly or you could find yourself raided by hungry pigs in the night.

The **gîte d'étape**, in the basement of the hotel, is just as shabby as the refuge though it does have steaming hot showers. Beds cost 13.70€, or 27.40€ half-board.

To be confident of a comfortable night's sleep indoors you'd have to shell out on a room in the **hotel**. Doubles with attached showers and toilets à l'étage cost 41€, or 41€ per head half-board; they're much better maintained than the dormitories but still a touch overpriced.

Meals are served in a spacious, bright dining hall on the ground floor with fishbowl windows overlooking Paglia Orba and Monte Cinto – a lovely sunny spot for breakfast (6.30–9am; 6.50€). In the evenings, suppers (menu fixe 15€) are dished up to long tables of hungry trekkers. The food is nothing to write home about but copious enough.

GR20 STAGE SEVEN: CASTEL DI VERGHIO → REFUGE DE MANGANU [MAP 9, p143; MAP 10, p145]

Overview

Another gentle but hugely scenic day's trekking awaits on stage seven, as the GR20 climbs out of the Niolu Valley via the Bocca San Pedru and follows the ridges above it to Lac de Nino – an exquisite high-altitude lake cradled by 2000m+ peaks. The lush green *pozzines* surrounding it, headwaters of the Tavignano River, are grazed by herds of wild horses. Together with the profile of snow-streaked Monte Rotondo nosing above the southern horizon this unique spot has an air curiously reminiscent of the Central Asian steppes.

From the lake the trail winds steadily downhill along the river, crossing a broad triangular-shaped plain, the Pianu di Campotile, on its approach to the refuge. The comparative easiness of the path, together with the temptation to linger on the idyllic shores of Lac de Nino, give this étape the feel of a day-off.

Bone breakers

The lammergeier or bearded vulture (*gypaète barbu* in French or *altore* in Corsican) is the B52 of the island's skies. Sporting a maximum wingspan of just under 3m, this majestic vulture is known locally as 'le casseur d'os' (bone breaker) after its ingenious feeding habits. When crows and other carrion feeders have cleaned up the carcasses left lying around the mountains, the lammergeier moves in to suck what goodness may be left from the bones. To do this, however, it first has to break them open by dropping them from a height of between 30 and 50 metres onto flat-topped rocks – one of the island's great natural spectacles.

In times past the bone breakers were persecuted almost to the point of extinction by shepherds, who mistakenly believed they preyed on lambs. Another cause for their decline was the disappearance of large sheep flocks from the Corsican mountains, which deprived them of their chief source of carrion. Only around eight couples survive here, despite recent attempts by the PNRC to revive the population with feeding stations, where carcasses are left for the lammergeiers to tuck into.

Sifting through the fragments left on their bone-breaking rocks has revealed that the vultures' territory may extend to 50 kilometres (scientists have even found remains in the mountains of southern Corsica brought across the sea from Sardinia).

Their pinkish-gold breasts, long diamond-shaped tail and colossal size (adults can weigh up to 6kg) make lammergeiers relatively easy to distinguish from golden eagles. Top spots to sight them along the GR20 are around Lac de Nino, where there are three nesting pairs, and the crags above the Refuge de Carrozzu.

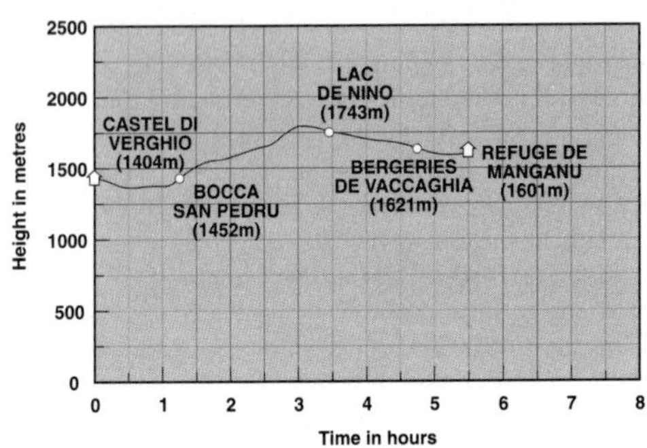

Route guide

To pick up the trail from Castel di Verghio, follow the D84 downhill for 20m or so until you see a signboard indicating the route onward through the forest, to the right-hand side of the road. After a steady drop through the forest the path hits a level gradient which it follows for the next hour or more around the contours of the hillside, passing through some wonderful Laricio pine and beech forest (for more on the history of the area's woodlands see p216).

The first ascent of the day, to the **Bocca San Pedru** (1452m), begins just over an hour into the étape, cutting up the dry hillside through a series of zig-zags. Laid down with horses and mules in mind, most of this stage's climbs are well paved and set at easy gradients, as you'll soon realize on leaving the small oratory at the col.

From the ridge south-east of the Bocca San Pedru the views improve, with Paglia Orba and the Monte Cinto massif dominating the horizon to the north. The sea is also visible for the first time since stage three.

Halfway to the summit of a subsidiary peak called U Tritore the path peels away across the hillside to the left, picking up the ridge again at 1800m. A gentle ascent over open, rocky terrain ensues. Just as the slope begins to steepen markedly on its run up to Capu a u Tozzu (2007m) the trail cuts off the ridge-line again, this time dropping slightly downhill to the right through a niche before striking a steady rising route to **Bocca â Rete** (1883m).

A leisurely descent over rolling stony ground leads you down from the pass to **Lac de Nino**, one of the most photographed landmarks of the GR20. Just under 400m long and 250m wide, it is the source of the Tavignano River, which flows down to Corte (this wonderful waymarked trekking route is described on pp229-230) where it merges with the Restonica River.

Although only 11m deep, the lake supports a thriving population of trout (hence all the local fishermen you'll see here at the weekend). The spongy grass banks and sinuous rivulets linking the pools dotted around it – known in Corsican as *pozzi* (whence their French name pozzines) – are home to a thriving population of wild horses and pigs. With the snow peaks reflected in the still water, this can be a dreamy spot. It is, however, rarely deserted. In addition to the flow of trekkers along the GR20, large numbers of day-hikers walk up here

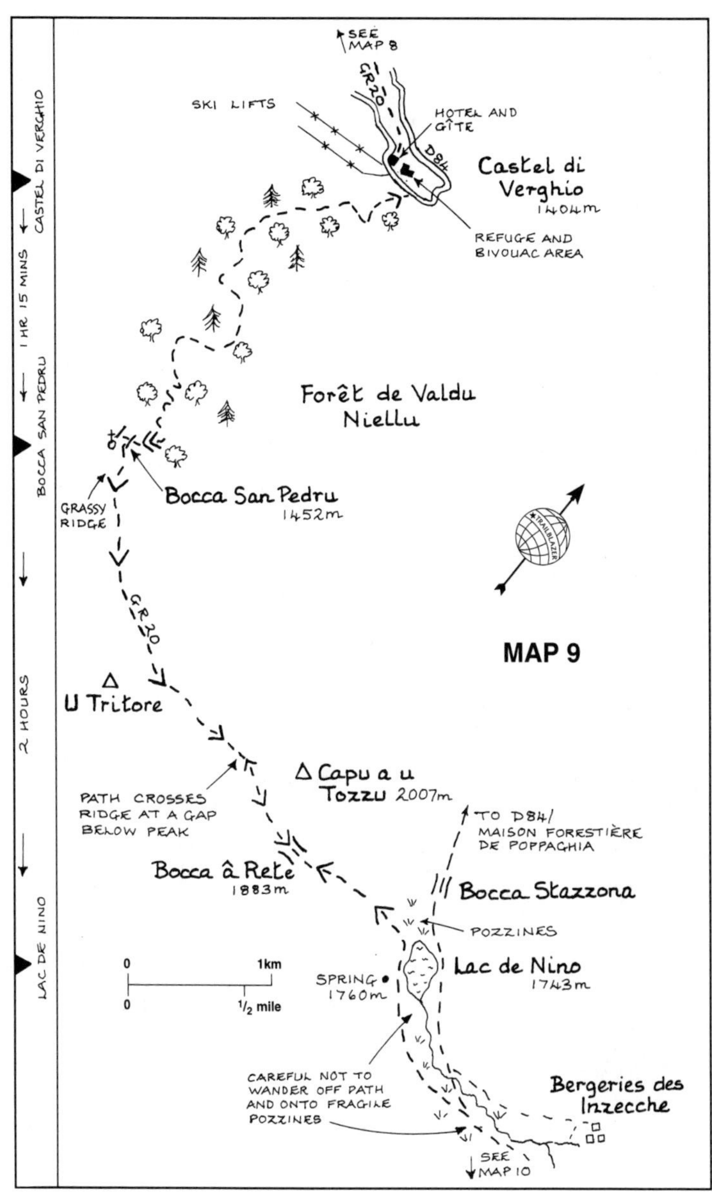
SEE MAP 8
GR20
SKI LIFTS
HOTEL AND GÎTE
D84
Castel di Verghio
1404m
REFUGE AND BIVOUAC AREA
Forêt de Valdu Niellu
Bocca San Pedru
1452m
GRASSY RIDGE
GR20
MAP 9
U Tritore
PATH CROSSES RIDGE AT A GAP BELOW PEAK
Capu a u Tozzu 2007m
TO D84/ MAISON FORESTIÈRE DE POPPAGHIA
Bocca â Rete
1883m
Bocca Stazzona
POZZINES
Lac de Nino
1743m
SPRING 1760m
0 1km
0 1/2 mile
CAREFUL NOT TO WANDER OFF PATH AND ONTO FRAGILE POZZINES
Bergeries des Inzecche
SEE MAP 10
CASTEL DI VERGHIO
1 HR 15 MINS
BOCCA SAN PEDRU
2 HOURS
LAC DE NINO

Pastori

Thousands of years before the first trekking boot stepped onto the island, Corsica's mountain trails were busy lines of communication between valleys. Modern waymarked routes such as the GR20 are only contemporary versions of ancient pathways along which shepherds (*pastori*) drove their flocks between the winter pastures at sea level (*a piaghja*) and the summer pastures high in the mountains (*a muntagna*).

Replicating the animals' own natural migratory cycle, this annual movement (transhumance) dictated patterns of rural life well into the 20th century. Until WWI cut a swath through the male population, the menfolk would spend half the year with their flocks three or more days' walk from home. For shepherds from high regions such as the Niolu Valley, the long separation from families and friends would take place on the coast during the cold months. The annual migration for shepherds in the arid south-east of the island, on the other hand, would occur in the summer, when the grass growing in the wake of receding snowfields provided an alternative to the sun-scorched grasses of their home patch.

In some parts of Corsica, families decamped en masse for the big migration, setting up home in their **bergeries** – tiny dry-stone cottages where the flocks would be driven to in the evenings and the milking carried out. Except for the introduction of metal implements, matches and rifles, life in the bergeries of the 1950s and 1960s had changed little since Neolithic times. Hunting, story-telling and traditional polyphonic singing (see p225) filled fireside hours at the end of the day, maintaining traditions that had virtually died out by the modern era.

From its high point in the mid-nineteenth century transhumance fell into a sharp decline as the pan-European economy gathered pace. Emigration also took its toll, along with the severe overgrazing that left whole forests and mountainsides scarred beyond recovery. Now, only 30 to 40 full-time shepherds remain on the island, dependent on EU subsidies and with rigid quotas limiting the ratio between grazing land and flock sizes.

Of the handful of bergeries still worked throughout the summer, **Vaccaghia**, overlooking the Pianu di Campotile near Refuge de Manganu, is one of only a few that survive along the line of the watershed (another is the **Bergeries de Gialgo** near Petra Piana). One of the reasons it continues to flourish is the number of trekkers streaming past its door, many of whom leave trailing the pungent aroma of a newly-acquired cheese behind them.

The modern shepherd's raison d'être, Corsica's famed **cheese**, is renowned throughout France for its overpowering smell (as you'll already know if you've read *Asterix in Corsica*, in which a cheese is so strong it spontaneously combusts – a play on the adjective 'explosif', which is often applied to describe the taste of *le fromage corse*). Its fresh and milder form, **brocciu**, is made by warming ewe's milk until it starts to coagulate into lumps, which are strained off and set in molds. Used to add flavour and texture to omelettes, flans, donuts and tiramisu, it is *the* quintessential ingredient of quality Corsican gastronomy and today enjoys its own prized Appelation Contrôlée status. Just don't, whatever you do, compare it to mozzarella in the presence of a shepherd.

For more background on traditional life in the Corsican mountains, see the box on p220.

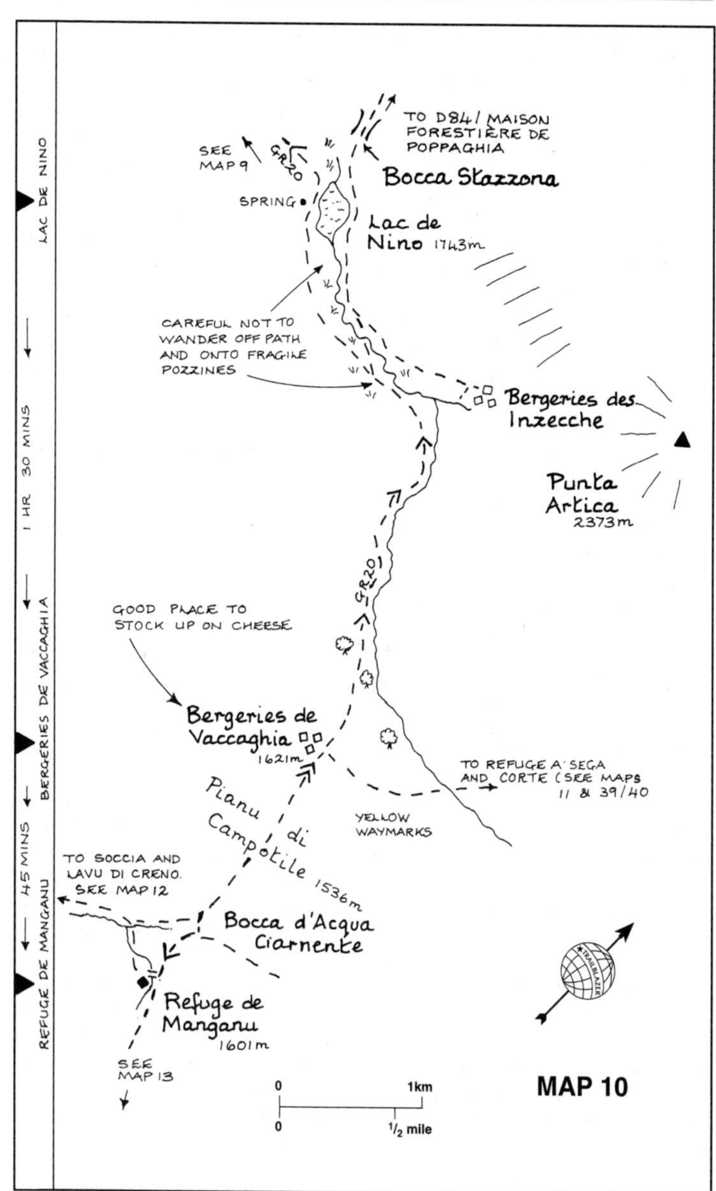
LAC DE NINO
1 HR 30 MINS
BERGERIES DE VACCAGHIA
45 MINS
REFUGE DE MANGANU
TO D84/ MAISON FORESTIÈRE DE POPPAGHIA
SEE MAP 9
GR20
Bocca Stazzona
SPRING
Lac de Nino 1743m
CAREFUL NOT TO WANDER OFF PATH AND ONTO FRAGILE POZZINES
Bergeries des Inzecche
Punta Artica 2373m
GR20
GOOD PLACE TO STOCK UP ON CHEESE
Bergeries de Vaccaghia 1621m
TO REFUGE A' SEGA AND CORTE (SEE MAPS 11 & 39/40
YELLOW WAYMARKS
Pianu di Campotile 1536m
TO SOCCIA AND LAVU DI CRENO. SEE MAP 12
Bocca d'Acqua Ciarnente
Refuge de Manganu 1601m
SEE MAP 13
TRAILBLAZER
0
1km
0
1/2 mile
MAP 10

from the Maison Forestière de Poppaghia on the main road. A young gardien is posted to the lake during the summer to ensure its fragile ecology is protected; camping, bivouacking and fires are strictly prohibited. You should also avoid leaving the path as the pozzines are easily eroded.

Having reached the lake the GR20 turns right and follows the shoreline past a **spring** and thence east along the valley floor. Ahead of you the serrated, snow-flecked ridges of the Rotondo massif are visible in the distance. Shortly after passing the ruined **Bergeries des Inzecche**, a cluster of stone huts clinging to the hill on the opposite side of the stream, the path bends decisively south-east to follow the wriggling course of the Tavignano across rougher, stonier ground interspersed with alder and beech. Not long after emerging from a large wood you'll crest a rocky ridge just below which, in a sheltered hollow facing across the valley, stand the **Bergeries de Vaccaghia**, one of the few working shepherds' camps on this route. Three varieties of ewe's cheese (from pungent to eye-wateringly strong) are sold here; express an interest and the *berger* might show you the cool underground **caves** where they mature on large planks.

From the bergeries you get a great view of the remaining stretch to the Refuge de Manganu across a dead-flat, grassy plain, the **Pianu di Campotile**, where the Tavignano bends north-east.

A **liaison path**, waymarked in yellow, turns left (east) off the GR just below the huts, winding along the northern side of the valley to the Refuge A Sega in around 3½ hours (see Map 11, opposite). From there you can head down the Tavignano Gorge to Corte, a route mapped on pp228-9.

At the **Bocca d'Aqua Ciarnente**, at the southern end of the plain, another yellow-waymarked route, indicated by a signboard, turns south-west down the Zoicu valley towards Soccia (see the box on p148), while the GR makes the short final ascent to the refuge.

Refuge de Manganu

Thanks to its proximity to both Lac de Nino and the roadhead at Soccia, Manganu is one of the busiest refuges on the GR20, attracting a mix of trout fishermen, fell runners and trekkers. Its dark but cosy interior accommodates 27 people and a dozen or more tents pitched around the back of the hut soak up the overspill during peak season. The refuge's terrace, which overlooks the Bocca d'Aqua Ciarente and Pianu di Campatile, is a great place to hang out, especially when the great pyramidal peak to the north, Punta Artica (2373m), is snow-covered.

The best ground behind the refuge is taken up by the gardien's tents, leaving campers and bivouackers little flat space to pitch on; you might have to hunt beyond the alder bushes for shelter. The toilet and shower block is to the right of the hut as you're facing it from the front terrace. A small selection of expensive **supplies** – from cheese and sausage to soft drinks and beers – are sold by the gardien; do your shopping in the evening as he doesn't open up the following morning.

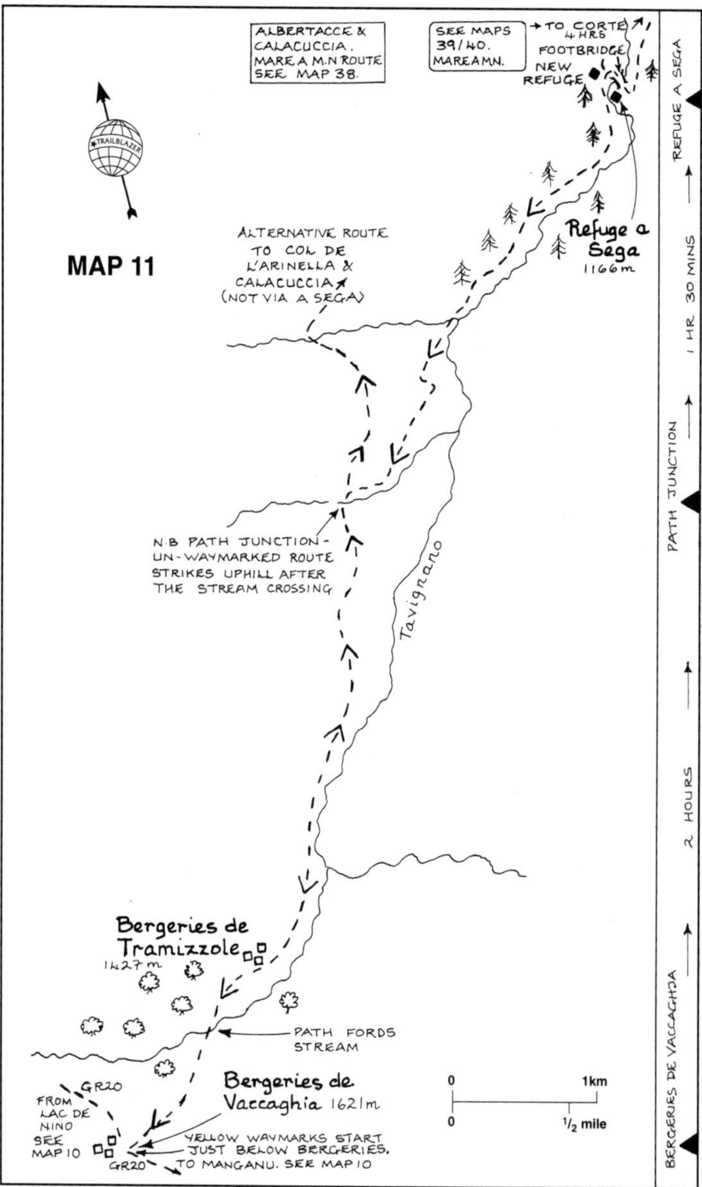
ALBERTACCE & CALACUCCIA. MAREA M.N ROUTE SEE MAP 38.
SEE MAPS 39/40. MAREAMN.
TO CORTE 4 HRS
FOOTBRIDGE
NEW REFUGE
MAP 11
ALTERNATIVE ROUTE TO COL DE L'ARINELLA & CALACUCCIA (NOT VIA A SEGA)
Refuge a Sega 1166m
N.B PATH JUNCTION - UN-WAYMARKED ROUTE STRIKES UPHILL AFTER THE STREAM CROSSING
Tavignano
Bergeries de Tramizzole 1427m
PATH FORDS STREAM
GR20
FROM LAC DE NINO SEE MAP 10
Bergeries de Vaccaghia 1621m
YELLOW WAYMARKS START JUST BELOW BERGERIES.
GR20
TO MANGANU. SEE MAP 10
0
1km
0
1/2 mile
BERGERIES DE VACCAGHJA
2 HOURS
PATH JUNCTION
1 HR 30 MINS
REFUGE A SEGA

Liaison route to Soccia via Lavu di Crenu and Monte Sant'Eliseo

Map 12, opposite

From Manganu it's possible to reach road level at the village of Soccia in a little under 2½ hours. The route, waymarked in yellow, peels west off the GR20 just below the refuge (a signboard shows the way), threading through the rocks above a rushing stream to cross the Rau de Zoicu on the floor of the valley. After winding above the right bank of the river through rough terrain for an hour or so, it switches to the left bank and from there rises gently through old-growth pine woods to the **Lavu di Crenu**. The only high-altitude lake in Corsica surrounded by Laricio pines, Crenu is a popular picnic spot in summer, when daytrippers hike up to admire the lotus flowers that bloom on it. A gardienne is on hand to ensure no-one camps, bivouacs or lights fires here.

Beyond the lake, a well-trodden path winds at contour level past a spring, the **Funtana di a Veduvella** which is renowned for the quality of its water, and later (at 1292m) a fork in the trail.

If you're not in a rush consider making the detour to **Monte Sant'Eliseo**, a superb viewpoint a little over 200 metres above you. Bearing left at the fork, the route to it continues downhill for 15 minutes as far as a ridge. At this point you reach another path that cuts back sharply to the left (you'll know you've missed this turning if you arrive at a large white crucifix). Follow this new path in a north-easterly direction as it drifts away from the ridge and then, around 15-minutes later, switches decisively to the south to begin a much steeper, zigzagging approach to the peak. A **chapel** sits on the summit, site of an annual pilgrimage in August when the inhabitants of the surrounding villages, their numbers swollen by relatives holidaying from the continent, follow the priest from Vico up here to celebrate mass. The view is magnificent, stretching from the snows of Monte D'Oro to the Golfe de Sagone, while to the north, Cimatella and Punta Artica flag the line of the watershed.

If you don't make the detour to Monte Sant'Eliseo keep heading straight on and you'll soon emerge from woods to start a long, easy descent through maquis to a **car park** where a *buvette* offers welcome shade and sustenance. From here you can either hitch the remaining few kilometres along the road to Soccia or pick up the path that continues steeply down the hillside.

Soccia, one of the most picturesque villages in the region, has neither a shop nor a bank, nor is it served by public transport. It does, however, have a hotel and a restaurant (see p241 for details). To reach the coast you'd have to hitch (ideally from the car park at the Lavu di Crenu trailhead, which sees more through traffic than the village). Alternatively, use this liaison route to pick up the Mare a Mare Nord *Variant* to Marignana, and from there trek either west to Cargèse or north into the Spelunca Valley.

GR20 STAGE EIGHT: REFUGE DE MANGANU → REFUGE DE PETRA PIANA

[MAP 13, p151]

Overview

Stage eight is one of the GR20's classic étapes. Taking you from the restrained environs of the Pianu di Campotile back to the extremes of the high watershed, the initial 650m ascent from Manganu strikes a stark contrast with the preceding day or two. But as recompense you'll have what many trekkers regard as the

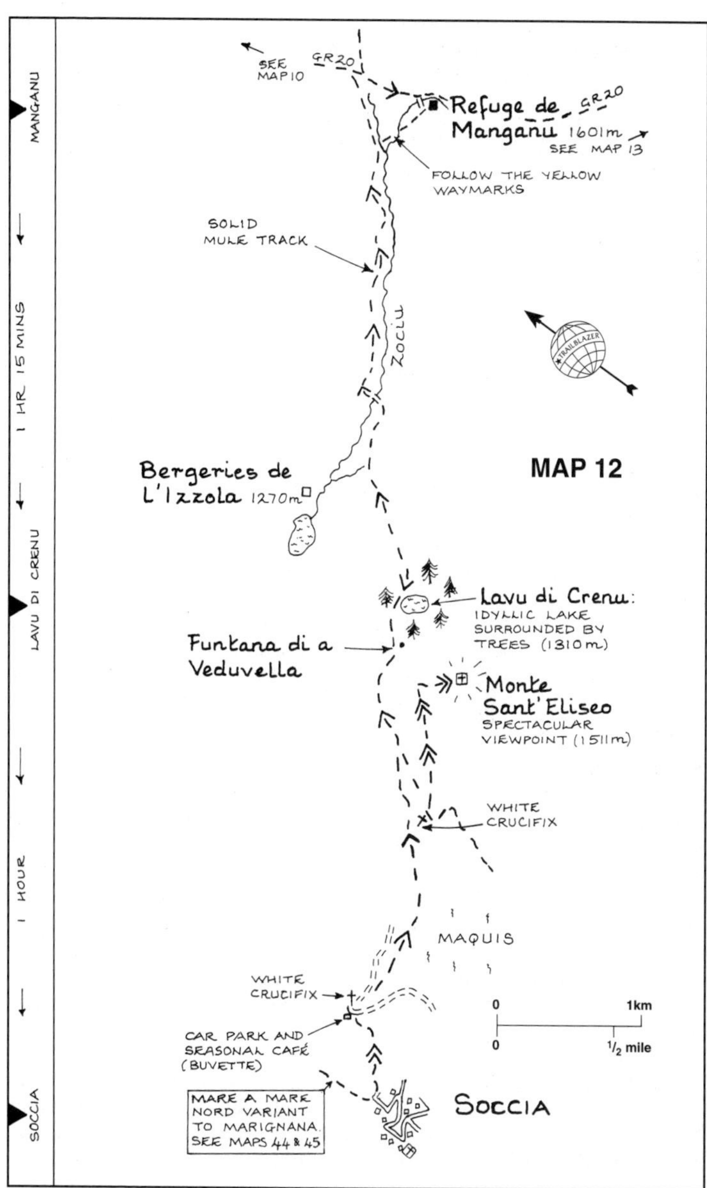
MANGANU
1 HR 15 MINS
LAVU DI CRENU
1 HOUR
SOCCIA
SEE MAP 10
GR20
Refuge de Manganu 1601m
GR20
SEE MAP 13
FOLLOW THE YELLOW WAYMARKS
SOLID MULE TRACK
ZOCCU
TRAILBLAZER
MAP 12
Bergeries de L'Izzola 1270m
Lavu di Crenu: IDYLLIC LAKE SURROUNDED BY TREES (1310m)
Funtana di a Veduvella
Monte Sant' Eliseo SPECTACULAR VIEWPOINT (1511m)
WHITE CRUCIFIX
MAQUIS
WHITE CRUCIFIX
CAR PARK AND SEASONAL CAFÉ (BUVETTE)
0
1km
0
1/2 mile
MARE A MARE NORD VARIANT TO MARIGNANA. SEE MAPS 44 & 45
SOCCIA

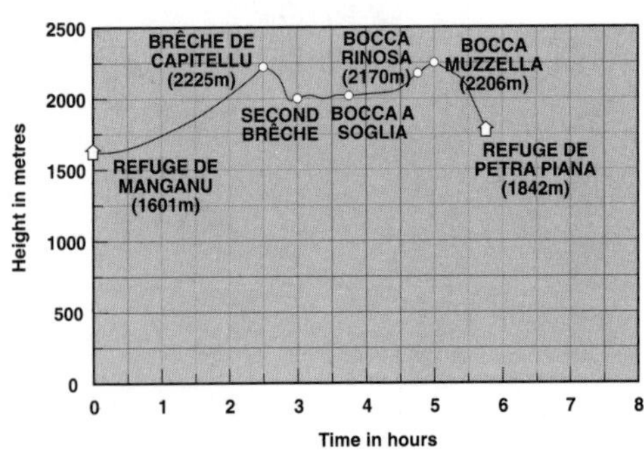

route's most dramatic landscapes to look forward to. In particular, the ridge section between the famous Brêche de Capitellu (at 2225m the GR's highest point) and Bocca Muzzella is a non-stop parade of stupendous scenery. Overlooking the head of the Restonica Valley on one side and the hinterland of the Golfe de Sagone on the other, the views stretch from glacial lakes surrounded by vast, vertical cliffs all the way to the sea, with glimpses of Monte Cinto and Paglia Orba in the distance.

On the downside, awaiting you during the descent from the *brêche* are a couple of especially steep passages that can be tricky in wet weather, as well as one or two large névés to negotiate early in the season. As you'll be more or less following the island's backbone, water is at a premium: take enough to last you most of the day (2–3 litres depending on the temperature). The étape's altitudes and high degree of exposure can also make this a difficult section in bad weather. If conditions look unstable seek the advice of the gardien at Manganu and be prepared to dig in for a day if storms or persistent rain are forecast. This is definitely one stage whose views you wouldn't want to miss out on.

Route guide

The day kicks off with a long climb that starts gently enough but steepens as you gain height. From the refuge the waymarks cross a **footbridge** and strike immediately uphill to the right along the stream bank. Crossing a succession of slabs and grassy slopes strewn with large boulders, you press on towards a more open area of pozzines at 1783m, the site of a now-drained glacial lake. Beyond this point the route steepens again, levelling off briefly at 1969m where there's a small lake. Above you a moraine splashed with patches of eternal snow stretches up to a cirque of peaks, interrupted by the distinct niche of **Brêche de Capitellu** (also called Bocca a e Porte; 2225m), which you should reach in around 2½ hours.

An amazing view opens up on the far side of the pass, dominated by **Lac de Capitellu** and **Lac de Melu**, which sit at the bottom of an awesome cirque. From this altitude an optical illusion makes them appear on the same level but Melu, to the right as seen from the brêche, is actually more than 200 metres below Capitellu. Both are popular targets for day trips from Corte. A paved

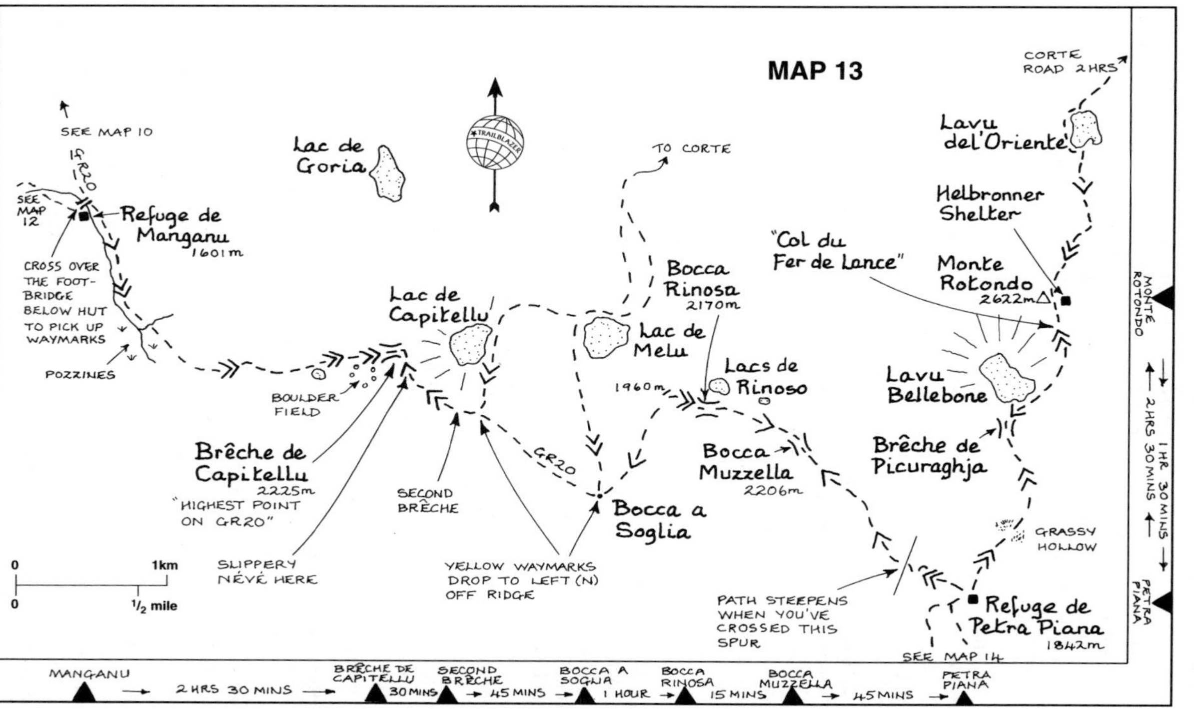
MAP 13
CORTE ROAD 2 HRS
SEE MAP 10
GR20
SEE MAP 12
Refuge de Manganu 1601m
CROSS OVER THE FOOT-BRIDGE BELOW HUT TO PICK UP WAYMARKS
POZZINES
Lac de Goria
TO CORTE
Lavu del'Oriente
Helbronner Shelter
"Col du Fer de Lance"
Monte Rotondo 2622m
Bocca Rinosa 2170m
Lac de Capitellu
Lac de Melu
Lacs de Rinoso
1960m
Lavu Bellebone
BOULDER FIELD
Brêche de Capitellu 2225m
"HIGHEST POINT ON GR20"
SECOND BRÊCHE
GR20
Bocca Muzzella 2206m
Brêche de Picuraghja
Bocca a Soglia
GRASSY HOLLOW
SLIPPERY NÉVÉ HERE
YELLOW WAYMARKS DROP TO LEFT (N) OFF RIDGE
PATH STEEPENS WHEN YOU'VE CROSSED THIS SPUR
Refuge de Petra Piana 1842m
SEE MAP 14
0
1km
0
1/2 mile
MANGANU
2 HRS 30 MINS
BRÊCHE DE CAPITELLU
30 MINS
SECOND BRÊCHE
45 MINS
BOCCA A SOGLIA
1 HOUR
BOCCA RINOSA
15 MINS
BOCCA MUZZELLA
45 MINS
PETRA PIANA
MONTE ROTONDO
1 HR 30 MINS
2 HRS 30 MINS
PETRA PIANA

road, recently revamped with a whopping EU grant, funnels traffic up to a car park at the head of the valley, from where a path (complete with stanchion cables and a steel ladder) provides access to the lakes. You can also reach the lakes from the GR20 via a waymarked path that drops steeply from the ridgetop (see below) but most trekkers prefer not to yield their hard-won height, instead admiring the water from above.

Leading to the right from the Brêche de Capitellu the descent involves several drops down steep crevices and over smooth slabs and boulders. It starts with a memorable névé crossing which, with the peaks of the watershed silhouetted to the south, provides one of the GR's more striking photo opportunities.

After a convoluted traverse, you arrive around 30 minutes later at the ridge. Its first landmark is a second **brêche**, flanked by a pair of pinnacles, from where yellow waymarks plunge steeply down to Lavu di Capitellu. The GR20, however, continues south-west, winding repeatedly to the sides of the ridgeline as it approaches **Bocca a Soglia** (2052m). Here another yellow-waymarked route, indicated by a sign, drops to the left; this one leads down to Lavu di Melu, offering a quick route off the mountain to Corte via the Restonica Valley.

Bocca a Soglia marks the point at which the GR20 bends decisively north-east to get stuck into another long, rocky traverse. At 1960m, however, it cuts suddenly into the line of the mountain and starts a short but stiff ascent through boulders and patches of alder scrub to **Bocca Rinosa** (2170m). Beyond here a spectacular moraine, crossed at a more gentle gradient, affords great views of the Lacs de Rinoso below and back along the range to Monte Cinto and Paglia Orba in the distance.

The best views come at **Bocca Muzzella** (2206m), where an impressive panorama to the south is revealed. Once across the pass, you start the hour-long descent to Petra Piana. Beginning with an easy traverse across compacted scree and boulders, the route steepens considerably once the waymarks switch left to cross a southerly spur of Punta Muzzella. From there on, you'll have the refuge firmly in your sights as you crisscross downhill through a messy mixture of granite boulders and alder scrub.

Refuge de Petra Piana

The Refuge de Petra Piana occupies a prime spot at the foot of Monte Rotondo, whose rugged south face forms an appropriately impressive backdrop after a memorable day spent clambering around the ridges. The hut, which accommodates up to 27 trekkers, is small but cosy with a rear terrace affording sublime views of Monte d'Oro across the valley and beyond towards the east coast. Close to the nexus of some of the island's key dividing ridges, it lies within comfortable walking distance of valleys that would be hours apart by car. This explains why the refuge becomes a de facto stray dogs' home in the summer: when they're not needed for hunting, the hounds tag along with trekkers for walkabouts that can take them into entirely different regions of the island. Somehow, a disproportionate number end up at Petra Piana.

Monte Rotondo [Map 13, p151]

The ascent of Monte Rotondo (2622m), Corsica's second highest mountain, is arguably the most dramatic day trek on the island. Starting out from the Refuge de Petra Piana, the route is considerably shorter and easier than the equivalent climb from Asco up its big sister, Monte Cinto (see p130-1). With a 6am departure you can be on the summit by 8.30am, well before the convection cloud blisters up and obscures the wonderful views. Well-equipped trekkers might consider making the climb towards the end of the day and bivouacking on top at the Helbronner shelter, to be there for sunrise.

Don't attempt this route in wet or misty weather. Most of it crosses exposed, rocky terrain that can be treacherous in bad conditions. Note, too, that there are three or four different cairned routes to the top. The one outlined below is the most straightforward. If you decide to go for it, consider leaving your name with the gardiens at Petra Piana as a precaution (in which case don't forget to let them know you've descended safely).

Marked at regular intervals by **cairns** (not paint waymarks), the standard approach follows the stream flowing past Refuge de Petra Piana north-east up a steep and rocky slope. Once past a small grassy hollow you ascend in a series of zigzags along the line of a rounded ridge to a little gap, the **Brêche de Picuraghja**. Beyond this, the south face of Rotondo is fully revealed, along with ice-encrusted **Lavu Bellebone** which often remains partly frozen until well into the summer. Dropping to skirt the south-east shore of the lake, the route then begins a steep traverse of the rugged scree- and boulder-covered cirque below the summit. It reaches the ridgetop at a prominent rock pinnacle marked on IGN maps as the **Col du Fer de Lance** and from there climbs steeply across large slabs and boulders to the top, which you should reach in around 2½ hours. The final little section, from the **Helbronner shelter** (a rough wood and tin shack left open year round) to the crow's nest summit, involves a bit of exposed scrambling.

From the top you can see all of Corsica's highest peaks, from Alcudina in the south to Monte Cinto in the north, as well as the Golfe de Ajaccio. Many Corsican mountaineers regard this as the island's ultimate viewpoint.

Allow around 1½ hours for the descent by the same route if you're aiming to pick up the GR again. Alternatively you could climb down the north flank of the mountain into the **Restonica Valley**. This is a considerably longer descent which drops steeply into a gloomy *couloir* just below the summit and then wriggles over a rough moraine to the exquisite **Lavu del'Oriente**. From there it more or less follows the course of the main stream northwards before switching to a north-east-running spur, which the path zigzags down to the Bergeries de Timozzo. Beyond this a long descent through pine forest (the latter part along a piste) brings you out on the Corte road. Well cairned as far as the lake, and thereafter waymarked in red and yellow, this northern descent takes around three hours.

The best way to savour the area's geography is to climb **Monte Rotondo** (see the box above). Considering Petra Piana is effectively halfway up surprisingly few GR20 trekkers bother, but a compelling ascent of just under 600m skirting the magnificent Lavu Bellebone, is all that separates you from one of Europe's finest viewpoints.

The one downside of Petra Piana's great location, at least for campers and bivouackers, is that it provides comparatively little **shelter**. If you're sleeping under the stars and arrive too late to get a decent pitch, hunt around on the far side of the stream running to the left of the hut, where some considerate souls have piled stone windbreaks.

A major makeover is planned for Petra Piana in the near future, but in the meantime this remains one of the GR20's more old-fashioned refuges, offering little in the way of **provisions** beyond overpriced beers and staple supplies such as pasta and biscuits, cheese and sausages.

GR20 STAGE NINE: PETRA PIANA → ONDA [MAP 14, OPPOSITE]

Overview

At Petra Piana the GR20 splits in two, offering a choice of routes to the next refuge at Onda. The conventional red-and-white waymarked one, followed by the majority of trekkers, drops south-east down the Manganello Valley to the passarelle de Tolla. There it crosses the river to follow a broad forestry piste south-west that gradually steepens as it nears the head of the Grottaccia Valley. Essentially a long forest walk passing a string of secluded bathing spots, this is the softer option and the obvious choice in poor weather or if you feel like an easy day.

The haute route, on the other hand, is a more challenging proposition following the ridges (*les crêtes*). Although much of it has been badly overgrazed, the landscape lining the path is unremittingly spectacular. With valleys falling steeply away to the sea on both sides, you get a strong sense of being at the sharp edge of the island's watershed – the essence of the GR20. There's quite a lot of scrambling – of much the same kind as on the previous day – but what sticks in the memory from this ridge route are the long, gloriously open sections.

The one thing that should deter you from choosing the latter path is bad weather. In winter this stretch becomes a full-on Alpine-style route requiring ropes and crampons; even in summer, snow patches persist until late in the year and the wind can whip over it at impressive speeds. If in doubt ask the advice of the gardiens at Petra Piana or, better still, trekkers arriving from the other direction.

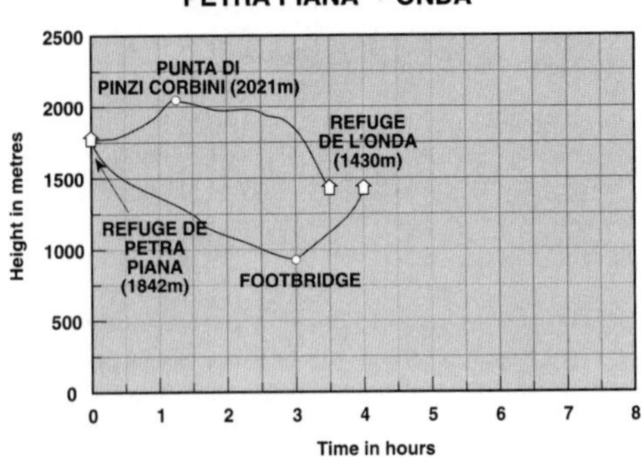

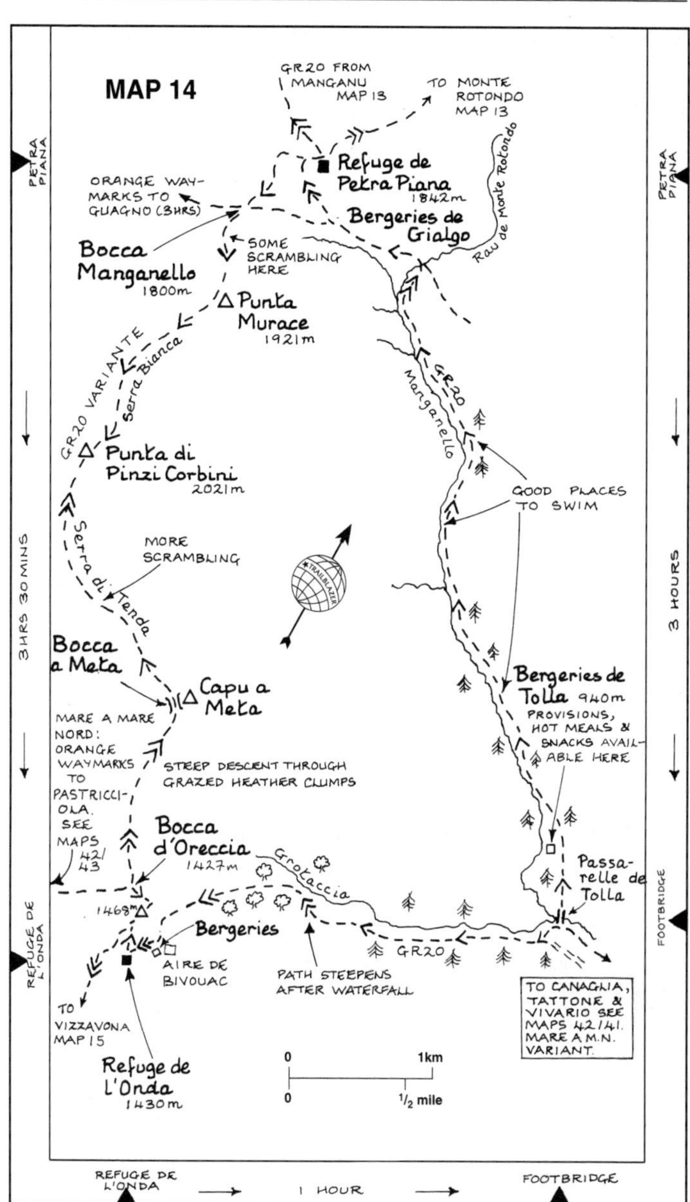
MAP 14
GR20 FROM MANGANU MAP 13
TO MONTE ROTONDO MAP 13
Refuge de Petra Piana 1842m
ORANGE WAYMARKS TO GUAGNO (3HRS)
Bergeries de Gialgo
Rau de Monte Rotondo
Bocca Manganello 1800m
SOME SCRAMBLING HERE
Punta Murace 1921m
GR20 VARIANTE
Serra Bianca
Manganello
GR20
Punta di Pinzi Corbini 2021m
GOOD PLACES TO SWIM
MORE SCRAMBLING
Serra di Tenda
Bocca a Meta
Capu a Meta
Bergeries de Tolla 940m
PROVISIONS, HOT MEALS & SNACKS AVAILABLE HERE
MARE A MARE NORD: ORANGE WAYMARKS TO PASTRICCIOLA. SEE MAPS 42/43
STEEP DESCENT THROUGH GRAZED HEATHER CLUMPS
Bocca d'Oreccia 1427m
Grotaccia
Passarelle de Tolla
1468m
Bergeries
AIRE DE BIVOUAC
GR20
PATH STEEPENS AFTER WATERFALL
TO CANAGLIA, TATTONE & VIVARIO SEE MAPS 42/41. MARE A M.N. VARIANT
TO VIZZAVONA MAP 15
Refuge de L'Onda 1430m
0 1km
0 1/2 mile
PETRA PIANA
3HRS 30 MINS
REFUGE DE L'ONDA
PETRA PIANA
3 HOURS
FOOTBRIDGE
REFUGE DE L'ONDA
1 HOUR
FOOTBRIDGE

Petra Piana → Onda: the low-level route

Running west along level ground from Petra Piana to begin with, the red-and-white waymarks drop downhill to the south-east at their bifurcation with the yellow marks of the haute route; the dividing point is indicated by a signboard. A steep descent through alder bushes brings you to the **Bergeries de Gialgo**, where you can buy ewe's cheese and top up your water bottle.

From there the path winds gently east to cross the Gialgo stream, whose true left bank it follows for a while before peeling away to the right at contour level. The descent starts again in earnest once you've forded the **Rau de Monte Rotondo**, which the route follows down to its confluence with the Manganello.

For the next 2½ hours or so a lovely old mule track winds along the approximate course of the Manganello as it crashes through a thickening forest of Laricio pine and beech. En route, a succession of tempting pools and waterfalls make perfect places to break the easy descent.

The **Bergeries de Tolla**, reached in just under three hours, sells its own delicious, freshly-made goats' cheese in addition to a better range of **provisions** than that found at Petra Piana. Hot stews, snacks and even full three-course meals are also available here, as well as bottled beers and wine.

About 10 minutes further down the hill you arrive at **la passarelle de Tolla**, the footbridge across the confluence of the Manganello and Grotaccia that marks the lowest point of the étape. A PNRC signboard on the far side indicates the route of the **Mare a Mare Nord *Variant***, veering left (east) towards Canaglia where a surfaced road winds out to Tattone and Vivario (see the box below).

The GR20, however, bends south-west here, following the Grotaccia upstream through more old-growth Laricio pine on a rough forestry piste. Having rounded a sharp bend near a large waterfall it grows considerably steeper and the pines gradually give way to gnarled beech trees. Only when you're clear of the woods, after around 1½ hours, is the refuge visible high above you at the head of the valley.

Petra Piana → Onda: the high-level *Variante*

The early part of this stage's high-level *Variante* can be traced from the Refuge de Petra Piana as the gently curving ridgeway curves south in a succession of

Liaison route to Tattone and Vivario

From the **passarelle de Tolla** it takes only 1¾ hours to trek downstream to Tattone via the hamlet of Canaglia. Waymarked with **orange** paint spots the path, which keeps to the true right bank of the river, follows the rocky route of the Mare a Mare Nord *Variant*, described (in reverse) on pp234-46; a map outlining the path between Tattone and Vivario appears on p236.

Tattone lies on the main railway line so you can hop on a train from there to Corte, Bastia or Ajaccio, or leap-frog to Vizzavona. The nearest shop, however, is at Vivario (see p234).

Liaison route to Guagno

At the **Bocca Manganello** a liaison path, marked by a signboard and orange paint spots, strikes steeply down the head of the Fiume Grossu Valley to Guagno – an easy three-hour descent with a final 4km stretch along the D23. This is a much longer exit from the GR than the one via Tolla and Canaglia and ultimately brings you out at a very remote village that is not connected to the rest of the island by public transport. Guagno does, however, have a gîte d'étape. For more on this area, see p240.

smooth-stepped summits. A pale line running along the top of the crest, the path presents a mouth-watering prospect for anyone who loves high, dry hiking, although it is far less of a straightforward yomp than it looks at this distance.

The first of the day's short scrambles begins just after the signboard showing the bifurcation of the main low route ('par la vallée') from the high one ('par les crêtes'). The yellow waymarks lead you through a jumble of granite up to the ridge, which you clamber onto for the first time just before the **Bocca Manganello**. From there an orange-waymarked liaison path drops into the Fiume Grossu Valley and, after three hours, the village of Guagno (see the box above).

More scrambling, interspersed with stretches of grassy ridge walking, takes you to just below the **Punta Murace**. From there the *Variante* runs along the aptly-named **Serra Bianca** crest to **Punta di Pinzi Corbini** (2021m), a star-shaped peak from where the views back to Petra Piana and Monte Rotondo are magnificent. A short, steep descent brings you to the **Bocca a Meta** where the waymarks drift to the east side of the ridge to avoid a sheer outcrop.

The next section involves a steep but enjoyable scramble to regain the crest of the **Serra di Tenda**. Once on the ridge, though, a more clearly-defined path takes over as the route drops 500m in a little over 1km.

The most sustained and steepest descent of the étape ends at the **Bocca d'Oreccia** (1427m), a broad, eroded saddle pass. Here the GR20 intersects the Mare a Mare Nord *Variant*, which falls steeply to the right (west) from the pass towards Pastricciola (see pp238-40). The yellow marks, however, climb again from the *bocca* to the top of the rise where they meet the red-and-white waymarks of the main GR20. Turn left here for Onda, or carry straight on to begin the long ascent up the north side of Monte d'Oro if you're continuing to Vizzavona.

Refuge de l'Onda

Perched at the head of the Grotaccia Valley, only metres below the line of the watershed, Refuge de l'Onda looks across the richly forested country above Vivario and Venaco to distant Monte Cardo, whose pale-grey humpbacked bulk dominates the north-east horizon. Above it the crags of Monte d'Oro surge sheer from the treeline, splashed with névés until well into the summer. The location is memorable enough, but the hut itself, which only has 14 beds, is decidedly poky. Most trekkers end up camping or bivouacking in the fenced (pig-proof) enclosure below it, where a rushing spring and *bloc sanitaire* (open mid-June–mid-Sept) are the only amenities. Overlooking the *aire de bivouac*, the **Bergeries de l'Onda** sells a good range of **supplies** including cheese, charcuterie, fresh fruit, bread and wine at the usual inflated prices.

Onda is not somewhere you'd relish spending much time. However, the next étape to Vizzavona is tougher than it might seem. To double up and leapfrog Onda you should reach here as early in the day as possible and, in hot weather, wait until the heat subsides before beginning the long initial climb to the Crête de Muratello. The refuge has a small kitchen where you can cook up lunch and there are plenty of shady spots around it for a restorative snooze.

GR20 STAGE TEN: ONDA → VIZZAVONA [MAP 15, OPPOSITE]

Overview

After the twists and turns of the previous étape, stage ten of the GR20 seems straightforward enough: a stiff ridge climb up to a pass, followed by a long descent down the valley on the other side. A close look at the map, however, reveals that the altitude changes involved are considerable. The 670m ascent from Onda to the Crête de Muratello might not be too intimidating by the standards of this route but the descent – at 1100m the longest on the whole GR20 – is a real knee-cruncher, especially if you've doubled up stages from Petra Piana.

For those with plenty more walking left in them when they reach the ridge, a superb high-level *Variante* beckons to the east. Routing you over the summit of Monte d'Oro, Corsica's fifth highest peak, it climbs to nearly 2400m before plunging down the forested flank of the mountain to Vizzavona. To get its most rugged, challenging sections behind you early in the day before the cloud forms, however, you have to start out from Onda rather than Petra Piana.

Whichever way you choose, be sure to take enough **water** as there are no springs along either route.

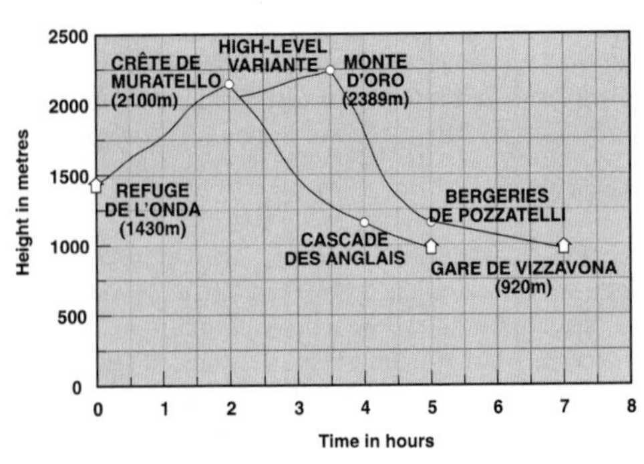

Route guide

The stage begins with a climb to ridge level, from where the path south towards the Crête de Muratello stretches steeply up the mountain above you.

Although relentlessly steep and rocky in places, the 2½ hour ascent is an enjoyable one, with superb views of Monte d'Oro, as

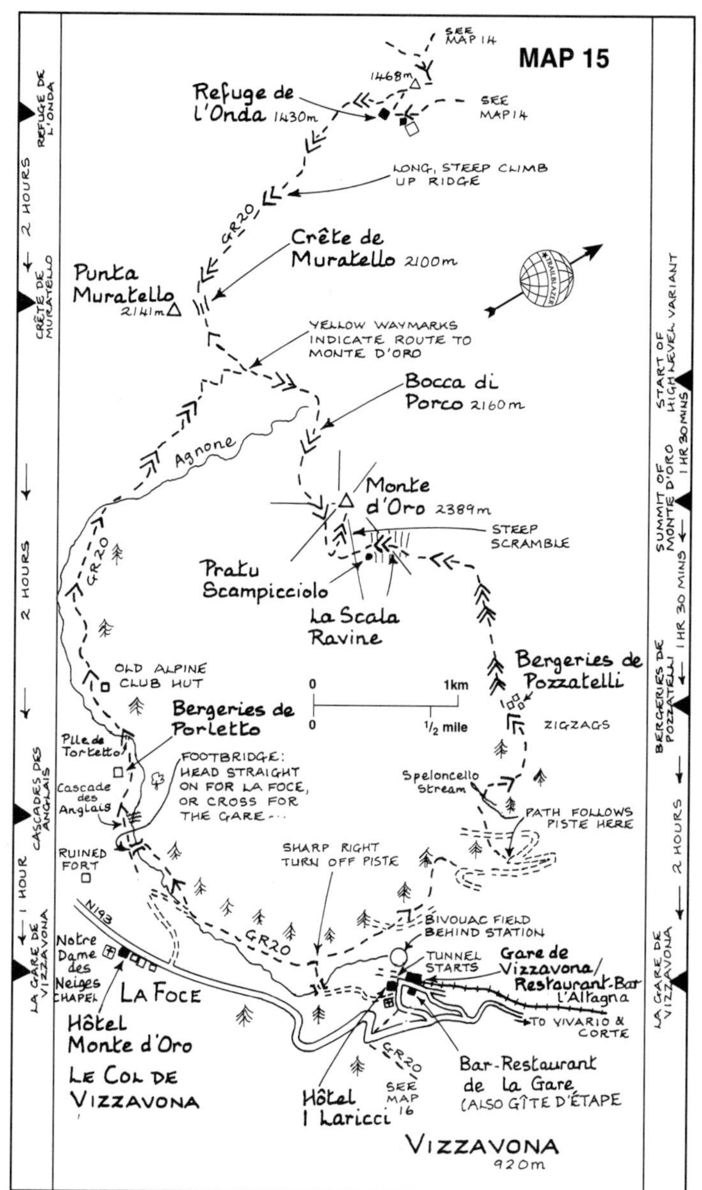
MAP 15
SEE MAP 14
1468m
Refuge de l'Onda 1430m
SEE MAP 14
LONG, STEEP CLIMB UP RIDGE
GR20
Crête de Muratello 2100m
Punta Muratello 2141m
YELLOW WAYMARKS INDICATE ROUTE TO MONTE D'ORO
Bocca di Porco 2160m
Agnone
Monte d'Oro 2389m
STEEP SCRAMBLE
Pratu Scampicciolo
La Scala Ravine
Bergeries de Pozzatelli
OLD ALPINE CLUB HUT
0 1km
0 1/2 mile
Bergeries de Porletto
ZIGZAGS
Pile de Tortetto
Cascade des Anglais
FOOTBRIDGE: HEAD STRAIGHT ON FOR LA FOCE, OR CROSS FOR THE GARE...
Speloncello Stream
PATH FOLLOWS PISTE HERE
RUINED FORT
SHARP RIGHT TURN OFF PISTE
N193
BIVOUAC FIELD BEHIND STATION
Notre Dame des Neiges CHAPEL
TUNNEL STARTS
Gare de Vizzavona/ Restaurant-Bar L'Altagna
LA FOCE
TO VIVARIO & CORTE
Hôtel Monte d'Oro
LE COL DE VIZZAVONA
Bar-Restaurant de la Gare (ALSO GÎTE D'ÉTAPE
Hôtel I Laricci
SEE MAP 16
VIZZAVONA 920m
REFUGE DE L'ONDA
2 HOURS
CRÊTE DE MURATELLO
2 HOURS
CASCADES DES ANGLAIS
1 HOUR
LA GARE DE VIZZAVONA
START OF HIGH LEVEL VARIANT
SUMMIT OF MONTE D'ORO 1 HR 30 MINS
1 HR 30 MINS
BERGERIES DE POZZATELLI
2 HOURS
LA GARE DE VIZZAVONA

Monte d'Oro High-level *Variante* [Map 15, p159]

Scaling Monte d'Oro, this high-level *Variante* presents a challenging alternative to the long and somewhat monotonous descent of the Vallée de l'Agnone. The massif, a huge pyramid of blue-grey granite whose crags tower above the railway line at Vizzavona, is among the island's most distinctive peaks. Climbing it offers a memorable culmination to the GR20 if you're quitting at Vizzavona. From the Crête de Muratello, only 300m and a bit of tricky scrambling separate you from the summit. The descent to Vizzavona, however, involves a hefty drop of 1469m – longer even than the descent from the top of Monte Cinto to Asco.

Note that the **exposed position** of this peak means that it's particularly vulnerable to sudden changes in weather, so carefully assess the likelihood of a storm before you set off.

The first part of the *Variante* follows the red-and-white waymarked route from Onda up to the Crête de Muratello and down the other side across the head of the Vallée de l'Agnone to the point where the **yellow waymarks** begin. These, along with a chain of cairns that are fairly regular but peter out in places, indicate the route to the summit, which completes the traverse of the valley head to scale the western spur of Monte d'Oro at **Bocca di Porco** (2160m), where you turn right. Apart from the occasional foray into the boulders below it, the waymarks keep more or less to the ridge. The final approach to the summit involves a scramble up the north (left) side of a gully on a bouldery incline. Allow 1½ hours for the whole ascent from the Crête de Muratello.

The **descent** initially doubles back the way you came, across the boulder field to a point where the waymarks run off to the left. Having crossed a little grassy plateau on the east flank of the mountain known as **Pratu Scampicciolo**, it penetrates the gloomy ravine of **La Scala** where you'll almost certainly have to contend with a large névé. Once clear of the gully and past a distinctive rock pinnacle dubbed, for obvious reasons, '**La Cafetière**', the route swings left to begin a steady, crisscrossing descent down the line of a stream over rough and rocky ground to the trees.

You should reach the ruined **Bergeries de Pozzatelli** around 90 minutes from the summit. Beyond there the path plunges into the forest proper, rounding the mountainside to reach the Speloncello stream. You cross a **piste** – part of a huge motorable track known as **La Grande Corniche** – shortly afterwards, and later join and follow the piste downhill for around 500m. A diagonal traverse through mature Laricio pine forest then takes you south across two of the Vecchio's main tributaries (via footbridges) to river level, where the yellow waymarks meet the red-and-white ones of the GR20 for the final half kilometre up to the gare de Vizzavona.

well as Monte Rotondo and the pale line of the GR20 winding across the ridges to the north.

From the **Crête de Muratello** (2100m), the red-and-white waymarks run down to the left (east), traversing the rocky head of the Vallée de l'Agnone. At the point where the yellow markers of the high-level *Variante* peel off to the left the main route cuts more steeply downhill. The next couple of hours or so take you across a mixture of steeply inclined slabs, boulders, streams and alder scrub. Later, patches of deciduous woodland create welcome shade as you approach the first real landmark of the descent, the **ruined refuge** of the Club Alpin Français, which stands close to an attractive waterfall. Beyond it the **passarelle de Tortetto**, where the path switches to the right bank of the Agnone, leads down to the **Bergeries de Porletto** and, once you've descended through a leafy beech wood, the famous **Cascades des Anglais**. These falls, where the Agnone crashes through a series of beautiful turquoise pools, have been a major tourist attraction since the nineteenth century and people continue to flock here from the nearby main road for picnics in the summer.

A short way below the cascades, after scrambling through a steep and rocky section deep in the woods, the GR20 reaches a second **footbridge** which you should cross for Vizzavona. Anyone intending to spend the night in Hôtel Monte d'Oro (see pp163-4) should head straight on here and follow the path until it meets a piste, where a right turn will bring you out after 10 to 15-minutes' level walking at the hamlet of La Foce (see Map 15, p159).

From the far (north) side of the footbridge the final section of the étape passes through some impressive old Laricio pine forest. Having followed a motorable piste for half a kilometre, you turn right onto a footpath, cross the Agnone for the last time and wind uphill to the **gare de Vizzavona**, reached a little over three hours after crossing the Crête de Muratello.

VIZZAVONA

Vizzavona is a scattering of hotels and tin-roofed forestry buildings littered around the col that divides Monte d'Oro and Punta dell'Oriente, where the main Ajaccio–Corte–Bastia artery crosses the Corsican watershed. Although long an important staging post on the journey across the mountains, the settlement only became a visitor attraction in its own right after the construction of the railway line at the end of the nineteenth century. A significant proportion of the first tourists to venture up here from the coast were wealthy English aristocrats (among them Edward Lear) for whom Vizzavona became something of a low-key hill station renowned for its salubrious cool air and invigorating forest walks (the most famous of them to the falls that would become known as the 'Cascades des Anglais'). A handful of elegant Edwardian hotels sprang up to cater for this influx; one of them, the Monte d'Oro, still survives, its fin-de-siècle atmosphere lovingly preserved.

For most trekkers, however, Vizzavona means the little clearing in the forest around the railway station, 700m below the *route nationale*. As the de facto midway point of the GR20, the station (famous in Corsica as the place where one of island's most notorious bandits, Antoine Bellacoscia, gave himself up to police in 1892) is a major landmark of the route. Lots of people leave or join it here by train, while those aiming to complete all 16 stages often celebrate getting this far with a cooked meal and few drinks at one of the terrace cafés outside the station.

If you're trekking on a tight budget the Gare de Vizzavona may leave a less than positive impression. Apart from the inevitable inflated prices (particularly galling given the convenient rail connection), the main gripe is the absence of refuge facilities, or even a bloc sanitaire, near the station. This forces many trekkers to camp or bivouac in a clearing across the rail tracks that lacks running water or toilets; in high season the resultant mess and congestion can be horrendous. The situation is compounded by the palpable reluctance of businesses at the station to allow walkers to use their toilets, or water sources. The politest solution if you're bent on staying here is, of course, to spend money as and where you're expected to. Alternatively, peel off the GR20 at the bridge over the Agnone and head up to the hamlet of La Foce, near the Col de Vizzavona, where the atmospheric Hôtel Monte d'Oro offers alternative accommodation, including a gîte d'étape (see pp163-4).

Orientation and services

Four **trains** per day pass through Vizzavona in both directions on the line between Bastia, Corte and Ajaccio, two of them connecting with services to Calvi. The next stop heading north down the valley is Tattone, site of the nearest **campsite** (see p235) in the area. The one after that is Vivario, the jumping-off place for the Mare a Mare Nord *Variant*, described on pp234-46. Trekkers arriving early in the day sometimes get on the train to Vivario to stock up with supplies at the village's excellent shop, or to call at the **post office**, the only one within easy reach of Vizzavona. To change money or get to an ATM cashpoint, however, you'd have to continue on to Corte (see pp230-4), an hour's ride to the north.

Where to stay and eat

A good range of food supplies and essential bits and bobs such as stove fuel, gas canisters, batteries, sticking plasters, blister pads and film (in short, the best selection of provisions on the GR20 between Calenzana and Conca) can be bought at Vizzavona's little **shop**, the Épicerie Rosy (open daily 7.30am–8pm) next to the station. It's run by the stationmaster and his wife, who also own the pleasant ***Restaurant-Bar l'Altagna*** next door, where you can order draught beer or a filling set-menu Corsican meal (12€ and

U Trinighellu

Even though few of them regularly use it, Corsicans love their narrow-gauge train line. When the government announced in 1972 that the coastal section between Ponte-Leccia and Calvi was to close, a massive public outcry blocked the plan. Bolstered by generous public funding and capacity tourist traffic in the summer, Le Chemin de Fer de la Corse (CFC) claims to transport nearly 800,000 passengers annually, many of them trekkers who use the line as a route to and from the heart of the island's mountains at Vizzavona.

Construction work began in 1855 but it wasn't until nearly 40 years later that Bastia, Ajaccio and Calvi were finally connected by rail. In all 230km of track were laid, requiring a total of 32 tunnels. The longest, the 3916m Tunnel de Vizzavona through the watershed, took seven years to hollow out with pick-axes and, until the completion of the Mont Blanc tunnel, was the longest in Europe. The line also crosses 75 viaducts, including the 30m-high Pont de Vecchio at Vivario, engineered by no less than Gustav Eiffel (of Eiffel tower fame).

Catching the *trinighellu* – or '*micheline*' as Corsica's pint-sized locomotives are known in French – can be a memorable if somewhat bone-shaking experience. The 1950s rolling stock and old diesel engines were recently replaced but the narrow-gauge track and typically Corsican speed at which the trains travel ensure a bouncy ride (whence the trinighellu's other, somewhat less felicitous nickname, the 'TGV' – Train de Grande Vibration).

The most scenic sections are between the Vizzavona tunnel and Corte, from where you get great views of Monte d'Oro and Monte Cardo, and the coastal stretch through the Balagne, which emerges from an olive-speckled hinterland to skirt one of the Mediterranean's most beautiful shorelines.

16€), served outdoors on a lively little terrace.

Far less appealing is ***Bar-Restaurant de la Gare*** (☎/🖹 04.95.47.22.20; open June–mid-Sept), directly opposite, whose meals, mostly dished up as part of their gîte's half-board deal, are poor value. Recently handed on to the younger generation of the family, this place has since gone decidedly downhill. The cramped six-bed dormitories and limited shower-toilet facilities of their gîte d'étape (28€ for obligatory half-board) also represent a worse deal than that offered by ***Hôtel I Laricci*** (☎ 04.95.47.21.12; open May–Oct), just up the lane from the station. Priced at 28€ per bed for (obligatory) half-board, dorms in this attractive period building, which has Alpine-style high-pitched roofs and a timber-lined interior, are much cleaner and airier, and there's the added attraction of a comfy lounge and garden to laze in. You can also check into more comfortable double rooms here for 56.80€ per head half-board (plus an extra 7€ for en suite). The I Laricci's one failing is its food, which is little better than that served at Bar-Restaurant de la Gare.

If you're happy to be away from the train line a far better choice, whatever your budget, is ***Hôtel Monte d'Oro*** (☎ 04 95.47.21.06, 🖹 04.95.47.22.05, 💻 www.sitec.fr/monte.oro), 3km south-west along the route nationale towards the col. Dating from the late-nineteenth century, when it was built to accommodate engineers working on the Vizzavona tunnel, the hotel epitomizes the genteel pre-war era when this area was popular with English aristos and a rich Parisian jet-set. Sepia photos of the building in its heyday, original hand-turned furniture and the pervasive scent of old-fashioned beeswax polish set the tone. The rooms are spacious and most enjoy fine views of the forest. You also get the run of the lovely conservatory and terrace looking across the valley to the mountain. Rates are 42–62.30€ in low season (April–May and

The roving stones

The proprietors of Hôtel Monte d'Oro at Col de Vizzavona love to regale guests with a family yarn dating from WWII, when the building was requisitioned by the occupying Italians. Much to the consternation of the *patronne*, Mme Plaisant, some of the soldiers stabled their mules in the tiny chapel behind the hotel, dedicated to Our Lady of the Snows. 'War is war' was the only explanation offered by the Italians for this act of sacrilege.

However, luckily for Our Lady and Mme Plaisant and for all those travellers whose safe passage across the notoriously weather-prone pass depended on both women's goodwill, help was at hand in the form of the High Chaplain of the occupying army. When he found out from the disgruntled patronne how his troops had accommodated their animals, he made them stand to attention in front of the wooden chapel and ordered that it be 'purified by fire' and then rebuilt by the offenders. Stones were transferred for the purpose from the ruins of a nearby French fort (remnants of which still stand at the col) and the new shrine to Notre Dame des Neiges was consecrated on Ascension Day, August 15, of that year. It still stands next to the road, beside the Hôtel Monte d'Oro.

The locals see in this chain of events the settling of even older scores by the stones themselves. Village lore holds that the seventeenth-century French fort was erected using material pillaged from an earlier chapel dedicated to Saint Peter. Thus Vizzavona's protective deities deviously outwitted their occupier foes by means of the island's granite – an interpretation that has an unmistakably Corsican ring to it.

mid-Sept–Oct) and 45.60–70€ from June to mid-September – very reasonable considering the location and atmosphere.

Hôtel Monte d'Oro has a small annexe offering basic but adequate gîte d'étape accommodation in three- or four-person dorms (13.70€ per bed, or 30€ for half-board) with a small kitchen for self-caterers. If you're staying in the refuge, where the dorms sleep only two people each (9.10€ per bed; no half-board), you can also use the kitchen but you'll need your own sleeping bags. All things considered, this is a more attractive budget option than the equivalent places near the station and you don't even have to walk here; phone from the station and they'll come and pick you up. The rates also include free transfer to the trailhead the following day after breakfast.

GR20 STAGE ELEVEN: VIZZAVONA → E'CAPANNELLE

[MAP 16, OPPOSITE]

Overview

A relatively undemanding stage gets the southern portion of the GR20 underway. From Vizzavona, the lowest point on the whole route, the inevitable ascent at the start of the étape follows old mule and foresters' tracks through deep, shady woodland. Easy gradients and springy, pine-needly paths make for a pleasant climb to the pass, Bocca Palmenti. From there an even gentler sentier contours around the west flank of the Fium' Orbu Valley and after a final short ascent reaches the ski station of E'Capannelle.

For once, water is plentiful throughout. From Vizzavona you'll only need enough to get you to the pass, just below which a gushing spring provides a perfect fill-up point. After that there is a string of bergeries and streams.

Anyone wishing to gain time and not intending to follow the high-level *Variante* over Monte Renoso from E'Capanelle might consider doubling up this stage and pressing on to Bocca di Verdi (Col de Verde) or Prati. Either would make for a long day but would also present a far less arduous option than combining the next two étapes between E'Capannelle and Usciolu.

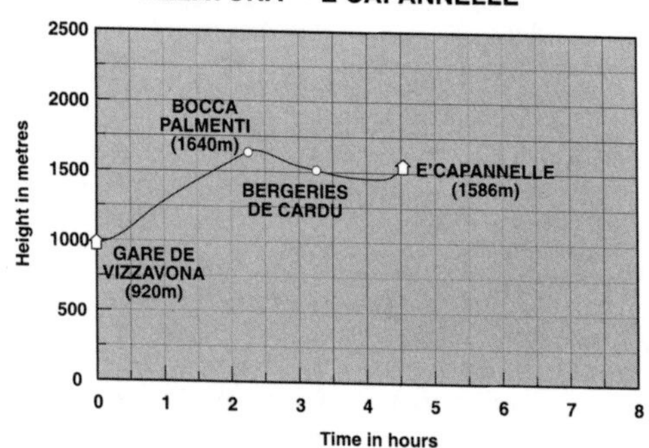

Route guide

From the Gare de Vizzavona the red-and-white waymarks lead you past Hôtel I Laricci and the roadside oratory of Notre Dame de la Forêt to cross a small bridge. Shortly after this they plunge to the right into the forest, emerging

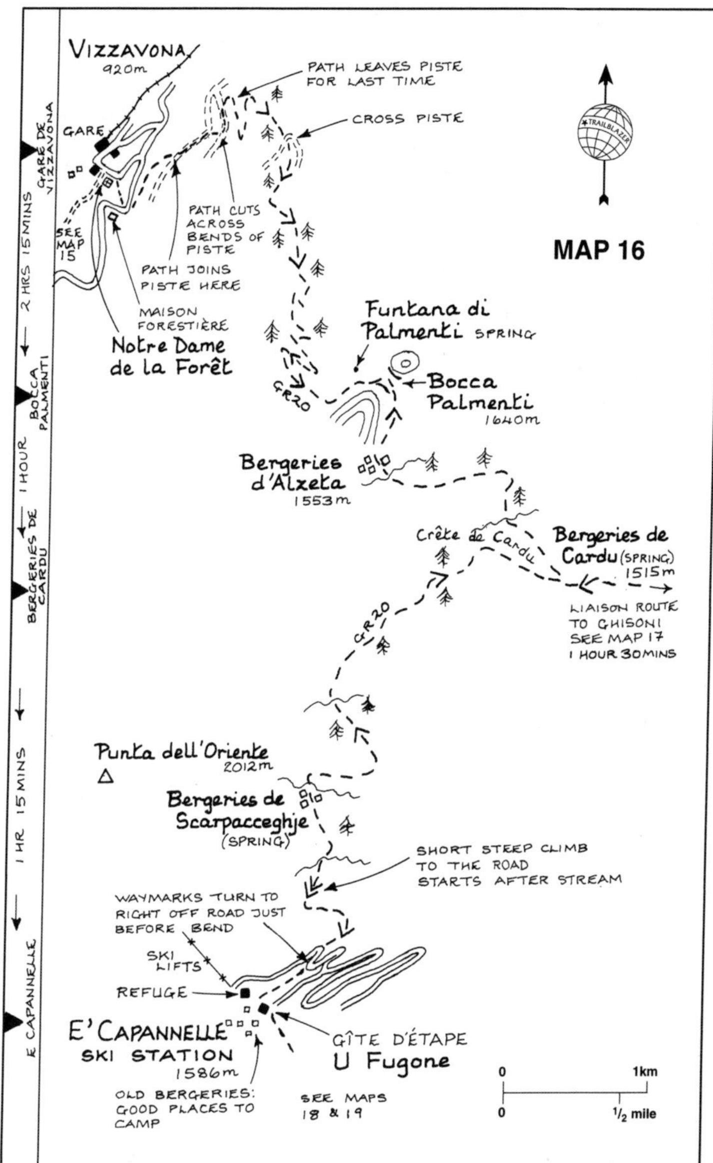

VIZZAVONA
920m
GARE
SEE MAP 15
PATH LEAVES PISTE FOR LAST TIME
CROSS PISTE
PATH CUTS ACROSS BENDS OF PISTE
PATH JOINS PISTE HERE
MAISON FORESTIÈRE
Notre Dame de la Forêt
MAP 16
Funtana di Palmenti SPRING
Bocca Palmenti
1640m
GR20
Bergeries d'Alzeta
1553m
Crête de Cardu
Bergeries de Cardu (SPRING)
1515m
LIAISON ROUTE TO GHISONI SEE MAP 17 1 HOUR 30MINS
Punta dell'Oriente
2012m
Bergeries de Scarpacceghje (SPRING)
SHORT STEEP CLIMB TO THE ROAD STARTS AFTER STREAM
WAYMARKS TURN TO RIGHT OFF ROAD JUST BEFORE BEND
SKI LIFTS
REFUGE
GÎTE D'ÉTAPE
U Fugone
E'CAPANNELLE SKI STATION
1586m
OLD BERGERIES: GOOD PLACES TO CAMP
SEE MAPS 18 & 19
0 1km
0 1/2 mile
GARE DE VIZZAVONA
2 HRS 15 MINS
BOCCA PALMENTI
1 HOUR
BERGERIES DE CARDU
1 HR 15 MINS
E'CAPANNELLE

after 10 minutes at a sharp bend on the route nationale. A piste on the opposite side of the road, to the left of the ONF **Maison Forestière**, takes you north-east on a traversing ascent to a sequence of steeper zigzags that criss-cross up a spur and then veer south. Another series of zigzags at the head of the valley keep the trail on a fairly gentle incline despite the steepening hillside. By the time the Laricio pines thin out only a short climb across scrubby, over-grazed ground remains before the pass, although anyone who started out late from Vizzavona may find the final shadeless stretch hot going. Thankfully, the perennial **Funtana di Palmenti**, just off the left side of the path, spews deliciously cold water throughout the summer: a perfect spot from which to admire the impressive views of Monte d'Oro and Monte Rotondo to the south.

Bocca Palmenti, a broad, flat saddle, heavily denuded by flocks from the nearby bergeries, yields the first views of the Fium' Orbu Valley, which runs down to the east coast. Beyond the pass, the GR20 swings south into a gently descending traverse to the **Bergeries d'Alzeta** (1553m), where it crosses the Alzitone stream. The next landmark is the distinctive **Crête de Cardu** (1515m), where you get your first good view of Monte Renoso and the high ridges running south.

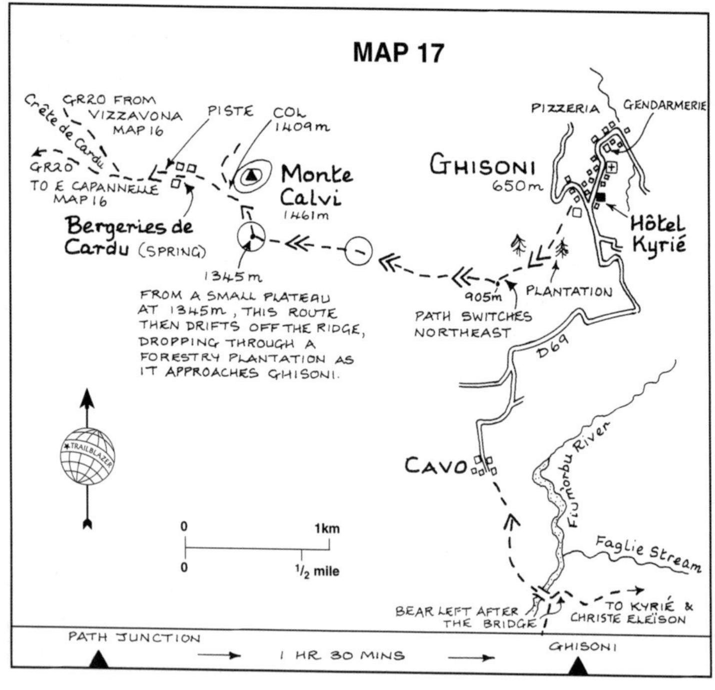

Liaison route to Ghisoni via the Bergeries de Cardu [Map 17 opp] At the ridge clearing on the Crête de Cardu, a PNRC signboard indicates the yellow-waymarked liaison route east down the crest to Ghisoni. Other than a small *épicerie* and hotel, the village holds little to detain trekkers; most people who stay here do so in order to complete the circular walk over Monte Renoso (described on pp170-2) without having to endure the relative discomforts of the station de ski at E'Capannelle.

Five minutes down the trail, the first landmark you come to is the **Bergeries de Cardu**, a cluster of shepherds' huts opposite conical Monte Calvi (1461m), which has a dependable **spring** and fine views down the Fium' Orbu Valley to the coast. Keeping to the ridge at the edge of the treeline you then drop down to a small saddle col, where the path divides, with the yellow waymarks leading to the right (east-south-east) around the side of Monte Cardo. At 1345m, this route then drifts off the ridge, crossing a small plateau and forestry plantation as it drops more steeply down to Ghisoni. The village centre lies five minutes' walk north of where the path meets the road. Allow around one-and-a-half hours for this descent (and two-and-a-half hours climbing in the other direction to rejoin the GR20).

Ghisoni Set against a grandiose backdrop of needle escarpments and Laricio pine woods, Ghisoni, the largest village in the upper Fium'Orbu, looks towards the east coast from its vantage point at a bend in the bottom of the valley. Dependent on pig rearing and forestry, it's an archetypal Corsican hill settlement: severely depopulated and with a floundering economy. Hope of a renaissance came in the 1980s with the creation of the ski station at nearby E'Capannelle but the expected winter tourist trade never materialized.

These days the few visitors that come here tend to be walkers who use Ghisoni's self-assuredly old-fashioned ***Hôtel Kyrié*** (☎ 04.95.57.60.33, 🖷 04.95.57.63.15; open April–mid-Oct) as a base for forays into the surrounding massifs. Situated on the main street near the centre of the village, this place has around 30 impeccably clean, en suite rooms, the best of them at the rear of the building.

In addition to the Kyrié's ***restaurant*** (open to non-residents) Ghisoni has a pleasant and much cheaper ***pizzeria*** at the bottom of the village out towards the *gendarmerie,* where you can tuck into copious wood-fired pizzas (5.30–10€) or plates of local charcuterie (11.40€) on a terrace overlooking the river.

Close to the church, **Libre-Service Micheli** (open year-round Mon–Sat 9am–noon and 4.30–6.45pm) is the best place for miles to stock up with supplies, though since the refuge at Bocca di Verdi (Col de Verde) opened few GR20 trekkers make the long detour just to shop here.

Ghisoni is not on a bus route. Other than hitching, the only way in or out is to phone **taxi** driver Michel Salviani (☎ 04.95.46.04.88, or mobile ☎ 06.03.49.15.24), who charges around 80€ one-way to Vizzavona.

Kyrié and Christe Eleïson Kyrié and Christe Eleïson, the magnificent granite escarpments that dominate Ghisoni to the south-east on the opposite side of the Fium'Orbu Valley, are inextricably associated with the **Giovannali** sect, an heretic splinter group of the Franciscans who were persecuted in the fourteenth century by Pope Urban V. Accused of conducting orgies in their churches, members of the sect were hunted down by emissaries from Avignon and killed at their strongholds across the island in 1362. *(cont'd overleaf)*

❑ **Liaison route to Ghisoni via the Bergeries de Cardu (cont'd)**
(cont'd from p167) The most famous of these massacres took place at **Carbini** in the Alta Rocca region, but a large group of Giovannalis were also burned to death in a giant pyre on the banks of the river below Ghisoni. It is said, however, that the villagers took pity on the heretics and persuaded their priest to administer last rites before the fire was lit. As the flames rose, the onlookers drowned the cries of the dying by intoning verses of the prayer *Kyrié eleïson, Christe eleïson*, which reverberated through the crags on the far side of the river. For more on the Giovannali sect, see the box on p292.

These days Kyrié (1535m) and Christe (1260m) Eleïson are more renowned for the Grade IV–V+ climbing routes offered by the numerous rock pillars and gullies that riddle their north-west faces than for their historic associations. You can also approach the summit of the former on a non-technical route that starts at the hamlet of **Cavo** (follow the D69 from Ghisoni for 2km until you see a signpost pointing left down a side turning). From there a path drops downhill to cross the Fium'Orbu. Once on the far side of the bridge do not follow the main path right (south); instead, turn left through the dense maquis above the Faglie stream, north-west of which a prominent gully rises to a notch in the summit ridge. Allow two hours for this ascent from Cavo.

The GR20, meanwhile, turns west-north-west here to begin a long, sweeping traverse of Punta Dell' Oriente's lower eastern flanks. Passing through a series of minor stream hollows and scrub-filled breaks in the forest, you round a succession of smooth spurs to reach the tongue-twisting **Bergeries de Scarpacceghje,** site of another spring. Fifteen minutes' walk further south the waymarks strike uphill for the first significant ascent since Bocca Palmenti, gaining 150m in just over half a kilometre.

This short, steep climb takes you over the thinly wooded Crête de Chufidu, where you briefly meet a surfaced road before dipping into the maquis for the last drop down to the ski station.

E'CAPANNELLE

The run-down winter sports complex of E'Capannelle ranks among the GR20's least inspiring locations. Its buildings may be less intrusive than those at Asco Stagnu and Castel di Verghio, but its overall aspect is blighted by clanking ski lifts and eroded hillsides hemming it in. E'Capannelle's only real plus is its bar-restaurant's rear terrace, which provides a congenial location to while away sunny afternoons over a beer and a hot meal. For trekkers whose budgets don't stretch to such luxuries the resort has little going for it, not least because of its deplorably poor refuge facilities, which might encourage anyone roughing it to press on to the comparative comforts of Bocca di Verdi (Col de Verde) or Usciolu.

Orientation and services

E'Capannelle is connected to Ghisoni by a tarmac road but no public transport runs up here, even during peak season.

To cover the 42km from Vizzavona (or 38km from Vivario), **taxis** charge upwards of 100€; call Michel Salviani (☎ 04.95.46.04.88, or mobile ☎ 06.03.49.15.24).

Dorm beds, breakfast and supper are available at ***Gîte d'étape 'U Fugone'*** (☎ 04 95.57.01.81, 🖷 04.95.56.39.34; open May–Sept), where obligatory half-board costs 25.80€. Meals are served in the lively downstairs bar.

Monte Renoso
E'Capennelle is the traditional starting point for the ascent of Monte Renoso (2352m), the highest peak in southern Corsica. You can incorporate the ascent into the GR20 by following the **high-level *Variante*** route outlined on pp170-2, which descends from the summit via the massif's famous pozzines. A less strenuous approach would be to leave your gear at the ski station and make the climb with a light daypack, returning to E'Capannelle for lunch and heading south along the main path afterwards.

The only other option is the grotty municipal **refuge**, two minutes further up the hill (to the right of the path as you approach E'Capannelle on the GR20). In order, one assumes, to funnel maximum business into the gîte, the refuge has been allowed to lapse into a dreadful state. You'd have to be desperate to sleep inside the hut, which accommodates 12 people but doesn't have running water. Nor are there washing or toilet facilities outside; instead you have to shell out 2.30€ to use the bathroom in the gîte (ask for a token at the bar).

Bivouackers and **campers** tend to pitch on the grassy patches below the old stone bergeries at E'Capannelle, or amid the trees below the refuge hut, but you have to get here fairly early in the day to be sure of nabbing some level ground.

Basic **supplies** are sold from the bar of Gîte d'étape U Fugone. In the same room you'll also find a coin-operated **telephone** that accepts incoming calls. The most convenient source of **drinking water** is the dressed spring immediately outside the gîte.

GR20 STAGE TWELVE: E'CAPANNELLE → BOCCA DI VERDI (COL DE VERDE) [MAP 18, p171; MAP 19, p173]

Overview

To reach the head of the Fium'Orbu Valley at Bocca di Verdi (or Col de Verde as it is marked on maps), where the GR20 begins its ascent to the Refuge de Prati, you've a choice of radically contrasting routes. The conventional one is an uncharacteristically monotonous plod at mostly contour level around the forested eastern base of the Monte Renoso massif; this is the path to follow if you want to notch up several étapes in one day. Alternatively, reacquaint yourself with

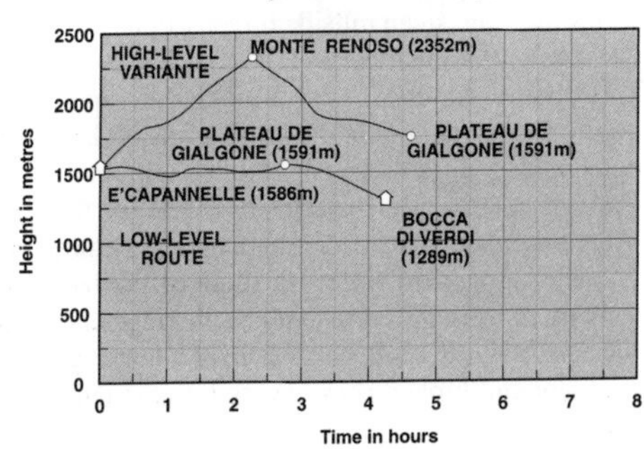

the extremes of the watershed via a more challenging ridge trek over the rocky, névé-encrusted summit of Monte Renoso itself. Following the line of the watershed, this was the route originally envisaged by Michel Fabrikant: it's wilder, tougher and altogether truer to the spirit of the GR20. It's also more vulnerable to sudden changes in weather and can get exceptionally windy. The pay-offs are some unforgettable views over the island's southern summits, from Rotondo to Alcudina, and the experience of descending into an exquisite suspended valley carpeted with lush green pozzines.

Route guide

E'Capannelle → Bocca di Verdi: the high-level *Variante*

[Map 18, opposite; Map 19, p173]

Stage twelve's high-level *Variante* represents a return to the kind of uncompromising mountain terrain you'll be familiar with if you've walked all the way from Calenzana. Cutting straight up the sharp side of Monte Renoso from E'Capannelle, the route arcs around the dividing ridge of the massif before shelving steeply down to a hanging valley on its southern side, lined with spongy pozzines. From there it veers east to rejoin the GR20 at the Plateau de Gialgone.

The only demanding section is the sheer descent from the summit ridge to the pozzines, which involves a stark drop over rugged, broken rock and alder scrub. The rest is surprisingly straightforward, following a well-worn, well-cairned route across rough but largely open ground. The views are superlative throughout.

Don't, however, attempt the high-level route in unstable conditions unless you have the compass skills to navigate in poor visibility. Exposed to strong winds off the sea, Monte Renoso sees a lot of wild weather and frequently gets misted up. If this happens, it's all too easy to wander off course and into one of the cwms that indent the east flank of the massif.

Allow around seven hours to reach Bocca di Verdi (Col de Verde) via the *Variante*, and as ever with high, exposed sections get a very early start so as to avoid the convection clouds that form in warm weather.

Zigzagging between the pylons of E'Capannelle's old chair lifts, the path scales the bare, steep hillside directly opposite gîte d'étape U Fugone, reaching the shoulder of the ridge at 1725m in just over half a kilometre. The cairns then lead you up the crest, with a rocky outcrop looming to the right, as far as a grassy depression where the route levels off briefly before tackling a more gradual, bouldery ascent. Shortly after crossing the 2000m contour line you round a rise and see **Lac de Bastiani** (2092m) for the first time, with the summit of Monte Renoso, which rises dramatically behind, reflected in its water.

The cairns skirt the north shore of the lake and begin a steeply ascending traverse of its rocky cwm to reach the ridge at roughly 2050m. From there a distinct path winds southwards across a huge, gently shelving crest strewn with boulders and broken rock, swinging gradually to the left as it approaches the summit.

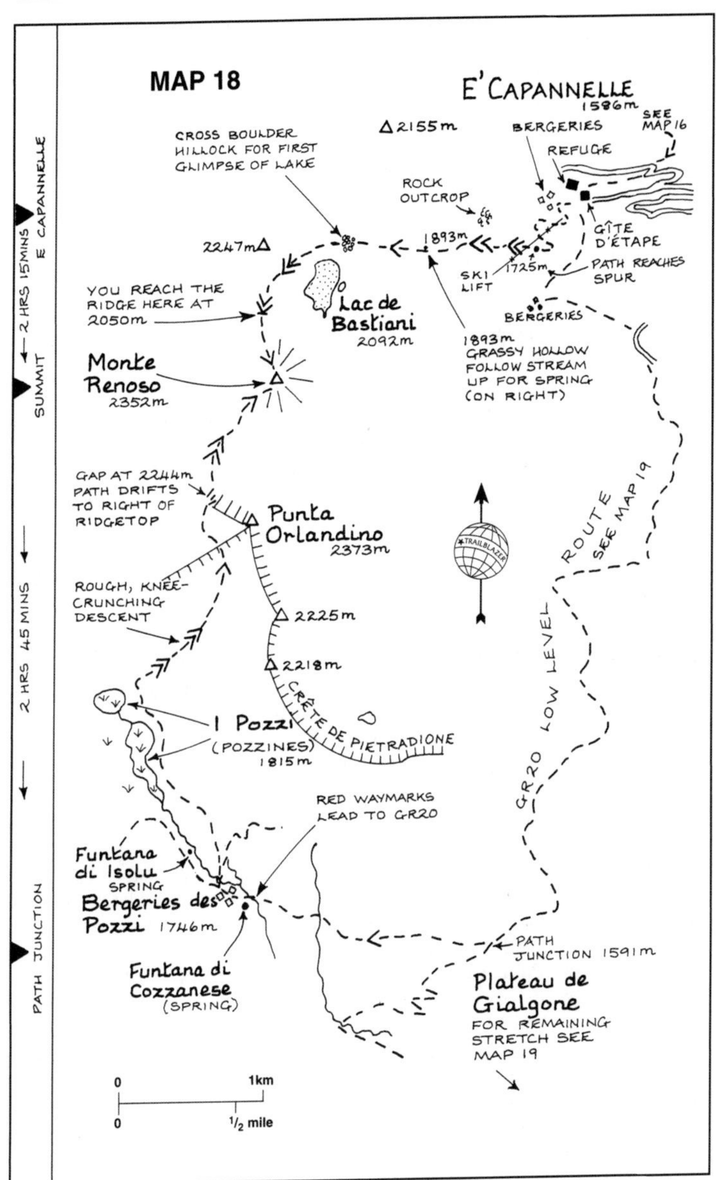
MAP 18
E'CAPANNELLE
1586m
SEE MAP 16
Δ2155m
BERGERIES
REFUGE
CROSS BOULDER HILLOCK FOR FIRST GLIMPSE OF LAKE
ROCK OUTCROP
GÎTE D'ÉTAPE
2247mΔ
1893m
1725m
SKI LIFT
PATH REACHES SPUR
YOU REACH THE RIDGE HERE AT 2050m
Lac de Bastiani
2092m
BERGERIES
1893m GRASSY HOLLOW FOLLOW STREAM UP FOR SPRING (ON RIGHT)
Monte Renoso
2352m
GAP AT 2244m PATH DRIFTS TO RIGHT OF RIDGETOP
Punta Orlandino
2373m
TRAILBLAZER
ROUTE SEE MAP 19
ROUGH, KNEE-CRUNCHING DESCENT
Δ2225m
Δ2218m
GR20 LOW LEVEL
CRÊTE DE PIETRADIONE
I Pozzi
(POZZINES)
1815m
RED WAYMARKS LEAD TO GR20
Funtana di Isolu
SPRING
Bergeries des Pozzi
1746m
PATH JUNCTION 1591m
Funtana di Cozzanese
(SPRING)
Plateau de Gialgone
FOR REMAINING STRETCH SEE MAP 19
0
1km
0
1/2 mile
E CAPANNELLE
← 2 HRS 15 MINS
SUMMIT
← 2 HRS 45 MINS ←
PATH JUNCTION

From the top of **Monte Renoso** (2352m) , a fine view extends north as far as Monte Cinto and south to Alcudina, with Monte d'Oro and Monte Rotondo dominating the mid-horizon. You can also see both the Golfe d'Ajaccio and the east coast on clear days.

The descent sticks close to the ridge for another kilometre until you reach a **gap at 2244m**, where the cairns swing right onto the more level dip slope of Punta Orlandino. Below you a *thalweg* (the line of steepest descent down a hill-side) plunges due south down the line of the mountain to I Pozzi, a tangle of sinuous water channels and pools lining the base of a beautiful suspended valley. The ensuing drop of 250 metres or so, where the cairns lead you through a mess of alder, juniper scrub and rock, is the trickiest section of the day.

The springy turf of I Pozzi comes as a relief after the rough descent and you'll probably be tempted to kick back for half an hour with the pigs and cows who graze these pastures in the summer. To the right of the path (now way-marked intermittently with red blobs of paint as well as cairns) a spring, the **Funtana di Isolu**, is a welcome source of drinking water. Shortly after it you arrive at a **path junction** where you should ignore the waymarks heading left and those veering sharply back to the right, and continue instead straight on to the **Bergeries des Pozzi** where there's a second spring, the **Funtana di Cozzanese**.

Once clear of the bergeries the route, marked with red paint blobs, bends east and crosses two streams on its gentle descending traverse to the **Plateau de Gialgone**, where it intersects the GR20. See p174 for the remaining section to Bocca di Verdi.

E'Capannelle → Bocca di Verdi: the low-level route

[Map 19, opposite]

The bulk of this étape is very much in the mould of the previous stretch from Bocca Palmenti, with a well-defined path that winds around a succession of shallow stream valleys and blunt spurs. It's well shaded throughout, and punctuated at regular intervals with water sources.

From E'Capannelle the red-and-white waymarks strike steeply up the mountainside initially, bearing left after the second ski-lift tower to cross a spur. Beyond the ridge you descend abruptly down a rugged path flanked by mature Laricio pines to the **Bergeries d'E'Traghjete**, whose immaculately restored stone cottages nestle beneath the open crags of Renoso. The path continues to descend on the left side of a stream from the bergeries, emerging after 15 minutes or so at the **Pont d'E Casaccie** on the D169, which you follow briefly before the route peels away to the right of the road.

The ensuing 2½ hours comprise a long traverse that's interrupted by a succession of easy ascents and descents to and from stream level, most of it through fragrant stands of pine and beech. Having forded the Cannareccia and Lischetto, and rounded the Crête de Scopina, the traverse comes to an end at the **Plateau de Gialgone**, an expanse of gently shelving grassland where a signboard marks the route up to the pozzines and Monte Renoso. To the south-west you can trace

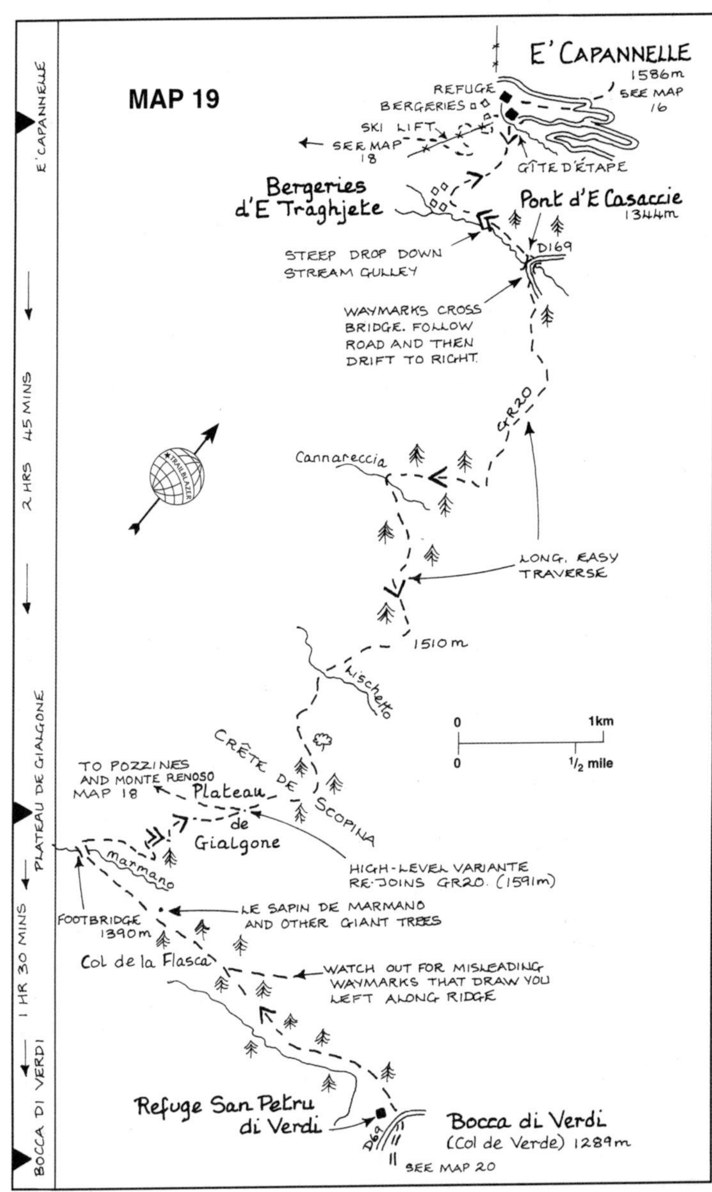
MAP 19
E'CAPANNELLE
1586m
SEE MAP 16
REFUGE
BERGERIES
SKI LIFT
SEE MAP 18
GÎTE D'ÉTAPE
Bergeries d'E Traghjete
Pont d'E Casaccie
1344m
D169
STEEP DROP DOWN STREAM GULLEY
WAYMARKS CROSS BRIDGE. FOLLOW ROAD AND THEN DRIFT TO RIGHT.
GR20
Cannareccia
LONG, EASY TRAVERSE
1510m
Lischetto
0 1km
0 1/2 mile
CRÊTE DE SCOPINA
TO POZZINES AND MONTE RENOSO MAP 18
Plateau de Gialgone
HIGH-LEVEL VARIANTE RE-JOINS GR20. (1591m)
Marmano
FOOTBRIDGE 1390m
LE SAPIN DE MARMANO AND OTHER GIANT TREES
Col de la Flasca
WATCH OUT FOR MISLEADING WAYMARKS THAT DRAW YOU LEFT ALONG RIDGE
Refuge San Petru di Verdi
Bocca di Verdi
(Col de Verde) 1289m
D69
SEE MAP 20
E'CAPANNELLE
2 HRS 45 MINS
PLATEAU DE GIALGONE
1 HR 30 MINS
BOCCA DI VERDI
TRAILBLAZER

the GR20 as it winds up the watershed and Bocca d'Oro, and then presses south along the ridgetops.

The high-level *Variante* rejoins the GR20 at Gialgone; shortly after this it begins a pronounced, zigzagging descent to the Marmano stream. At the **foot-bridge** the path swings sharply to the left (east). The giant spruce trees lining the route here are reputedly some of the most ancient in the Mediterranean; some are about 500 years old. A rusty plaque pinned to one especially grand specimen distinguishes it as the tallest tree in Europe. Until 2.8m was chopped off its top by lightning a few years back, the **Sapin de Marmaro** measured a staggering 56m with a circumference of 6.3m.

After an almost imperceptible ascent to the **Col de la Flasca** the path starts to give ground, winding down to a stream which it follows by means of a piste. However, the route becomes repeatedly confused with other red-and-white waymarked paths (the most misleading of which takes you left from the Col de la Flasca along the line of the ridge to approach Bocca di Verdi from the north). Stay close to the stream, though, and you'll be led along a clear piste most of the way to the col.

Bocca di Verdi (Col de Verde)

Flanked by windy 2000m ridgetops and swaths of dense coniferous forest, Bocca di Verdi forms a low pass through the watershed mountain range between the Fium'Orbu and Taravo valleys. From here the rivers flow in opposite directions, debouching into the sea on the east and west coasts respectively. Although hidden from view by only a single curtain of hills, the sea feels far off (you'll be seeing it again in the course of the next étape, once over the Bocca d'Oro).

For GR20 trekkers Bocca di Verdi is significant as the place where the route makes its penultimate descent to road level. On hand to help you make the most of your relative proximity to civilization is a well-kept bar-cum-refuge, the ***Refuge San Petru di Verdi*** (☎ 04.95.24.46.82; open late-May–mid-Oct), whose shady garden terrace is a very pleasant spot to eat, drink and laze around contemplating the stiff hike ahead. The patron is a local man who spent some time studying in Leeds, where he met his wife. The resulting Anglo-Corsican hybrid atmosphere makes this one of the most unusual and convivial stops on the GR20. You can sleep in immaculately clean, wood-panelled dorms (9.50€ per bed) or rented tents (4.70€ per person). Campers are charged 4€ to pitch in the garden (bivouacking is free); rates include the use of a bathroom equipped with piping-hot, solar-heated showers (bivouackers pay 1.50€ for these). Half-board is good value at 26€ per head; copious Corsican meals, based on produce from the Taravo Valley, are served on the terrace or in the cosy dining room. Note that it is possible to make **reservations** by telephone and that basic **provisions**, including quality charcuterie and ewe's cheese, are sold from the bar.

No public transport runs to Bocca di Verdi. The nearest village with a bus service is Cozzano (see the box on p180), 18km to the south, from where Autocars Santoni's service (daily except Sun; ☎ 04.95.22.64.44 or 04.95.24.51.56) departs at 6.30am for Ajaccio. In July and August only you can arrange **taxis** through the owner of the refuge.

GR20 STAGE THIRTEEN: BOCCA DI VERDI (COL DE VERDE) → USCIOLU [MAP 20, BELOW]

Overview

After an initial climb of 550m, stage thirteen of the GR20 settles into a long but highly varied ridge walk following the rocky spine of the watershed due south. To avoid the more problematic *puntas* and sheer rock outcrops that punctuate the crest, the waymarks regularly switch from one side to the other. The route thus affords constantly changing views of both the spectacular Taravo Valley to the west (right) and the east coast to your left.

Don't, however, be lulled by the comparative lack of sustained ascents into thinking this is an easy day's walk. Some of

GR20 STAGE THIRTEEN
BOCCA DI VERDI (COL DE VERDE) → USCIOLU

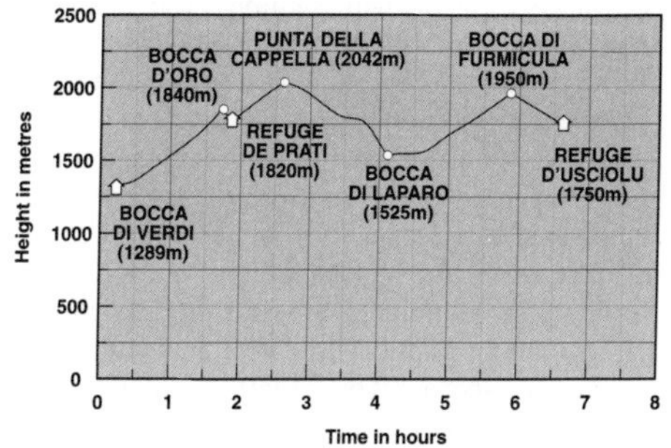

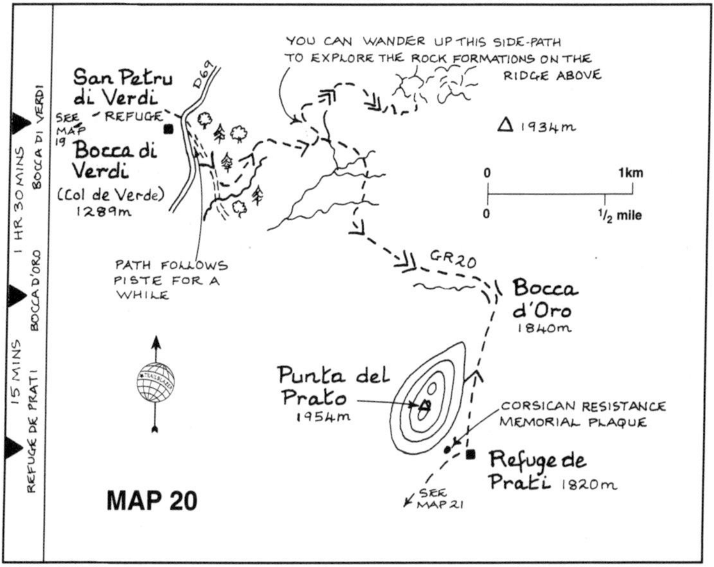

the rockier passages are quite physical and the stage is long (16km), with a total of more than 2100m of altitude change. For this reason it isn't advisable to double up stage thirteen; lots of trekkers do walk to Usciolu from E'Capannelle in a day but they invariably regret it.

Two refuges, one run by the PNRC and the other privately owned, provide shelter and supply points along the way. They're also virtually the only places on the étape where you can refill your water bottles. This stage, perhaps more than any other, underlines the fact that the GR20 is essentially a ridge walk along the island's parched *partage des eaux*.

Route guide

The stage kicks off with a climb through shady mixed beech and pine woodland. From Bocca di Verdi (Col de Verde) you cross the road and follow the forestry piste to the right as it traverses the hillside at a gentle angle and later swings east into a much steeper gradient, zigzagging up the line of a shallow stream valley. Once clear of the tree line, with impressive views of the Renoso massif opening up to the west, you pick your way around a valley head via a succession of seasonal streams. Later the waymarks cut more decisively uphill to crest a shoulder beyond which the GR20 begins its steep approach across a bouldery slope to the pass, visible to the right of a towering rock outcrop.

A rounded gap scattered with boulders and clumps of heavily-grazed vegetation, the **Bocca d'Oro** (1840m), around 1½ hours from Bocca di Verdi, is marked with a large cairn and a PNRC signboard. Looking north-west you can see back along the route of the GR20, dominated by Monte d'Oro and Monte Renoso, while an even more amazing view of the eastern plain is revealed in front. Far to the north-east, Elba rises from the Tyrrhenian Sea and on a clear day you might be able to pick out the shadowy profile of the Tuscan coast.

Refuge de Prati

A leisurely 15-minute stroll down from the pass brings you to the superbly sited Refuge de Prati, from whose sunny deck you have a wonderful panoramic view over the island's coastal plain. Damaged by lightning a few years back, the hut was entirely rebuilt by the PNRC in 2000 and it's now a well-set-up place with 22 beds. If you sleep inside you can use the kitchen, which has a good range of utensils and a large wooden dining table; bivouackers, however, have to make do with the gas hob in the shelter next to the main hut. People who are just passing through technically don't have the right to use any of these facilities.

A scenic spot this might be but it's not a great place to sleep outside as there's precious little cover, so peg in your tent well and expect a strong wind off the sea in the night. The spread of open ground along this stretch of the ridge made a perfect site for parachute drops to the Corsican Resistance in the WWII, as a nearby plaque recalls. British and American planes, guided in by fires lit by local shepherds, landed supplies of arms, ammunition and money that were hidden and later deployed to harass the German retreat along the east coast in September 1943. More background on the Corsican Resistance appears on pp54-6 and p210.

Prati → Usciolu [Map 21, p178; Map 22, p179]

Following the waymarks south-west from the refuge, a short walk across closely-cropped turf takes you back to the ridgeline, which you follow through a steepening ascent. At the 1788m mark the GR drifts left onto the rim of a small cirque where you might find patches of snow clinging to the shadier crevices. The peak above, **Punta della Cappella** (2042m), is bypassed by the route, which cuts across a shoulder on its east flank, but you can easily scramble up to the bouldery summit for a superb view of the Taravo Valley and the watershed tapering south. Apart from Monte Alcudina, crossed a couple of étapes further on, this is the final point above 2000 metres on the GR20 and a good place to get your bearings for the day ahead.

Dipping down the south-east side of the pyramidal punta, the path rejoins the ridge at a small rocky depression known as the **Bocca di Campitello**. From there it skirts the side of another peak to begin a precipitous 200m descent over exposed granite, most of it on the west side of the crest. There are a few tricky passages along this stretch.

At **Punta di Latoncello**, the route briefly levels off then continues downhill through clumps of stunted beech trees on its approach, via the east side of the ridge, to **Col de Rapari** (1614m), a broad, open pass that looks directly down onto the village of Palneca on the floor of the Taravo Valley. From the col another steady traverse across the eastern flank of the mountain brings you to a saddle pass below **Punta di Campolongo**, where the GR switches to the west side of the ridge and falls sharply through a wood of ancient beech trees, wonderfully contorted by the wind.

At **Bocca di Laparo** (1525m), the lowest point of the étape, the GR20 intersects the Mare a Mare Centre, by means of which you can reach **Cozzano** in 2½ hours of easy downhill walking. For more on Cozzano and this liaison route see the box on p180.

Once clear of the Bocca de Laparo, the GR20 takes on a completely different aspect as it penetrates a gloomy beech wood lined with mossy boulders. Five minutes down the trail you pass a **private refuge** offering basic accommodation, supplies, camping space and a water point. At the start of the 2001 trekking season it was burned down by arsonists but the owner was busily rebuilding the hut when we last passed through. This kind of thing happens a lot in Corsica when one person's entrepreneurial initiative impinges on another's monopoly. Generally described as 'une affaire politique', such attacks tend to be repeated unless some kind of arrangement can be made to placate the perpetrators – so don't count on the refuge being here.

A gradually ascending traverse through the forest, which avoids the craggy summit of Punta Mozza, comes to an abrupt end just under one kilometre beyond the refuge when the path cuts into the line of the hillside to begin a steep, zigzagging ascent. Pestered by clouds of flies, many trekkers find this leg along an old mule path the toughest of the day despite most of it being in shade by mid-morning.

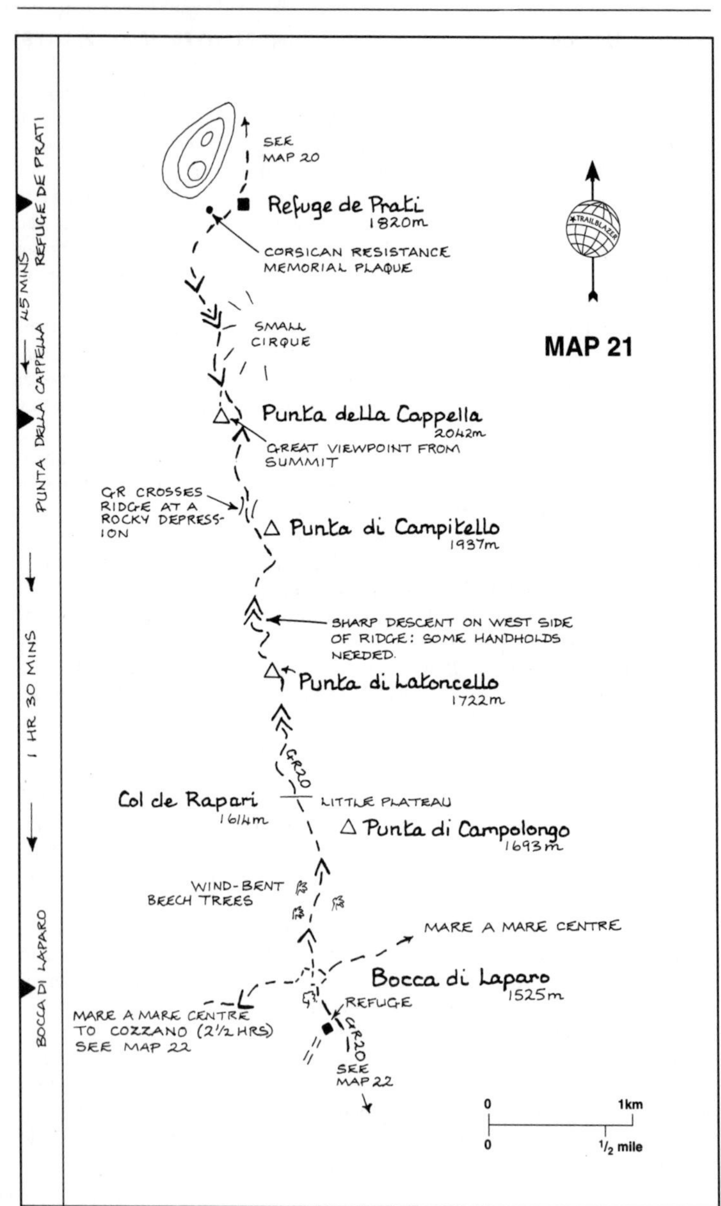
REFUGE DE PRATI
45 MINS
PUNTA DELLA CAPPELLA
1 HR 30 MINS
BOCCA DI LAPARO
SEE MAP 20
Refuge de Prati
1820m
CORSICAN RESISTANCE MEMORIAL PLAQUE
SMALL CIRQUE
MAP 21
Punta della Cappella
2042m
GREAT VIEWPOINT FROM SUMMIT
GR CROSSES RIDGE AT A ROCKY DEPRESS-ION
Punta di Campitello
1937m
SHARP DESCENT ON WEST SIDE OF RIDGE: SOME HANDHOLDS NEEDED.
Punta di Latoncello
1722m
GR20
Col de Rapari
1614m
LITTLE PLATEAU
Punta di Campolongo
1693m
WIND-BENT BEECH TREES
MARE A MARE CENTRE
Bocca di Laparo
1525m
REFUGE
MARE A MARE CENTRE TO COZZANO (2½ HRS) SEE MAP 22
GR20
SEE MAP 22
0
1km
0
½ mile

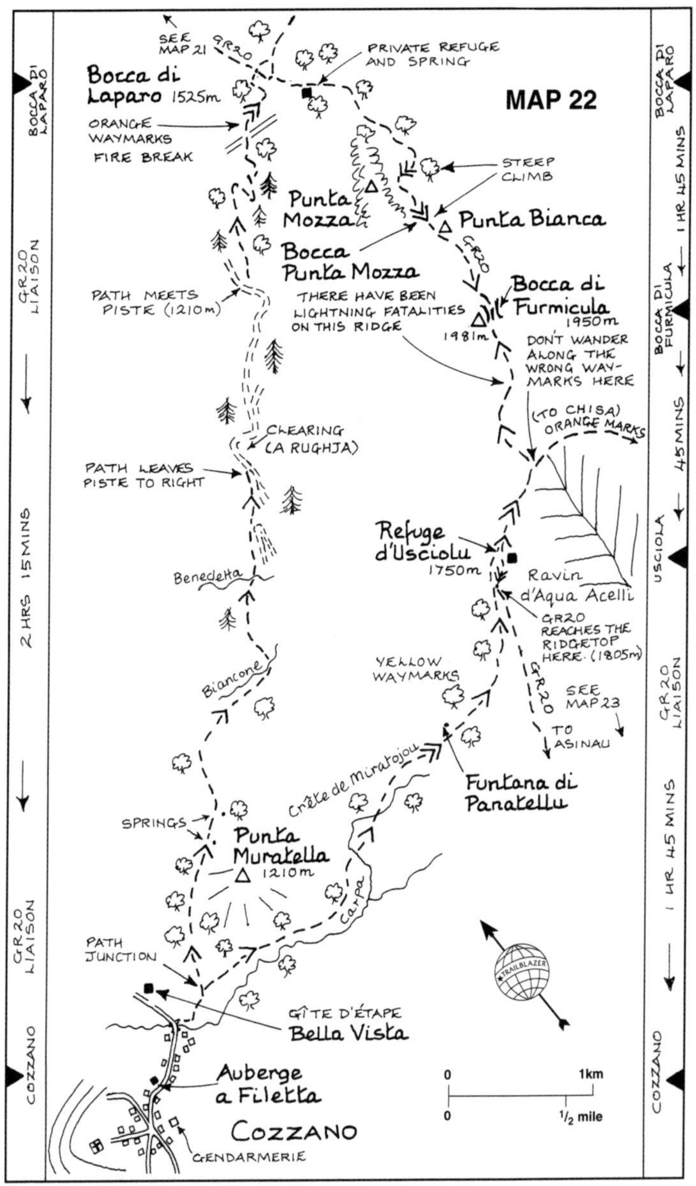
MAP 22
SEE MAP 21
GR20
Bocca di Laparo 1525m
PRIVATE REFUGE AND SPRING
ORANGE WAYMARKS
FIRE BREAK
STEEP CLIMB
Punta Mozza
Punta Bianca
Bocca Punta Mozza
GR20
Bocca di Furmicula 1950m
1981m
THERE HAVE BEEN LIGHTNING FATALITIES ON THIS RIDGE
PATH MEETS PISTE (1210m)
DON'T WANDER ALONG THE WRONG WAY-MARKS HERE
(TO CHISA) ORANGE MARKS
CLEARING (A RUGHJA)
PATH LEAVES PISTE TO RIGHT
Refuge d'Usciolu 1750m
Ravin d'Aqua Acelli
Benedetta
GR20 REACHES THE RIDGETOP HERE. (1805m)
YELLOW WAYMARKS
Biancone
GR20
SEE MAP 23
TO ASINAU
Crête de Miratojou
Funtana di Panatellu
SPRINGS
Punta Muratella 1210m
Carpa
PATH JUNCTION
GÎTE D'ÉTAPE Bella Vista
Auberge a Filetta
COZZANO
GENDARMERIE
TRAILBLAZER
0 1km
0 1/2 mile
BOCCA DI LAPARO
GR20 LIAISON
2 HRS 15 MINS
GR20 LIAISON
COZZANO
BOCCA DI LAPARO
1 HR 45 MINS
BOCCA DI FURMICULA
45 MINS
USCIOLA
GR20 LIAISON
1 HR 45 MINS
COZZANO

Liaison route: Bocca di Laparo → Cozzano [Map 22, p179]

Trekkers sometimes use the Mare a Mare Centre, which cuts across the GR20 at Bocca di Laparo, to escape the high ridge if bad weather suddenly halts progress towards Usciolu. The pharmacy at Cozzano, on this liaison route, is also the region's most accessible source of medical supplies.

The route, clearly waymarked with blobs of orange paint, follows a gently descending traverse through a dense forest of mature pine and beech, crossing a succession of streams before it meets a *piste forestière* at 1210m. The waymarks follow this for nearly 2km until the track, bending sharply to the left around a spur, arrives at a large clearing known locally at **A Rughja** (1240m). Immediately after this, look out for the orange paint marks leading to the right, back into the forest. The long, gradual descent along a clear path continues from there, passing two perennial streams – the Benedetta and the Biancone – and two springs as it drops below the rocky peak of Punta Muratella. Ten minutes before Cozzano, in an old chestnut forest, you join the GR20's liaison path from Usciolu (see box opposite). This takes you onto the D69 where you should turn left for the village or right for the gîte d'étape. The descent of around 800 metres shouldn't take more than 2½ hours in normal conditions.

Cozzano, clustered on a spur overlooking the Taravo River, is a pretty granite village that sees a good deal of trekking traffic thanks to its prominence as a staging point for the Mare a Mare Centre. Most people who pass through stay in ***Gîte d'étape Bella Vista*** (☎ 04.95.24.41.59; open June–Sept), on the north-east outskirts of the village. The gîte has 36 beds (10.70€ per person), a couple of double rooms (26.70€ for two people) and camping space (5.30€ per person, including use of the kitchen). They also offer evening meals (15€) and half-board for 27.40€.

A more comfortable option, and the only other place to stay in Cozzano, is the bright and cheerful ***Auberge A Filetta*** (☎ 04.95.24.45.61, 🖷 04.95.24.47.05), on your right as you enter the village. The hospitable owners, M and Mme Renucci, have six double rooms costing 28€ for two persons (plus 8€ for extra beds). They also do evening meals of quality local cuisine for only 12.20€ per head (56.50€ half-board for two people or 42€ for one).

Cozzano's **pharmacy**, on the square, is open daily except Sundays. You can buy groceries at the **shop** nearby (which also opens on Sunday mornings in summer).

The village also boasts a year-round **bus** service to Ajaccio, which leaves at between 6.30 and 6.50am, Monday to Saturday, arriving one hour and forty minutes later (Autocars Santoni ☎ 04.95.22.64.44 or 04.95.24.51.56)

Roughly halfway through the climb you get a short breathing space at a magical little hollow dotted with asphodel and wizened trees, after which the final steep stretch begins.

A series of endless switchbacks takes you rapidly back to the ridge at **Bocca Punta Mozza**, but the ascent continues in earnest after the col, only levelling off when it reaches a bare saddle just below the peak of **Punta Bianca**. The views from this point are wonderful, encompassing the Taravo Valley all the way up to Bocca di Verdi and beyond; it's a particularly atmospheric spot late in the day, with the sun setting over the ridge opposite.

The remaining ascent to the last pass of the étape is an easy amble over eroded, grazed ground. Fabrikant dubbed the **Bocca di Furmicula** (1950m) the 'Fog Pass' with good reason: the whole ridge section from here to the Plateau de Coscione is often shrouded in mist and cloud or else scoured by incredibly strong winds.

With the bouldery summit of Monte Furmicula on your right, you begin a steady traverse across the east flank of the mountain towards the head of a sheer gully, the ravin d'Acqua Acelli. Close to its edge the GR intersects another path, waymarked in orange, which runs left (east) in a tortuous descent to the village of Chisa. The red-and-white paint blobs, however, fall steeply downhill in the opposite direction towards the Refuge d'Usciolu, reached after a tumbling drop of nearly 200m across loose stone and messy rocks.

Refuge d'Usciolu

Usciolu ranks among the PNRC's best-run refuges, thanks to the efforts of its long-time gardien, whose marathon mule treks to and from Cozzano each day ensure the hut is outstandingly well provisioned. Its shop stocks an amazing range of supplies (including fresh bread) at fair prices. You can even buy post-cards and stamps here, franked with a special 'Refuge d'Usciolu GR20' post-mark, which will be delivered to the post office down in the valley the next day. Copious mixed vegetable pasta stews are also served up each evening (7€ per portion); if you want one, order it in advance on arrival.

The only catch is the shortage of space. The hut, which has room for 32 people, is comfortable enough but the bivouac and camping area below it strain to accommodate the crowds in summer. Most tents end up pitched cheek-by-jowl on the grassy patches between rocks.

However, the welcoming personality of the gardien, who likes to serenade trekkers with stirring Corsican polyphonic music from his solar-powered hi-fi at dusk, is ample compensation, as are the superb views of Alcudina to the south. If you feel like stretching your legs before bedding down, a good incentive is the panorama from the ridge above the refuge, from where the sunsets over the Taravo Valley and distant Golfe d'Ajaccio are magnificent.

Liaison route: Usciolu → Cozzano

It's possible to reach the village of Cozzano in around 1¾ hours from the Refuge d'Usciolu. To pick up the path follow the GR20 in the direction of Asinau to the ridgetop above the refuge, where a PNRC signboard indicates the liaison route; the first part comprises a steep, sustained descent through old beech forest. At the end of a long thin clearing the path passes the **Funtana di Panatellu** (on your right) and drops straight down a ridge called the Crête de Miratojou to cross a second clearing. Shortly after this you twice ford the **Carpa stream**, which the route then follows at a gradually levelling gradient as far as its intersection with the Mare a Mare Centre, arriving from the north-east. When you reach the road turn left for the village or right for the gîte. More details of accommodation and services available in Cozzano appear in the box opposite.

GR20 STAGE FOURTEEN: USCIOLU → ASINAU

[MAP 23, OPPOSITE; MAP 26, p190]

Overview

Stage fourteen comprises three wildly contrasting sections. The first, a sustained ridge trek along the famous Arête a Monda, takes you through a jumble of wind-eroded outcrops that are fully exposed to the vagaries of the Corsican weather: if you get caught in cloud or by a storm anywhere on the GR20 it'll probably be here. Once off the ridge, however, you cross much less harsh, undulating moorland, the Plateau de Coscione, which is grazed by cows and sheep in the summer. The third part is the traverse of Monte Alcudina (2134m; Monte Incudine in French), the last of the 2000m+ peaks along the route, which involves what might be your final protracted ascent of the walk. The climb takes you to the surreal, bouldery world of the mountain's domed summit, a superb vantage point marked by a crucifix, from where southern Corsica's rolling maquis and oak woods are revealed for the first time.

A long étape requiring a total of 1900m of altitude change, stage fourteen is usually more than enough of a day's work for most trekkers. However, with an early start and short rest breaks it is possible to double up and reach Bavella by nightfall, especially if you take the shorter *Variante Alpine* over the needles (see p195). For once, water isn't a problem – at least once you're clear of the ridge section. There are two perennial springs on the route: one on the north edge of Coscione and the other at the foot of Alcudina, perfectly placed for a top-up ahead of the climb.

Before the era when most refuges stocked supplies, many trekkers would quit the GR20 during this stage for a re-provisioning detour to Zicavo, two hours' walk down a side valley. Comparatively few do so these days but the path, which peels away from the main route at the end of the ridge traverse, provides a quick way to one of the region's larger mountain settlements, where you can enjoy the comforts of Corsican village life before getting stuck into the ascent of Alcudina.

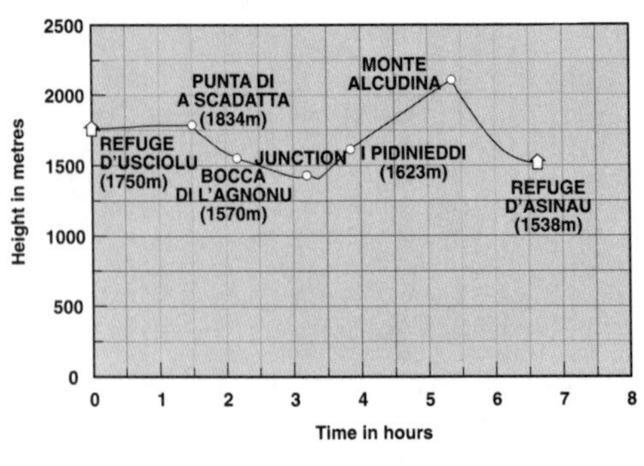

Route guide

The stage begins with a short but gritty climb to the ridgetop followed by the first of the day's real challenges: the traverse of the **Arête a Monda** (also called the 'Arête des Statues' after the spooky rock forma-

SEE MAP 22
Refuge d'Usciolu
1750m
YELLOW WAYMARKS: LIAISON PATH TO COZZANO
SEE MAP 22
GR20
GR20 REACHES THE RIDGETOP HERE (1805m)
ARÊTE A MONDA
Punta d'Usciolu
1815m
THIS STRETCH ACROSS THE ROCKY ARÊTE IS SLOW GOING
Punta di a Scadatta
1834m
Brêche di a Petra di Leva: END OF ARÊTE
SPRING
Bocca di l'Agnonu
1570m
1556m
TRAILBLAZER
GR20
MAP 23
YELLOW WAYMARKS: LIAISON PATH TO ZICAVO. SEE MAP 24
PLATEAU DE COSCIONE
Furcinchesu
0
1km
0
1/2 mile
PATH JUNCTION
1450m
GR20
YELLOW WAYMARKS: LIAISON PATH FROM ZICAVO SEE MAP 25
PISTE
SUSPENSION FOOTBRIDGE (1434m)
SEE MAP 26
PATH JUNCTION
1 HOUR
BOCCA DI L'AGNONU
40 MINS
PUNTA DI A SCADATTA
1 HR 30 MINS
USCIOLU

tions punctuating it). The giant, ribbon-thin outcrop lining the ridge, a mass of smooth-backed boulders, steeply angled slabs and pinnacles sculpted into weird shapes by the wind, would be a formidable obstacle were it not for some clever waymarking. The path traced by the paint blobs along the *arête*, which snake continually from one side of the ridge to the other by means of open rock, narrow gullies and gangways, is a vivid testimony to the ingenuity of the GR20's originators.

The end of the ridge section comes quite abruptly. Having rounded the *arête*'s highest point, the **Punta di a Scadatta** (1834m), the waymarks squeeze through a distinctively shaped gap (known as the **Brêche di a Petra di Leva**) to the east side of the ridge, and from there drop sharply downhill, passing through the treeline into a depression lined by twisted old beech trees. At the point where the path more or less levels off, a sign points out the site (to your right) of a welcome **spring** where you can refill your bottle for the crossing of Coscione.

Another sharp drop through the trees brings you to a second, much larger wooded hollow, called the **Bocca di l'Agnonu**, where a prominent PNRC signboard marks the start of the **liaison route to Zicavo**, heading down the valley to the right. The main route, meanwhile, veers left over a rise covered in more

Plateau de Coscione

The Plateau de Coscione, which the GR20 traverses between Bocca di l'Agnonu and Monte Alcudina, provides a rare grassy interlude along this relentlessly rocky route. For northern European walkers, trekking over its rolling moorland, riddled by hundreds of small streams and splashed with patches of purple monksfoot, will feel an oddly familiar experience, especially when the mist and drizzle is down and the typically Corsican summits and ridges that surround it are shrouded in cloud.

Known locally as 'U Pianu' ('the table'), the lush depression hidden at the heart of the island was the linchpin of the local economy for many centuries. During the summer months, 600 to 700 shepherds used to live up here, tending their flocks and herds of cattle as they fed on the lush pasture. Nowadays, however, only a handful of working bergeries remain inhabited. The decline of transhumance in the region at the beginning of the twentieth century (see p144) became terminal after WWII, when a large timber company moved in to harvest the beech in order to replace railway sleepers damaged by the fighting on the continent. When it pulled out, hundreds of men found themselves without work and were forced to emigrate, having allowed their ancestral flocks to dwindle.

The few shepherds that still work Coscione tend to do so using pick-up trucks, travelling up here once or twice each week from the villages of the Taravo Valley to check on their animals. EU subsidies rather than sales of brocciu account for the bulk of their income but you can still buy top-quality cheese made in the traditional way (with milk from the plateau) at the bergeries along the liaison path to Zicavo (see p188).

Apart from mid-summer when Coscione is crossed by an unending stream of GR20 trekkers, the only time of year when the plateau sees visitors is after heavy snow when it becomes a paradise for cross-country skiers.

fairy-tale beech forest. By the time you've crossed it you're technically in the Coscione basin proper, but the defining feel of the plateau doesn't become apparent until you emerge from the trees, from where the grassland rolls south to the foot of Monte Alcudina, interrupted by pozzines and winding brooks.

Liaison route: Bocca di l'Agnonu → Zicavo [Map 24, p186]

One of the more worthwhile forays off the GR20 begins at Bocca di l'Agnonu, from where an easy, well-shaded path winds down the mountainside to Zicavo. If you're not in a hurry this detour warrants consideration not only because it provides an opportunity to visit a very pretty, unspoilt Corsican village (of which there are few within easy reach of the route) but also for the chance to trek across the most scenic corner of the Plateau de Coscione on your return via the second liaison path.

At Boccia di l'Agnonu a PNRC sign points the way to the right off the GR down the Padulelli Valley; the route is waymarked with **yellow** paint flashes. After half an hour following these through beech woods you emerge at a clearing where the route swings north-west and crosses a stream flowing off Monte Ucchjatu, whose crags rise to the north. Running alongside an old dry-stone wall for a while, the path then penetrates oak forest and, shortly after intersecting a waymarked path from Cozzano, a large wood of chestnut trees. Allow two hours to cover this stretch from Bocca di l'Agnonu, which brings you out at the north side of the village.

Zicavo With over 300 permanent residents, Zicavo, *chef-lieu* of the upper Taravo Valley, remains one of the few populous villages in this remote corner of the island. The source of its relative prosperity are the legions of semi-wild pigs you'll doubtless have encountered on the way down here. They fatten on windfall chestnuts in the surrounding forest in the autumn and are then slaughtered in prodigious numbers during December. The result is outstanding charcuterie, and aficionados shouldn't miss the opportunity to sample the local figatellu. The Zicavais' long-standing association with the bloody art of sausage-making may in part account for the other phenomenon for which the village is renowned. On foggy nights it is said that female **vampires**, or *streghe*, swoop down in search of infants' blood. Another word for them is *gramantis*, which probably derives from the name of a much-feared Saracen pirate, d'Agramante, who terrorized the region in the fourteenth century from his base on the coast. Lone trekkers should also beware of the Zicavais zombies – *i acciacciatori* – who are said to crush the skulls of solitary travellers.

If you can forget its tongue-twisting occult associations, Zicavo is a great place to relax and recover from the travails of life on the GR. Among its picturesque huddle of old granite houses (many of them over 500 years old) are a handful of pleasant **places to stay**. The cheapest and most welcoming is the ***Gîte d'étape Le Paradis*** (☎ 04.95.24.41.20; open May–Oct, and out of season with advance booking), just north of where the yellow GR20-liaison waymarks hit the D69. Taking its name from the cemetery next door (home of the aforementioned acciacciatori, one imagines), the gîte is impeccably managed by its garrulous patronne, Mme Pirany, who uses home-grown produce to create sumptuous Mediterranean cuisine for guests in the evening. Her breakfasts are equally copious, comprising some 10 different kinds of jam and bread fresh from the bakery. Double rooms cost from 30.50€ to 33.50€, depending on the level of comfort, and there are beds in four-person dorms (10.70€). Book in advance if you can as the gîte is very popular with trekkers. *(cont'd p188)*

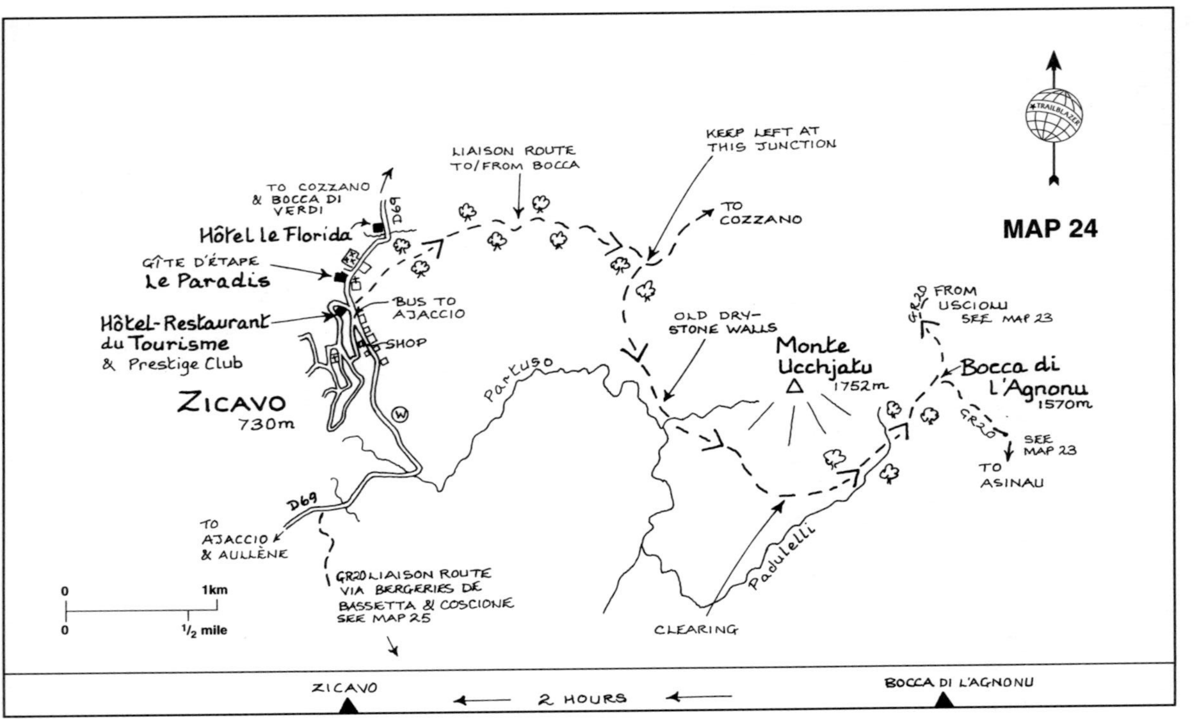
MAP 24
TRAILBLAZER
TO COZZANO & BOCCA DI VERDI
D69
Hôtel le Florida
GÎTE D'ÉTAPE Le Paradis
Hôtel-Restaurant du Tourisme & Prestige Club
BUS TO AJACCIO
SHOP
ZICAVO 730m
LIAISON ROUTE TO/FROM BOCCA
KEEP LEFT AT THIS JUNCTION
TO COZZANO
Partuso
OLD DRY-STONE WALLS
Monte Ucchjatu 1752m
GR20 FROM USCIOLU SEE MAP 23
Bocca di L'Agnonu 1570m
GR20
SEE MAP 23
TO ASINAU
D69
TO AJACCIO & AULLÈNE
GR20 LIAISON ROUTE VIA BERGERIES DE BASSETTA & COSCIONE SEE MAP 25
Padulelli
CLEARING
0
1km
0
1/2 mile
ZICAVO
2 HOURS
BOCCA DI L'AGNONU

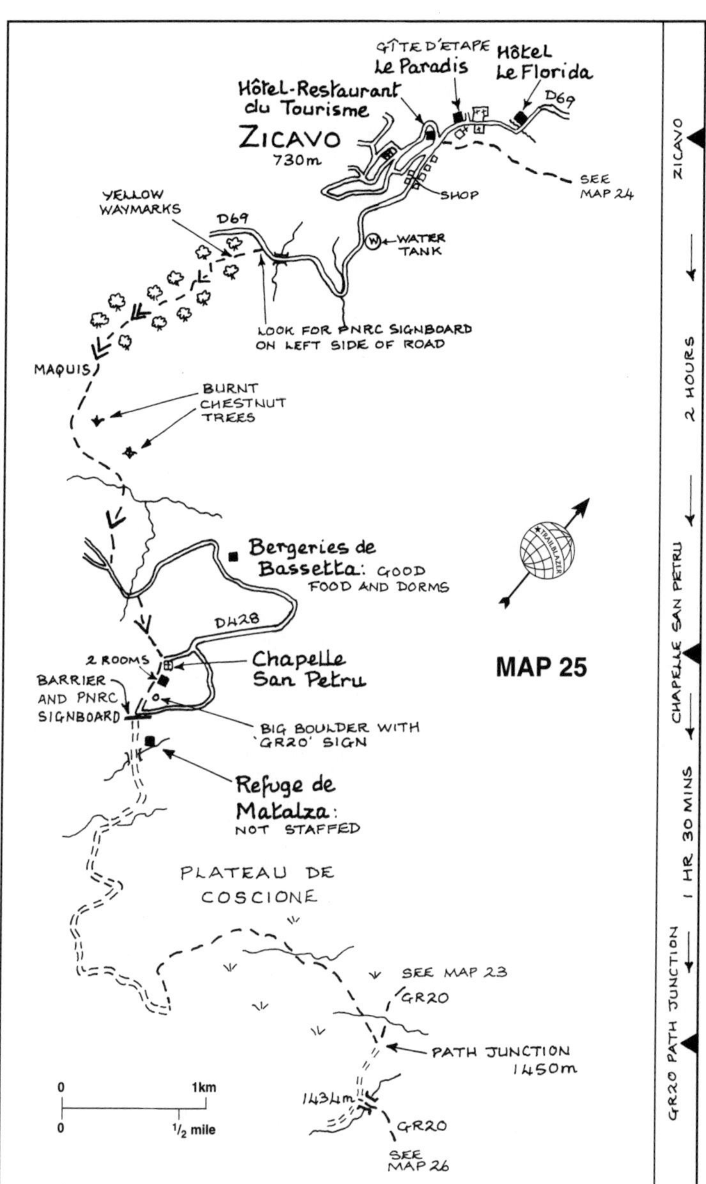
GÎTE D'ETAPE
Le Paradis
Hôtel
Le Florida
Hôtel-Restaurant
du Tourisme
D69
ZICAVO
730m
SEE
MAP 24
SHOP
YELLOW
WAYMARKS
D69
WATER
TANK
LOOK FOR PNRC SIGNBOARD
ON LEFT SIDE OF ROAD
MAQUIS
BURNT
CHESTNUT
TREES
Bergeries de
Bassetta: GOOD
FOOD AND DORMS
TRAILBLAZER
D428
2 ROOMS
Chapelle
San Petru
MAP 25
BARRIER
AND PNRC
SIGNBOARD
BIG BOULDER WITH
'GR20' SIGN
Refuge de
Matalza:
NOT STAFFED
PLATEAU DE
COSCIONE
SEE MAP 23
GR20
PATH JUNCTION
1450m
1434m
GR20
SEE
MAP 26
0
1km
0
1/2 mile
ZICAVO
2 HOURS
CHAPELLE SAN PETRU
1 HR 30 MINS
GR20 PATH JUNCTION

❑ Liaison route: Bocca di l'Agnonu → Zicavo (cont'd from p185)
Just up the road from Le Paradis, ***Hôtel Le Florida*** (☎ 04.95.23.43.11; open all year) is another inviting option with en suite double rooms for 38€. The same family also has a rudimentary camping field 20 minutes' walk further north towards Cozzano (5€ per head). Otherwise there's the homely ***Hôtel-Restaurant du Tourisme*** (☎ 04.95.24.40.06), a short way below the chapel San Roccu, where doubles with shower and toilet are good value at 31€. Next door, the ***Prestige Club*** is a cheap and cheerful pizzeria where you can eat al fresco with views over the valley for under 8€.

Zicavo's **shop**, which stocks a good range of trekker-friendly food (including delicious, locally-made chestnut-flour biscuits), stands at the south side of the village on the Ajaccio road. For anyone wishing to leave the GR20 at this point, a **bus** departs for Ajaccio each morning except Sunday (Autocars Santoni ☎ 04.95.22.64.44 or 04.95.24.51.56).

Returning to the GR20 [Map 25, p187] The only drawback with dipping down to Zicavo is that you have to slog all the way back up to Coscione afterwards. Rather than retrace your steps to Bocca di l'Agnonu, however, it is possible to follow another liaison path that arcs south from the village to rejoin the GR20 at the foot of Monte Alcudina – a hike of around 3¼ hours.

The first stretch of the path is, it has to be said, an extremely dull plod by the standards of the GR20. You'd do well to avoid it by hitching a lift up the mountain with one of the shepherds who make the journey by jeep most days during the summer: ask at the village shop for anyone planning to go past the Bergeries de Bassetta the next day.

If you don't manage to arrange a ride you'll have to follow the D69 south towards Aullène/Ajaccio, past the shop and on for another 1.5km until you reach a PNRC signboard on the left side of the road. **Yellow waymarks** lead into the forest, striking steeply uphill through the woods and later swinging over open, flatter ground around the foot of Punta di l'Erta. Shortly after crossing a stream, you arrive at the D428 which has zigzagged up here from its junction with the D69 14km below. Where it bends to the left the waymarks head straight on up the line of a stream but if you're feeling peckish, follow the road instead to the **Bergeries de Bassetta** (☎ 04.95.25.74.20), which serves top-notch Corsican-speciality meals of Zicavias charcuterie and Coscione cheese (count on 18€ for three courses). They also offer simpler *plats du jour* such as mint-and-brocciu omelettes or bowls of filling pork stew flavoured with herbes du maquis for around 9€. Set in an idyllic spot on the edge of the Coscione plateau, the converted bergerie makes a great place to stay the night: a bed in one of the impeccably maintained dorms costs 12€.

From Bassetta the quickest way back to the path is to retrace your steps to the bend in the D428 and from there continue south-west along the yellow waymarks to the **Chapelle San Petru**. This tiny church is said to have been built in fulfilment of a vow by three brothers from Sartène who were locked in a bloody vendetta with a rival family. While hiding out in the woods above Zicavo, Saint Peter appeared to them in a dream to tell them their pursuers were approaching. Thus warned, they escaped and ultimately survived the feud, which was resolved some years later. Saint Peter, however, made a second nocturnal appearance to demand that the brothers, by way of thanks for his having saved their skins, erect a chapel at a spot on the Plateau de Coscione where an 'iron stake sprouted from a boulder'.

❑ Liaison route: Bocca di l'Agnonu → Zicavo (cont'd from opposite)
After its legendary foundation in the sixteenth century, the Chapelle San Petru became the patron shrine of the region's shepherds, who traditionally gather here for a festival on 1st August each year. Two simple rooms provide basic shelter.

Pressing on south-west up a stony slope, you soon pass a large boulder pointing the way to the GR20. Beyond this a PNRC signboard and vehicle barrier herald your arrival at the unstaffed **Refuge de Matalza** which has two dingy rooms but no water source. From this point you're on the Plateau de Coscione proper as the path crosses a succession of streams and hollows drained by beautiful little pozzines. Cairns and intermittent yellow paint flashes reassure you that you're on the correct track, which around 1½ hours after the Chapelle San Petru intersects the GR20, as indicated by a prominent PNRC sign.

The route onwards to Asinau is described on pp189-92.

The enjoyable plod across the heart of the **Plateau de Coscione** (see the box on p184), in the course of which you cross a succession of shallow streams and grassy gullies, takes around one hour. You'll know you're nearing the edge of it when you arrive at a second PNRC signboard for Zicavo; where the liaison route rejoins the GR20.

Ten minutes further along the trail, after following a piste for a short way, the waymarks drop down to the Furcinchesu stream, crossed by means of a suspension **footbridge**. From the far bank they zigzag quite steeply uphill through the woods, emerging 20 to 30 minutes later at a denuded hollow known as **I Pidinieddi** (1623m). The large pile of rubble to the right of the path is all that remains of a refuge that once occupied the old bergeries, whose stones have now been piled into makeshift windbreaks. Bivouacking and camping are allowed but in practice few trekkers spend the night here unless bad weather blocks the route over Alcudina, as that is extremely exposed and most definitely not a path you'd want to be on in an electrical storm.

Another five minutes or so uphill from the ruined refuge, a **spring** sheltered by a coppice of trees is your last dependable water source before Asinau. Beyond it the GR20 presses on across more denuded hillside to a sharp ridge, reached at a point known as the **Bocca di Luana**, where the waymarks switch southwards to tackle the crux of the climb. This comprises a long, steady ascent up a stony path, with an occasional easy clamber over outcrops. Above you, Alcudina's twin forepeaks bring the wild head of the Luvana Valley to an abrupt, dramatic end.

The final haul to the top starts after the path drifts temporarily to the right of the ridgeline and then back towards it again. Crowned with a large crucifix, the summit of **Monte Alcudina**, reached around 1½ hours after leaving the river, rises from the middle of a smooth granite dome, surrounded by a mass of gently tilting slabs. In good weather it provides one of Corsica's most extraordinary viewpoints. To the south-east the spectacular Aiguilles de Bavella, seen here for the first time, dominate the landscape, while beyond them you might

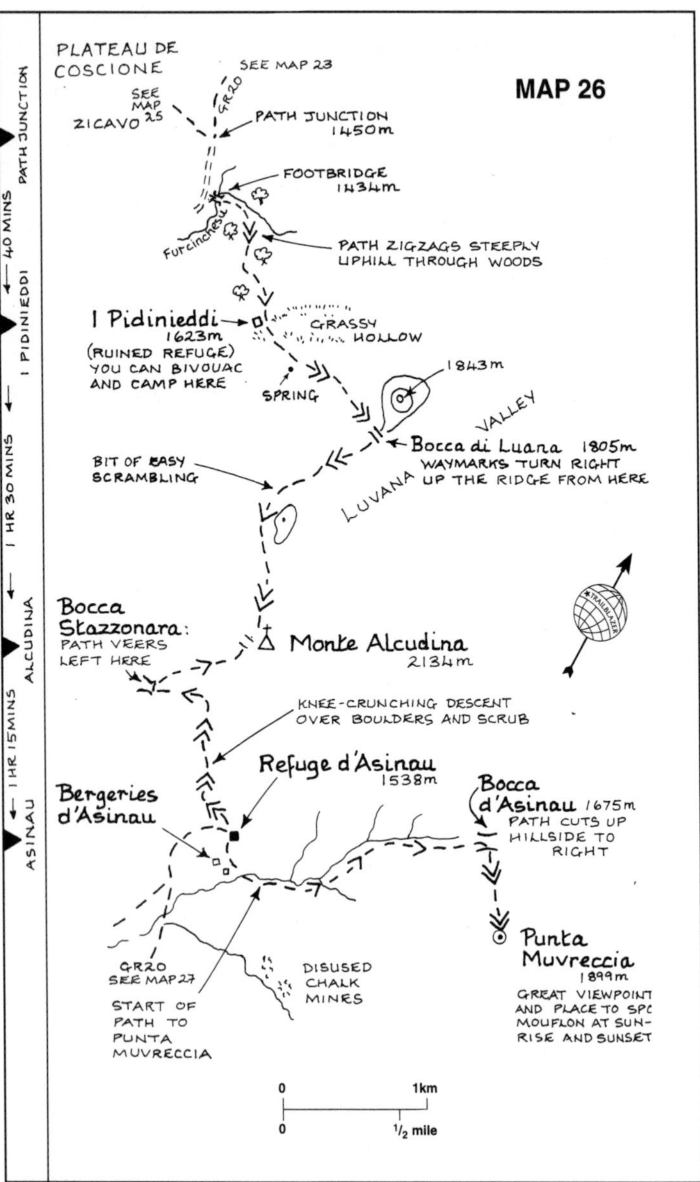

MAP 26
PLATEAU DE COSCIONE
SEE MAP 23
GR20
SEE MAP 25
ZICAVO
PATH JUNCTION 1450m
FOOTBRIDGE 1434m
Furcinchesu
PATH ZIGZAGS STEEPLY UPHILL THROUGH WOODS
I Pidinieddi 1623m
(RUINED REFUGE) YOU CAN BIVOUAC AND CAMP HERE
GRASSY HOLLOW
SPRING
1843m
LUVANA VALLEY
Bocca di Luana 1805m
WAYMARKS TURN RIGHT UP THE RIDGE FROM HERE
BIT OF EASY SCRAMBLING
Bocca Stazzonara:
PATH VEERS LEFT HERE
Monte Alcudina 2134m
KNEE-CRUNCHING DESCENT OVER BOULDERS AND SCRUB
Refuge d'Asinau 1538m
Bergeries d'Asinau
Bocca d'Asinau 1675m
PATH CUTS UP HILLSIDE TO RIGHT
Punta Muvreccia 1899m
GREAT VIEWPOINT AND PLACE TO SPOT MOUFLON AT SUNRISE AND SUNSET
GR20 SEE MAP 27
START OF PATH TO PUNTA MUVRECCIA
DISUSED CHALK MINES
0
1km
0
1/2 mile
PATH JUNCTION
40 MINS
I PIDINIEDDI
1 HR 30 MINS
ALCUDINA
1 HR 15 MINS
ASINAU

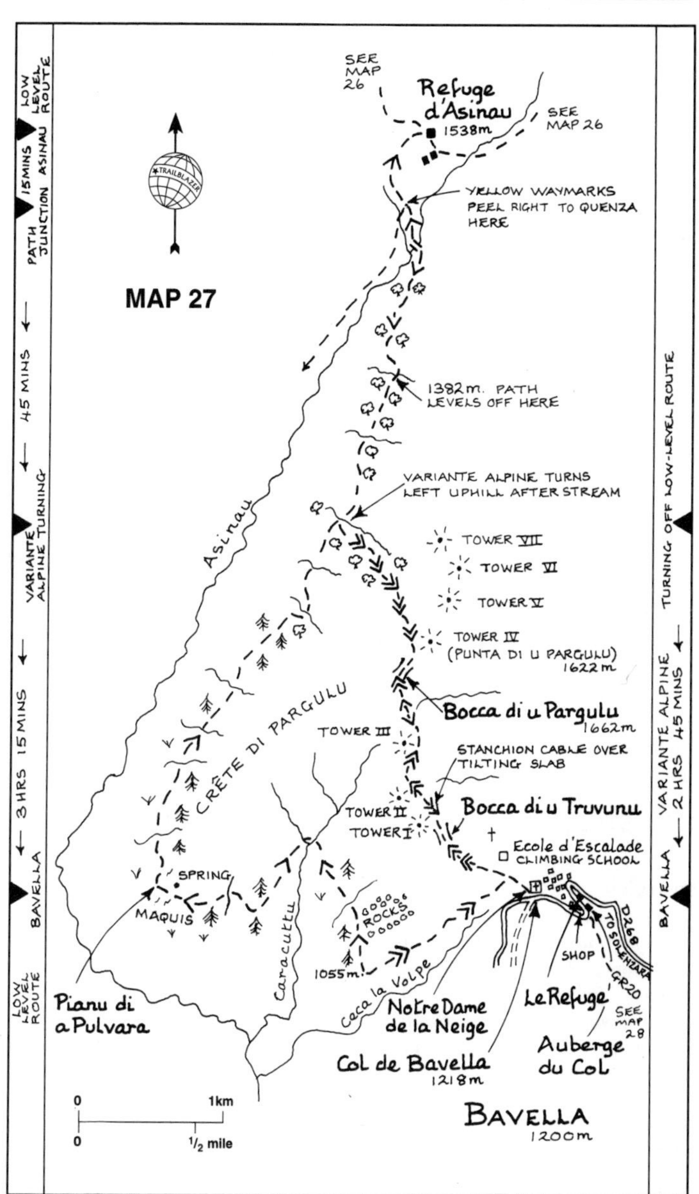
MAP 27
SEE MAP 26
Refuge d'Asinau
1538m
SEE MAP 26
YELLOW WAYMARKS PEEL RIGHT TO QUENZA HERE
1382m. PATH LEVELS OFF HERE
VARIANTE ALPINE TURNS LEFT UPHILL AFTER STREAM
Asinau
TOWER VII
TOWER VI
TOWER V
TOWER IV
(PUNTA DI U PARGULU)
1622m
Bocca di u Pargulu
1662m
CRÊTE DI PARGULU
TOWER III
STANCHION CABLE OVER TILTING SLAB
TOWER II
TOWER I
Bocca di u Truvunu
Ecole d'Escalade
CLIMBING SCHOOL
SPRING
MAQUIS
ROCKS
Caracuttu
1055m
Caca la Volpe
D268
TO SOLENZARA
SHOP
GR20
SEE MAP 28
Pianu di a Pulvara
Notre Dame de la Neige
Le Refuge
Col de Bavella
1218m
Auberge du Col
BAVELLA
1200m
0
1km
0
1/2 mile
LOW LEVEL ROUTE
15 MINS
ASINAU
PATH JUNCTION
45 MINS
VARIANTE ALPINE TURNING
3 HRS 15 MINS
BAVELLA
LOW LEVEL ROUTE
TURNING OFF LOW-LEVEL ROUTE
VARIANTE ALPINE
2 HRS 45 MINS
BAVELLA

be able to make out the east coast running down to the Golfe de Porto-Vecchio, and in the opposite direction, the Golfe de Valinco on the island's west side. Between them the dark oak woods and ridges of the Alta Rocca region ripple away towards Sardinia, obscured by the massif of Uomo di Cagni.

Explore the fringes of the summit area and you might be lucky enough to spot a herd of mouflon scouring the rocky slopes for vegetation. This is also a good spot for sighting lammergeier vultures (see the box on p141) and golden eagles, who exploit the hot thermals rising from the granite slabs lining the mountain.

The descent starts with a gentle drop through rocky outcrops along the ridge running south-west from the summit. At a niche known as **Bocca Stazzonara** (2025m) it cuts sharply back to traverse Alcudina's southern flank, a mass of sharp-edged boulders and scrub. Seeming to lose interest in their leisurely course, the waymarks then plunge straight down the line of the mountain – an exceptionally abrupt descent (the steepest part of the GR20's southern section). In dry conditions, you should reach Asinau between 60 and 75 minutes after leaving the summit.

Refuge d'Asinau

Asinau clings to the hem of Alcudina's southern skirts, at the head of a wonderfully wild valley. Enfolded by ridges, it's the last of the GR20's refuges situated amid high-mountain terrain. Once again, bivouackers and campers will find little flat ground to pitch on at the height of the season, an inconvenience that prompts many trekkers to press on towards Bavella. Nevertheless the hut, with bunks for 30 people and a large kitchen area, makes a good base from which to savour the atmosphere of the watershed. Its gardiens keep a stock of basic supplies (including tins of cold Pietra beer) and from the wooden deck, which looks south down the valley towards the majestic Aiguilles de Bavella, you may glimpse a mouflon or two grazing on the ridgetops opposite (see the box opposite).

GR20 STAGE FIFTEEN: ASINAU → BAVELLA → PALIRI

[MAP 27, p191; MAP 28, p199]

Overview

Whether you trek around their base or scramble over the top of them on the *Variante Alpine*, the Herculean pinnacles of the Aiguilles de Bavella, which soar sheer from a gently undulating sea of deep green maquis, form the defining feature of Stage fifteen and are the GR20's last major cadence before Conca. Once past them the watershed disintegrates into a chaos of bizarrely-eroded orange cliffs.

The GR, however, is far from over, especially for those who opt to reach the Col de Bavella the hard way, by clambering over the crags of the Aiguilles.

Opposite: Bergeries d'E Traghjete at dawn, GR20; see p172. (Photo © David Abram).

Mouflon-spotting walk from Asinau **[Map 26, p190]**

Refuge d'Asinau stands less than an hour's walk from one of Corsica's top mouflon-spotting locations. If you haven't yet seen one of the island's rare mountain sheep (see the box on p134) consider slotting in the following walk as it takes you to a viewpoint from where you get a matchless (and rarely seen) vista of the Alcudina massif and Bavella crags.

Rather than following the red-and-white waymarks to the right (west) of the hut, drop straight down the line of the mountain to the **Bergeries d'Asinau**. From there, a cairned path drifts left to cross the stream at the base of the valley and then winds along its true left (south-east) bank towards the **Bocca d'Asinau** (1675m), which you should reach in around half an hour from the bergeries.

Once at the col, turn 90° to your right and keep to the ridgeline as it climbs more steeply south-east across denuded ground to the **Punta Muvreccia** (1899m), a superb vantage point overlooking the mass of cliffs and crags on the north rim of the Fiumicelli Valley. Far below you can trace the line of the D268 – which many claim to be Corsica's most scenic road – as it winds from Bavella down to the east coast.

The far (south-east) side of the ridge running from the Punta Muvreccia is where you're almost certain to sight mouflon if you reach it early enough on a summer's morning. The crête runs along the top of a row of spectacularly rugged little cirques, sliced by narrow stream ravines by means of which the animals ascend to these high pastures.

It's best to start the hike from the refuge at first light, not only because dawn and dusk are the most promising times for wildlife watching but because in good weather you'll be able to catch the extraordinary spectacle of the sun's first rays illuminating the rocky summit of Alcudina.

Some imposing landscape stands between you and a late breakfast at the pass. That said, the *Variante Alpine* is a far less intimidating proposition that it might look from Asinau. There's a fair bit of scrambling over steep rock to contend with but in dry conditions the high-level route poses no obstacles that anyone

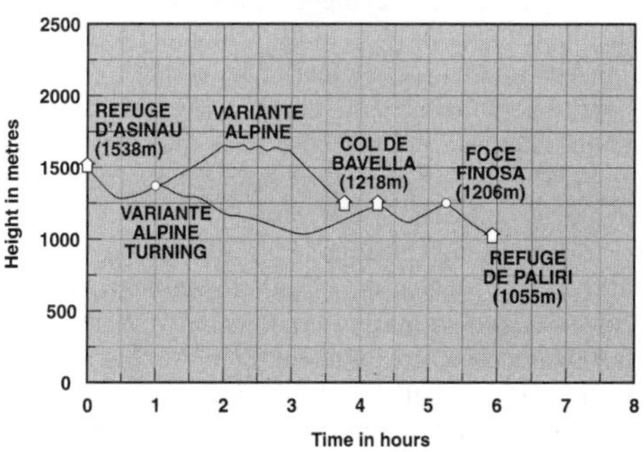

Opposite Top: Crossing an early summer névé on the GR20. **Bottom:** Sunrise at the mouth of the Asco valley (see p172). (Photos © David Abram).

who's made it this far should shy from. Apart from the stupendous views and intense feeling of wilderness you get from the needles, a further incentive to take the *Variante* is that the low-level route is basically a monotonous yomp with little to recommend it unless you're mad for pine forest. Winding around the base of the Aiguilles in a huge semi-circle it's also a much longer route to the col.

However you get there, the seasonally-inhabited village that spills from the far side of the pass comes as a bit of a shock if you've not seen a café since Bocca di Verdi. A popular target for bus tours and car trippers, it is usually swarming by mid-morning, although compensation comes in the form of fresh croissants and real coffee at the sunny roadside terraces, and you can pen a few last-minute postcards while bracing yourself for the final leg.

Route guide

Asinau → Bavella: the low-level route [Map 27, p191]

It's hard to be enthusiastic about this stretch, which seems to drag on far longer than it should, but it does offer some pleasantly level walking through what, if you hadn't just spent a week or two high on the Corsican watershed, would be an impressive valley. The forest covering much of the route offers plenty of shade and water sources but the last half of the étape, where the well-worn path winds through maquis carpeting the south-west base of the Aiguilles, is exposed to the full glare of the afternoon sun and should thus be avoided during hot weather.

After a level stretch across boulders and scrub from the Refuge d'Asinau, the red-and-white waymarks turn at a gradually steepening gradient down the line of the hillside to a **path junction**, where a liaison route peels off the GR20 to the village of Quenza (see p286). Shortly below this point you cross the Asinau and begin a steady climb up the opposite flank of the valley through shady silver-birch woods. At the **1382m mark** (only 70m higher than the river crossing) the path, having traversed up a series of stream thalwegs, hits a level that it sticks to for most of the remaining route to the mouth of the valley.

The first major landmark beyond the river, after around 45 minutes, is the point where the *Variante Alpine* turns left off the main path, as indicated by a PNRC signboard. Once past here, the route emerges from the birch trees to cross a broad band of deforested hillside, rising and falling slightly as it winds in and out of shallow side valleys.

The definitive change of direction comes after a long, very gradual descent, at the end of which the GR20 crosses the **Crête di Pargulu**, the spine of the Bavella ridge, to reach a small maquis-covered plateau known as the **Pianu di a Pulvara** (1046m). Look out for the **spring** to the left of the path here. Beyond it the maquis, dotted with the odd maritime pine, closes in as the waymarks swing north-east to enter the Caracutu ravine. From there they turn south-east and zigzag steeply uphill for 50 metres or so to a new contour level.

With the cliffs of the Aiguilles towering above, you then enter a much rockier landscape where the path begins its approach to the col along the side of the Ceca la Volpe stream valley. This is one stretch where you should keep an eye on the waymarks; lose your concentration and you could find yourself following one of the many sheep trails that run down to stream level.

The final ascent over rock and scrub takes you up just under 200m. Towards its end, the *Variante Alpine* rejoins the main route at a small forested plateau from where you can see the statue of Notre Dame de la Neige through the trees.

Asinau–Bavella: the high-level *Variante Alpine*

The final yellow-waymarked portion of the GR20, dubbed the *Variante Alpine*, marks a radical shift in tone after the restrained scenery of Coscione and the Asinau Valley. Don't be put off by its nickname. Some of the gradients (notably the initial approach section) are undeniably strenuous and the terrain as harsh as any on the GR but none of the passages is any more technical or vertigo-inducing than those of the first three days. Threading around the base of the immense Bavella needles, this portion offers the last real thrills of the walk, and some dramatic views. The only reason you'd regret choosing it is if the weather took a nasty turn; some of the steep, exposed rock around the *aiguilles* can get very slippery when wet.

The *Variante*, clearly marked with conspicuous yellow flashes, begins 45 minutes into the étape, zigzagging steeply to the left of the main path through a long ribbon of silver birch. The sheer gradient eases up once you're clear of the trees as the route drifts to the right (south) into a long traverse across boulders and juniper scrub below towers VII, VI and V of the Aiguilles. Having skirted the base of tower IV (Punta di u Pargulu) you reach the precise line of the watershed at a spectacular pass called **Bocca di u Pargulu** (1662m). From there the yellow flashes descend steadily to the south, past the east side of towers III and II. An especially steep stretch over an awkwardly tilting slab, negotiated with the help of a 10m **chain** secured to posts, is followed by a short, stepped descent and then an easier passage up a pine-covered boulder slope to a second pass, **Bocca di u Truvunu**, below tower I. From there a sustained, rocky scramble down a sheer-walled gully takes you back to the treeline at the Col de Bavella.

BAVELLA

With its parking lot full of hire cars, camper vans and luxury coaches, Bavella can come as a disappointment after the trek from Asinau. The bulk of the day-tripper traffic congregates at the **col**, where a large white statue of **Notre Dame de la Neige** looks benignly down on the main road from her boulder pedestal, scattered with miniature effigies of tin limbs and red plastic candle offerings.

Bavella itself lies 300m beyond the rise. The settlement, a scattering of corrugated-iron and felt-roofed huts that nestle in the shade of huge Laricio pines, has served as a bolthole from the summer heat for the villagers of Conca since the land was gifted to the *commune* by Napoléon III in the nineteenth century. Deserted for six months of the year, it sees an overwhelming amount of through traffic in the summer months because of its position at the head of the D268, to Solenzara on the east coast; tourist literature loves to call this 'Corsica's most beautiful road', an accolade it thoroughly deserves. Flanked by spectacular cliffs and rock formations, the entire area is a paradise for climbers. After peering up at the mighty buttresses, towers, and 200m faces from the comfort of a café terrace you might feel inspired to tackle one or two of them with the help of the climbing school located here (see the box on p197).

Where to stay and eat

Among GR20 trekkers not desperate to get onto the rock, opinion is divided over whether Bavella warrants a stopover, but most people take the opportunity to buy provisions for the last leg to Conca. A single **shop**, on the left just past the bend in the road, sells top-grade charcuterie, cheese and other edible supplies (at inflated tourist prices) but little else.

The *boulanger*'s van from nearby Zonza doesn't make it this far but you might be able to rustle up a baguette at the friendly ***Auberge du Col*** (☎ 04.95 57.43.87; open April–Oct), opposite the shop. Offering three *menus corses* from 12€ to 21.50€, in addition to an exhaustive à la carte selection, this is much the best place in the village for a sit-down meal. House specialities include local-style lasagna made with fresh brocciu, lamb aux herbes du maquis, and sweet chestnut flan, and they serve delicious chilled Cap Corse muscat as an aperitif. Around the back of the restaurant, an annexe of six-berth dorms provides basic gîte d'étape accommodation for 13€ per bed (29€ for half-board).

The only other place to stay in Bavella is ***Le Refuge*** (☎ 04.95.57.40.26; open May–Sept) a couple of doors down, which also has a handful of simple dorms (with shared showers and toilets) costing the same as those at the Auberge. You can order wood-fired pizzas in their small restaurant, as well as a range of inexpensive snacks and freshly-made sandwiches.

For those who can't face the last étape and a half to Conca it's worth knowing that a **bus** departs from Bavella for Ajaccio via Levie, Propriano and other villages in the Alta Rocca. The service, run by Autocars Ricci (☎ 04.95.51.08.19 or ☎ 04.95 76.25.59), operates daily (including Sundays and holidays) from July 1 until September 15; outside these dates it starts from Zonza, 7km south-west down the D268 (daily except Sun).

Bavella → Paliri [Map 28, p199]

The GR20 leaves Bavella on the piste behind the Auberge du Col. Once you've filled up your water bottle at the Funtana di u Canone, follow the track at contour level for 450m to where the orange waymarked trail to Trou de la Bombe (a popular picnic spot) peels away to the right. The red-and-white flashes drop quite steeply downhill from here to cross a stream and, after another short descent down a wooded spur, meet a motorable piste forestière. This crosses the Ravin de Volpajola via a bridge from which a right turn and a five-minute detour upstream takes you to a beautiful but little-known bathing spot.

Thus refreshed, you can look forward to the last climb of the day, which strikes uphill to the right of the piste, 20m after the bridge. From here to Conca you'll be following an ancient transhumant path along which shepherds used to drive their flocks from the coastal plains north of Porto-Vecchio to the high valleys around Alcudina and the Plateau de Coscione. Much of the well-engineered route has retained its original, time-worn paving slabs and buttressed bends, now maintained by the PNRC.

Winding north-east from the piste at a gradually steepening gradient, the old path crests the Crête de Punta Tafonata ('Pierced Peak Ridge') at the **Foce Finosa** (1206m) where a superb view south-west over the wild valleys below greets you. Beyond it the stream-eroded route drops sharply down, switching first to the right and then to the left to begin a descending traverse of a hillside that's dwarfed by the massive cliffs of Punta Tafonata di Paliri.

Climbing in Bavella

Since its awesome crags were first explored by Belgian, Swiss and Austrian mountaineers in the late 1920s, Bavella has become *the* top climbing destination in Corsica. An amazing array of routes, ranging from low-grade scrambles to longer multi-pitch *grandes voies*, wriggle up the rock faces looming above both sides of the main road here. Apart from the spectacular rock on offer, one of the main reasons for Bavella's enormous popularity is the unusual accessibility of its more challenging climbs, some of which literally overlook the car park at the col.

The area boasts roughly 120 named, graded (and in many cases bolted) routes. Beginners usually stick to the training pitches accessed from the bottom of the GR20's *Variante Alpine*, where the yellow and red-and-white waymarks merge (see map p191). This is where the German-run climbing school, L'École d'Escalade de Bavella, is based. Here, novices can get instruction and more experienced climbers can rent gear. The school also publishes a technical route guide to help you find your own way around if you don't wish to join an organized group. Reached by following the *Variante Alpine* to the top of the massif, some of Bavella's most famous routes scale the buttressed Aiguilles themselves. Across the valley, another classic is the ascent of the **Campanile Ste Lucie**, a colossal monolith from the top of which you get a magnificent view of the wild country crossed by the final stage of the GR20.

Perfectly placed for exploring this area's wonderful rock possibilities, the tiny Refuge de Paliri is dominated by a massive cliff rising to its north. From its top you can make out the enigmatic **Punta Tafonata di Paliri,** a large hole piercing the ridgetop. Overlooking a rugged nexus of valleys, the standard route to it (level 6a+ on the French mountaineering scale) is known as 'La Maravigliosa' ('The Wonder') because of the intense sense of exposure you gain from it.

The toughest route of all in the Bavella area is **Octogenese 8c**, opened up by Arnaud and François Petit. A 9-pitch route that cuts up the majestic east face of the Teghie Lisce cliff, it boasts imposing vital statistics of 6a+, 8c, 8a, 7a, 7b, 6a, 6a, 7a, 8a, 7a and has yet to be completed as a one-day, ground-up ascent.

Apart from calling in at the École d'Escalade for a chat, the best way to get to grips with the innumerable route options is to consult J-P Quilichi and B Vaucher's *Le Massif de Bavella*, which is crammed with essential technical tips and detailed descriptions of all the major climbs. For non-French speakers, Colomb's *Corsica Mountains* gives a rundown of the main routes and their approaches, although without illustrations.

Whatever level you're climbing at, an early start is essential during the summer when the temperature on the Bavella rock faces builds rapidly. Take as much water as you can to avoid dehydration and, as ever, make sure you check the weather forecast at one of the cafés before leaving, particularly if you plan to attempt one of the longer, higher grandes voies in the massif itself. Bavella enjoys an exceptionally sunny, dry climate for a climbing destination of its calibre, but when storms sweep in they tend to do so rapidly.

Refuge de Paliri

Less than five hours from Conca, Paliri is often leapfrogged by trekkers eager to polish off the last, easy stage of the GR20. But the hut, which stands on a beautiful belvédère dominated by the awesome east wall of Punta Tafonata, makes an ideal base for exploring one of the island's truly unique landscapes. With your pack stashed in the hut you can amble unencumbered up the approach trail through maritime pine forests to the mighty pierced peak itself (whose amazing hole is visible high above at the head of the cliffs), or simply laze around enjoying the sublime views over the Vallée du Carciara.

The refuge is a small one, with bunks for only 20 people, but the bivouac area is spacious and superbly sited. To reach the water source you've a bit of a trek back down the path, where a sign points the way to a spring and shower area.

GR20 STAGE SIXTEEN: PALIRI → CONCA

[MAP 28, OPPOSITE; MAP 29, p201]

Overview

The concluding stage of the GR20 holds no unpleasant surprises. With the splendour of Bavella receding behind you, resinous maritime pine forest gives way to a landscape of blasted, orange-tinted rock, charred trees and brittle, spiny maquis. Underfoot, the crystalline gravel of the Corsican coast begins to reassert itself as you press through a belt of rock outcrops eroded into phantasmagorical shapes. By the time the door-sized niche of the Bocca d'Usciolu heralds the start of the final descent to Conca, the high peaks will seem like a distant memory and you'll probably have your mind fixed firmly on the prospect of a hot shower.

The one danger you really do have to be aware of on this leg is the **heat**. Most of the path from Paliri faces south-east and is thus exposed to the full glare of the morning sun – a force to be reckoned with from June onwards. After the cooler climes of the interior, the temperatures here can come as a surprise. With only one (easily missed) source of drinking water on the route, the risk of **dehydration** is significant. Bear in mind that if you're hit by sunstroke you'll have a very long, dry

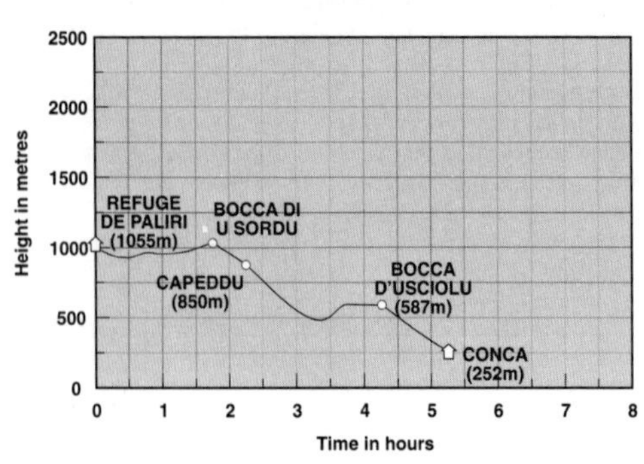

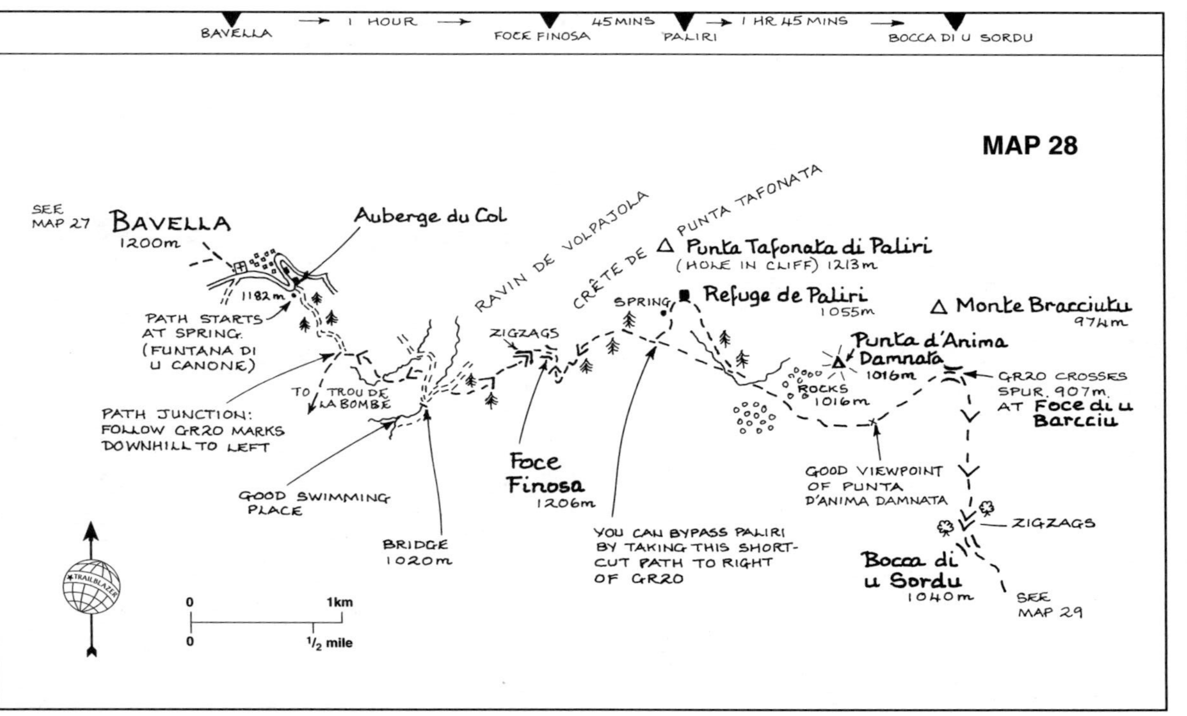
BAVELLA → 1 HOUR → FOCE FINOSA 45MINS PALIRI → 1 HR 45 MINS → BOCCA DI U SORDU
MAP 28
SEE MAP 27
BAVELLA 1200m
Auberge du Col
1182m
PATH STARTS AT SPRING (FUNTANA DI U CANONE)
PATH JUNCTION: FOLLOW GR20 MARKS DOWNHILL TO LEFT
TO TROU DE LA BOMBE
GOOD SWIMMING PLACE
BRIDGE 1020m
RAVIN DE VOLPAJOLA
ZIGZAGS
Foce Finosa 1206m
CRÊTE DE PUNTA TAFONATA
Punta Tafonata di Paliri (HOLE IN CLIFF) 1213m
SPRING
Refuge de Paliri 1055m
YOU CAN BYPASS PALIRI BY TAKING THIS SHORT-CUT PATH TO RIGHT OF GR20
Monte Bracciutu 974m
Punta d'Anima Damnata 1016m
ROCKS 1016m
GR20 CROSSES SPUR, 907m, AT Foce di u Barcciu
GOOD VIEWPOINT OF PUNTA D'ANIMA DAMNATA
ZIGZAGS
Bocca di u Sordu 1040m
SEE MAP 29
TRAILBLAZER
0
1km
0
1/2 mile

and shadeless walk to safety. So if the weather's hot, force down as much liquid as you can and carry at least two litres of spare.

Route guide

A steepish descent through the narrow, pine-forested stream valley that runs south-east from the Refuge de Paliri is followed by a short ascent to a rocky gap from where you have an impressive view of the witches-hat-shaped **Punta d'Anima Damnata** ('Peak of the Damned Soul'; 1016m), a renowned climbing spot. Having crossed through the gap in the rocks above, you penetrate the edge of a broad cirque, dominated by the mass of Monte Bracciutu (974m) that rises from the centre of the amphitheatre.

The old transhumant path keeps faithfully to contour level as it swings north around the flank of the basin to round a sharp shoulder at a pass called **Foce di u Barcciu** (907m). Once around the spur the waymarks veer decisively south into an ascending traverse that culminates with a strenuous, zigzagging climb to **Bocca di u Sordu** (1040m), the last serious climb of the GR20. From the top you can see the sea and trace most of the onward route, which

Les Faux Éleveurs

The kind of fire damage encountered on the GR20 in the hills above Conca is sadly typical of the landscape in Corsica these days; each year upwards of 15,000 hectares of forest and maquis are consumed by flames. This calamity appears all the more shocking when you realize that the vast majority of fires are started intentionally – not by lone pyromaniacs or thoughtless trekkers but by ordinary Corsicans.

The truth behind the annual infernos, which together account for one-fifth of all the land laid waste by fire in France, was exposed by a visionary (some would say reckless) fire service chief in 1994 after he noticed that a disproportionate number of the blazes occurred on common land near villages. By cross-referencing his statistics with farming patterns he showed that the most likely culprits were the owners of cattle.

Fire has for centuries been used on the island as a means of clearing unproductive land so that green shoots may grow back to provide fodder for animals. But this ancient transhumant practice spiralled out of control in the 1990s following the introduction of dairy **subsidies**, since when Corsican villagers have acquired more cows than they know what to do with. Rather than dip into the 1140€ most receive each month from Brussels to buy in fodder, the so-called 'Faux Éleveurs' ('Fake Cattle Rearers') simply torch the hillsides around their villages where the animals that nominally belong to them roam free.

When the EU was informed about this destructive abuse of the Common Agricultural Policy it suspended all aid to Corsica. The move slashed the incidence of wild fires almost overnight. Payments have since been re-instated but the problem persists, not least of all because of the wide-ranging economic benefits fires bring to an island plagued by unemployment for most of the year. When a mountain burns in Corsica, firemen, foresters, builders, council workers and Canadair pilots (who douse the flames with water from specially converted tanker planes) all get a lot of overtime pay.

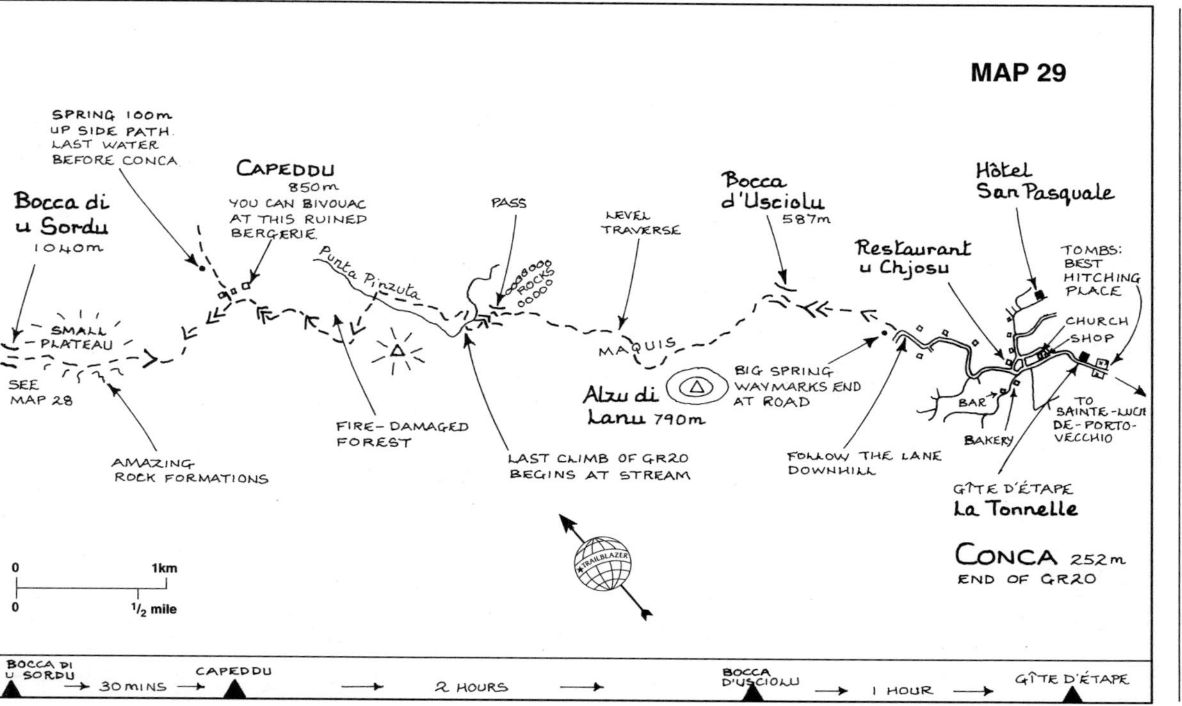
MAP 29
SPRING 100m UP SIDE PATH. LAST WATER BEFORE CONCA
CAPEDDU 850m
YOU CAN BIVOUAC AT THIS RUINED BERGERIE
Bocca di u Sordu 1040m
SMALL PLATEAU
SEE MAP 28
AMAZING ROCK FORMATIONS
Punta Pinzuta
FIRE-DAMAGED FOREST
PASS
ROCKS
LAST CLIMB OF GR20 BEGINS AT STREAM
LEVEL TRAVERSE
MAQUIS
Alzu di Lanu 790m
Bocca d'Usciolu 587m
BIG SPRING WAYMARKS END AT ROAD
FOLLOW THE LANE DOWNHILL
Restaurant u Chjosu
Hôtel San Pasquale
TOMBS: BEST HITCHING PLACE
CHURCH
SHOP
BAR
BAKERY
TO SAINTE-LUCIE DE-PORTO-VECCHIO
GÎTE D'ÉTAPE La Tonnelle
CONCA 252m
END OF GR20
TRAILBLAZER
0
1km
0
1/2 mile
BOCCA DI U SORDU → 30 MINS → CAPEDDU → 2 HOURS → BOCCA D'USCIOLU → 1 HOUR → GÎTE D'ÉTAPE

descends from here across a large depression cluttered by eroded slabs of white granite. Clinging to the sandy soil between them are the first of many scorched trees – the result of the fire that laid waste to much of Conca's deserted hinterland in 1985.

At the end of a fairly long, steep descent through maquis on a rain-rutted, gravelly path the trail cuts past ruined stone huts at **Capeddu**, where a sign points the way through the bushes to the only **spring** of the étape. There's also a rubbish point here, installed primarily for walkers heading north on the GR20, that's periodically emptied by helicopter (and rummaged by stray dogs and pigs).

From Capeddu the descent continues in earnest down the side of a shallow valley, over a low, broad ridge and thence more steeply down the side of another valley to cross the **Punta Pinzuta** stream, beyond which the path swings right to follow the bank southwards. This whole section of former Laricio pine forest is blighted by ghoulish fire-blackened trees.

After fording the stream a second time the GR20 climbs in a short series of tight switchbacks to another pass, beyond which it contours through more dense maquis around the lower north-eastern slopes of a hill called Alzu di Lanu (769m). Ahead of you to the south-east you can make out at last the niche of **Bocca d'Usciolu** (587m), a gap in the ridge that feels like a ceremonial gateway marking the end of the GR20. Once through it, you'll lose sight of the high mountains for the last time. From here on it's downhill all the way to Conca.

CONCA

Were it not at the end of the big GR, Conca, spread around the head of a valley below an amphitheatre of crags and maquis, would be a largely undistinguished place – picturesque enough but not somewhere you'd go out of your way to visit. As it is, though, thousands of trekkers pour through here annually, most of them via the gîte d'étape at the bottom of the village, which benefits from a remarkable (although typically Corsican) absence of competition. Once you've showered off, had a nose around the centre and swapped a few yarns with fellow GR veterans, there's precious little to do other than savour the prospect of a dip in the sea, only 9km down the valley.

Where to stay and eat

Trekking traffic through Conca is all but monopolized by the large ***Gîte d'étape La Tonnelle*** (☎ 04.95.71.40.09; open June–Sept), a one-stop establishment which, with well-oiled efficiency, provides for the specific needs of *nouveaux arrivées* off the GR. Rates range from 12.20€ for a dorm bunk to 16.80€ for a bed in a double room. You can also camp in their very large, well-shaded garden for 4.60€. The rates all include access to hot showers.

Most people who stay here celebrate with a slap-up meal; the cheapest way to do this is to opt for half-board (an extra 17€ on top of your accommodation), which buys you a three-course supper and French breakfast with fresh bread, jam and croissants. The food is nothing special but the portions are generous and the atmosphere well worth shelling out for, even if this would normally be beyond your budget.

The only other accommodation in Conca is ***Hôtel San Pasquale*** (☎ 04 95.71.56.13; open May–Oct), at the opposite end of the village. The hotel offers very comfortable studio apartments with large balconies, or smaller en suite rooms, opening onto a central courtyard. Rates for a double range from 42€ to 60€ depending on the kind of room and time of year; tariffs are at their highest in July and August.

The San Pasquale doesn't offer meals but you can eat well at the ***Restaurant U Chjosu***, down on the main street, whose 17€ menu corse is a notch above the cheap and cheerful food dished up in the gîte d'étape.

Conca also has a couple of **grocery shops** (in summer the one just below the church near the gîte stays open the latest) and a **bakery**.

Onward transport

Predictably, the only public transport between Conca and the coast road is laid on by the owner of the gîte d'étape, who boasts of never leaving anyone stranded in the village. Straight after breakfast he begins to shuttle trekkers down the valley in his minibus to Sainte-Lucie-de-Porto-Vecchio (3.50€), from where you can pick up one of Rapides Bleues' two daily services up the east coast to Bastia via Solenzara and Aléria. Timetables for this route may be consulted in the gîte. Alternatively, pay a bit more to be driven all the way to Porto-Vecchio (7.60€) where buses leave for Ajaccio, stopping at Sartène and Propriano en route.

For more details on transport, accommodation and services in Porto-Vecchio, see pp296-9.

Which beach?

If you've walked all the way to Conca from Calenzana, you can pride yourself on having covered 140km across some of the most rugged mountain terrain in Europe, notching up 19,000m of ascent and descent over the 16 stages. After such a mammoth trek, few can resist the lure of the beaches that line the nearby coast, which comprise some of the most beautiful shorelines in the entire Mediterranean.

Unfortunately, without your own transport little of it is easily accessible unless you've got time to spare. You'd need at least a day to reach the pick of the beaches **south of Porto-Vecchio** (see the box on p299).

All things considered your quickest route to pearl-white sand and turquoise water is to head 4km south-east of Sainte-Lucie-de-Porto-Vecchio on the main N198, to the **plage de Pinarellu**. A long, gently curving bay enfolded by headlands and overlooked by a Genoan watchtower, it has ticks in all the right boxes and is large enough to soak up the crowds of holidaymakers and the campers from the site behind it who descend there in July and August. Best of all, the owner of Conca's gîte d'étape 'La Tonnelle' will drop you slap on the beach in his minibus.

Further north, the bays of the **Côte des Nacres** – Solenara and Anse de Favone – are mediocre by Corsican standards and really not worth breaking the journey to Bastia for.

If, on the other hand, you're heading up the other side of the island towards Ajaccio, one more option stands out. You'll have to walk 4km from the main road to reach it, but **Roccapina** is a real gem. The simplest way to get there is to jump on any Eurocorse Voyage bus heading between Porto-Vecchio and the capital Ajaccio, and ask to be dropped off at the turning for the beach, exactly 42km south-west along the N196. A piste leads from the main road past a pleasant little campsite to a bay backed by a band of shell sand that's easily one of the most spectacular and undeveloped beaches in southern Corsica.

For more on Roccapina, see p310.

PART 5: MARE A MARE NORD

Overview

Starting at Moriani on Corsica's eastern seaboard, the official Mare a Mare Nord, waymarked in orange, cleaves south-west across the island via Corte and Col de Veghio to Cargèse on the west coast in 10 relatively easy stages. Its less travelled, slightly tougher *variant* peels south after three days to cross the watershed at Onda on the GR20 then rejoins the main path at Marignana for the final two days to the sea.

The route described in this chapter, however, is not the one you'll find in FFRP Topoguides. Instead it runs from west to east, cuts out three relatively dull sections (between Moriani and Corte), and strings together the most memorable *étapes* to create **a long loop** that would take between seven and ten days to complete, depending on how hard you walk.

For most trekkers, particularly those eager for a taste of the deep interior, the first four or five days of this route are reason enough to choose it and many are content to wind up the walk at Corte. The less frequented *variant* section (see pp234-46), along which gîtes, shops and villages are comparatively few and far between, will appeal to anyone really wanting to get away from it all. A short train ride from Corte provides a convenient liaison between the end of the previous étape and the onward trailhead at Vivario – closing a gap in our circular itinerary that would otherwise require three days of dull walking to cover. From Vivario, however, you have to be largely self-sufficient for three days, taking food and accommodation where you can find it. The pay-off is a sense of isolation that you'll rarely experience on other routes at these altitudes.

The other big plus with the Mare a Mare Nord is the scenery, which even by Corsican standards is spectacular and astonishingly diverse. No two days are alike. From the coastal maquis above Cargèse you climb above gradually deep-

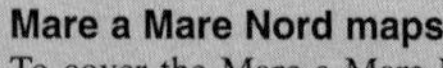

Mare a Mare Nord maps
To cover the Mare a Mare Nord between Cargèse and Corte, cartophiles will need IGN maps 4151OT (Vico/Cargèse), 4150OT (Porto) and 4250OT (Corte/Monte Cinto). Anyone intending to follow the alternative route to Corte from Col de Verghio might also want the 4251OT (Monte D'Oro/Monte Rotondo) which covers the path over the Col de St Pierre and past Lac de Nino to A Sega. The latter also includes most of the *variant* section west of Vivario.

L'Indivision

The remote, depopulated villages that punctuate the Mare a Mare Nord – particularly those along its *variant* section, such as Soccia, Pastricciola and Renno – are evidence of the decline in Corsica's rural economy. But they are also victims of a cultural conundrum that has, since the first wave of mass emigration following WWI, perennially suffocated attempts to revitalize village life on the island.

Many young people from continental France, among them second-generation Corsicans, wish to resettle in their ancestral villages but are unable to do so for want of accommodation; this despite the glut of empty houses. The problem, known locally as *l'indivision*, is that according to Corsican tradition parental estates must be divided equally between all surviving children, male and female. Thus, over time, the homes of grandparents end up co-owned by several families who in most cases refuse to be bought out. As a result, the houses stand empty except for a few weeks during the summer holidays.

With each succeeding generation the problem grows worse, compounded by the enormous emotional value given to old family homes in Corsica. Even when indivision disputes have been resolved, the prices for which houses are put on the market tend to be far higher than anyone hoping to earn a living in the village can afford. Consequently they are bought by wealthy Parisians as second homes, forcing prices up still further. Nor can the FLNC intervene in its customary way, by blowing up houses acquired by outsiders as holiday properties; the destruction of a traditional family home would be bound to infuriate relatives still living in the area, and could ignite a feud.

ening valleys and chestnut forests to Marignana, overlooking the rugged Spelunca gorge. Once beyond the giant Laricio pines of the Forêt d'Aïtone, you press on across the Col de Verghio – Corsica's highest motorable pass – to the Niolu Valley, an alpine-style valley flanked by the snow-flecked massifs of Paglia Orba and Monte Cinto. Separating the Niolu from the neighbour Tavignano Valley, the Col de l'Arinella marks the next stage's transition to a weird world of soaring vertical cliffs and ancient pines which you penetrate via a wonderful an old Genoan mule path.

The *variant*, though passing through less dramatic mountains, leads into one of the island's least populated regions, the hinterland of the Golfe de Sagone. Carpeted by swathes of unbroken forest and gloriously unpolluted rivers, the area is littered with near-deserted villages, poignant reminders of a more prosperous past. In recent times the region has become notorious as the home patch of the island's most radical separatists, a faction of whom are suspected of having murdered the island's *Préfet*, Claude Erignac, in February 1998 (see p58) – Corsica's most infamous terrorist atrocity. The former goatherd wanted for the shooting, Yvan Colonna, is still at large and thought to be hiding out somewhere in this wild tangle of valleys.

The route

CARGÈSE

Straddling the main west-coast road, Cargèse is a pretty, prosperous village with a population of just under one thousand, most of whom earn a living from tourism or related businesses. Its inhabitants are renowned throughout the island for being descendants both of old shepherds and Greek refugees who came here to escape Turkish persecution in the late seventeenth century. The 730 settlers from Mani in the Peloponnese (invited by Genoan overlords in part to dilute resistance to Italian rule) weathered the inevitable local resistance to their arrival and dug themselves in on the windy headland at the top of the Golfe de Sagone. This explains why the village has two churches: one Greek Orthodox, the other Roman Catholic. They share the same priest, an Albanian expatriate called Père Florent who claims to be the only man in the world permitted by the Pope to pronounce rites in both Greek and Latin.

For trekkers Cargèse is primarily a springboard for the Mare a Mare Nord and Tra Mare e Monti (see pp247-71). Connected to Ajaccio by regular buses, it has a good crop of small hotels, cafés and restaurants for its size, as well as a supermarket and post office. Get here on SAIB's early morning service from the capital, however, and you could have time for a nose around (the Greek church is especially worth a visit), shop for last-minute supplies and still be on the trail on the same day.

What to see

The pretty stone houses of Cargèse's old quarter, splashed with bright bougainvillea, look down on the silent stand-off between the village's two churches. The Greek church is the more interesting; gaudily restored in the 1990s, it houses a collection of splendid icons, painted by monks on Mt Athos and brought here by the Maniot refugees in 1676. The 'Virgin and Child', on the right as you face the altar, is believed to be 900 years old.

Orientation and services

Buses from Ajaccio via Sagone (SAIB ☎ 04.95.22.41.99 or 04.95.21.02.07; Sept–June one to two daily Mon–Sat; July–Aug two daily) can either drop you at the bottom of the village, opposite the Proxi supermarket, or further up the hill on place St Jean. The latter stop is nearer the trailhead. The service continues up the coast to Porto, turning around at Ota for the return journey.

There are three **ATMs:** one at the **post office,** just below the main road at the bottom of the hill; another half-way up the hill at the Crédit Agricole **bank;** and the third outside the large Shopi **supermarket** just off place St Jean. Shopi has the best all-round source of supplies including stove fuels and other useful hardware. The staff at the **tourist office** (July–Sept daily 9am–noon and 4–7pm, Oct–June Mon–Fri 3–5pm), at the bottom of the village near the post office, are welcoming but can't offer much advice about trekking in the area. You can, however, get Topoguides, IGN maps and English guidebooks at either the newsagents or the small **book and photographic shop** on the main road.

Where to stay and eat

The nearest campsite to the village is ***Camping Toraccia*** (☎ 04.95.26.42.39; open Easter–Oct), 4km north along the main Porto/Calvi road.

The cheapest place to stay in Cargèse is ***Hôtel de France*** (☎ 04.95.26.41.07; April–Oct), on the main street just east of place St Jean. It's spartan and run-down and the front rooms can suffer from traffic

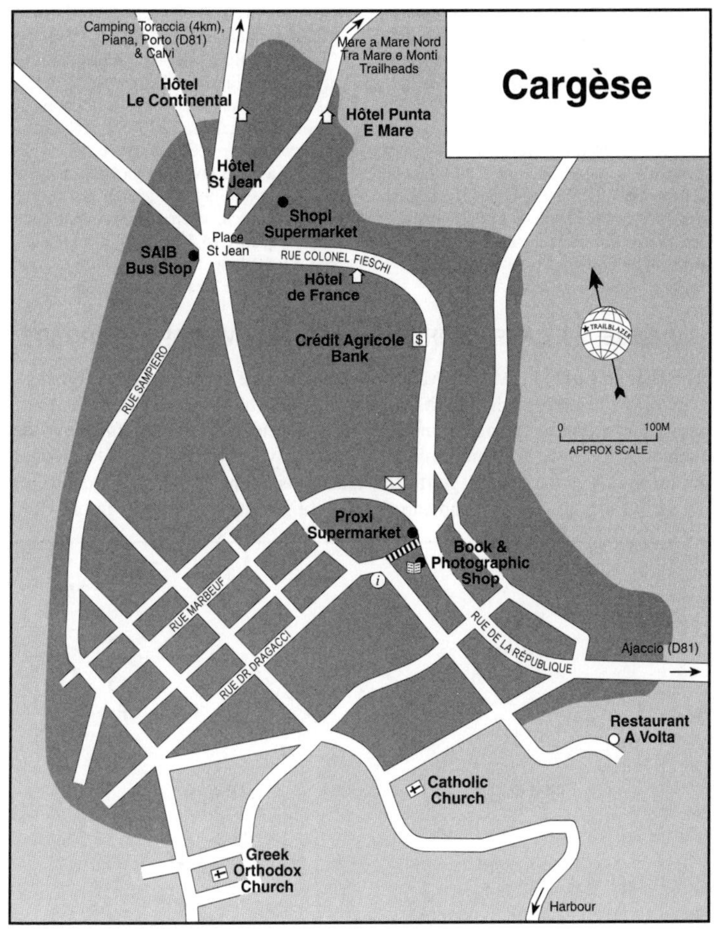

noise, but rates are rock bottom (24.30–30.40€ depending on the season) and there's a lively pizzeria and bar downstairs.

A notch pricier and more comfortable, ***Hôtel Le Continental*** (☎ 04.95 26.42.24, 🖹 04.95.26.46.81, 💻 grand carg@aol.com; closed Dec-Jan), on the right-hand side of the main road out of the village towards Porto, is a popular option with walkers. This friendly family-run hotel has large, impeccably clean en suite rooms, a busy restaurant on the ground floor, and views across the bay. Tariffs start at 40€ for a double in low season, rising to 48.60€ in July and August. They also do good half-board deals (41.80/45.60€ low/high season).

Hôtel Punta e Mare (☎ 04.95.26.44.33, 🖹 04.95.26.49.54, 💻 punta.e.mare.@wandoo.fr; closed Dec–Jan), 300m above place St Jean along the road to the trailhead, occupies a quieter spot on the outskirts of the village. A room with a balcony costs 38.80€ in low season or 57.70€ in mid-summer.

A swisher choice, also at the top of the village, is ***Hôtel Saint-Jean*** (☎ 04.95 26.46.68, 🖹 04.95.26.43.93, 🖳 s.zanettacci@wanadoo.fr). You can opt for a standard rear-facing room here, or a pricier one with sea views and mezzanine floors. Rates go from 39.50€ in low season to 69.90€ in July and August.

Eating out in Cargèse usually boils down to a choice between Saint-Jean and Le Continental. Both cater for a broad range of budgets, offering wood-fired pizzas, copious salads, or the usual selection of Corsican specialities and fresh seafood on their variously priced *menus fixes*.

For a more inspiring location, however, stroll over to the old quarter next to the Catholic church, where ***Restaurant A Volta*** serves a quality 16.70€ menu on a little terrace overlooking the bay. This is a good place to sample locally-caught fish.

CARGÈSE → E CASE/REVINDA [MAP 30, BELOW; MAP 31,OPPOSITE]

The first étape of the Mare a Mare Nord/Tra Mare e Monti is relatively short, with only one noteworthy climb. Most trekkers are happy to take their time and spend the afternoon lazing around E Case, a particularly peaceful *gîte* above the hamlet of Revinda. Anyone wishing to press on will probably have to bivouac in the woods as the next stage (to Marignana) is a long one. You'd have to get an early start, be pretty fit and carrying a light rucksack to do both in one day.

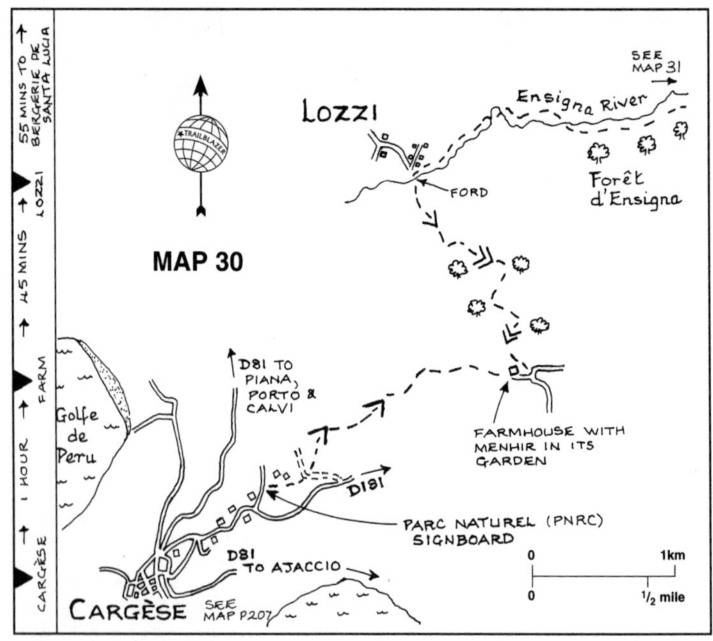

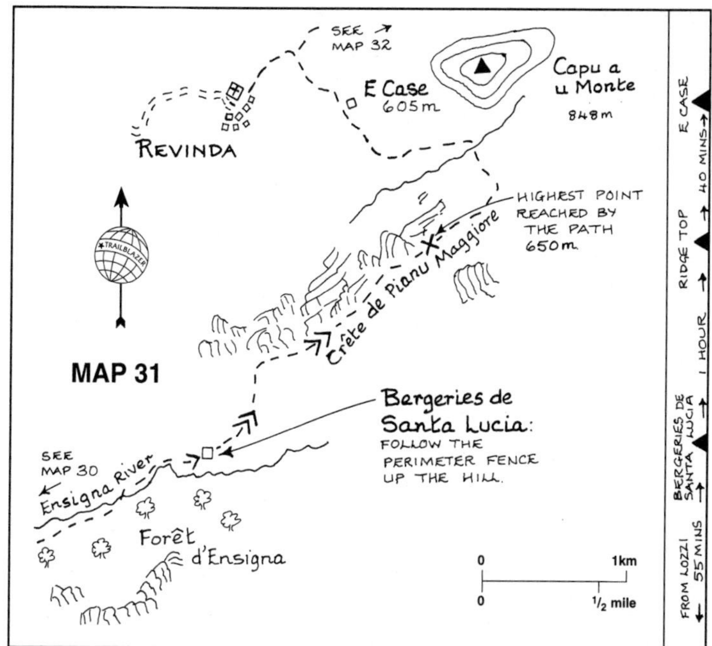

The official trailhead lies on the upper fringes of Cargèse. From place St Jean follow the lane uphill past the Shopi supermarket for around 10 minutes (the route is waymarked sporadically), until you arrive at the first prominent left turn, shortly after a bend in the road. Head down it for 250m, keeping an eye out for the Parc Naturel (PNRC) signboard on the right, which indicates the route to Revinda/E Case.

Plunging immediately into dense maquis, the path twists steeply up a ridge from which you get occasional glimpses of the Golfe de Peru to the west. After a climb of roughly 300 metres, the undergrowth thins out into patches of open pasture as you approach a small **farm** (in the garden of which stands a splendid ancient menhir).

Pass through the gate and turn left at the farm, from where a surfaced lane drops downhill. At this point the route turns sharply north to begin a longish, steep descent through woodland, re-crossing the lane further down and then entering a series of zigzags as it approaches the hamlet of **Lozzi**, stacked up the hillside above you. There's no shop here, so most hikers ford the stream and continue up the valley.

The next hour comprises a gentle walk through mixed deciduous forest – formerly a centre of charcoal production – during which you ford the stream

Le Chemin des Résistants

The old transhumant route between Cargèse and Marignana, which nowadays forms the first two étapes of the Mare a Mare Nord and Tra Mare e Monti footpaths, featured prominently in the creation of Corsica's famous Resistance network in WWII. It was along its winding woodland trails and granite ridges that a team of undercover agents were led by local patriots in 1942, their mission to establish an armed guerrilla movement that could mount an insurrection against the 90,000 or so Axis troops occupying the island at that time.

Code-named 'Pearl Harbour', the American-backed operation nearly floundered at the outset, however, when the submarine in which the agents travelled from North Africa surfaced in the wrong bay. Choppy water in the **Golfe de Topiti**, just north of Cargèse, capsized one of their inflatable dinghies, stranding several submariners on shore. Unable to return to their vessel, three ratings had to join the agents as they made their way at dawn inland through the maquis to search for help.

The expedition's big break came when they crossed paths with the local *curé* who was riding to Revinda on his donkey. Quick to realize the danger they were in, the priest smuggled the men into his church while he arranged for some local shepherds to shelter them.

The members of the Pearl Harbour mission spent their first night ashore in a dry-stone *bergerie* below the village, crammed with the Nesa family around a single fire. Led by one of the elder brothers, Benoît, the four principal agents left early the next day, following the old path up to Marignana and over the Col de St Pierre to Corte where they met Resistance chiefs. The young sailors, meanwhile, remained in the shepherds' hut for months until arrangements were made to smuggle them back aboard their submarine.

Corsica became the first *départment* of Metropolitan France to be liberated in September 1943, by which time Pearl Harbour's radio operators had broadcast 202 messages to Free French command in Algiers. The mission proved a valuable prototype for future landings, when arms, munitions and supplies for the Resistance were beached by the *Casabianca*. It remains a source of considerable pride for those involved, particularly the elderly villagers of Revinda and Marignana who put their lives in very real danger to help the mission.

Two plaques – one on the church at Revinda, and the other on the Nesa's winter house in Marignana – record the names of those who took part in Pearl Harbour. Following the mission's success, and that of the Corsican insurgency as a whole, the term Maquis, which until then referred only to the Corsican partisans, was adopted as a collective title for the entire French Resistance movement. The seminal role played by the old transhumant path in the early days of the armed struggle has led to calls from some locals to have the route re-named as Le Chemin des Résistants.

several times. Towards the head of the valley, the crags looming above the trees of the Forêt d'Ensigna start to close in and the hillsides show the scars of intensive grazing.

After crossing the stream one last time the Mare a Mare leaves the valley floor and climbs to the **Bergeries de Santa Lucia**. The shepherd has re-routed the path around his goat enclosure so keep an eye on the waymarks, which lead you along the fence and up a steep maquis-covered incline via a series of switchbacks. Fine views down the valley provide ample excuses to pause on this sharp haul of over 200m to the **Crête de Pianu Maggiore**.

The ensuing ridge climb, across low granite outcrops, grass patches and occasional coppices of gnarled oak and strawberry trees, affords the most impressive views of the day, with the mountains of the interior tumbling into Chiuni Bay.

From the culminating point at 650m, the path bends north and drops down from the plateau to ford the head of the Fornellu stream. This marks the start of the last ascent of the day, a gentle climb through thick maquis to the gîte of **E Case** (☎ 04.95.26.48.19). Situated on a sheltered balcony above Revinda village, the small hostel, housed in a converted stone farm, is among Corsica's most congenial, with sweeping views from its cosy little garden and terrace. The *gérant*, from Revinda, offers copious Corsican meals in the evening (15.24€); breakfast costs (4.57€). They have a total of 22 beds, in 6- or 8-person dormitories. Rates are 9.15€ per bed, or 27.40€ for half-board. Campers pay 7.62€ per tent. Book ahead by phone if you want a bed as this place tends to fill up early in the day.

E CASE/REVINDA → MARIGNANA [MAP 32, p212; MAP 33, p213]

This stage of the Tra Mare e Monti/Mare a Mare Nord takes you through a gloriously wild corner of the island, with the path keeping well away from villages and roads throughout. Growing gradually more grandiose as the day progresses, the scenery is also magnificent, although you pay for it with some longish ascents.

From E Case the path winds downhill for 10 minutes to a prominent fork. A left turn here will take you into **Revinda** – a village of a dozen or so (mostly uninhabited) houses that holds little of interest beyond its small church, where a wall plaque records the building's role in the Pearl Harbour mission of 1942 (see box opposite). Head right at the fork and, after an initial drop, follow the more or less level gradient up the Sulleoni Valley, with old-growth maquis and the crags of Punta di a Scavata combining to create a gloomy atmosphere.

The first landmark you come to, around 40 minutes after the fork, is an enigmatic **circle of stones**. This is a *chiostru* (or *séchoir* in French), used in former times to store and dry chestnuts gathered in the surrounding woods. The small clearing about 15 minutes beyond it is the best spot along this stretch to bivouac. A clump of exposed boulders just visible through the trees gives you a great view west over the valley.

After the clearing the path drops slightly as it approaches the river. On the far side, hollowed from the rocky slope, you can make out the blackened caves and scree of an old copper mine. One of the day's main climbs begins here. Lasting approximately 1½ hours, the ascent takes you 500 metres up the narrow Riogna Valley through more thick, tall maquis. The last section, zigzagging out of the undergrowth to a cluster of ruined shepherd's huts known as **Casta**, is particularly steep. Spread over a patch of open grassy ground, with panoramic

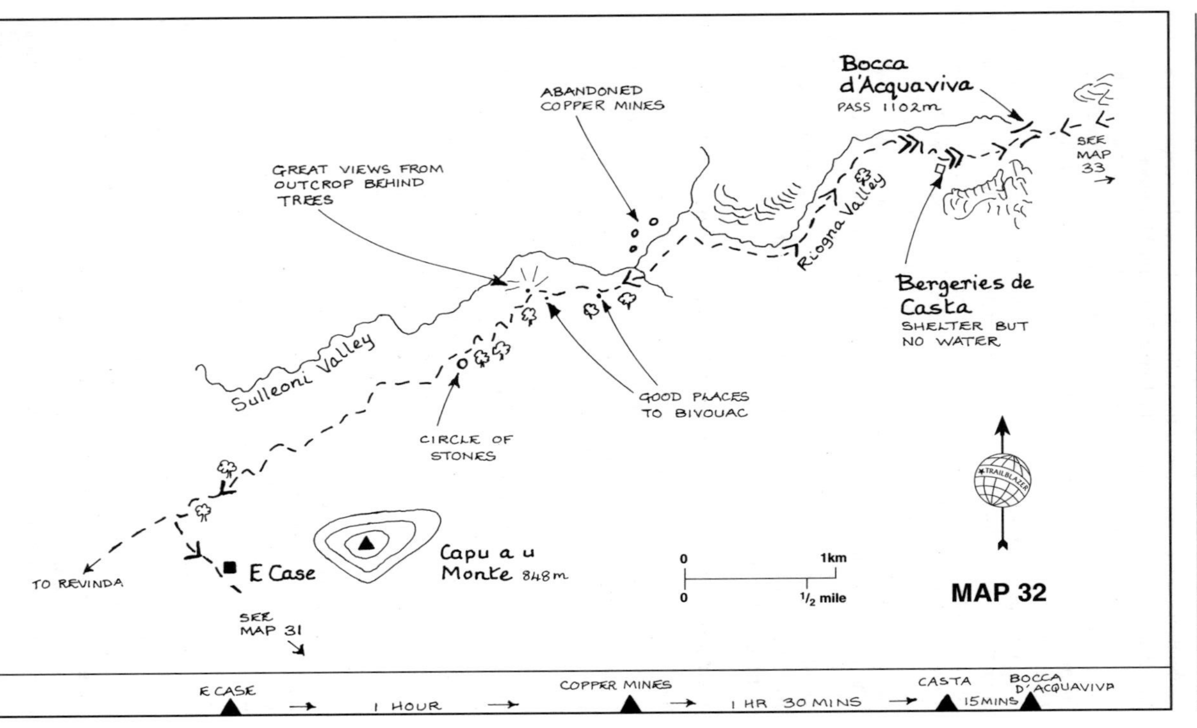
Bocca d'Acquaviva
PASS 1102m
SEE MAP 33
ABANDONED COPPER MINES
GREAT VIEWS FROM OUTCROP BEHIND TREES
Riogna Valley
Bergeries de Casta
SHELTER BUT NO WATER
Sulleoni Valley
GOOD PLACES TO BIVOUAC
CIRCLE OF STONES
TRAILBLAZER
Capu a u Monte 848m
TO REVINDA
E Case
SEE MAP 31
0
1km
0
1/2 mile
MAP 32
E CASE
1 HOUR
COPPER MINES
1 HR 30 MINS
CASTA
15MINS
BOCCA D'ACQUAVIVA

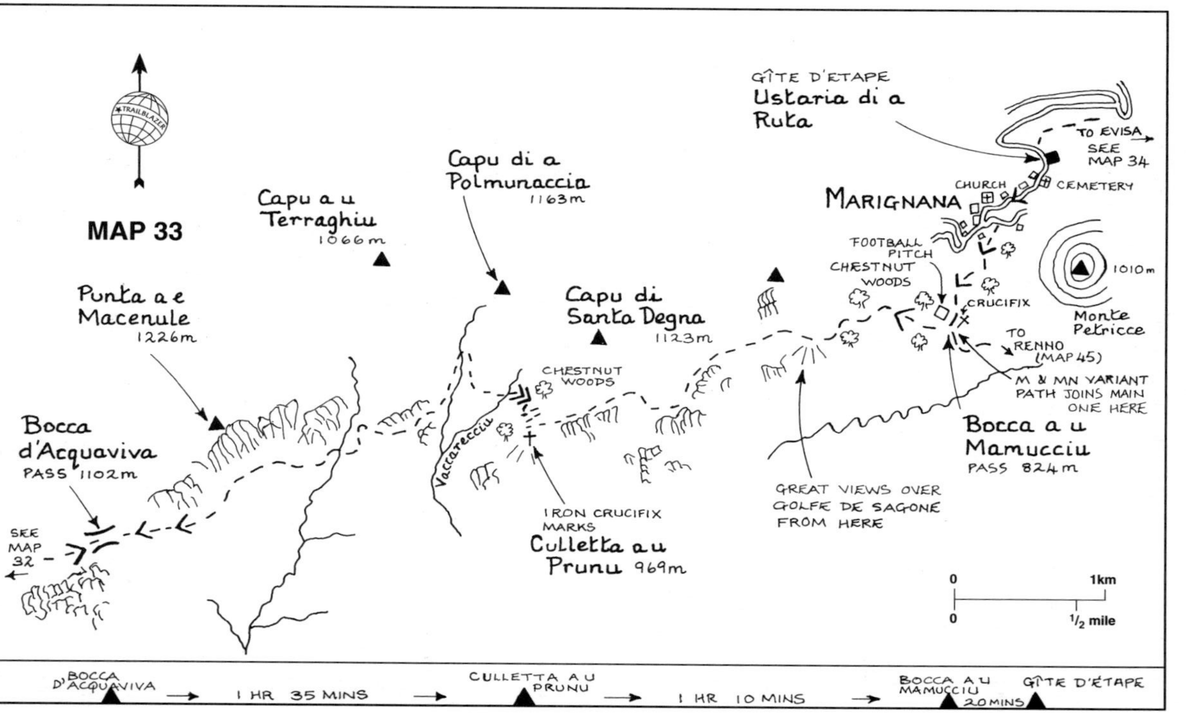
MAP 33
TRAILBLAZER
GÎTE D'ETAPE
Ustaria di a Ruta
TO EVISA
SEE MAP 34
CHURCH
CEMETERY
MARIGNANA
Capu di a Polmunaccia 1163m
Capu a u Terraghiu 1066m
Punta a e Macenule 1226m
Capu di Santa Degna 1123m
FOOTBALL PITCH
CHESTNUT WOODS
CRUCIFIX
1010m
Monte Petricce
TO RENNO (MAP 45)
M & MN VARIANT PATH JOINS MAIN ONE HERE
CHESTNUT WOODS
Bocca d'Acquaviva
PASS 1102m
Vaccareccia
Bocca a u Mamucciu
PASS 824m
SEE MAP 32
IRON CRUCIFIX MARKS
Culletta a u Prunu 969m
GREAT VIEWS OVER GOLFE DE SAGONE FROM HERE
0 1km
0 1/2 mile
BOCCA D'ACQUAVIVA → 1 HR 35 MINS → CULLETTA A U PRUNU → 1 HR 10 MINS → BOCCA A U MAMUCCIU 20 MINS GÎTE D'ÉTAPE

views, the bergeries would make an ideal spot to bivouac or camp if water were available; a signboard points to a spring but we couldn't find it.

Ten to fifteen minutes' more climbing brings you to **Bocca d'Acquaviva** pass (1102m), a saddle-shaped niche below the summit of Punta a e Macenule (1226m). Beyond it the path, descending steeply at first, makes a long, sweeping traverse of the valley head and then winds through rocks on its northern rim to penetrate a wilder ravine.

The route to the far side of this valley involves a succession of short descents to and climbs from easy stream crossings. Once over the **Vaccarecciu**, you start a more protracted 140m climb through lovely old chestnut forest emerging eventually at a ridgetop crowned by a cairn and crucifix. Known as **Culletta a u Prunu** (969m), this windblown spot high above the roadless Fiuminale Valley affords the day's most spectacular view, encompassing the distant Golfe de Sagone.

The great views continue uninterrupted for the next hour or so as you wriggle via a well-preserved mule path along the top of the valley to **Bocca a u Mamucciu** (824m). Marked by a large white crucifix, this pass forms the gateway into the Spelunca Valley system; it also marks the place where the Mare a Mare Nord *Variant* rejoins the main path. If you intend to complete the whole of the grand loop from Corte to Guango and Renno, you'll return here in a week or more.

MARIGNANA

The remaining 20- to 30-minute amble into Marignana passes through stately old-growth chestnut forest, where gangs of snuffling pigs forage, and past the village football pitch. After skirting the first row of houses, turn left at the surfaced road and then right at the main junction a little further on. This brings you to the church at the centre of the village.

Practical information

For ***Gîte d'étape Ustaria di a Rota*** (☎ 04 95.26.21.21) keep going down the road past the church for another five or ten minutes; the hostel stands just above the bend, after the cemetery. Some trekkers give this place a miss, preferring to press on to Évisa, but it's one of the nicest gîtes on the island, renowned both for the conviviality of its owners, the Ceccaldi family, and for the wonderful food, which attracts a strong local clientele. The owner's brother is a butcher, which assures a supply of top quality *charcuterie*. You could also be served old-fashioned *polenda* or succulent wild boar stew. Evening meals cost around 15.20€; half-board is good value at 25.80€. The rate for beds in the large dormitories upstairs is 10.70€, or you can camp or bivouac in the rear garden for 5.20€. For anyone craving a bit of luxury there are also a dozen or so en suite 'studio' rooms further up the lane for 30€.

Even if you decide not to stop for the night in Marignana, don't miss out on a drink in the gîte's bar, which is one of the few places in Corsica where locals and visitors mingle easily. From its terrace, the sunsets over Spelunca gorge and the Golfe de Porto are sublime.

The only public transport serving Marignana is Autocars Ceccaldi's bus service (☎ 04.95.21.38.06 or 04.95.21.01.24; Mon–Sat 1–3 daily), which runs to Ajaccio via Évisa and Vico. There are no taxis so if you miss the bus and want to leave by road your only alternative is to hitch – in which case, walk downhill out of the village (past the gîte) for 3km until you meet the main Évisa–Porto road, which sees a lot more through traffic.

MARIGNANA → ÉVISA [MAP 34, BELOW]

The path to Évisa begins just past the gîte. After a short rise, it contours through maquis and later chestnut woods to the deserted hamlet of **Tassu.** When you reach the stream just below the ruined houses, follow the waymarks left and keep to the nearside (true left) bank until you come to the first of three crossing points. This sequence is poorly marked in places and can be confusing but after fording the stream for the third time you arrive at a major confluence with the Tavulella River, where a **suspension bridge** (marked 'Plle' for *passarelle* on the IGN map) provides a somewhat awkward crossing point (getting off the bridge under the cables at the far end is a bit tricky with a rucksack).

From the passarelle, a mainly gentle 45-minute climb across more maquis-covered crags and chestnut woodland, through which views of Capu d'Ortu and

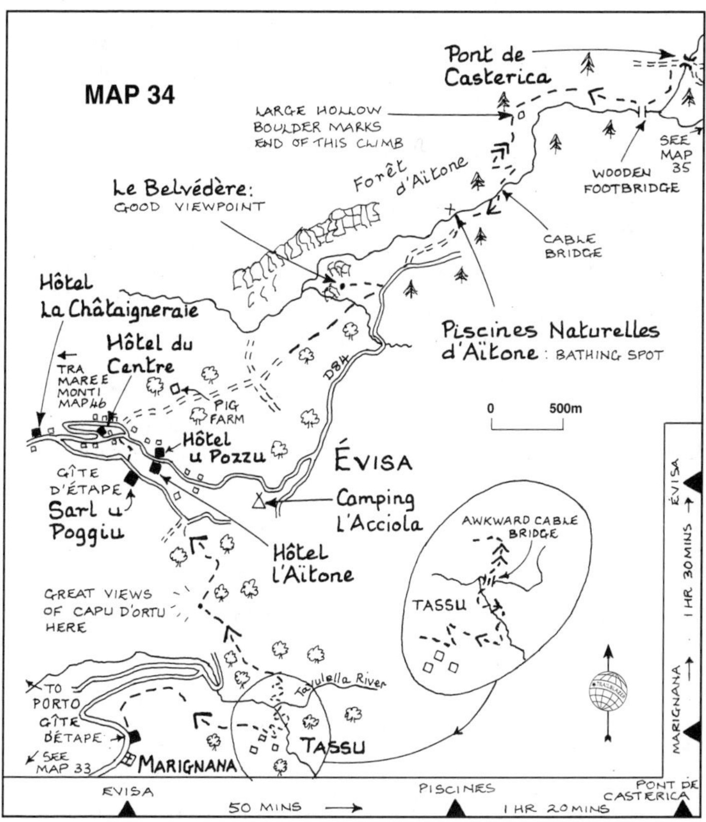

The Forêt d'Aïtone

Extending north-east from Évisa to the rim of the Col de Verghio, the Forêt d'Aïtone is often claimed to be Corsica's most spectacular forest thanks to the wealth of **Laricio pines** spread over the valley floor and sides. These were the trees prized above all others by the timber-hungry Genoans, who felled them in prodigious quantities to feed their shipbuilding industry. Towering to a height of 50m or more (ideal for mast poles), mature Laricios yield a strong, supple and storm-resistant wood. Nowhere else in the world has so many, despite the rapacious clear felling that denuded vast swathes of the island in the fifteenth and sixteenth centuries. The Genoan timber industry explains why valleys such as this – the reason why valleys such as this and the Tavignano were lined with immaculate mule tracks, which were built to facilitate the extraction of the wood .

The Forêt d'Aïtone also supports an uncommonly rich profusion of **fauna**. Wild boar, stoats and foxes are fairly numerous, though your chances of spotting the enigmatic *ghjattu volpe* (cat-fox), Corsica's rarest and most exotic mammal, are even slimmer than the odds of sighting a mouflon foraging on the rocks high above. *Ghjattu volpes* were thought to be extinct until French Customs recently discovered several carcasses in a haul of poachers' booty.

Banditry rather than poaching was the speciality of the criminal most closely associated with the Aïtone forest, where he made his hideout. Dubbed 'Le Roi des Montagnes' (the King of the Mountains) by his French adversaries, **Tiadore Poli** ranked among the island's most notorious outlaws. For nearly a decade in the early nineteenth century he and his band of 150 roughnecks terrorized the local clergy and nobility, from whom they extracted their own brand of revolutionary tax. The gang's anti-French activities, which extended to murdering unpopular local governors and gendarmes, earned them a Robin-Hood-like reputation among the local population. A special corps of crack trackers and troops was eventually raised to capture Poli. Local legend has it that he died after being lured into a deadly ambush by a beautiful woman who fed him an apple laced with cyanide.

its surrounding peaks open up to the west, brings you to the lower fringes of **Évisa**. The Mare a Mare Nord and Tra Mare e Monti paths diverge here.

ÉVISA

This region's two long-distance trails cross at Évisa, making the village an important staging post for walkers. Scattered over a high balcony above the Spelunca Valley, at the head of a famous paved Genoan timber track (which connects it with nearby Ota) it is also a major target for day walkers. Once they've gone, however, Évisa reverts to being a sleepy hill village. Additional reasons to stay here are the wonderful sunsets, the views of the peaks above Porto, and the batch of exceptionally good restaurants where you can sample the area's speciality chestnut dishes.

Orientation and services

Évisa lies on Autocar Ceccaldi's year-round **bus** route Ajaccio (☎ 04.95.21.38.06 or 04.95.21.01.24; Mon–Sat 1–3 daily) to and from Ajaccio, which calls at Marignana, Vico and Tiuccia. Between July and mid-September you can also get here from Porto on Autocar Mordiconi's (☎ 04 95 48 00 04) once-daily service to Corte, via Col de Verghio, Albertacce and Calacuccia in the Niolu Valley. Ask at the Café-Bar de la Poste, in the middle of the village where the buses stop, for the exact timings.

Where to stay and eat

Évisa's smart ***Gîte d'étape Sarl u Poggiu*** (☎ 04.95.26.21.88; open April–Oct) stands at the bottom of the village, slap on the Mare a Mare Nord. Like most businesses hereabouts, it's run by the entrepreneurial Ceccaldi family, whose food is a cut above your average hostel fare and relatively inexpensive: 11.40€ for supper, 6€ for breakfast or 25.84€ for half-board. Dorm beds cost 10.64€.

For a little more comfort, you won't do better than the welcoming ***Hôtel La Châtaigneraie*** (☎ 04.95.26.24.47, 🖹 04.95 26.23.11, 🖳 hotellachataigneraie@wanadoo.fr; open April–Oct), on the western edge of the village, overlooking the main Porto road and surrounded as its name implies by chestnut woods. Tastefully furnished rooms in this traditional stone building range from 30.40 to 45.60€. The hotel's restaurant, whose set 16.70€ menu includes local dishes such as chestnut-flour doughnuts made with fresh *brocciu* and melt-in-the-mouth *fiadone*, is open to non-residents. This is a particularly good option for non-French speakers as the proprietress is American.

Serious foodies, however, might try for a bed at the smaller ***Hôtel du Centre*** (☎ 04.95.26.20.92; open April–mid-Oct) in the middle of the village. At 36.48€ per double or 82€ for half-board (regardless of the season), the four rooms here are well priced, but cooking is the real reason to stay. Downstairs in the cosy dining room, you can tuck into house specialties such as wild boar in chocolate sauce or fillet of local pork in basil. Their chestnut *parfait* is also a dream. The set menu is 21.28€ in the evening and a little cheaper at lunch time; be sure to book a table as far in advance as possible as this restaurant is extremely popular.

Évisa's two remaining places to stay and eat are both at the eastern end of the village on the Col de Verghio road. ***Hôtel U Pozzu*** (☎ 04.95.21.11.45; open May–Sept) offers half a dozen impeccably clean rooms for 38/42.56€ low/high season. Directly opposite and run by the same family is the much grander ***Hôtel L'Aïtone*** (☎ 04.95 26.20.04, 🖹 04.95.26.24.18; open June–Nov), which boasts a pool and a terrace from where the views of the sunset are superb. Off season, rates here drop as low as 30.40€ for a room with shared toilet but for most of the year, half-board (85.12€ for the basic rooms or 129.20€ for the en suite ones) is obligatory.

Campers have an uphill trudge to reach the village's only campsite, the rudimentary but cheap ***Camping L'Acciola*** (☎ 04 95.26.03.01; May–Sept), 1.5km east along the Col de Verghio road. During the season they open a small wood-fired pizzeria here.

ÉVISA → ALBERTACCE [MAP 34, p215; MAP 35, p219; MAP 36, p221; MAP 37, p222]

Crossing the island's watershed at Col de Verghio (1477m), this third stage of the Mare a Mare Nord between Évisa and Albertacce in the Niolu Valley is a long one, involving seven or eight hours of trekking. Most of it crosses simple terrain, the only significant ascent being the well-shaded climb through the upper reaches of the Forêt d'Aïtone to the col, where you can refuel at a seasonal produce stall before the long drop down into the Niolu Valley. Crossing point of the Mare a Mare Nord and the GR20, Col de Verghio is also where anyone wishing to follow the more challenging route to Corte via Lac de Nino (see the box on p218) has to peel south towards the Col de St Pierre.

At Évisa the Mare a Mare Nord recommences directly opposite Café-Bar de la Poste, near the middle of the village, scaling a flight of steps between the houses. Follow the waymarks up the lane beyond these, then north-west past a pig farm and into the shade of the last chestnut trees of the day. After 45 minutes' easy walking you rejoin the main **D84**, at which point a **subsidiary path** doubles back to your left, winding for 20 minutes through the forest to a massive granite outcrop known as **Le Belvédère**, a well-known viewpoint overlooking the Spelunca Valley. The orange Mare a Mare waymarks, meanwhile, follow the main road for around 40m before dropping off it onto a piste to the left that goes down to the **Piscines Naturelles d'Aïtone**, a popular picnic spot where you can swim in pools of crystal-clear water.

Cross the stream here via the cable bridge to your right to begin a stiff 40-minute corkscrew climb. Near the top, you reach another wonderful belvédère formed by a large hollow boulder. Shortly beyond it the path improves, becoming a proper mule way paved with large flat stones. A long, gentle downhill section winds under imperious old pines to a wooden footbridge (marked with a sign for the holiday village on the far bank). Don't cross it; continue instead above the true right bank of the Aïtone and its confluence with the Casterica to arrive at a second bridge, the **Pont de Casterica**.

Most of the remaining route up to the col follows a very even, broad foresters' piste, only quitting it for the final steep pull to the pass, winding alongside the Verghio stream.

The Lac de Nino *Variant*

Just below the Col de Verghio, the Mare a Mare Nord crosses the GR20 as it approaches the end of its descent from the Golo Valley. By turning onto it and heading south, you can bypass Albertacce, Calacuccia and the Col de l'Arinella in favour of a wilder route that takes you over the Col de St Pierre to and around Lac de Nino, the island's most beautiful high-altitude lake, where wild horses and pigs graze a landscape oddly reminiscent of a Tibetan plateau. Around 75 minutes beyond the lake, at the Bergeries de Vaccaghia, a liaison path, waymarked in yellow, turns left (north-east) down the headwaters of the Tavignano to rejoin the Mare a Mare Nord at the A Sega refuge.

The section from Castel di Verghio to the Bergeries de Vaccaghia is described in detail on pp141-6. Although arguably the least strenuous stage of the entire GR20, the étape crosses some unforgettable terrain and affords much more impressive views of Paglia Orba and the Cinto Massif than you get from Col de l'Arinella on the conventional route. To complete it in a day, though, you'll have to overnight at Castel di Verghio and get a very early start.

From **Bergeries de Vaccaghia**, reached after roughly 3½ hours' walking from Verghio (see p141), you drop down 120m to the valley floor and follow a clearly defined, well-waymarked path that undulates north-east above the left bank of the Tavignano, past the **Bergeries de Tramizzole** (1427m). After around 1¾ hours, it crosses into a small side valley, at the bottom of which it splits. Follow the right fork along the stream (the other traverses the valley flank to the Col de l'Arinella). The fringes of the Tavignano forest, where the path levels out on its run in to **A Sega**, are reached shortly before the three-hour mark. This link section, between Vaccaghia and A Sega, shouldn't take more than 3½ hours. It's covered on IGN Map 4251OT (Monte D'Oro/Monte Rotondo).

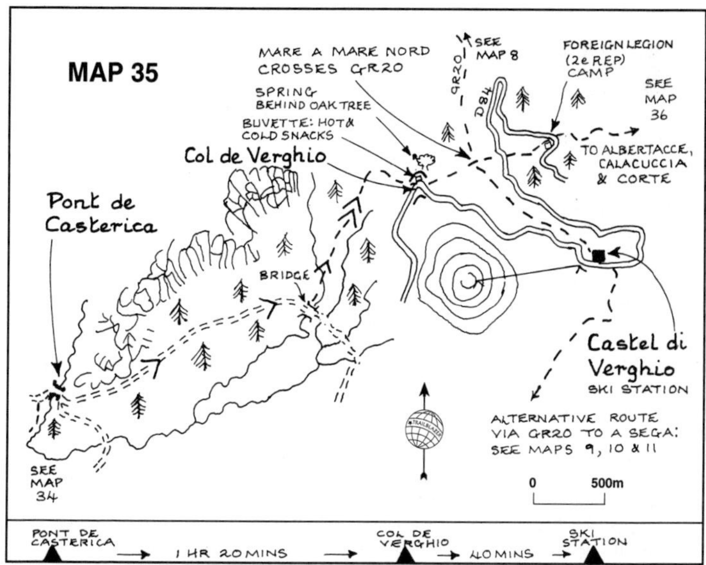

After the effort to reach it, the **Col de Verghio** (1477m) comes as something of a disappointment, despite the impressive views east into Niolu. The highest point on the island crossed by a tarmac road, it tends to be swarming with bus parties, German bikers and jazzily-dressed French cyclists. The main incentive to linger is the cold beer sold at the *buvette*, where you can also stock up on fresh spinach and brocciu pasties, local charcuterie and eye-wateringly strong ewe's cheese from the valley.

The buvette doesn't provide drinking water for trekkers, so to fill up your water bottles you'll have to seek out the **spring** 50 metres above it, behind the solitary oak tree.

The **Castel di Verghio** ski station lies a dull 20-minute plod down the D84 from the pass. A key landmark on the GR20, it relies on trekkers rather than skiers for its custom these days: there hasn't been enough snow up here to keep the place going through the winter for years. For details of its generally shabby facilities, see p140.

The Mare a Mare bypasses the ski station and plunges east downhill through the Laricio pine forest, cutting across the GR20 and then two switch-backs of the D89. At the second road crossing look out for the camp of the **French Foreign Legion**'s 2nd Parachute Regiment, the 2e REP. Based at Calvi, this élite force of mountain-warfare specialists, picked from the cream of the legion's international recruits, trains in the rugged terrain to the north. You'll occasionally meet them on the trail; they are recognizable by their

U Niolu

One of the very few corners of Corsica where you feel truly far from the sea is the **Niolu**, an oval-shaped plateau hidden deep in the island's rocky heart. Surrounded on three sides by jagged rows of peaks rising above 2500m (among them Monte Cinto, Paglia Orba and the Cinque Frati, or 'Five Monks'), the 21km-long basin, where the headwaters of the Golo flow into the Calacuccia barrage, is sealed off on the fourth side by the long, tortuous ravine of Scala di Santa Regina – dubbed by those obliged in times past to lead their mule trains up its vertiginous rock-cut steps as A Scala, 'The Ladder'.

The Niolu's physical isolation, compounded by winter snows, has always ensured the valley has remained distanced from the mainstream of island life. When the French novelist Guy de Maupassant ventured up here at the end of the eighteenth century he found a society seemingly little altered since prehistoric times. Its inhabitants were still primarily transhumant shepherds. The men, notoriously violent, vindictive and independent-minded, migrated with their flocks between the high pastures around Monte Cinto in the summer, and over the shoulder of Capu Tafonatu through the Fangu Valley to the coast in winter. The women, meanwhile, remained at home to spin wool, rear pigs and chickens, and coax crops of flax and vegetables from the impoverished soil. To Maupassant's amazement many Niolins were uncommonly tall, sandy-haired and blue-eyed, claiming descent from Corsica's original Megalthic tribes.

Smothered in more central regions by centuries of Christianity and oppressive colonial rule, many ancient traditions, whose standing stones and tombs are still strewn across the hillsides, had been miraculously preserved. Among them were the valley's pure polyphonic singing which, with its swirling harmonies and bleak emotional intensity, powerfully conveyed to the young novelist the austerity of life in the Niolu, which he later characterized in his best selling novel of 1892, *Un Bandit Corse* (A Corsican Bandit), as 'this wild trench'.

Today, Niolu is no longer the lost world it was. The first road through the Scala penetrated the valley shortly after Maupassant's first visit, while a high-spec Route Nationale now runs over the Col de Verghio to the west coast. Engulfing the valley floor, and some of its oldest monuments, a reservoir formed to supply Bastia has also, local environmentalists claim, altered the microclimate of the plateau, giving rise to strange mists and ruining crops with mysterious fungal diseases. In addition, the once massive Forêt de Valdoniello, crossed by the Mare a Mare Nord, has been decimated by fire, scarring the south side of the plateau with giant patches of barren earth.

Even so, entering the Niolu on one of the old paths across the cols de Verghio, l'Arinella or St Pierre, you'll still be struck by the wild setting of its villages, clustered in red-tiled clumps on the shores of the lake or clinging to the awesome bulk of the Cinto massif. And it may sound a cliché to say so, but the Niolins' traditional hospitality has also endured, most evidently in the pride they show for their cuisine. At one time the valley supplied most of the milk used by the Roquefort company, and cheese is still a big thing here, as is the dark art of charcuterie making. Vegetarians considering a visit in mid-December might want to think again. The local patron saint, Saint Francis, would turn in his grave at the gruesome din of pig slaughter that echoes through the valley before the onset of the first snows.

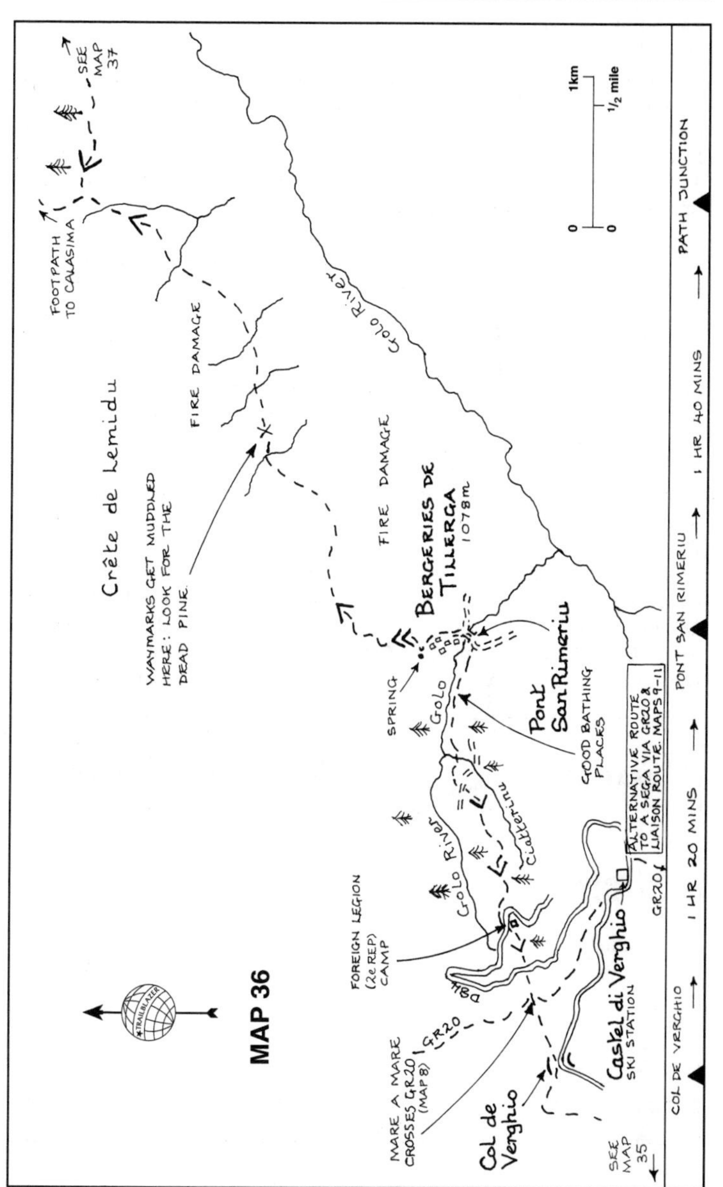
MAP 36
TRAILBLAZER
Crête de Lemidu
FIRE DAMAGE
FIRE DAMAGE
FOOTPATH TO CALASIMA
SEE MAP 37
Golo River
WAYMARKS GET MUDDLED HERE: LOOK FOR THE DEAD PINE
BERGERIES DE TILLERGA
1078m
SPRING
Golo
Pont San Rimeriu
GOOD BATHING PLACES
Ciatterinu
Golo River
FOREIGN LEGION (2e REP) CAMP
D84
ALTERNATIVE ROUTE TO A SEGA VIA GR20 & LIAISON ROUTE. MAPS 9-11
GR20
Castel di Verghio
SKI STATION
GR20
MARE A MARE CROSSES GR20 (MAP 8)
Col de Verghio
SEE MAP 35
1km
1/2 mile
0
0
COL DE VERGHIO
1 HR 20 MINS
PONT SAN RIMERIU
1 HR 40 MINS
PATH JUNCTION

Rambo-like physiques, crew cuts and green berets, which bear the famous winged-dagger ensignia.

Twenty minutes or so below the army camp, the path fords the Ciatterinu stream and follows the Golo River as it crashes eastward, creating a series of perfect swimming pools. It eventually crosses the river at the **Pont San Rimeriu**, an old stone bridge built to provide access to the **Bergeries de Tillerga**, now a cluster of holiday cottages. Follow the lane uphill through the settlement past its **spring** at the foot of a large concrete tank.

A short, sharp pull from here brings you to a level gradient that the route sticks to more or less constantly for the next couple of hours during its long, gradual descent of the Niolu Valley. The only blots on an otherwise idyllic landscape are the expanses of fire damage, which have necessitated several re-routings. At one stage, just after the first of three stream crossings, the path gets muddled with its old waymarks, drawing you into dense maquis around the foot of a granite outcrop. Forget the cairns that are meant to lead you out of it and head instead for the prominent dead pine, from where the correct path leads into a coppice of spruce trees.

From here on the absence of forest makes for open, easy walking and impressive views. In clear weather you'll have an uninterrupted panorama of the 2000+m ridge to the south, which culminates in the snow-capped summit of Punta Artica (2327m).

Before dropping back to river level, the Mare a Mare Nord scales the **Crête de Lemidu**, an arcing spur of Paglia Orba dividing the Niolu and Viru valleys. Once over the ridge (1115m), you come face to face with the south flank of Monte Cinto. Calasima (1110m) – Corsica's highest permanently inhabited village – clings to the mountain's denuded lower slopes in the middle distance.

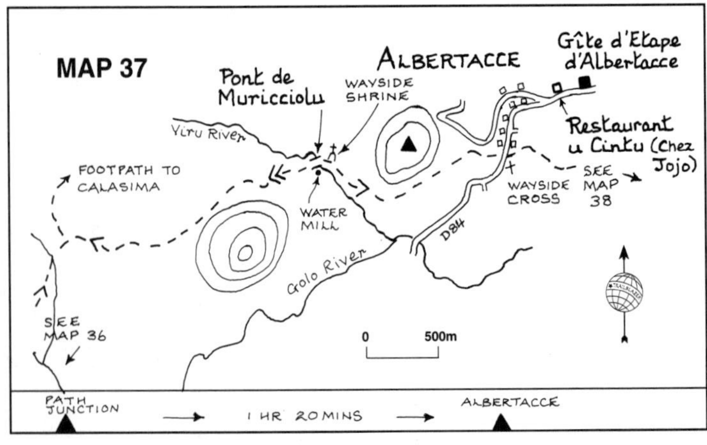

At the fork in the path reached a short way beyond the ridgetop, bear right and follow the orange waymarks down through the last of the pines to the Viru River, which you cross via a gracefully-arched Genoan footbridge, the **Pont de Muricciolu**. Upstream the mighty shark's tooth summit of Paglia Orba looms at the head of a superbly glaciated valley. With its dramatic situation and excellent bathing places, this makes a good bivouac spot as any if you have enough supplies.

To reach Albertacce, however, you still have one more rise to negotiate via the paved mule track that runs most of the way to the village.

ALBERTACCE

Huddled at the foot of Capu di Manganu, a subsidiary peak of the Cinto massif, Albertacce is the second largest settlement in the Niolu Valley after Calacuccia. During the summer months its solid grey granite houses dotted along the D84 see streams of through traffic. But in winter, when the pass is often blocked by snow and the valley becomes a giant cul de sac, the village feels like a remote outpost, inhabited by a hard core of resilient pensioners. Its populous is, however, too small to support a store; the nearest source of supplies is Calacuccia.

As somewhere to rest before the haul over the Col de l'Arinella, however, Albertacce has the edge over its neighbour – at least if you're happy with the basic comforts of the local gîte. In addition to fine views over the valley, it boasts an especially good (and inexpensive) restaurant where you can tuck into platefuls of top-notch Niolu home cooking.

Practical information

Accommodation is limited to the run-of-the-mill ***Gîte d'étape d'Albertacce*** (☎ 04 95.48.05.60 or 04.95.48.08.05; open April–mid-October), on the east side of the village, where a bed in a six- or nine-person dorm costs 10.60€ plus 3.80€ for breakfast, or 27.40€ for half-board. The kitchen is well set up for self-caterers, and there's a washing line in the back garden, but no terrace or balcony. Walkers tend to hang around in the somewhat spartan dining hall in the evening. Campers may stick their tents in the back garden, but if you want to bivouac, you'll have to find a secluded spot well out of sight of the village down by the side of the lake.

A more congenial place (and the best possible excuse for skipping supper at the gîte) is the wonderful ***Restaurant U Cintu 'Chez Jo Jo'*** (open May–Oct, and out-of-season with a few hours advance warning), five minutes' walk back towards the centre of the village, on the right (north) side of the main road. Served in a little front room that probably doubles as a sitting room in winter, two menus are on offer: a no-frills 11.40€ option comprising three courses, or 15.20€ for the works. Go for the works, which basically means as much sublime Corsican mountain cuisine – such as home-made ravioli brocciu, tender local lamb, and dessert such as chestnut flan with honey – as you can cram in, with *eau de vie* on the house. The couple who run it are refreshingly down-to-earth and justifiably proud of their local cuisine. Wherever possible, ingredients are sourced locally: this includes the sublime charcuterie served as a starter for the pricier menu, and the wonderfully strong local cheeses. Express an interest and Jo Jo will take you through the whole gamut of different Niolin sausages, including a pungent *figatellu* which he makes himself.

Albertacce is on Autocars Mordiconi's seasonal bus route, to Calacuccia and Corte in one direction, and cols de Verghio, Évisa and Porto in the other (☎ 04 95 48 00 04; July–mid-Sept one daily).

The Massacre of 1774

The Couvent Saint François di Niolu witnessed a grizzly massacre on June 25, 1774, when 11 local men (one of whom was only 15 years old) were broken on cartwheels and hanged from trees in its grounds. They had been accused by the French, who were desperately attempting to consolidate their new rule of the island, of being ringleaders of an armed insurrection. Doomed from the outset, the uprising has become emblematic of the Niolins' resistance against colonial occupation. This has always been a staunchly independent region, marshalling on several occasions local opposition to the French.

ALBERTACCE → CALACUCCIA [MAP 38, p227]

It takes around an hour to walk along the north shore of the lake from Albertacce to Calacuccia. The path begins diagonally opposite the spot where the previous day's trail emerges on the main road, next to a large wayside cross. About 50 metres down the track you enter a triangular clearing. Bear left here and follow the waymarks to the lakeside. The next half hour is a leisurely amble along old paths, flanked here and there by drystone walls and chestnut trees, with views of Monte Cinto and its neighbouring peaks to the north.

In the hamlet of **Sidossi**, roughly the midway point, there's another excellent restaurant. Renowned across the island as the home of definitive Niolin cuisine, ***L'Auberge du Lac*** (☎ 04.95.48.02.73; open June–Sept) occupies a tranquil spot slap on the lake, with a large dining hall looking south across the water to the mountains. Menus are fixed at 15.20€ and 19.80€ and include top-quality local charcuterie and cheeses; main dishes are usually simple grilled meat or stews flavoured with fragrant Niolin mushrooms, maquis herbs or brocciu, and their mint omelettes are out of this world.

The area's nicest ***gîte d'étape*** (☎ 04.95.48.00.11; open year-round) lies a short walk north of Sidossi in an old converted convent – **Couvent Saint François di Niolu** – on the north side of the main road, 2km west of Calacuccia and roughly the same from Albertacce. Dorms beds cost 10.64€, or you could splash out on an en suite double room for 35€. Use of the kitchen is included in these prices, but the *patronne* doesn't provide supper. For that, you'll have to cross the road to ***Auberge Casa Balduina*** (☎ 04.95.48.08.57; open Easter–Sept), another unpretentious place that serves delicious, home-cooked local specialities such as veal pan-fried with olives, cêpes or morelle mushrooms. They also do a melt-in-the-mouth *fiadone* made with soft brocciu and honey from down the valley. Menus are priced at 13.70€ and 19€.

To get to the convent from Sidossi you can cut along the path between two houses on the west side of the hamlet and turn left at the fork shortly afterwards

Opposite: Statue of General Gian' Pietri Gaffori, Corte (see p231); notice the Genoan bullet holes in the façade behind. (Photo © David Abram).

REFUGE SEGA
CALACUCCIA

Corsican polyphony

'It was like hearing a voice from the depths of the earth; a song from the dawn of time; from a beginning that one never dares believe is accessible', wrote historian and traveller Dorothy Carrington in 1948 of her first encounter with Corsican *polyphonies*.

The island's extraordinary *a cappella* singing tradition encapsulates perhaps better than anything else Corsica's essential otherness. Derived from a mixture of Roman-Christian liturgy, Genoan madrigals, Islamic prayer and pagan chant, its characteristic blend of soaring harmonies overlaid with transient, eerie dissonances seem to bear the imprint of every invading culture since Megalithic times.

The region most closely associated with Corsican singing is the **Niolu Valley**, whose remote churches remained bastions of the art long after it had died out almost everywhere else. Its greatest exponents were always shepherds, which may account for the melancholic tone of much polyphony, premature death (as often as not through vendetta or exposure to the elements) and perennial separation from loved ones being integral to transhumant life.

Bleakest of all the island's vocal forms, and the Niolu's speciality, is the **paghjella**, a lament usually performed by three male voices: a bass, or *bassu*; a mid-range singer, *a secunda*; and *a terza* above them, providing heavily ornamented improvisations over the basic chords and cadences. Before the advent of organs in village churches, mass was sung in this style, with the three vocalists leaning together, often with their elbows resting on each others shoulders and hands shielding their ears – the classic Corsican polyphony pose.

You can be guaranteed to hear live singing at the annual **Santa di u Niolu** fair, held on 8th September at **Casamaccioli**, across the lake from Calacuccia. Its centrepiece is a typically Corsican contest between local bards called **chiami e rispondi**, literally 'call and response'. Contestants improvise a stream of invective, political parody and insult, strictly phrased in 16-syllable lines and designed to outwit their opponent. When one of them fails to respond, the other is declared the winner.

In recent years Corsican polyphony has enjoyed a remarkable renaissance. Having become almost extinct after WWII, it was revived by the nascent nationalist movement in the early 1970s, when its rousing patriotic strains stirred crowds at political rallies.

The power of polyphony was considered so potent by Giscard d'Estaing's government that at one stage several of the most respected young groups, including Cantu u Populu Corsu and Bastia's I Muvrini, were banned. Since then both have become household names in France while a younger generation of singers, notably Les Nouvelles Polyphonies Corses, has experimented with traditional forms to produce platinum-selling World Music albums. More groundbreaking still, an all-women group, Donnisulana, formed in the mid-1990s and shocked traditionalists, who insisted polyphony was an exclusively male art, by recording the CD of the decade, *Per Agata* (on the Silex label and available at good record shops in most towns in Corsica). Other commendable compilations include the *Voce di Corsica: Polyphonies* (Olivi/Sony) and *L'Âme Corse* (Audivis).

Opposite Top: Orto (see p241), with Monte d'Oro just visible on the horizon; Mare a Mare Nord Variant (see p234). **Bottom left:** The ascent to Col de l'Arinella; see p228. **Bottom right:** Scrambling around Lac de Capitellu; see p150. (Photo © Tim Glasby).

to reach a lane that reaches the D84 opposite the gîte (see map). The first part of this shortcut is waymarked in orange.

Having rejoined tarmac shortly before reaching Sidossi, the Mare A Mare Nord, meanwhile, continues along the D218, rounding a sharp bend before veering north-east to the left of the road and uphill towards Calacuccia. When you reach the D84, just after the small cemetery full of rusting iron crucifixes, turn right for the village centre, or left for the Hôtel Acquaviva (see below).

CALACUCCIA

Niolu's tiny capital is made up of four separate hamlets, scattered across the mountainside above the north-east corner of the lake. It lacks the charm of Albertacce but does boast the valley's only supermarket, the last source of supplies before Corte. The only noteworthy monument is an excruciatingly realistic carved-wood crucifix in the whitewashed **Church of Saints Pierre et Paul**, on the western outskirts next to the main road. Notice the flights of steps on the exterior of many houses. These are an architectural trait almost unique to Niolu, where *vindittas* were traditionally pursued in the hills rather than the villages, rendering unnecessary the fortified or raised entrances seen in similarly remote settlements elsewhere on the island.

Orientation and services

Between July and mid-September, Autocars Mordiconi (☎ 04.95.48.00.04) runs a **bus** service between Corte and Porto, via Col de Verghio, which passes through here.

You can consult timetables at the Hôtel des Touristes in the middle of the village, at several of the bars along the main street, and at the **tourist office** (☎ 04 95.48.05.22; mid-June–Sept Mon–Fri 9am–noon and 2–7pm, Sat 9am–noon), inconveniently situated 1km out on the main road to the Scala di Santa Regina. Here you can gather information on the network of **short walks** around Calacuccia. The trails, which link the most prominent of many **prehistoric sites**, were recently cleared and waymarked to tempt people passing through to stay in the area for a day or two.

Both of the village's two **shops**, an **ATM**, and the **post office** stand on the main street, along with several cafés and knick-knack shops.

Where to stay and eat

In addition to the gîte d'étape at Couvent Saint François di Niolu (see p224), Calacuccia has two good value hotels. The most popular option with hikers is the old-fashioned ***Hôtel des Touristes*** (☎ 04.95 48.00.04, 🖷 04.95.48.05.92; open May–Oct) at the top of the main street. Behind a somewhat forbidding 1930s facade, the rooms are spacious and light, with comfy modern beds, and cost 30.49€ year round. By the petrol station, on the western edge of Calacuccia, the pricier ***Hôtel Acquaviva*** (☎ 04 95.48.06.90 or 04.95.48.00.08, 🖷 04.95 08.82; open year round) offers more comfort; the well-appointed rooms have cable tv, individual balconies and valley views (ask for one at the rear of the building). Rates start at 48.70€ for an en suite double, rising to 65.60€ in peak season.

For food, avoid the places in the village centre in favour of ***L'Auberge du Lac***, 2km out of the centre on the lakeside (see p224), where you can eat well from around 15.20€ per head (without wine).

CALACUCCIA → CORTE [MAP 38, p227; MAP 39, p228; MAP 40, p229]

Zigzagging up what looks like a near vertical mountainside on the far side of the valley, the path over the Col de l'Arinella can seem a daunting prospect from the comfort of Calacuccia. Once past the dam and the messy refuse dump

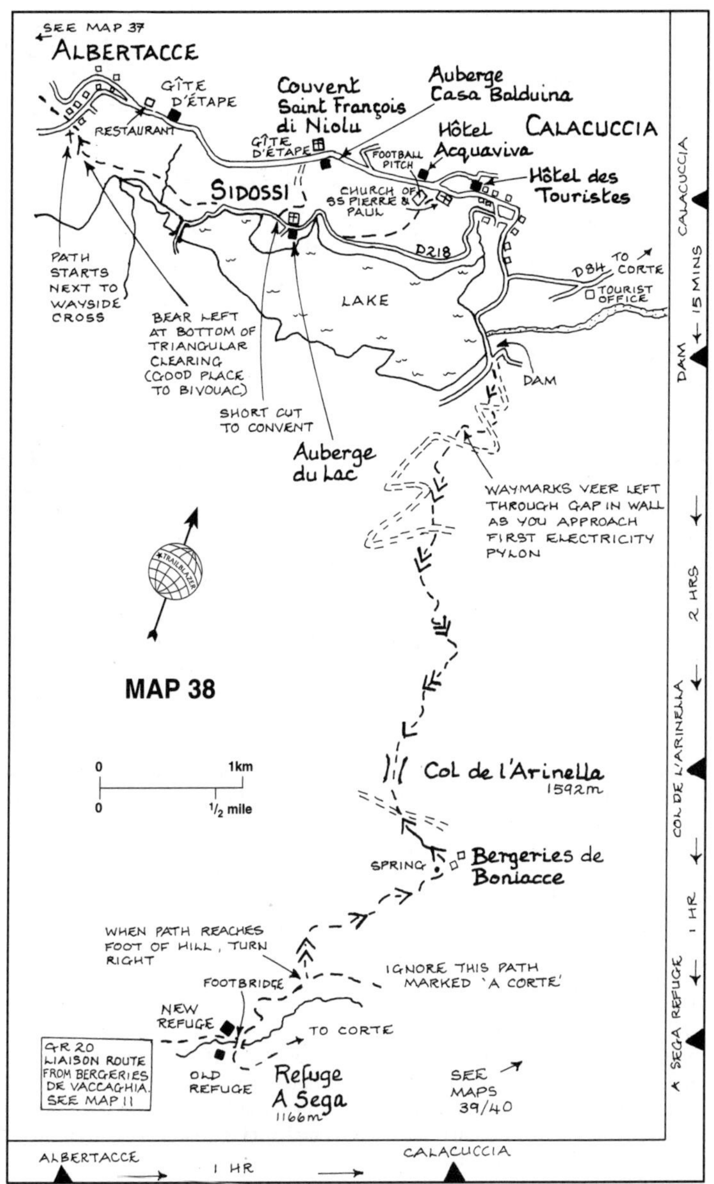

SEE MAP 37
ALBERTACCE
GÎTE D'ÉTAPE
RESTAURANT
Couvent Saint François di Niolu
Auberge Casa Balduina
Hôtel Acquaviva
CALACUCCIA
GÎTE D'ÉTAPE
FOOTBALL PITCH
Hôtel des Touristes
SIDOSSI
CHURCH OF SS PIERRE & PAUL
D218
TO CORTE
D84
TOURIST OFFICE
PATH STARTS NEXT TO WAYSIDE CROSS
BEAR LEFT AT BOTTOM OF TRIANGULAR CLEARING (GOOD PLACE TO BIVOUAC)
LAKE
DAM
SHORT CUT TO CONVENT
Auberge du Lac
WAYMARKS VEER LEFT THROUGH GAP IN WALL AS YOU APPROACH FIRST ELECTRICITY PYLON
TRAILBLAZER
MAP 38
0
1km
0
1/2 mile
Col de l'Arinella
1592m
SPRING
Bergeries de Boniacce
WHEN PATH REACHES FOOT OF HILL, TURN RIGHT
FOOTBRIDGE
IGNORE THIS PATH MARKED 'A CORTE'
NEW REFUGE
TO CORTE
GR 20 LIAISON ROUTE FROM BERGERIES DE VACCAGHIA. SEE MAP 11
OLD REFUGE
Refuge A Sega
1166m
SEE MAPS 39/40
CALACUCCIA
15 MINS
DAM
2 HRS
COL DE L'ARINELLA
1 HR
A SEGA REFUGE
ALBERTACCE
1 HR
CALACUCCIA

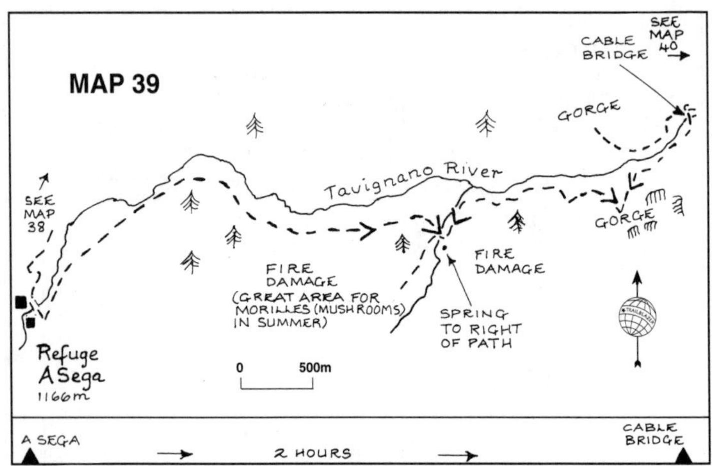

on its far side, however, the climb turns out to be a lot more enjoyable than it looks and – provided you start early enough to beat the clouds that usually bubble up over the Cinto massif by mid-morning – yields a sublime panorama over the Niolu. As a reward for this, the hardest ascent of the Mare a Mare Nord, you can also look forward to trekking down the Tavignano Valley, on the far side of the pass, through some of the most outstanding scenery in Europe.

Leave Calacuccia via the main road and cross the **dam** below the village. From the far end of the dam the orange waymarks pick their way uphill through a wasteland of discarded rubbish and goat sheds. A little over half-an-hour up (as you approach the foot of an electricity pylon), look out for a left turn off the old path you've been following through a niche in a dry stone wall; the Mare a Mare waymarks are easy to miss. From here on the gradient steepens as the path cuts between bends of a hairpin piste and then zigzags via a series of sharp switchbacks through forest littered with megalithic boulder shelters.

Reached after an ascent of a little under 800m, taking around 2¼ hours, the **Col de l'Arinella** (1592m) is a broad hilltop severely denuded by centuries of intensive grazing. Ahead, the dark grey mass of Punta di Castelli (2180m) looms above the Tavignano Valley, the needles of Monte Rotondo's serrated summit just visible behind. It's easy to see why this remote spot was chosen by the Corsican Maquis in 1943 for a parachute drop of arms. Flares to guide the pilots could be lit without being seen from any village, while the isolated bergeries dotted across the mountains nearby provided perfect caches. The plaque next to the piste just below the pass commemorates the 40th anniversary reunion held here by surviving members of the local Resistance in 1993. Below it, the **Bergeries de Boniacce** has a perennial **spring** (on the opposite side of the path from the stone huts).

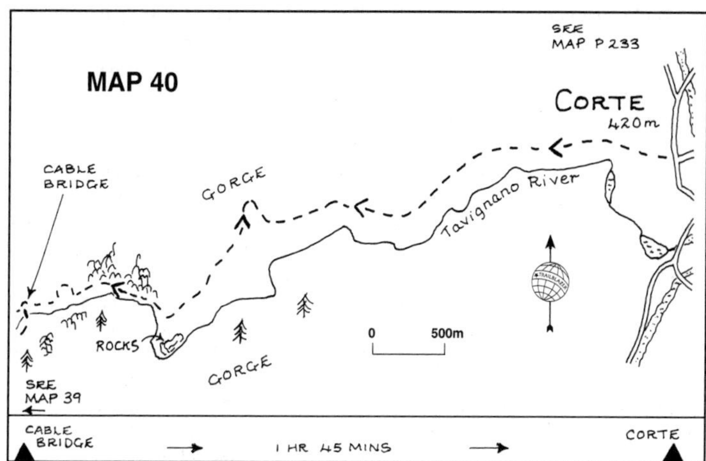

The descent from the col to river level, across a sheer mountainside dotted with clumps of sea daffodils (*Pancratium maritimum*), juniper and fern, takes around 1½ hours. At the bottom a sign sprayed in fluorescent ink onto a pine trunk points left to Corte. This route along the north side of the Tavignano Valley was opened in 2001 to bypass the fire-blacked forest that now mars the traditional route, but it's neither particularly easy to follow nor well waymarked. By using it, you'd also miss out on the old Genoan paved pathway down the gorge, one of the real highlights of this trek.

To cross the Tavignano, head right from the bottom of the path, through a depression in the Laricio forest to the **A Sega refuge**. The original building here was blown up by the FLNC in the mid-1990s; it has been replaced by a state-of-the-art structure that's monstrous from the outside but much airier, more comfortable (and a good deal less crowded) than most other mountain huts. As it's officially a refuge and not a gîte, the bunk beds (8.36€) are allotted on a first-come-first-served basis, with a dingier, grubbier annexe on the far side of the footbridge taking the overspill. You can also bivouac in the woods outside for 6€, which includes the use of a gas stove.

From the far side of the footbridge, follow the waymarks left down the valley. For the next 15km or so to Corte it is virtually impossible to lose your way thanks to the remarkably intact old pack path, the most extraordinary of its kind of the island, that threads down the entire length of the Tavignano. How long the walk takes will depend on how often you pause to admire the landscape, which will probably be more often than you intend so allow plenty of time – three-and-a-half to four hours if you hike non stop – to complete this stretch.

Paved with timeworn granite slabs, the mule track winds around a succession of steep, densely-wooded spurs, climbing high above the river as it does so to avoid some vertigo-inducing crags. Relatively restrained at first, the sides of the gorge, flanked by ridges of 1500–2000m, surge to a height of 800m in the middle of the valley, where the vast cliffs are streaked with pale green mineral traces. On some of the higher ledges, lone Laricio pine trees cut striking silhouettes. Sadly, many were lost in the devastating fire that swept through here in the summer of 2000, and you'll probably have to negotiate a succession of fallen trees along the route. Look out as you do so for morelle mushrooms (see opposite p65 for photo), which thrive in pine cinders during early summer. A rare, fragrant fungus that's highly prized for the magic it works with meat sauces, *morilles* sell for insane sums in the markets of Lyon and Paris. On a good day here, you can literally fill rucksacks with them.

The first major landmark about halfway along the Tavignano is the **cable bridge** (*passarelle suspendue*), beneath which a small beach provides an ideal camping or bivouac spot (though flooding is possible in wet weather). More spectacular scenery awaits beyond the bridge, as the forest gradually gives way to low maquis. By the time you get your first glimpse of Corte at the distant mouth of the valley you'll probably be exposed to the full strength of the sun on this south-facing slope – another good reason you should get an early start and carry plenty of water.

CORTE

As the seat of the island's independent government in the eighteenth century and now the home of its only university, Corte occupies a unique position in the Corsican psyche. Ajaccio and Bastia may be the main economic centres but this is the undisputed spiritual capital. When the FLNC decided to stage a mass show of strength prior to its ceasefire of 1996 it's no coincidence that the site they chose lay on the opposite side of the valley from the town. Rising above its Tibetan-monastery-like tumble of tiled rooftops, Corte's citadel, where Faustina Gaffory and her rebels held out against a Genoan siege in 1750, is dwarfed by an appropriately epic mountain backdrop – a vision that for many Corsicans symbolizes the island's defiant essence.

Despite an abundance of political graffiti, Corte strikes a more peaceful profile than its nationalist significance would suggest. Bombings and machine-gun attacks on civic buildings are actually much rarer here than in Ajaccio, Bastia and Calvi, and the presence of so many students gives the town a lived-in atmosphere missing from much of the interior.

Corte also occupies a pivotal position for trekkers. The Mare a Mare Nord passes through, and the GR20 is a day's hike away up the Restonica Valley. Corte is linked by train with the rest of the island, including the village of Vivario from where the Mare a Mare Nord *Variant* route, see pp234-46, strikes west towards the watershed. If you've been on the trail for some days this is the perfect place to see a bit of island life, especially during term time when Corte's main drag, café-lined cours Paoli, is the liveliest spot for miles. Cours Paoli is also the home of Corsica's best-stocked outdoor equipment shop, Omnisports Gabrielli, see p232.

What to see

The logical place to begin a walk around Corte's historic *haute ville* is **place Paoli**, dominated by the statue of the man affectionately dubbed 'Babu di a Patria, or 'Father of the Nation' by Corsicans. Although originally from the Castagniccia region in the north-west of the island, Pascal Paoli is most closely associated with Corte, the town from where he launched the rebellion of 1754 and where he revived the island's National Assembly the following year (see p51).

Heading up the stepped ramp on the south side of the square brings you to the smaller **place Gaffori**, where the seeds of Paoli's success were sown. The house flanking its north side belonged to the first leader of independent Corsica, General Gian' Pietri Gaffori, whose wife Faustina famously defended it against a Genoan attack long enough for her husband to arrive with reinforcements (she allegedly threatened to ignite a keg of gunpowder and blow both herself and her troops up if they failed to fight to the last). You can still see the old Genoan bullet marks on its facade.

The seat of Paoli's first government, **U Palazzu Naziunale**, stands just above place Gaffori, to the left of the entrance to the citadel. After serving as a parliament building, it was handed over to the Franciscan Order to become Corsica's first university, and today houses the Corsican Studies department.

Beyond the ornamental gateway the Genoan **citadel**, dating from the early fifteenth century, was recently given a massive makeover to accommodate the state-of-the-art **Museu di a Corsica** (summer daily 10am–8pm, winter Tues–Sat 10am–6pm; 5.30€). The complex, designed by Italian architect Andréa Bruno, forms an incongruously modern counterpoint to the collection inside it, dominated by farm implements and peasant costumes collected by the ethnographer Révérend Père Luois Doazan, but the admission price includes entrance into the citadel proper, from where the views over Corte's hinterland and its convoluted roofscape are spectacular.

Orientation and services

The Mare a Mare Nord approaches Corte from the west, arriving in town on the north side of the citadel. Follow the lane downhill and you'll eventually hit cours Paoli, running from place du Duc de Padoue in the north to place Paoli in the south; this is Corte's principal thoroughfare. On its south-west side, the old quarter, a mildewing mass of Genoan-era tenements stacked up the hillside below the university and citadel, holds most of the town's picturesque buildings and atmosphere.

Buses from Ajaccio and Bastia, operated by Eurocorse Voyages (☎ 04 95.21.06.30) stop at the top of ave Xavier Luciani, just off the south side of cours Paoli. Autocars Mordiconi's (☎ 04.95. 48.00.04) seasonal bus to and from Calccuccia in the Niolu Valley leaves from around the corner, on the east side of cours Paoli.

The **train** station (☎ 04.95.46.00.97), on the eastern edge of town, has four services daily from Ajaccio and Bastia (via Vizzavona and Vivario). The station is within easy walking distance of the town centre; the quickest route on foot is to turn right out of the main exit and follow allée du 9 Septembre past the sports stadium, shortly after which a lane cuts on your right down to a footbridge across the confluence of the Tavignano and Restonica rivers. The steps on the opposite side bring you out on ave Président Pierucci, five minutes from the bottom of cours Paoli.

Taxis (☎ 04.95.46.07.90 and 04.95 61.01.41) queue at the rank outside the train station. You can **leave luggage** at the *consigne* in the ticket office, or better still lug it up the hill to the Café du Cours, on cours Paoli, which keeps rucksacks in its locked store room while you wander around town. The service is free but it's a good idea to return the favour by ordering a drink at the bar if you've time. In another of this café's backrooms you'll find Corte's only **Internet access**, where you can send and receive email for nominal rates.

Information on current bus and train timings is the main reason you might want to visit the town's main **tourist office** (☎ 04 95.46.26.70; Mon–Sat 9am–1pm and 3–6pm, also Sun 3–6pm from mid-June–Sept); it's just inside the entrance to the citadel, on your right. Of more use to trekkers is **Parc Naturel**'s little information bureau (☎ 04.95.46.27.44; June–Sept daily 9am-1pm and 4.30–7pm), tucked away on Fontaine des Quatre-Canons, a small square between the citadel and cours Paoli. Staff can help with route planning and gîte reservations and they sell a selection of maps and guide books.

FFRP **Topoguides** and IGN **maps** of the island are also sold at all the newsagents and bookstores dotted along cours Paoli. In the same street, you'll find a string of **ATMs** and **banks** where you can change money (normal hours Mon–Fri 8.15am–noon and 2–4.30pm). The **post office** (Mon–Fri 8am–noon and 2–5pm, Sat 8am–noon), on a road leading north off place du Duc de Padoue, also has an ATM.

The best and cheapest place for provisions is the Casino **supermarket** on the southern edge of town near the train station. In the same complex you'll find a **launderette** (daily 7am–7pm).

Omnisports Gabrielli, at the top of cours Paoli, is the place to go for trekking and camping gear. Run by irrepressible outdoor enthusiast Phillipe Gabrielli, it's a unique resource for hikers and climbers in Corsica. Phillipe, born and bred in Corte, is a fund of knowledge and pertinent advice about the local mountains and the best kit for exploring them.

Where to stay

On the whole, accommodation is cheaper here than on the coast and there's plenty of it. After Ferme Équestre L'Albadu (see below) the best of the many **campsites** dotted around the town (see map, opposite) is ***U Sognu*** (☎ 04.95.46.09.07; open May–Sept), 15 minutes' walk from the centre at the bottom of the road leading up the Restonica Valley. It has views of the citadel, a seasonal wood-fired pizzeria and is altogether cleaner and more congenial than the nearby ***Restonica*** and ***Alivetu*** sites across the bridge.

Gîte d'étape 'U Tavignanu' (☎ 04.95 46.16.85; Easter–Oct), secluded in the woods behind the citadel, is the most convenient budget option for trekkers. Peaceful, close to the centre and yet inaccessible by road, it has a leafy garden terrace overlooking the valley and a ping-pong table, and offers half-board for 25.80€. Dorm beds cost 12.90€ (breakfast included).

For those happy to walk a little further, the pleasant ***Ferme Équestre L'Albadu*** (☎ 04.95.46.24.55; open year-round), a horse-riding centre and working sheep farm, offers inexpensive bed and breakfast accommodation for 30.40€ per double room (shared shower and toilets), or 27.36€ half-board. Located on the hillside above the town, the farm enjoys fine views over the hills from its olive orchards, where you can pitch tents or bivouac for 7.60€; this includes unlimited hot showers and use of the clean toilet block. Don't miss the wonderful evening meals here (see p234). To reach it, follow the old Ajaccio road uphill for 15 minutes.

Other accommodation in Corte is serviceable but largely uninspiring. For rock bottom rates try ***Hôtel HR***, near the train station on allée du 9 Septembre (☎ 04.95 45.11.11, 🖹 04.95.61.02.85; open all year). Basic double rooms in this vast, institutional block (a converted gendarmerie) go for as little as 22.80€, or 30.40€ en suite. Up in the centre of town, the little ***Hôtel de la Poste***, on place du Duc de Padoue (☎ 04.95 46.01.37, 🖹 04.95.46.13.08; open year round) has a lot more character. On the ground floor of an old building, its rooms range from simple doubles with WC on the corridor (32€) to larger en suites (39.50€). They also have a few triple-bedded rooms (again, with washbasins but no toilets) for 41€. It's open year round and rates do not fluctuate according to the season.

In a similar mould though much larger is ***Hôtel du Nord et de L'Europe*** (☎ 04.95 46.00.68, 🖹 04.95.46.03.40, 💻 www.hotel dunord-corte.com; open year round), on cours Paoli. The building has lots of period feel, with original stone steps and wood floors. Rooms start at 27.36€ for the most basic options (wash basin but shared toilets) and are 38€ for en suite. The priciest rooms (41€) have TVs and valley views from the rear of the building. Triples cost from 44€ to 51.70€ depending on the level of comfort. This is a smart, friendly, efficient place within easy reach of the train station and bus stops.

Moving upscale slightly, ***Hôtel de la Paix*** (☎ 04.95.46.06.72, 🖹 04.95.46.23.84, 💻 socoget@aol.com; open year round), on

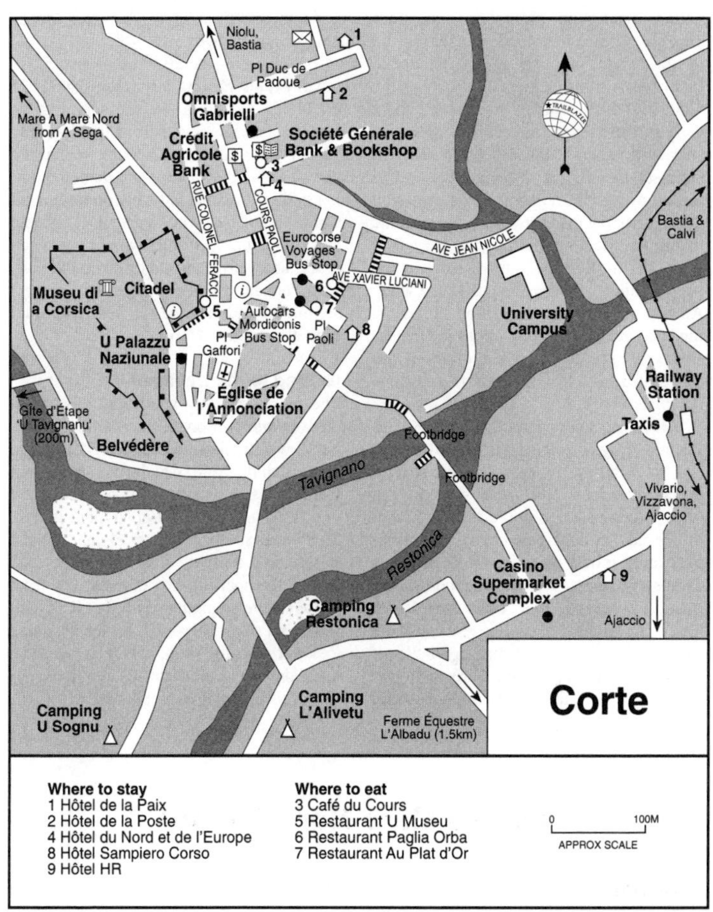

the north side of place du Duc de Padoue, was recently spruced up and is a notch plusher than the competition. Rates range from 35/50€ to 45/56€ in the low/high season; the pricier rooms have a TV and balcony overlooking the square. If it's fully booked, try the modern ***Hôtel Sampiero Corso*** (☎ 04.95.46.09.76, 🖹 04 95.46.00.08; open April–Oct) at the other end of town on ave du Président Pierucci; its rates remain more or less constant at 42.60€ for a double, or 61€ for a triple.

Where to eat

When looking for somewhere to eat in Corte, the golden rule is to avoid anywhere with photos outside it. These places, dotted around the squares, cater solely for tourists and are not in the same league as the town's four bona fide restaurants, which offer fine dining for no more expense. The best situated is ***U Museu***, up in the haute ville on rampe Ribanelle (open year round, except Sun during the winter). It does a roaring trade so get there early in the evening to secure a table outside with views of the valley. The cost of their set menus – 11.50–13.70€ – varies according to the number of courses you choose, not the dishes on offer. Most of the mains are local specialities, such as wild boar and myrtle stew, stuffed trout in red pepper sauce, and sweetmeats in red wine. Among their copious selection of salads, the *chèvre chaud* (hot goat's cheese) stands out; served on a bed of croutons and cubes of bacon, it's filling enough to be a complete meal.

Just off cours Paoli on ave Xavier Luciani, ***Paglia Orba*** (☎ 04.95.61.07.89) is a safe choice for a cheap and cheerful pizza, or pricier à la carte splurge. For once, vegetarians are well catered for, with dishes such as aubergine baked with chestnuts and stuffed onions, and a generous choice of salads. Around the corner, on place Paoli, ***Au Plat D'Or*** (☎ 04.95 46.27.16) is the classiest restaurant in Corte. Wild river trout and brochette of local beef with mushrooms are their two specialities (15€ à la carte), and they offer a tempting selection of desserts. Menus range from 10.60€ to 18.30€.

Well worth the 20-minute walk out of town, ***Ferme Équestre L'Albadu*** (☎ 04.95 46.24.55) is the most sociable option. Evening meals (fantastic value at only 12.20€ for a fixed three-course menu) are served on a long table in a communal dining hall. The accent is firmly on traditional Corsican cuisine, with superb local cheese and charcuterie, as much wine as you can drink, and warm hospitality from the host, Jean Pulicani. Book in advance as numbers are limited and the food is prepared to order each afternoon.

Getting to the trailhead

The most straightforward way to pick up the *variant* portion of the Mare a Mare Nord, which takes you back to Marignana, is to catch the train, which runs south from Corte four times daily. Jump on the earliest one you can and get off at **Vivario** station, 20 minutes south. Alternatively, the official waymarked footpath follows a wide loop around the opposite side of the valley from Corte before swinging south, but it's a dull route that's best bypassed. By leapfrogging to Vivario on the train, it is possible to be high on the watershed in the heart of Corsica's mountains, by lunch time.

Mare a Mare Nord *Variant*

OVERVIEW

From Vivario the Mare a Mare Nord *Variant* plunges straight into Corsica's mountain spine, entering the roadless Gruzini Valley via the watershed at Onda. With Monte D'Oro dominating the southern horizon, it then winds through a succession of forested valleys, dotted with villages that stand near deserted amid old chestnut trees, before rejoining the main path at Marignana. Trekkers usually walk from east to west and choose one or another of the waymarked routes described here, but we've spliced them together to create a circular itinerary that, with the help of a short hop by train from Corte, cuts out several rather tedious stages.

This southern route, from Vivario to Marignana, passes through some of Corsica's least visited regions. Its appeal lies both in the proximity of Monte Rotondo and Monte D'Oro – both spectacular massifs – and in the overall feeling of remoteness. Apart from on the initial stretch, which crosses the GR20, you'd be unlikely to come across more than half a dozen fellow trekkers all day.

This *variant* route is also less strenuous than the northern one, with relatively few long ascents and descents. That said, it definitely has its drawbacks. Day one involves some long plods along surfaced roads – albeit unfrequented ones – and there are very few shops or gîtes along the way. Consequently, you either have to carry three days' worth of provisions and bivouac, or else put in two very long stages at the start, overnighting at Pastricciola and Letzia, with a short final leg to Marignana. In the latter case, be sure to book accommodation in advance, as there are no fallbacks in either village.

VIVARIO → ONDA → PASTRICCIOLA [MAP 41, p236; MAP 42, p237; MAP 43, p239]

The first day of the Mare a Mare Nord *Variant* is a long one, requiring an early start from Corte if you're catching the train to the trailhead. Alternatively, travel down the evening before and get off at Savaggio (one stop after Vivario), where there's a pleasant campsite (although you'll have to tell the conductor in advance that you wish to do this or the train won't stop there) only five minutes' walk from the path (see Map 41); ***Abri et Camping Savaggio*** (☎ 04.95 47.22.14; May–Sept) has a couple of dozen well-shaded pitches and refuge accommodation for 22 persons. It's close to the road and is used almost entirely by trekkers.

From Vivario station, a left turn will bring you onto the main Ajaccio–Bastia road, N193. The village centre, with a spring and a well-stocked shop, lies 1km south. To pick up the path, head through the gap in the buildings opposite the spring (to the left of the shop as you're looking at it) and follow the steps until a footpath (the one you should take) turns right. Once past a cluster of small houses the route, well-waymarked from here on, winds around a steep, fire-damaged hillside from which you gain increasingly spectacular views of Monte Cardo (2453m) to the north. At the ridgetop you meet a piste from which it's possible to make a rewarding 500m detour north to visit the **Fortin de Paschiola**, a square tower erected by the French in 1770 to imprison Corsican rebels. Its crumbling ruins crown a bare hilltop that looks north across a dramatic wall of grey scree and granite. This would be a memorable spot to bivouac, but there doesn't seem to be any water source.

Back where the path from Vivario crosses the piste, look out for a derelict white van slumped in the verge. For some reason, the waymarks dry up at this point, but the piste is easy enough to follow. Keep walking down it until you reach the train line on your right (you'll know you've gone too far if you reach a stream crossing after a short rise). Follow the footpath running alongside the railway for roughly 500m until it reaches a small clearing. This is where you

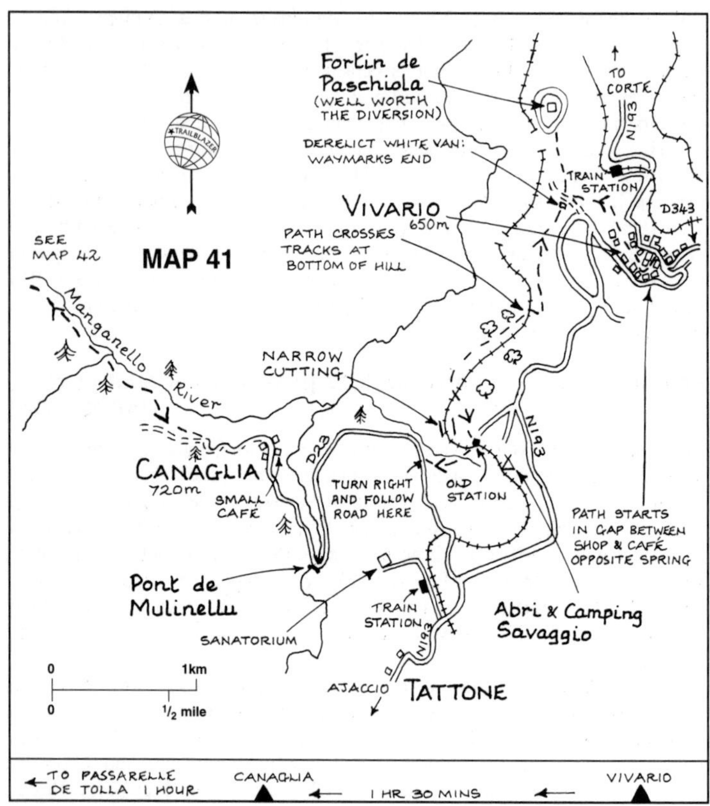

have to recross the tracks and follow the path that rises through the woods on their far side; look for the orange waymarks (the first since the wrecked van) on tree trunks.

Once over the rise, the path drops downhill and re-crosses the railway line next to an old station. A left turn along the tracks will take you to the Savaggio campsite (see p235). Continue straight on and you'll cross a stream soon after, and then gain ground to reach the D23; the route follows this for 3km or so as it rounds the base of a wooded hill to cross the Vecchio River at **Pont de Mulinellu**. Shortly after, you reach the hamlet of **Canaglia**, where there's nothing much beyond a clutch of houses, a spring, and one café that serves sandwiches and snacks during the trekking season.

At Canaglia the road peters into a dirt forestry track which, after crossing a bridge, forks in two. Dropping to the right, the waymarked trail becomes a prop-

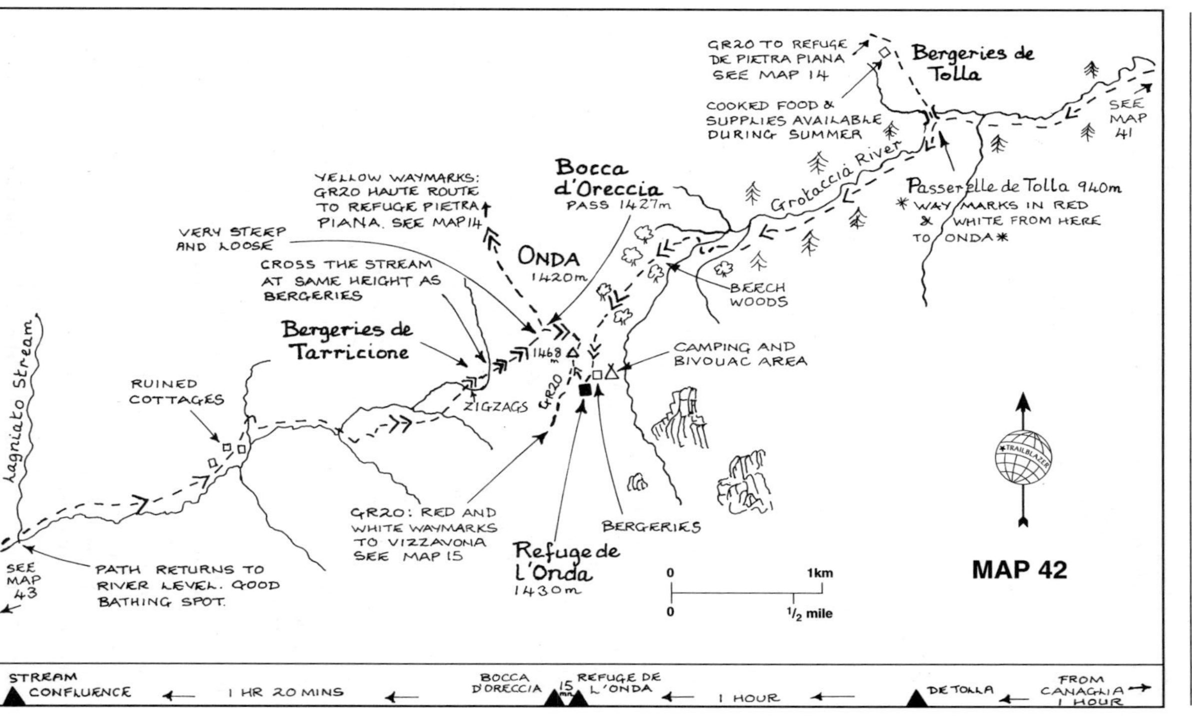
MAP 42
SEE MAP 41
Bergeries de Tolla
Passerelle de Tolla 940m
* WAY MARKS IN RED & WHITE FROM HERE TO ONDA *
GR20 TO REFUGE DE PIETRA PIANA SEE MAP 14
COOKED FOOD & SUPPLIES AVAILABLE DURING SUMMER
Grotaccia River
BEECH WOODS
CAMPING AND BIVOUAC AREA
BERGERIES
Bocca d'Oreccia PASS 1427m
ONDA 1420m
1468m
GR20
Refuge de l'Onda 1430m
ZIGZAGS
YELLOW WAYMARKS: GR20 HAUTE ROUTE TO REFUGE PIETRA PIANA. SEE MAP 14
CROSS THE STREAM AT SAME HEIGHT AS BERGERIES
VERY STEEP AND LOOSE
Bergeries de Tarricione
GR20: RED AND WHITE WAYMARKS TO VIZZAVONA SEE MAP 15
RUINED COTTAGES
PATH RETURNS TO RIVER LEVEL. GOOD BATHING SPOT.
Lagniato Stream
SEE MAP 43
0 1km
0 1/2 mile
STREAM CONFLUENCE
1 HR 20 MINS
BOCCA D'ORECCIA
15 min
REFUGE DE L'ONDA
1 HOUR
DE TOLLA
FROM CANAGLIA 1 HOUR

er footpath here, rising at a gentle gradient from river level through a jumble of boulders and loose rock lining the true right bank of the Manganello River.

One hour beyond the village, you arrive at the confluence with the Grottaccia River – meeting point of the GR20 and the Mare a Mare Nord. Surrounded by Laricio pines, the **passerelle de Tolla** gives access to the Manganello Valley and, high above it on the northern flank of Monte Rotondo, to the refuge de Pietra Piana. But the Mare a Mare Nord, indicated from here with **red-and-white waymarks**, peels south-west above the passarelle to begin its climb through the forest to Onda via a broad forestry *piste*. Gradually the Laricio pines give way to beech and the path narrows and steepens. The final pull up to the bergeries begins shortly after the waterfall and lasts around 40 minutes.

Perched on a lateral moraine at the head of the Grotaccia Valley, the **Refuge de L'Onda** (1431m; see pp157-8) ranks among the smallest and least appealing of the shelters along the GR20 route but you may want to stop here to fill water bottles or cook lunch (there's a well-equipped, dingy kitchen inside). During the trekking season, the bergeries below it sell cheese, charcuterie and other essentials at GR20 prices. If you want to bivouac or camp, find a place in the pig-proof enclosure below the shepherds' huts, which are serviced with a toilet block and perennial spring. Shade and shelter are both in short supply here.

Still waymarked in red-and-white, the path zigzags uphill from the refuge to the **Bocca d'Oreccia** pass (1468m), at which point the GR20 veers south to tackle Monte D'Oro. The Mare a Mare Nord *Variant*, meanwhile, continues a little way further north. Follow the yellow and orange markers for around 150m, past a signboard, until you see faded orange markers dropping steeply to the left towards a stream. The first section of the descent is very steep and slippery in places, with poor waymarking towards the bottom. You eventually cross it level with the **Bergeries de Tarricione** (1225m) – a ford that's easy to miss thanks to a tangle of goat tracks that will lead you down into a rough gully if you're not vigilant.

Shortly after the bergeries a shady, mixed-deciduous forest is broken briefly by a sunny clearing beyond which the path follows the course of the Coracchia in a sheer ravine. Loose stone underfoot makes for some uncomfortable walking along this stretch, compounded by a series of landslides and fallen pines that block the way.

Having climbed high above the Gruzini, the path drops to river level again at the confluence with the Lagniato stream, passing a string of ruined chestnut mills and cottages en route. From here on the going gets a lot easier as you approach the first inhabited settlement on this side of the pass, **Chiusa** (542m), reached roughly three hours after Onda. On the edge of the hamlet look out for a signboard on the right-hand side of the road, indicating the onward route up a lane between dry-stone walls. The stream flowing down it originates in a tiny but very welcome **spring**, a minute or so up the path, which emerges shortly afterwards on the D104 at the hamlet of L'Ugnica.

The last leg of this section follows the surfaced road at contour level around the valley to the area's most populated village, **Pastricciola**, whose well-

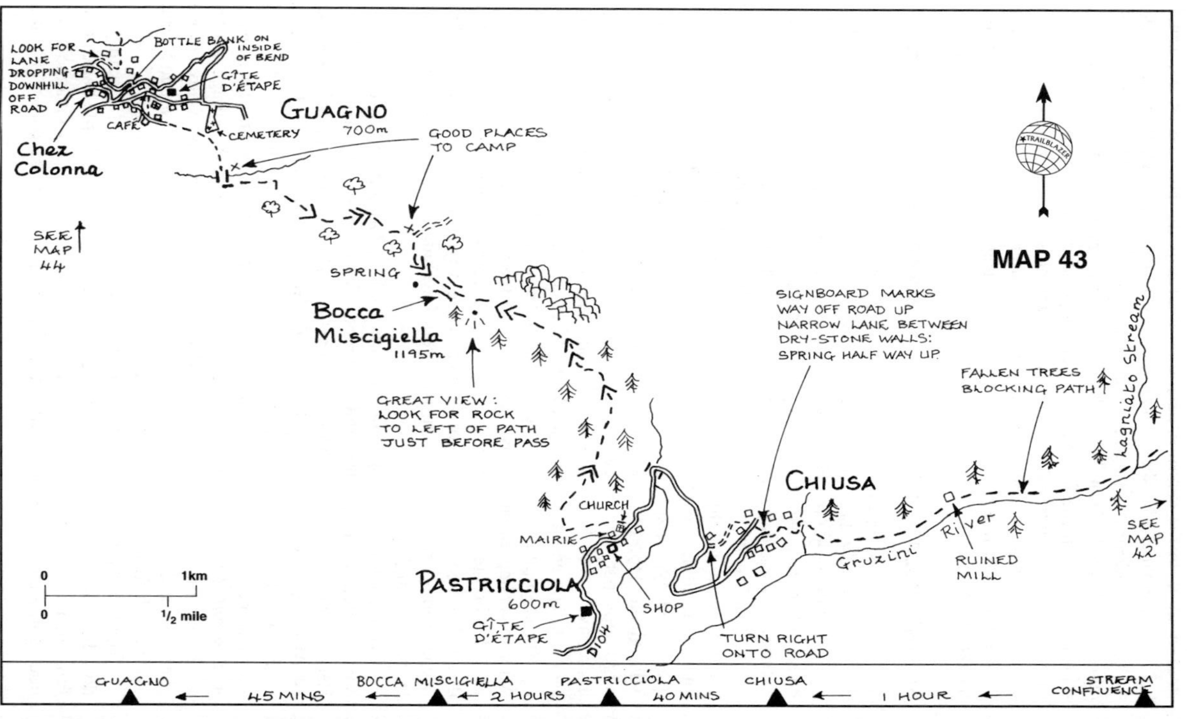
LOOK FOR LANE DROPPING DOWNHILL OFF ROAD
BOTTLE BANK ON INSIDE OF BEND
GÎTE D'ÉTAPE
GUAGNO
700m
CAFÉ
CEMETERY
Chez Colonna
GOOD PLACES TO CAMP
MAP 43
TRAILBLAZER
SEE MAP 44
SPRING
Bocca Miscigiella
1195m
GREAT VIEW: LOOK FOR ROCK TO LEFT OF PATH JUST BEFORE PASS
SIGNBOARD MARKS WAY OFF ROAD UP NARROW LANE BETWEEN DRY-STONE WALLS: SPRING HALF WAY UP.
FALLEN TREES BLOCKING PATH
Lagniato Stream
CHIUSA
CHURCH
MAIRIE
PASTRICCIOLA
600m
GÎTE D'ÉTAPE
D104
SHOP
TURN RIGHT ONTO ROAD
Gruzini River
RUINED MILL
SEE MAP 42
0
1km
0
1/2 mile
GUAGNO
45 MINS
BOCCA MISCIGIELLA
2 HOURS
PASTRICCIOLA
40 MINS
CHIUSA
1 HOUR
STREAM CONFLUENCE

stocked **shop**, in the centre opposite the mairie, is the last one on this route before Marignana. The shop's hours are Tues, Thurs and Sat 9am–noon and 4–7pm; if it's closed try ringing the bell on the doorway next to it. The ***gîte d'étape*** (☎ 04.95.28.91.88 or 04.95.91.60, or leave a message on ☎ 04.95.28.96.34) stands 1km out on the far south-western edge of the village, overlooking the road. It's a bit institutional and dark but the gérant is exceptionally amiable and a good cook. Use of a washing machine and drier are included in the prices (7.60€ for a dorm bed; 15.20€ for evening meal or 26.60€ for half-board; breakfast 3.80€).

PASTRICCIOLA → LETZIA [MAP 43, p239; MAP 44, p243]

You'll have to be up early and made of sturdy stuff to complete this stage in a day. Alternatively, break it at Guagno, where there's a gîte or, better still if you're not on a tight budget, at Soccia where you can check into a comfortable hotel. Either way, take along plenty of water (there's a spring next to the mairie) as the start of the day involves the *variant*'s hardest ascent.

The path continues from the centre of the village, just past the church. Climbing west initially, it switches north-east on reaching the ridge and starts a long, unrelenting ascent through maritime pines up the left flank of a valley overlooked by a giant outcrop of granite. The final haul to the pass, **Bocca Miscigiella** (1195m), takes you up a sequence of switchbacks. Just before the ridge, look out for a large rock on the left, which offers the last and most impressive views back over the Gruzini Valley, with the craggy summits of Monte D'Oro and its sister peak, Punta Migliarello, to the south-west.

The ensuing descent is steep initially but eases off towards the valley floor. After traversing an enormous chestnut forest the path crosses the Albelli river via a footbridge, where there's a pig-scoured patch of level, secluded ground that makes a good bivouac spot. From here the waymarks are a bit muddled but if you keep the cemetery to your right you'll eventually hit a surfaced lane that leads to the middle of Guagno.

With a permanent population of around 150, **Guagno**, renowned as the home of arch-bandit **Tiadore Poli** (more on whom appears on p216), is today a sleepy backwater. It does, however, boast a well-kept municipal ***gîte d'étape*** (☎ 04.95.28.33.47; open May–Sept), with two 14-bed dormitories. Rates are a little lower than average at 9.20€ per person. Meals are not available here but you can order sandwiches and other snacks at the café opposite the church. ***Restaurant 'Chez Colonna'*** (open all year), at the bottom of the village, serves a selection of Corsican specialities indoors or across the road on a tiny terrace overlooking the valley. A bread van also passes through here at around 8am, loaded with fresh croissants, pains au raisins and delicious *bastelles*.

The trail starts again from the bottom of the village. Follow the main road downhill and look for the first turning after the bend with the bottle bank on it. From there the orange waymarkers lead you down a lane below Guagno's last houses to a stream crossing. After a stiff 15-minute climb the path winds at a more-or-less even gradient around a chestnut-wooded spur and down the other side to cross the **Fiume Grossu** River.

The hamlet of **Orto** (700m), reached after a steep zigzagging ascent from the wooden suspension bridge over the river, clings to the mountainside, looking south-west up a wonderfully wild valley to the Bocca Manganello pass. The most tranquil of all the villages on this route, Orto has neither a shop nor anywhere to stay but you could do a lot worse than stop for a drink at the snug little ***Café de la Paix***, on the right of the road as you enter the village. Dominated by a mural of a very youthful-looking Général de Gaulle, its interior is locked in a beguiling 1950s time warp.

The orange waymarks start again at the top of Orto from behind a disused laundry shelter (*lavoir*). Be careful here not to follow the yellow marks striking uphill to the right; these indicate the route of a GR20 liaison path that winds over a ridge of Monte Sant' Eliseo (whose summit is crowned by a chapel) to Lavu di Creno (see p148) and thence to the Refuge de Manganu (see p146).

The Mare a Mare Nord *Variant* continues steeply up through dense maquis, with the crags of the Fiume Grossu Valley forming an increasingly spectacular backdrop. By the time the path starts to level off the Monte D'Oro massif and its sister peak are visible beyond the ridges to the south-west, while the red-tiled rooftops of Orto below are virtually the only signs of human life.

The descent into **Soccia** is a mostly gentle one through more old chestnut woods. Nestled on a fertile ridge against an impressive backdrop of grey granite, the village ranks among the most picturesque on the island. It's also one of liveliest hereabouts, with an untypically young, year-round population. Several families now depend for a living on tourists passing through en route to the Lavu di Creno trail (see Map 12, p149), which starts from the car park high above Soccia. A prime beneficiary of this seasonal influx is the excellent ***Restaurant A Merendella*** (☎ 04.95.28.34.91, 🖷 04.95.28.35.03; open all year), on rue u Chiassu near the church, whose little grassy terrace makes the most of the fine valley views. This is a great place to break for lunch; the restaurant serves a good-value 13.68€ menu of fresh local organic produce prepared according to traditional mountain recipes. For a quick snack, try their sublime charcuterie. You can also stay here in one of three cosy en suite rooms (45.60€ per double). The only other accommodation in the village is offered by ***Hôtel U Paese*** (☎ 04.95.28.31.92, 🖷 04.95.28.35.19), down the hill beside the main road. It's an ugly modern building but the views from the little balconies in front of its rooms over the Guagno basin are impressive. Doubles cost from 34.20€ to 50.90€ depending on the time of year.

Worth a visit while you're in Soccia is the village **church**, built in 1875 on a ledge overlooking the valley; pride of place is given to a splendid wood triptych of the Virgin and Child thought to date from the fifteenth century.

From Soccia the Mare a Mare Nord *Variant* follows the main D123 downhill for around 2km. Some compensation for the long trudge on tarmac are the fine views of the village above, the best of which are from the helipad.

The footpath proper begins again at a row of green cement silos (look for waymarks on the breeze blocks behind them), from which it follows a rough littered piste for an uninspiring half an hour or so. At the bottom of hill, just before the track emerges onto the D123 again, you'll see a **spring** on the left-side of the path – the last source of drinking water for some time.

Turn left here and cross the bridge, and you'll find yourself on the edge of **Guagno-les-Bains**, an incongruously French-style thermal resort, established in the 19th century but nowadays dominated by the modern ***Hôtel les Thermes*** (☎ 04.95.26.80.50, 🖹 04.95.28.34.02; open May–Oct). Tariffs here range from 67€ to 79€, depending on the season, and include various water therapies. Non-residents are welcome to eat at their smart little restaurant, where the menu is fixed at 21.30€. The hotel is virtually the only sign of life in Guagno-les-Bains; most hikers bypass it all together by turning right before they cross the bridge and following the waymarks west along the right bank of the Guagno River. Passing through some magnificent old holm oak forest, with the river crashing nearby, this is among the most pleasant stretches of the day.

Close to the confluence with the **Filiccioni River** you encounter the first of two bridges – a good place to swim. Once across it the path gradually gains ground in more dense, dark forest, before dropping down to cross the **Liamone River** via the second passarelle of the day. This one occupies a gloomier and less enticing spot, hemmed in by steeply wooded slopes. You'll probably want to get stuck straight into the ensuing climb which zigzags sharply from river level to a clearing from where you gain uninterrupted views up the rugged Liamone Valley and its tributaries, encircled by an impressive wall of mountains. Not so much as a path nor ruined shepherd's hut is visible from this distance, but the now remote valley was once an important transhumant corridor and remains littered with deserted bergeries. Old trails wind up it to the foot of Cimatella (2098m), the horizon's most prominent peak, and beyond it to the rich pastures around Lac de Nino, on the GR20 (see p142).

From the clearing, the path proceeds at a level gradient around the contours of the hillside to Porta, the first hamlet of **Letzia**, which you enter shortly after passing a **spring** on your right. Waymarks lead you up past empty houses and between switchbacks of the main road, bringing you out finally at **St Roch**, the village's topmost hamlet. Just before a little bridge and second spring, you pass a Butagaz sign on the left side of the road, diagonally opposite an orange-waymarked path striking to the right into dense maquis. These, however, are old waymarks and should be ignored.

Continue instead along the road until you come to a turning on the right for a **Centre Équestre** (riding school). Run by the local municipality, a campus of a dozen or so wooden chalets provides clean, comfortable and cheap **accommodation**. Each has a small kitchen, bathroom, toilet and balcony with valley views. Priced at 9.10€ (or 12.20€ in July/August), the bungalows are the best bargain on this route and well worth pressing on from Soccia for. As this is the only place to stay for miles, it's a good idea to book in advance by telephoning the mairie (☎ 04.95.26.63.24) during working hours; ask to speak to Carole Paoli.

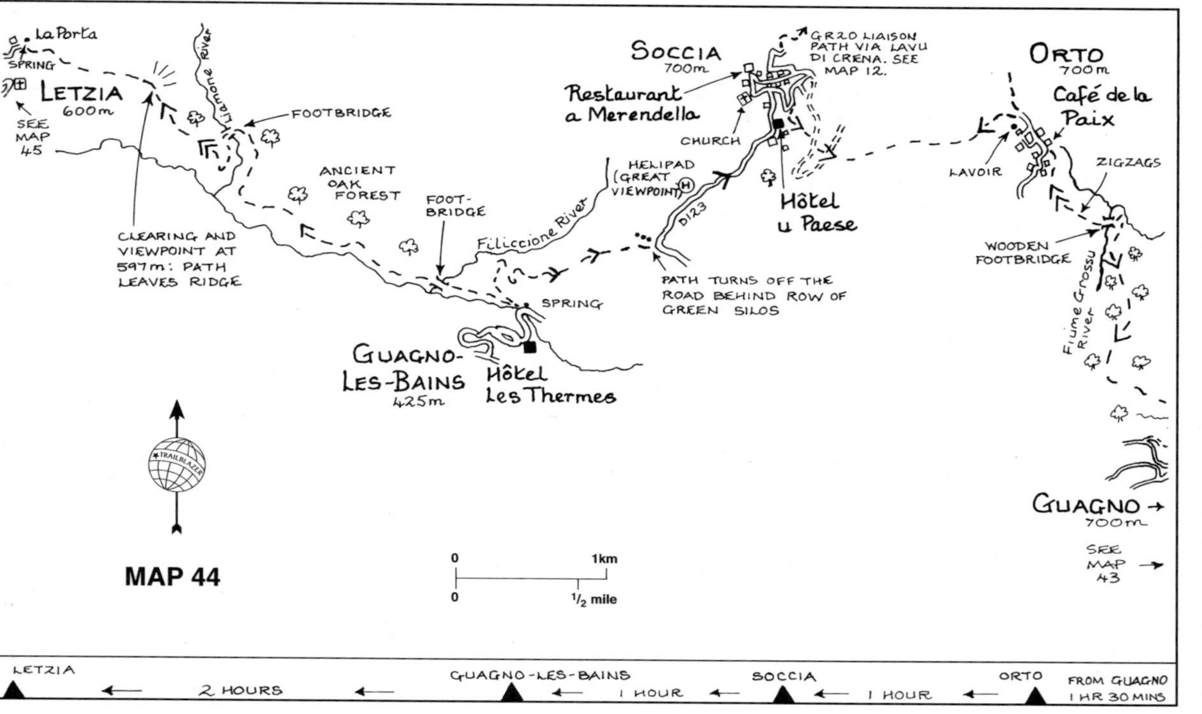
La Porta
SPRING
LETZIA
600m
SEE MAP 45
Liamone River
FOOTBRIDGE
CLEARING AND VIEWPOINT AT 597m: PATH LEAVES RIDGE
ANCIENT OAK FOREST
FOOT-BRIDGE
Filiccione River
SPRING
GUAGNO-LES-BAINS
425m
Hôtel Les Thermes
HELIPAD (GREAT VIEWPOINT)
D123
PATH TURNS OFF THE ROAD BEHIND ROW OF GREEN SILOS
SOCCIA
700m
Restaurant a Merendella
CHURCH
Hôtel u Paese
GR20 LIAISON PATH VIA LAVU DI CRENA. SEE MAP 12.
ORTO
700m
Café de la Paix
LAVOIR
ZIGZAGS
WOODEN FOOTBRIDGE
Fiume Grossu River
GUAGNO →
700m
SEE MAP 43
MAP 44
TRAILBLAZER
0
1km
0
½ mile
LETZIA
2 HOURS
GUAGNO-LES-BAINS
1 HOUR
SOCCIA
1 HOUR
ORTO
FROM GUAGNO 1 HR 30 MINS

Chestnuts

The extensive chestnut forests crossed by the Mare a Mare Nord at altitudes of 500-800m are vestiges of an era when the ***castagna*** (*châtaigne* in French) formed the essence of Corsica's rural economy. Originally planted by the Genoans in the fifteenth century, the trees thrived on the island's granitic soil and moist, warm climate, providing villagers not only with building wood but a ready source of food. Once harvested in late autumn and dried, chestnuts can be ground into a rich, nutritious flour (*farina* in Corsican) that until recent times was the island's main staple. Many of the delicious speciality dishes served in restaurants along the trekking routes – including polenda, a calorific porridge made by mixing meat stock and salt with chestnut flour – derives from the time when the castagna was king.

Sadly, 50 years of depopulation have seen many thousands of trees die from neglect and today the massive hollow hulks of dead *châtaigniers* are a defining feature of the interior's landscape. It was hoped that renewed demand for chestnut flour in the cities, as Corsican cuisine is rediscovered by a second generation of urban emigrants, would lead to a renaissance of the chestnut economy. However, too few people remain in the villages to tend and harvest the trees, which have suffered an additional threat from a fungal disease, and much of what passes for Corsican farina these days is merely imported from the continent and packaged here. Nowhere has been so utterly transformed by this economic downturn as the region around Marignana and Renno, swathed in forests of dead and dying trees. The only real beneficiaries of the blight are Corsica's legion of semi-wild pigs, for whom the millions of windfall castagnas provide a month of mad feasting in November – the secret of the area's supremely tasty charcuterie.

Note that there is neither a shop nor a café in Letzia; the nearest supermarket is in Sagone, an hour's drive down to the coast. The only place you might be able to talk into rustling you up some kind of a meal is the Centre Équestre, which has a small dining room for clients.

LETZIA → RENNO → MARIGNANA [MAP 45, OPPOSITE]

The final stage of the Mare a Mare Nord *Variant*, which takes you onto the saucer-shaped plateau of Renno and beyond to the edges of the Spelunca Valley, presents no real physical challenges, but the end of the walk is heralded by a succession of superb views. Once again there's nowhere to stock up with supplies, nor a café or restaurant outside peak season.

The path resumes at the top of the piste above the chalets, following a track uphill past a solitary chestnut tree and then swinging east, seemingly back towards the village. After meeting up with the old route, it then keeps to a broad, rough track for a while before plunging into ferns. The rest of the ascent hops between rock outcrops, zigzagging finally across open ground to gain the ridge from where you have marvellous views over the Golfe de Sagone and its hinterland villages.

Topoguides and the IGN map here indicate that the path drops immediately downhill from the ridge towards the first village. In fact it turns sharp right

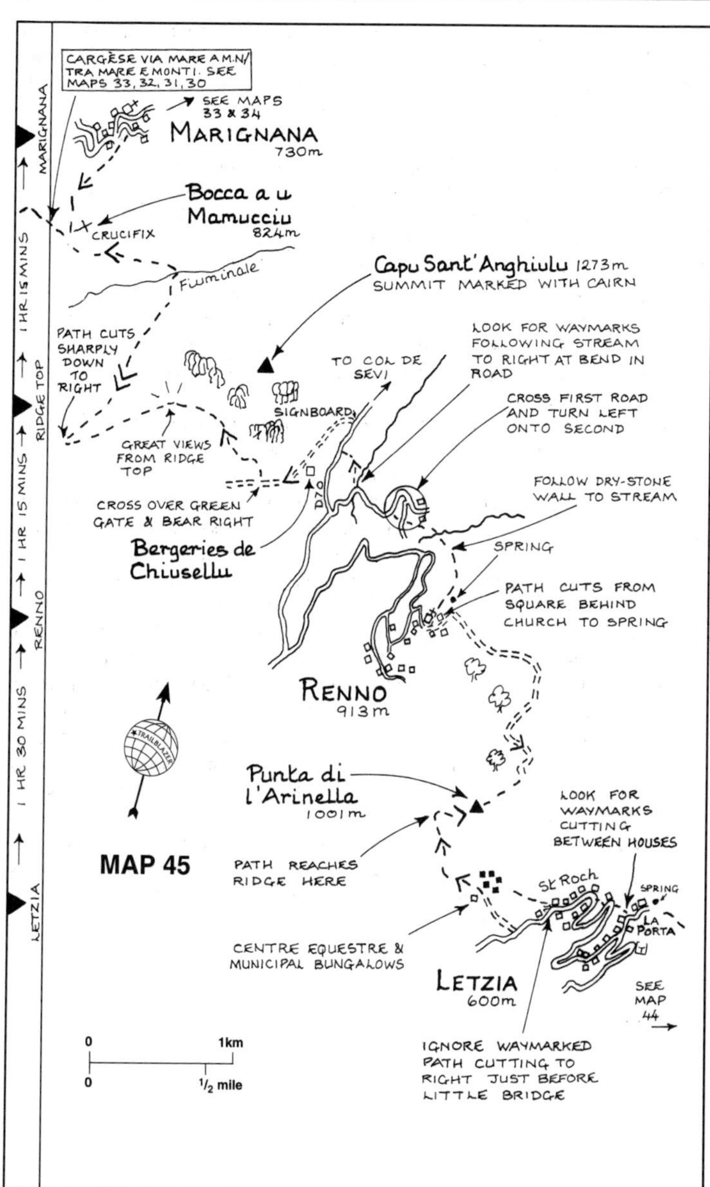
CARGÈSE VIA MARE A M.N/ TRA MARE E MONTI. SEE MAPS 33, 32, 31, 30
SEE MAPS 33 & 34
MARIGNANA
730m
Bocca a u Mamucciu
824m
CRUCIFIX
Fiuminale
Capu Sant'Anghiulu 1273m
SUMMIT MARKED WITH CAIRN
PATH CUTS SHARPLY DOWN TO RIGHT
GREAT VIEWS FROM RIDGE TOP
TO COL DE SEVI
SIGNBOARD
LOOK FOR WAYMARKS FOLLOWING STREAM TO RIGHT AT BEND IN ROAD
CROSS FIRST ROAD AND TURN LEFT ONTO SECOND
CROSS OVER GREEN GATE & BEAR RIGHT
D70
FOLLOW DRY-STONE WALL TO STREAM
Bergeries de Chiusellu
SPRING
PATH CUTS FROM SQUARE BEHIND CHURCH TO SPRING
RENNO
913m
Punta di l'Arinella
1001m
LOOK FOR WAYMARKS CUTTING BETWEEN HOUSES
MAP 45
PATH REACHES RIDGE HERE
St Roch
SPRING
LA PORTA
CENTRE EQUESTRE & MUNICIPAL BUNGALOWS
LETZIA
600m
SEE MAP 44
0
1km
0
1/2 mile
IGNORE WAYMARKED PATH CUTTING TO RIGHT JUST BEFORE LITTLE BRIDGE
MARIGNANA
1 HR 15 MINS
RIDGE TOP
1 HR 15 MINS
RENNO
1 HR 30 MINS
LETZIA

(the way is shown by a new signboard) and follows the ridgeline up to the summit of **Punta di l'Arinella** (1001m), before picking up a piste that winds around the east flank of the Renno depression, through thickening chestnut woods. Keep to this track and you'll eventually drop into **Renno**.

Once in the tiny square beside the church you'll see a narrow (non-waymarked) lane leading off to the right, 50 metres beyond which stands a dressed **spring**. The path continues diagonally opposite this, crossing a piste and dense chestnut forest as it winds in a wide semi-circle around the Renno plateau, skirting the hamlets. Eventually you'll come to a drystone wall, which the path follows steeply downhill to a stream.

The next section is poorly waymarked. Having climbed up the other side, the route emerges onto a road, which it crosses shortly before arriving at a second road. Turn left onto this and follow the tarmac for roughly 50 metres until it crosses a stream, where clearly discernable orange waymarks indicate a path uphill through the ferns.

If you lose the waymarks again, just keep heading uphill and you'll end up on another, larger road, the D70. A right turn onto this, in the direction of Col de Sevi, will bring you after five minutes to a signboard on the left side of the road pointing the way up a clear track leading to the **Bergeries de Chiusellu**. Having forded the stream at the bergeries, the track picks its way through thick bracken, crossing a piste a couple of times before arriving at a wide clearing on a ridge, where you should see a green gate on your right. Once over it, via the steel ladder installed for the purpose, bear right (the waymarks disappear again) and make for the large outcrop just above you on the right. The route cuts up from this to a high ridge from where sweeping views extend over Évisa and the Spelunca Valley on one side, and out towards the Golfe de Sagone on the other.

Once at the ridge the waymarks become more regular, switching direction to the south-west to follow the crest of the hill. Twenty minutes later the path drops sharply to the right and descends into the Fiuminale Valley, along whose northern flank you'll have walked days before if you've completed the entire Mare a Mare Nord loop.

The final leg to Marignana, from the stream at the bottom of the valley to the large white crucifix that marks the conjunction of the Mare a Mare Nord and Mare e Monti, takes another 20 minutes or so. For details of accommodation and transport in Marignana see p214.

PART 6: TRA MARE E MONTI

Overview

Nothing epitomizes Corsica's unique scenery as vividly as the red cliffs of Scandola, and the Tra Mare e Monti, zigzagging up the west coast from Cargèse to Calenzana, takes you to within a stone's throw of the famous promontory. To do so, it arcs through one of Europe's most dramatic marine landscapes: a convoluted hinterland of deep valleys and *maquis*-covered hills overlooked by the serrated profile of Paglia Orba and the Cinq Frati, which peak at an improbably short distance from the shore. Combine this unforgettable scenery with the prospect of some of Corsica's most picturesque villages, not to mention roadless valleys carpeted in ancient oak forest, and you'll understand why the route is regarded by French *randonneurs* as a classic.

Few trekkers, however, attempt this path's most memorable stages – between Ota and Galéria – at the height of summer, when the lack of shade at sea level renders the heat unbearable. On the other hand, this is among the few routes on the island which you can, if adequately equipped, safely cover throughout the winter, even when the mountains a short way inland are plastered in snow.

The FFRP advises 10 days to complete all 10 stages but if you're in reasonable shape and flexible about accommodation you should be able to finish in a week. No fewer than 10 *gîtes d'étape* punctuate the route but don't be complacent about finding beds: the Tra Mare e Monti's popularity almost guarantees the hostels will be fully booked throughout May, June, September and October. Reserve well in advance at these times and be prepared for a night or two under canvas or in a hotel.

Although each stage of the route passes through at least one village, banks and ATMs are rare. Once you've left Cargèse the only places to change money are at Porto and Galéria.

If you're planning to cut the route short do it at Galéria, two or three days from the end and connected to Calvi by bus. Running inland up the Fango Valley and thence over the Bocca Bonassa pass to Bonifatu and Calenzana, the final few stages lack the intensity of earlier ones, making for an anti-climatic end to the trek. With more time you can combine the early part of this route with the Mare e Mare Nord in reverse from Corte to Évisa. An even more challenging alternative would be to approach Calenzana via the GR20, swapping the last, easy stage from Bonifatu for the GR's *variant* route to the Refuge d'Ortu di u Piobbu (see p118).

The first two stages of the Tra Mare e Monti – which run in tandem with those of the Mare a Mare Nord – are described on pp206-214. For advice on how to get to and from the trailheads, see Cargèse (pp206-8) and Calenzana (pp113-5).

The route

ÉVISA → OTA [MAP 46, OPPOSITE]

Running down the spectacular Spelunca Gorge, this stretch follows a cobbled mule track used in past centuries to transport timber from the Forêt d'Aïtone to the harbour at Porto. A popular day-hike, it's famous above all for its two gracefully-arched Genoan bridges, the Pont de Zaglia and Ponte Vecchiu. Once over them, Corsica's own Pillars of Hercules, Capu d'Ota and Capu d'Ortu, flanking the mouth of the valley, herald the route's return to the coast.

It's possible to do this and the next stage (to Serriera) in one long day. But starting out from Marignana (see the Mare a Mare Nord section, p214) you'd be better off stopping for at Ota, which would leave plenty of time to swim and laze around en route.

Orange waymarks lead you west out of **Évisa**, past Hôtel la Châtaigneraie and the *gendarmerie* to the turning off the main Porto road, marked with a signboard. Shaded by chestnut trees at first, the path descends sharply from the outset, plunging in a series of tight switchbacks through moss-covered oak and pine forest towards the confluence of the Aïtone and Tavulella rivers, overlooked by stands of alder. Once across the **Pont de Zaglia** you climb above the left bank of the river, through the bottom of a steeply-sided ravine, and then drop gently down to meet and cross the D84 at river level.

A right turn here will take you over the road bridge to the head of a trail up the right bank of the Lonca River that leads eventually to a series of beautiful natural bathing pools, crowded in summer but off the beaten track in spring and autumn. The Tra Mare e Monti, meanwhile, hedges around a football pitch to cross the river again at **Ponte Vecchiu**, from where it begins a steady ascent through broken maquis to Ota.

OTA

Before the rise of Porto as a tourist centre, Ota, ranged in terraces up the flank of a precipitous, pirate-proof hillside beneath Capu d'Ota, was the valley's principal village. Fringed by clumps of grand Corsican tombs, it's a sleepy place these days with a permanent population of only 150, most of them retired. In summer, however, the village livens up considerably, with trekkers and a steady trickle of beach tourists lured up from Porto by the prospect of Ota's renowned mountain cuisine.

Practical information

Looking south across the Porto Valley to the towering crags of Capu d'Ortu (1294m), the terrace of ***Chez Félix*** (☎ 04 95.26.12.92; open year-round) is the perfect spot to enjoy Ota's spectacular views and local specialities such as rabbit stew, *figatellu* (liver sausage) or wild-boar terrine,

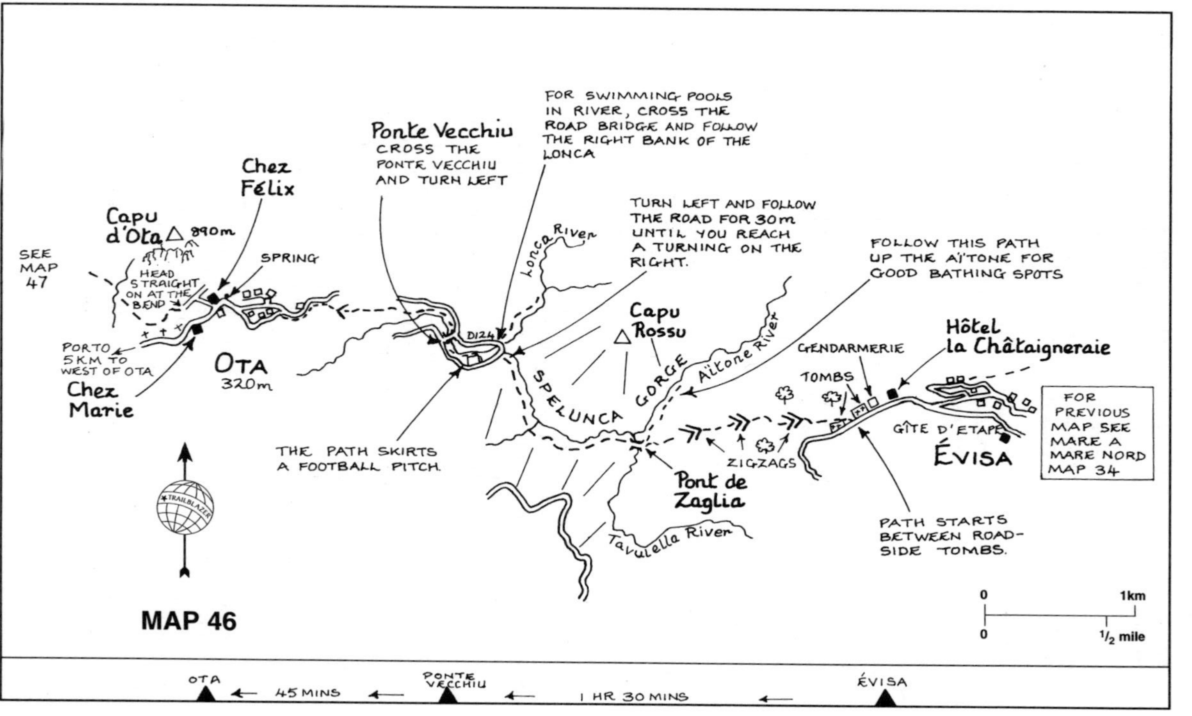
Ponte Vecchiu
CROSS THE PONTE VECCHIU AND TURN LEFT
FOR SWIMMING POOLS IN RIVER, CROSS THE ROAD BRIDGE AND FOLLOW THE RIGHT BANK OF THE LONCA
Chez Félix
Capu d'Ota 890m
SEE MAP 47
HEAD STRAIGHT ON AT THE BEND
SPRING
PORTO 5KM TO WEST OF OTA
OTA
320m
Chez Marie
Lonca River
D124
TURN LEFT AND FOLLOW THE ROAD FOR 30m UNTIL YOU REACH A TURNING ON THE RIGHT.
FOLLOW THIS PATH UP THE AÏTONE FOR GOOD BATHING SPOTS
Capu Rossu
Aïtone River
SPELUNCA
GORGE
THE PATH SKIRTS A FOOTBALL PITCH.
Pont de Zaglia
ZIGZAGS
Tavulella River
GENDARMERIE
TOMBS
Hôtel la Châtaigneraie
GÎTE D'ETAPE
ÉVISA
FOR PREVIOUS MAP SEE MARE A MARE NORD MAP 34
PATH STARTS BETWEEN ROAD-SIDE TOMBS.
TRAILBLAZER
MAP 46
0
1km
0
1/2 mile
OTA
45 MINS
PONTE VECCHIU
1 HR 30 MINS
ÉVISA

rounded off with chestnut-heavy desserts. The set menu, which includes the *plat du jour*, costs around 18€. If you're staying in Félix's *gîte*, however, go for the good value half-board at 29€. Beds in the six-person dorms in an old stone house across the road from the restaurant cost 10.60€.

Ota's other gîte, ***Chez Marie*** (☎ 04.95 26.11.37; open year-round) a little further down the lane at the Bar des Chasseurs has identical prices and facilities (though not such good views).

Ota is served by SAIB's bus (☎ 04.95 22.41.99 or 04.95.21.02.07; Sept–June one to two daily Mon–Sat; July–Aug two daily) from Ajaccio which terminates here after calling at Sagone, Cargèse, Piana and Porto. You can consult the timetable at either gîte.

PORTO/PORTU

Five kilometres west of Ota and spread around the far eastern end of the Golfe de Porto, the village, with its photogenic, square-topped watchtower, was established by the Genoans as a timber harbour in the sixteenth century. Over the years its population was all but wiped out by malaria and had dwindled to virtually nothing by the time Porto was revived as a resort after WWII. A rash of modern buildings followed hot on the heels of a new marina. The result was an untypically soulless, artificial place whose raison d'être seems to be to relieve German campers and French pensioners of their euros – which it accomplishes with far less panache than most other resorts.

For trekkers, Porto offers a rare opportunity on this route to re-provision; it has an ATM, bureau de change, pharmacy, supermarkets and a bumper crops of hotels, campsites and restaurants. Unless you're happy to hitch or walk 5km along the road, SAIB's bus is the most convenient way to get here from Ota.

What to see

Porto's dramatic location is its principal attraction and the best place to get to grips with the surrounding landscape is the top of the **Genoan tower** (daily 11am–7pm, or 9am–10pm in July and August; admission 2.30€). It was erected in 1549 as a part of an island-wide initiative against Moorish pirates plaguing the coast (for more on this see p49). The ticket price includes an engaging guided tour (in French only) about the island's Genoan *torri* and how this effective early-warning and defence system functioned.

Visible from the tower, the village's grey pebble **beach**, reached via the footbridge down in the marina, is nothing to write home about. It lacks any shade and with the slightest wind can turn into a dust bowl. More worryingly, the undertow claims lives each year. For a swim and sunbathe you're better off heading inland along the Tra Mare e Monti to the Spelunca or Lonca valleys, which are dotted with exquisite pools.

The Golfe de Porto's best-known natural features, however, are only accessible by boat. Two companies, Nave Va (☎ 04.95.26.15.16) and Porto Linea (☎ 04.95.26.11.50), run excursions out of Porto harbour to the **Scandola Nature Reserve** (see p262) and the massive red cliffs and outlandish rock formations, known as **Les Calanches de Piana**, lining the south shore of the gulf. A three-hour cruise to Scandola, calling briefly at Girolata (see pp258-60) costs 30€; the shorter foray west to the Calanches costs 15€. Timetable information is available from Nave Va's booking booth and Porto Linea's counter in Hôtel Monte Rosso, both down in the harbour, or from the tourist office nearby. Excursions run from April until mid-October.

Alternatively you could explore the gulf by hiring an inflatable **Zodiac** boat from one of the outfits at the marina; around 70€ for a half day.

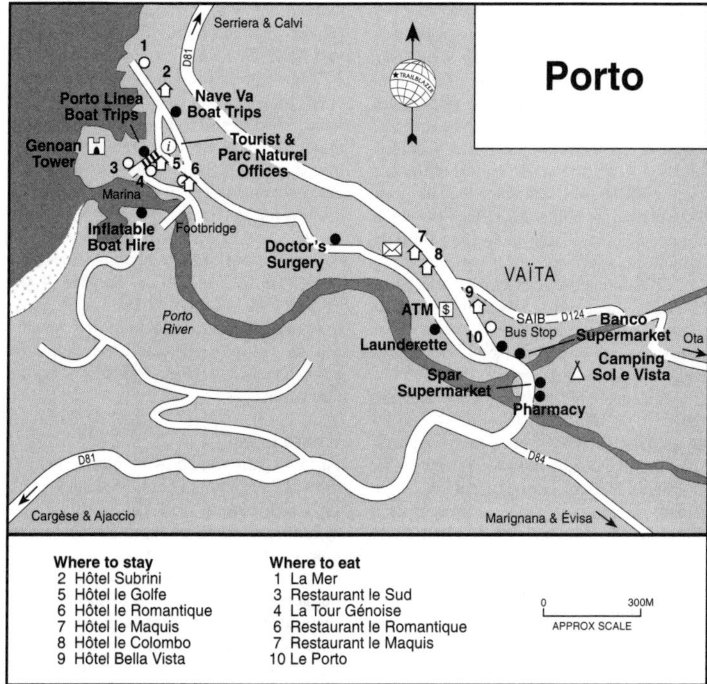

Orientation and services

Porto has two distinct centres of gravity. The first, known as **Vaïta**, straddles the coast road just after it crosses the river. This is where you'll find the village's campsites and two large supermarkets. From here, another road drops downhill to the marina, 1.5km west, passing the **launderette** (8am–10pm), **ATM**, **post office** (Mon–Fri 9am–12.30pm and 2–4pm, Sat 8.30–11am), bakery and ranks of hotels and pizzerias.

The other centre is the modern seafront square, overlooked by the old Genoan tower, at the far end of town. Nearby stands the **tourist office** (July and Aug daily 9am–7pm, Sept–June Mon–Fri 9am–noon and 2–6pm) and the **Parc Naturel office** (same hours as the tourist office).

The **marina**, with its diving school stalls and boat rental agencies, is two minutes' walk south off the square. A footbridge gives access to the beach and scruffy *camping municipal* across the river.

Getting there and away

SAIB's buses run year-round between Ajaccio and Ota via Sagone, Cargèse and Piana (☎ 04.95.22.41.99 or 04.95.21.02.07; Sept–June one or two daily Mon–Sat; July–Aug two daily).

During the summer, SAIB also runs services to and from Calvi, via Galéria, Bocca a Croce, Curzu, Partinello and Serriera (mid-May–Oct Mon–Sat one daily).

The only other bus service to Porto is Autocars Mordiconi's seasonal service to Corte, via Évisa, Col de Verghio, Albertacce and Calacuccia (☎ 04 95 48 00 04; July–mid-Sept, one daily).

Where to stay

Porto boasts four large campsites, but easily the nicest of them is ***Camping Sol e Vista*** (☎ 04.95.25.15.71), just behind the supermarkets at Vaïta. Ranged up the sides of the valley in the shade of an old olive orchard, it enjoys the best views and most secluded situation. It's also the one closest to the Tra Mare e Monti. You can enter the site from the Ota road, or lower down the hillside via a gateway just off the main drag through the village (near the Spar).

Stiff competition among Porto's many hotels has kept tariffs low compared with most of the island's resorts. However, from mid-July until the end of August, rates typically rise by a third or more.

A dependable budget choice near the seafront is ***Hôtel le Golfe*** (☎ 04.95 26.13.33; open May–Oct), where simple en suite rooms opening onto the square go for as little as 30€ off season, or 53.20€ at the height of summer. Only a little pricier, ***Hôtel Le Maquis*** (☎ 04.95.26.12.19, 🖹 04 95.26.12.77; open Feb–mid-Nov), up on the outskirts of Vaïta to the left of the main road as you head out towards Calvi, is a welcoming, family-run place. Rooms are basic (most have shared bathrooms and toilets on the corridor), but clean and comfortable. Prices range from 36.50€ to 45.60€; half-board (42.60–53.20€) is obligatory in August.

On the same road, ***Hôtel Bella Vista*** (☎ 04.95.26.11.08, 🖹 04.95.26.15.18; open April–Oct), an attractive pink granite place with views over the valley and gulf, offers a notch more comfort. Rates here range from 45.60€ to 68.40€ depending on the season. Once again, half-board (63€ per head) is obligatory in August. In a similar bracket, but closer to the seafront, ***Hôtel le Romantique*** (☎ 04.95.26.10.85, 🖹 04.95 26.14.04; April–mid-Oct) offers good value for money in the mid-range category. Costing from 57.70€ to 63.80€, most of its comfortable air-conditioned rooms overlook the marina. The hotel has a small restaurant. Half-board is optional, even in peak season, when prices remain reasonable.

Decked out with driftwood sculpture and nautical bits and bobs, ***Hôtel le Colombo*** (☎ 04.95.26.10.14, 🖹 04.95.26.19.90; 💻 www.porto.tourisme.com/Colombo/; open May–Oct), next to Le Maquis in Vaïta, is an even more pleasant mid-price option if you don't mind being away from the shore. The difference between its cheaper rooms (50.20/74.50€ low/peak season) and pricier ones (60.80/88.20€) is a spacious terrace overlooking the valley.

At the top of the range you won't do better than the swish ***Hôtel Subrini*** (☎ 04 95.26.14.94, 🖹 04.95.26.11.57; open Easter–20 Oct), overlooking the square near the seafront, where air-con rooms with all mod cons cost 76–83.60€ depending on the season.

Where to eat

Porto is jam-packed with places to eat, most of them churning out formulaic menus for coach parties. You can, however, eat extremely well here, especially if you're prepared to splash out a bit.

Among the many cheap-and-cheerful budget restaurants ranged around the seafront, ***La Tour Génoise*** is a safe option. On a raised terrace overlooking the harbour, it serves a huge selection of pizzas from 6€, as well as largely unexciting set menus.

For better local cuisine and a lofty location with valley views, book a terrace table at ***Le Maquis*** (see Where to stay). This place enjoys a strong reputation for good-value Corsican set menus (13.70€ and 23€), which draw on local seafood and pork reared in the Spelunca Valley. Scorpion fish in mussel sauce is a perennial favourite but vegetarians are well catered for with south Corsican-style baked aubergine, prepared with *brocciu* and crême fraiche.

Classic *cuisine continentale* is the hallmark of popular ***Le Porto*** (☎ 04.95.26 11.20), just down the road. Its two set menus (15€ and 20€) feature more typically French gourmet dishes such as duck in orange and rabbit or veal in mustard sauce; meals are served on a terrace overlooking the valley.

Le Sud (☎ 04.95.26.14.11) offers Porto's most stylish fine dining. Served on a high deck surveying the marina and beach, the beautifully presented dishes give local ingredients an imaginative North African twist. Apricot and lamb *tagine* is a filling alternative to the delicate seafood choices, which change daily according to what the local fisherman have caught. They also offer a selection of designer salads and starters such as octopus marinated in maquis herbs. The set menu is 19.70€; count on around 45€ if you eat à la carte. If Le Sud seems too contrived, ***La Mer*** (☎ 04.95.26.11.27), across the square, might appeal more for a splurge. Top-grade Corsican seafood – east-coast oysters, crayfish, lobsters, anemones and mullet out of the gulf – is prepared in definitively traditional style. Prices reflect La Mer's reputation as the poshest restaurant this side of Calvi. With a chilled bottle of Patrimonio white you could easily spend 75€ or more per head.

OTA → SERRIERA [MAP 47, p254]

Still well waymarked in orange, the Tra Mare e Monti continues from next to the gîte d'étape Chez Félix, striking uphill along a narrow lane. At the sharp bend directly above Chez Marie, go straight on past the point where the tarmac gives way to the dirt and cobbles of an old mule track. Gaining height gradually, the trail bends around the base of Capu d'Ota via a succession of rocky spurs, with views over the maquis to Ota, Porto and across the valley to Capu d'Ortu.

The first sustained ascent begins after you cross the Enova stream, as the path zigzags into the **Vitrone Ravine**, a very steep stream bed hemmed in by bare, pale orange porphyry. South-facing and with very little shade, the corridor is exposed to the full force of the mid-afternoon sun and should thus be tackled as early in the day as possible.

After around an hour things start to level off as you approach a *belvédère* with superb views west over the distant Calanches de Piana to Capu Rossu, the sugar-loaf mountain at the mouth of the gulf. A short way beyond the viewpoint the first chestnut trees shade the trail, which passes a **spring** on your right, smothered in wild peonies. By now you've reached the edge of a magical hidden plateau known locally as Pedua, where villagers from Ota used to graze their pigs in late summer. Only one cottage, a converted *séchoir*, still stands here, hidden amid the chestnut trees and maritime pines. You pass a turning for it on your left as you drop down through the forest towards the **Bocca San Petru** pass (900m), from where the route north across a rippling mass of maquis-covered hillside is revealed.

An unusually steep descent ensues, plunging from 900 metres to 30 in little over one hour. A good spot to break it up is a prominent outcrop on the right of the path, roughly half-way down, which affords a dramatic view of the west face of Paglia Orba and trio of lesser peaks below it. By now Serriera is clearly visible below, crouched in a shaded valley. Once you're through the last of the tall maquis and forest lining the descent, a motorable *piste* runs the rest of the way into the village, past a row of scruffy hunting kennels.

The gîte d'étape ***U me Mulinu*** (☎ 04.95.26.10.67; March–Oct) stands on the south-west side of Serriera, a 10- to 15-minute walk downhill from the

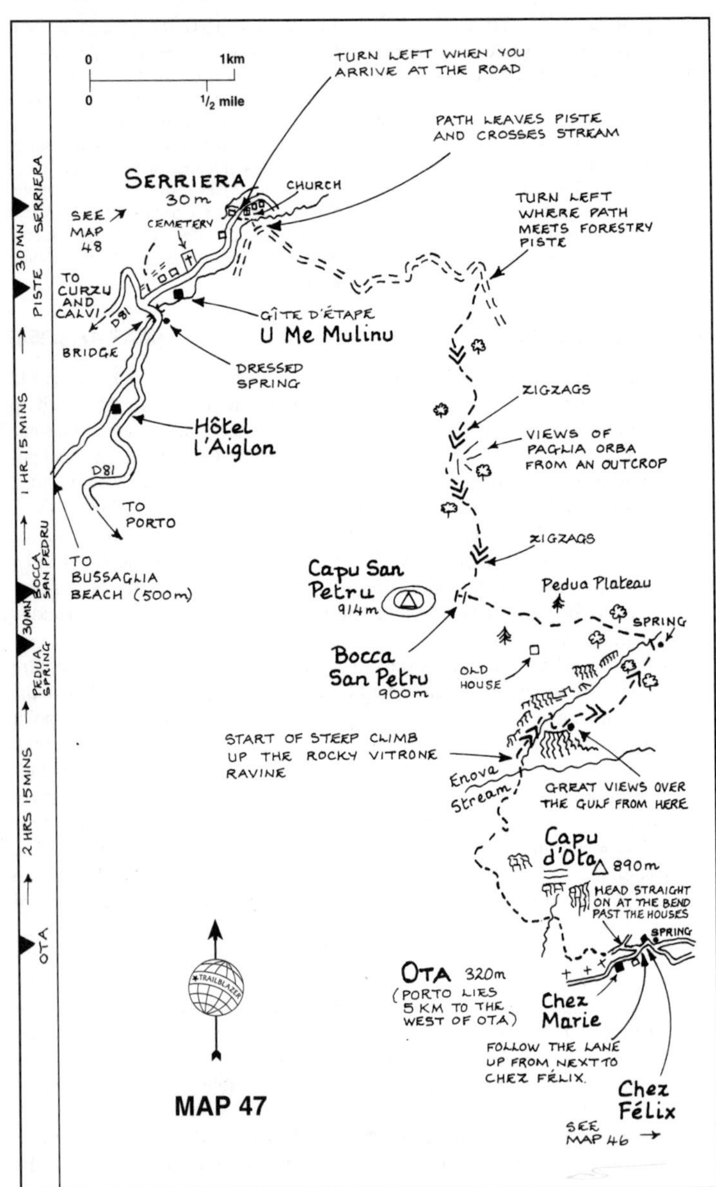

0 1km
0 1/2 mile
TURN LEFT WHEN YOU ARRIVE AT THE ROAD
PATH LEAVES PISTE AND CROSSES STREAM
SERRIERA 30m
CHURCH
SEE MAP 48
CEMETERY
TURN LEFT WHERE PATH MEETS FORESTRY PISTE
TO CURZU AND CALVI
D81
GÎTE D'ÉTAPE U Me Mulinu
BRIDGE
DRESSED SPRING
ZIGZAGS
Hôtel L'Aiglon
VIEWS OF PAGLIA ORBA FROM AN OUTCROP
D81
TO PORTO
ZIGZAGS
TO BUSSAGLIA BEACH (500m)
Capu San Petru 914m
Pedua Plateau
SPRING
Bocca San Petru 900m
OLD HOUSE
START OF STEEP CLIMB UP THE ROCKY VITRONE RAVINE
Enova Stream
GREAT VIEWS OVER THE GULF FROM HERE
Capu d'Ota 890m
HEAD STRAIGHT ON AT THE BEND PAST THE HOUSES
SPRING
OTA 320m
(PORTO LIES 5 KM TO THE WEST OF OTA)
Chez Marie
FOLLOW THE LANE UP FROM NEXT TO CHEZ FÉLIX
Chez Félix
SEE MAP 46
TRAILBLAZER
MAP 47
SERRIERA
30MN
PISTE
1 HR 15 MINS
BOCCA SAN PEDRU
30MN
PEDUA SPRING
2 HRS 15MINS
OTA

church towards the main road. It's neither particularly well set up nor welcoming, with run-down dorms opening onto a row of rear terraces. However, the dining hall, where meals are served on large wooden tables, is more convivial. Half-board costs 27.40€, or 10.60€ for just a bed. There are no self-catering facilities but you can cook on your camping stove behind the dorms.

The only alternative hereabouts is the posher ***Hôtel L'Aiglon*** (☎ 04.95.26.10.65, 🖷 04.95.26.14.77; open April–mid-Oct), 1.5km down the road to Bussaglia beach (see below). To find it, continue past the gîte, turn left onto the main road and follow it over the bridge and past the spring (on your left) until you reach a turning to the right. The hotel, an attractive stone building with its own tennis courts and large terrace overlooking the valley, lies 200m past the junction. Simple but well-furnished rooms with toilets *à l'étage* cost 41/42.60€ (low/high season); for en suite you're looking at 55/62.30€. Triples go for 57.80/68.40€ (prices include breakfast). They also offer good half-board deals from 33.40€ to 45.60€ per head, depending on the time of year and type of room.

Carry on past the hotel for another kilometre to Bussaglia **beach**, a small but beautiful spread of pale grey pebbles flanked by slopes shrouded in maquis. Quiet and secluded for most of the year, it's a good spot to swim and there's a decent restaurant, ***Les Galets*** (☎ 04.95.26.10.49), whose terrace makes the most of the views across the gulf. Set menus, dominated by local seafood, range from 13€ to 19€. They also offer salads (try the delicious octopus salad at 6.80€) and budget-priced pasta and pizzas. This is a particularly pleasant spot at sunset.

SERRIERA → CURZU [MAP 48, p256]

The route onward from Serriera is tricky to locate. The orange marks start below the village on the main road, but the way was recently blocked, obliging you to cut up the bulldozed track that runs from just past the time-share complex (see Map 48, p256). Once off the road, cut across the piste and head diagonally over the field until you pick up the waymarks, which run more or less parallel with the ridge up the hill.

Around 45 minutes on, the path levels off as it reaches a clearly defined fork with a signboard pointing north to Tuarelli. The Tra Mare e Monti bears left here to start a long descent. If you've run out of water keep an eye out for a right turn, about 10 minutes after the fork, marked with sporadic orange spots and sprayed 'S' symbols. This side path takes you to the ruined, deserted hamlet of **Pinetu**, whose old spring is hard to find: make for the two prominent chestnut trees below the houses, where cattle congregate.

Beyond the Pinetu turning, the main path drops steadily to ford the **Vetricella stream**, then follows a wooded gully uphill, emerging in dense maquis that hedges the route for the next half hour or so as you climb to a saddle in the ridge above the village of Partinellu. Having crossed the ridge beyond a hilltop called **Sant' Angelu**, the path climbs slightly and then keeps more or less to the contours across the Pilatri stream gully. Beyond this it drops down to the village of **Curzu**, piled up in steep terraces above the main D81 coast road.

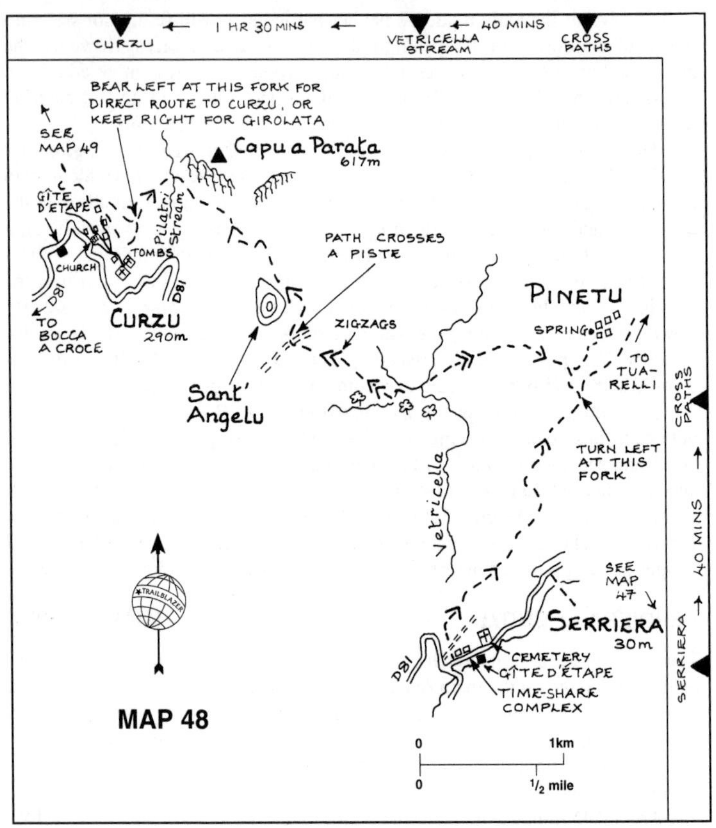

There's little to detain you here beyond the pleasant ***gîte d'étape*** (☎ 04 95.27.31.70; March–Oct), a modern three-storey house at the south-west exit of the village, just below the main road. A bed in its dorms, which accommodate between eight and fourteen people, costs 10.60€, or 30€ for half-board. Curzu doesn't have a shop, but Monsieur and Mme Sangny, who run the gîte, keep a store of essential supplies for guests.

From mid-May to the end of October the village is served by SAIB's Calvi to **Porto bus** (☎ 04.95.22.41.99 or 04.95.21.02.07), which also passes through Serriera, Bocca a Croce and Galéria. A timetable is pinned to the wall of the dining room in the gîte.

CURZU → GIROLATA [MAP 48, p256; MAP 49, p259]

This *étape*, undisputed highpoint of the Tra Mare e Monti, takes you through some of the most memorable scenery in Corsica, if not in all Europe. From the ridge above Curzu the blue expanse of the Golfe de Porto, bounded by its serene red promontories, is spread out below you, while the mountains of the island's watershed – among them the distinctive shark's tooth summit of Paglia Orba – are visible a short way away inland.

The icing on the cake is the village of Girolata. This superbly picturesque cluster of red-tiled houses, tucked away in a shell-shaped bay against the backdrop of Scandola's poryphry cliffs, is the last remaining, permanently inhabited village in Corsica not accessible by road. Spend the night there and you'll get to appreciate its essential tranquillity after the boat trippers have all gone home.

Two possible routes run between Curzu and Girolata. The main path, completing a circuit of the high ridges inland, offers superb views. An alternative itinerary (see the box on p258), keeping close to the coast via Bocca a Croce, is considerably shorter and easier. The main incentive to attempt the former are the superb views of the gulf and interior mountains to be had from the Capu di Curzu and the Crête de Salisei. Whichever route you choose, set off as early as possible to experience first light over the sea – an unforgettable spectacle – and take your time. Landscape doesn't get much more extraordinary than this.

Steel yourself for a stiff start as the path from Curzu ascends nearly 550m from the top of the village to the ridge high above it. At the crest a signboard indicates the fork where the alternative route to Girolata drops south-west towards Bocca a Croce (see box p258). The main path, meanwhile, swings east, following the edge of a wonderful holm oak forest up the ridge to **Capu di Curzu**, the day's most striking viewpoint, where a panel names the peaks and other major landmarks visible from it.

Beyond Capu di Curzu the route bends north-east and winds in and out of a succession of large granite outcrops and clumps of gnarled oak lining the rugged Crête de Salisei. At the **Bergeries de Salisei**, where the path peels away from the ridge, a stone shepherd's hut makes an ideal place to stop for a break, with a dressed spring providing fresh water a short way further along the trail.

From here on, the Tra Mare e Monti rises and falls constantly as it continues the giant circuit around the ridges. At **Punta di a Tartavellu** (825m) it reaches its final highpoint of the day and turns west to begin a sustained, gradual descent through more broken granite boulders and wild maquis to rejoin the road (352m).

The path runs northward along the D81 for 200m then drops westward into tall maquis. The rest of the descent to Girolata sticks closely to the ridge top until the Tra Mare e Monti meets its alternative path, arriving from the south, at which point it veers north to wind gently down to sea level.

Alternative route to Girolata **[Map 49, opposite]**

This *variant* of the Tra Mare e Monti more or less halves the walking time between Curzu and Girolata and takes you past a wild beach where you can swim and snorkel, but by following it you miss out on the main trail's best ridge section. A compromise would be to make a quick detour north-east from the place where the two paths diverge (see p257), to Capu di Curzu, for a taste of the magnificent views from the higher route.

From the fork in the paths the *variant* drops south-west down the ridge to Bocca a Croce (served by SAIB's daily Calvi to Porto bus; ☎ 04.95.22.41.99 or 04.95.21.02.07; mid-May–Oct Mon–Sat), where it meets the main road (D81). The onward path (indicated by a signboard) heads into the maquis beyond the seasonal snack hut (*buvette*) in the car park. A **spring**, the Funtana de Spana, appears roughly one-third of the way down to the cove of **Cala di Tuara**, where the trail emerges from the undergrowth onto a secluded bay lined with pebbles and flotsam: the best swimming spot lies on the north side of the beach. Waymarks lead across the streambed and up the far side of the hill to rejoin the main Tra Mare e Monti path, though a more scenic route runs west from the beach around the headland immediately to the north. Climbing high above the rocky shore it takes you through swathes of wind-bent maquis, gorse and broom to approach Girolata from the south – a great angle from which to photograph the village's Genoan tower, with the backdrop of the red cliffs behind.

Allow 40 minutes to reach Cala di Tuara from Bocca a Croce, and roughly the same for the remaining section to the village.

GIROLATA

After the white cliffs of Bonifacio in the far south, Girolata is probably the island's most photographed location, and for good reason. Clinging to a sheltered promontory beneath its crenellated Genoan tower, the village sits at a fault line of giant colour blocks: the sapphire-blue of the gulf, the rich greens of the maquis spread in a vast amphitheatre behind and, most improbable of all, the red rock of Scandola to the west, which at sunset seems to glow like molten iron.

Thanks to this scenery and the blissful absence of a road link, the approach to Girolata feels like the culmination of an adventure, no more so that after a day rock-hopping along the high ridges inland. The only thing likely to sour your experience of its epic setting and essential isolation are the crowds of boat trippers that descend here during the day. You can, however, avoid them by arriving after 5pm, by which time only a handful of yachties and hikers remain.

Until the advent of excursion boats in the 1960s, life in Girolata had remained largely unchanged for hundreds of years, its inhabitants dependent on the lobsters they haul in now depleted numbers from the abysses beneath Scandola's cliffs. Aside from the odd pirate raid, the only event to have troubled its peaceful existence was the arrival in 1530 of the infamous corsair Dragut and his fleet of nine galleons. When the Genoan admiral, Andrea Doria, got word of what had happened he dispatched a fleet of his own to capture the Barbary privateer. Dragut, however, managed to bribe his way out of prison and 11 years later returned to wreak revenge on those who had denounced him by slaughtering the entire population of Girolata.

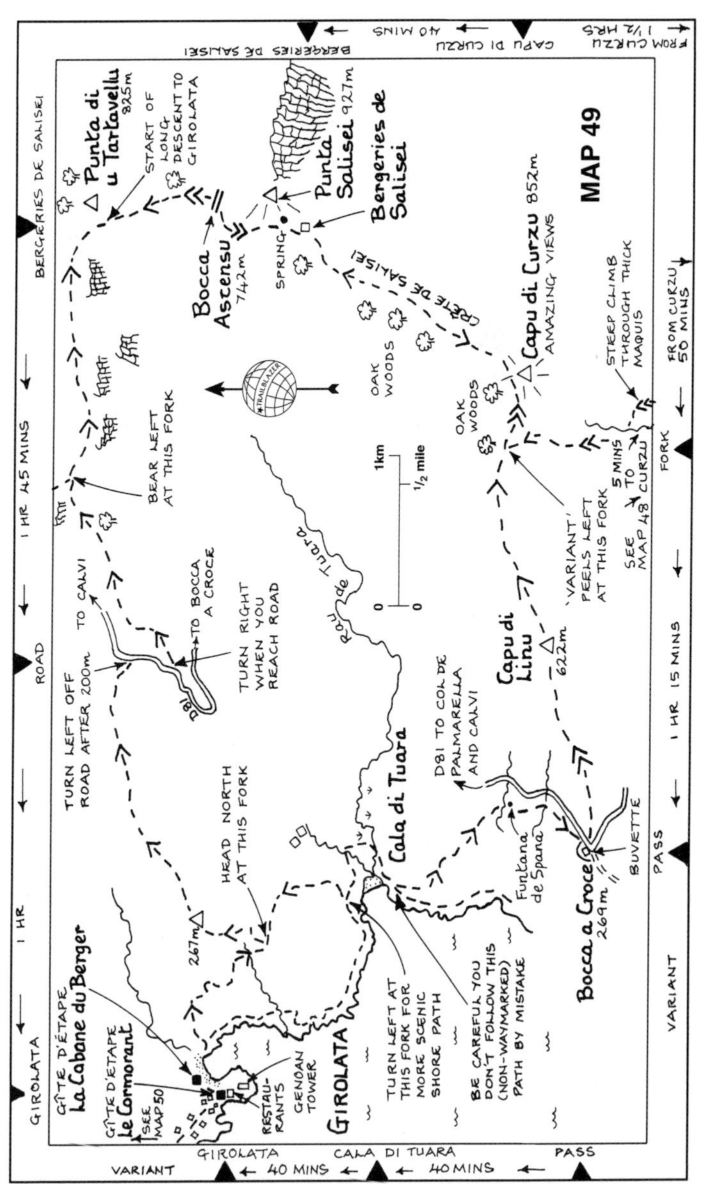
MAP 49
FROM CURZU 1 1/2 HRS
CAPU DI CURZU
40 MINS
BERGERIES DE SALISEI
1 HR 45 MINS
ROAD
1 HR
GIROLATA
VARIANT
40 MINS
CALA DI TUARA
40 MINS
PASS
FROM CURZU 50 MINS
FORK
1 HR 15 MINS
Punta di u Tartavellu 825m
START OF LONG DESCENT TO GIROLATA
Punta Salisei 927m
Bergeries de Salisei
Bocca Ascensu 742m
SPRING
CRETE DE SALISEI
OAK WOODS
Capu di Curzu 852m
AMAZING VIEWS
STEEP CLIMB THROUGH THICK MAQUIS
OAK WOODS
BEAR LEFT AT THIS FORK
'VARIANT' PEELS LEFT AT THIS FORK
SEE MAP 48
5 MINS TO CURZU
1km
1/2 mile
0
0
Rau de Tuara
TO CALVI
TO BOCCA A CROCE
TURN RIGHT WHEN YOU REACH ROAD
TURN LEFT OFF ROAD AFTER 200m
D81
Capu di Linu
622m
D81 TO COL DE PALMARELLA AND CALVI
Cala di Tuara
HEAD NORTH AT THIS FORK
267m
Funtana de Spana
Bocca a Croce 269m
BUVETTE
GÎTE D'ÉTAPE La Cabane du Berger
GÎTE D'ÉTAPE Le Cormorant
SEE MAP 50
RESTAU-RANTS
GENOAN TOWER
GIROLATA
TURN LEFT AT THIS FORK FOR MORE SCENIC SHORE PATH
BE CAREFUL YOU DON'T FOLLOW THIS (NON-WAYMARKED) PATH BY MISTAKE

Practical information

As befits its roadless status Girolata is well set up for walkers, with a tiny shop (March–Oct) selling basic trekking supplies, a telephone cabin and a couple of gîtes d'étape, in addition to restaurants and cafés that cater for the day trippers. Prices are on the high side, reflecting the fact that everything has to brought here by boat.

Directly behind the beach, ***La Cabane du Berger*** (☎ 04.95.20.16.98; open April–mid-Oct; no credit cards) is the first gîte you pass on entering the village. The wooden cabins in the rear garden provide Girolata's most comfortable accommodation; beds cost 16.70€ per head, or 38€ for half-board. There are also a few dorm beds at 13€ (27.40€ for half-board). Campers and bivouackers are charged 7.60€. The food served in the restaurant is nothing special; opt for half-board and you'll probably regret it.

The same applies to the second gîte, ***Le Cormorant*** (☎ 04.95.20.15.55; open April–mid-Oct; no credit cards), overlooking the jetty. The six-bed dorms (identical rates to La Cabane du Berger) are a bit musty and not all that well maintained. Moreover, half-board (29€) is obligatory.

Both of Girolata's **restaurants** stand above Le Cormorant, overlooking the beach and bay. On a spacious terrace, decked out with teak furniture, ***Le Bel Ombra*** serves two set menus (20€ and 25.80€) dominated by local seafood dishes, including Scandola lobster. Next door, ***Le Bon Espoir*** is a slightly smaller, less expensive alternative, with menus at 15€, 21.30€ (Corsican) and 24.30€ (the serious seafood option). Both places accept credit cards.

GIROLATA → GALÉRIA [MAP 50, OPPOSITE]

Another wonderful day's walking lies in store as the Tra Mare e Monti scales the ridge behind Girolata and then, after following its spine for 3km, drops down the other side to follow the Tavulaghiu Valley north to Galéria. This is a relatively short and easy stage which, with an early start (recommended in any case to make the most of the sunrise light over the gulf), could be combined with the following one to Fango or Tuarelli.

Once clear of the houses at the top of Girolata, the path runs down the shore into the **Cavone ravine**, overgrown with thick maquis. From here the steady, enjoyable climb that yields increasingly spectacular views south over the gulf. A gentle traverse of the west flank of the **Calanchelle ravine**, which funnels down to Girolata, brings you after around 1½ hours to the ridge top, where you veer east along the watershed. The maquis is soon interrupted by low outcrops of broken granite and the path steepens considerably as you approach a radio mast. Around it oak trees spill south down a totally wild hillside, fringed in the distance by the red rocks and blue waters of the Baie de Focolara.

The path for the next few kilometres is a succession of superb panoramas over the mostly deserted country between Scandola and Paglia Orba, with the rocky coast stretching away north towards Calvi. Granite outcrops provide a string of viewpoints as the path wriggles east along the ridge via a series of clearings dotted with flat-bottomed oaks. Shortly after the largest of these open patches (**Punta di a Literniccia**), a sign indicates a fork in the path where a right turn takes you down to the D81 at Col de la Palmarella; the Tra Mare e Monti, however, bears left to begin its two-hour descent of the Tavulaghiu Valley.

Zigzagging down a spur through a mixture of oak wood and maquis, the path is steep until you reach the stream, where it levels off. After switching

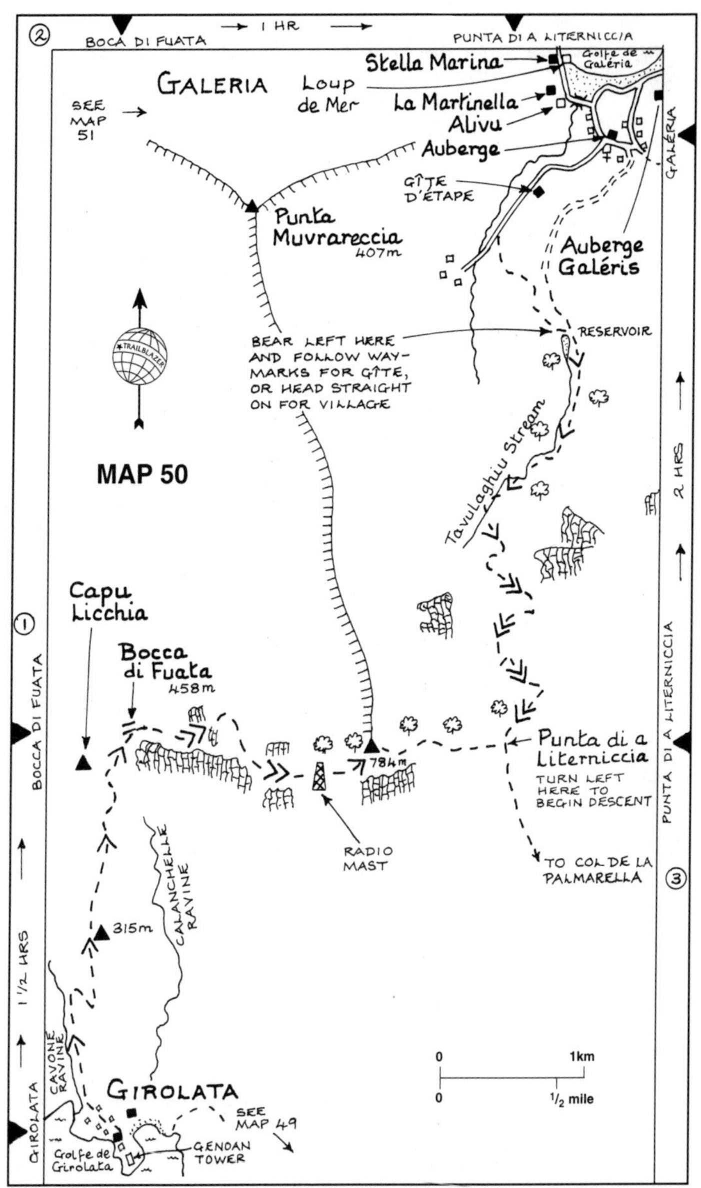

BOCA DI FUATA
1 HR
PUNTA DI A LITERNICCIA
GALERIA
SEE MAP 51
Stella Marina
Golfe de Galéria
Loup de Mer
La Martinella
Alivu
Auberge
GÎTE D'ETAPE
GALÉRIA
Punta Muvrareccia 407m
Auberge Galéris
BEAR LEFT HERE AND FOLLOW WAY-MARKS FOR GÎTE, OR HEAD STRAIGHT ON FOR VILLAGE
RESERVOIR
Tavulaghiu Stream
2 HRS
MAP 50
Capu Licchia
Bocca di Fuata 458m
784m
Punta di a Literniccia
TURN LEFT HERE TO BEGIN DESCENT
BOCCA DI FUATA
PUNTA DI A LITERNICCIA
RADIO MAST
TO COL DE LA PALMARELLA
CALANCHELLE RAVINE
315m
1 1/2 HRS
CAVONE RAVINE
GIROLATA
SEE MAP 49
GENOAN TOWER
Golfe de Girolata
0
1km
0
1/2 mile

Scandola Nature Reserve (Réserve Naturelle de Scandola)

Forming the northern limits of the Golfe de Porto, the distinctive red peninsula of Scandola (named after the island's traditional terracotta rooftiles, *scandule*), comprises one of the Mediterranean's richest biospheres. In 1975, after the disappearance of the monk seal, 7800 hectares of its wind-lashed tip and 4200 hectares of water were accorded special protection; today, as a UNESCO World Heritage site, the area supports a wealth of wildlife, both above and below sea level.

The promontory is believed to have been formed by a volcanic eruption 200–250 million years ago when lava from the crater of Monte Cinto flowed into the sea. Since then, wind, waves and wet weather have been hard at work sculpting its cliffs, which rise to 900m in places, into an astonishingly convoluted mass of fissures, pinnacles, creeks, arches and caves.

As Scandola is strictly off-limits to casual visitors, you'll have to be content with a boat trip from Porto or Calvi (see p250 and p103). Birders shouldn't pass up the chance to see some of the 24 pairs of ospreys who nest here (most of them on rocky columns rising out of the sea), as well as andouin gulls, bearded vultures, peregrine falcons and the large flocks of Mediterranean shearwaters.

The clear seas around Scandola harbour a correspondingly rich subaquatic ecosystem, underpinned by deep fields of **poseidonion** (*Posidonia oceanica*), a grass that is able because of the water's exceptional clarity to photosynthesize at 35m – and thus supply life-giving oxygen to the many creatures who live at that depth (you'll come across banks of the stuff on Girolata beach and Cala di Tuara on the Tra Mare e Monti).

Grazing the reefs of exquisite red coral beneath the cliffs, chubby-lipped **grouper**, two-metre barracuda, scorpion fish, moray and conger eels and carnivorous dentex all flourish here, as do three species of lobster, seahorses and a vivid red plant called gorgonian that glows blue when illuminated by diving lights.

Divers are not allowed inside Scandola's exclusion zone but the **sub-aqua schools** in Porto marina lead groups to a string of superb sites nearby. Rates for exploratory dives range from 27€ to 42€; the schools also offer instruction for beginners, leading to PADI accreditation. For more information, check out 💻 www.plongeeporto.com or www.generation-bleue.com, or call at the dive schools on the quayside.

banks several times it arrives at a small **reservoir**, at the far end of which anyone heading for the gîte d'étape (see Galeria below) should turn left and follow the orange waymarks across the front of the reservoir onto the road. For the most direct route to Galéria, however, head straight on from the reservoir along a concrete-covered water channel; this will lead you first to a broad path and then to a motorable piste that runs all the way into the centre of the village. The latter route is not well waymarked.

GALÉRIA

Identified by archaeologists as the ancient Greek port of Kalaris, Galéria occupies a wonderfully sheltered bay backed by a rugged hinterland of eroded hills. Although a thriving town in the sixth century BC when it was first colonized by the Phoenicians, the settlement went into a decline hastened by malaria, which was only wiped out by DDT-spraying American soldiers in 1947. These days, despite its promising position at the heart of

Corsica's wild north-west, the village lacks the fishing-port atmosphere it must once have possessed, and is a bit of an anticlimax after the landscape you cross to get here. Scattered over a wide area behind its curving shingle beach, most of its houses – with the exception of those lining the main street – are modern villas with little charm.

On the plus side, Galéria remains relatively quiet even at the height of summer and offers a number of useful services for trekkers, including the first supermarket since Porto (or Cargèse if you didn't call there en route) – as well as a post office where you can change money. During the summer a daily bus connects the village with Calvi, an hour away to the north. Trekkers sometimes jump on it to cut short the remaining, less scenic stage of the Tra Mare e Monti.

Orientation and services

From July to mid-September Autocars Les Beaux Voyages (☎ 04.95.65.15.02 or 04.95.65.11.35) provides a daily bus link from the church square to Calvi. You can pick up SAIB's bus south to Porto via Col de la Croix, Curzu and Serriera (Aug daily, mid-May–July and Sept–mid-Oct one/two daily) from the intersection of the D81 and D351, 4km east of Galéria. During term times there's a school bus from Galéria to Calvi too. For timetable information on all these, ask at one of the bars in the village, telephone the company direct, or contact the **tourist office** (June–Sept Mon–Sat 9.30–noon and 5–8pm), 4km east where the SAIB Calvi to Porto bus stops.

Galéria's well-stocked supermarket stands at the heart of the village, next to the church. Nearby, the post office (Mon–Fri 9am–noon and 2–4pm) doesn't have an ATM but will undertake credit card encashments.

Where to stay and eat

Most trekkers check into Galéria's excellent ***gîte d'étape*** (☎ 04.95.62.00.46; open April–Oct), 1km south-west of the village centre (the waymarks run right past it as you approach from Girolata). Served in a light and airy, wood-panelled dining room, the food here is copious and of a high standard, and the animal-loving *gérants* are very hospitable. Half-board costs 29.60€. Dorm beds cost 11.40€ and campers pay 6.10€ per person to pitch in the small garden behind the hostel, which includes use of a hot shower and gas stove.

The next best budget option is the ***Auberge*** (☎ 04.95.62.00.15, 🖹 04.95.60 00.63; open Feb–mid-Dec), an unpretentious, old-fashioned village inn on the main street opposite the church. Small double rooms with shared toilets go for between 31€ and 38€ depending on the season. The restaurant also does a commendable *menu corse* for 17€, with a choice of three starters, mains and desserts. If you plan to stay here ask about their rates for half-board.

As a fallback, ***Auberge Galéris*** (☎ 04 95.62.02.89; open May–Sept) is worth a try. Tucked away just off the road running behind the beach, it comprises six modest rooms with terraces on the ground floor of a modern house. Tariffs start at a bargain 28€ off-season, rising to 38€ in July and August.

Two other very pleasant places stand at the opposite end of the village, above the jetty. ***La Martinella*** (☎ 04.95.62.00.44; open March–Oct) charges 39.50€ for its spacious, well-presented rooms, which all have refrigerators and sea-facing balconies. This is a particularly good choice for anyone travelling in a group of three or four, as the landlady will put up extra beds in the rooms for only 10.70€. Breakfast is included in these rates.

A short way further up the lane, the ***Stella Marina*** (☎ 04.95.62.00.03, 🖹 04.95 62.04.29) is a swisher place with correspondingly higher prices. Its rooms (47–64€ depending on the month) are large, light and impeccably maintained. Those on the top floor enjoy the best views over the bay. There's also a very pleasant restaurant here, serving Scandola lobster and crayfish, and a wonderful apple pie *flambée* in local *eau de vie*. Count on around 25€ per head à la carte.

Immediately below Stella Marina is the ***Loup de Mer*** restaurant, where you can sample the top-quality seafood landed on the jetty next to it. Get here early so you can sit on the rear terrace, which juts out over the sea. Set menus start at 18€, which usually includes the freshest fish plat du jour. For those on tighter budgets ***Alivu***, behind the beach at the bend in the road, knocks up tasty, inexpensive pizzas and a range of salads, served under an old olive tree outside.

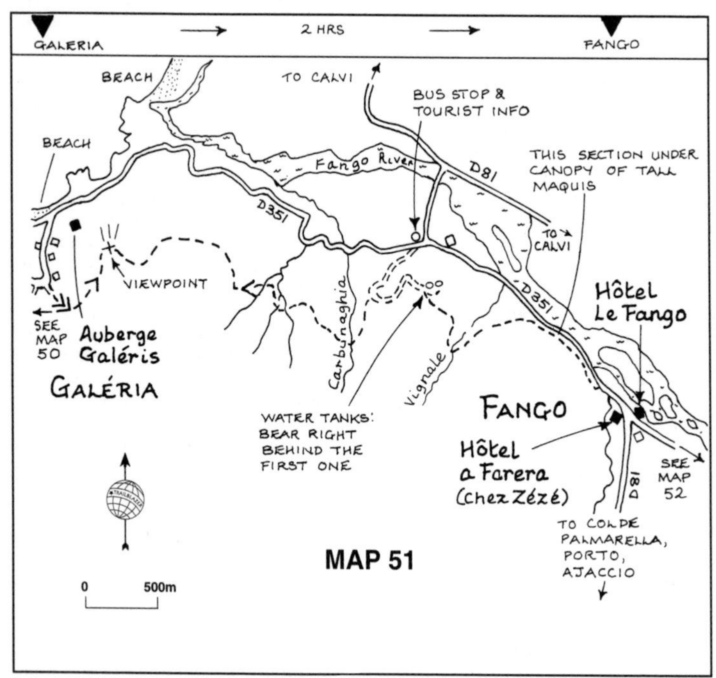

GALÉRIA → FANGO → TUARELLI [MAP 51, ABOVE; MAP 52, OPP]

This étape, for some the penultimate day of the Tra Mare a Monti, is essentially a transitionary one, taking you inland via the mighty Fango Valley to the mountains, a route traditionally followed to drive flocks between winter pastures around Galéria to the Niolu Valley (see p220). Its prettiest section meanders along an idyllic river bank, worn smooth by centuries of transhumant use, toward the seemingly impregnable Paglia Orba massif, whose near-vertical west face brings the valley to a breathtakingly abrupt end. The proximity of what Corsicans call '*La Grande Barrière*' is the stage's only scenic distinction. For much of the time you'll be plodding through dull maquis, below vast swathes of fire-damaged hillside – especially onerous in bad weather, or when the peaks are shrouded in cloud.

To pick up the path from Galéria (coming from the south of the town), follow the main street northward until you arrive at its first major bend, from where the waymarks lead you to the right between two old granite houses. The lane soon degenerates into a footpath that strikes uphill into the maquis quite steeply at first. The end of this first short ascent is marked by a bluff giving fine views over the beaches to the north. From here on the trail levels off, winding at more or less contour level through low scrub around a series of minor stream valleys. After fording the largest of them, the **Carbunaghia**, you arrive at a piste where you should turn right and walk for 400m towards a couple of large water tanks. The Tra Mare e Monti cuts to the right beside the first of these and shortly after descends to and fords the **Vignale** stream.

Twisting in parallel with the D351 for one kilometre under a dense canopy of old maquis, the track follows the valley south-west, reaching Fango after a five-minute walk on the main road. There are two places to stay on the crossroads here, neither particularly inviting but convenient if you've started in Girolata and run out of steam before Tuarelli. On the south side, ***Hôtel A Farera (Chez Zézé)*** (☎ 04.95.62.01.87; open April–mid-Oct) has en suite rooms tucked away above a small bar for 36.50–45.60€. The slightly larger ***Hôtel Le Fango*** (☎ 04.95.62.01.92; open April–mid-Oct) has double en suite rooms from 38€ to 46€, and a good restaurant where specialities include *canelloni al brocciu* and lasagna in wild boar sauce. Count on around 20€ per head for three courses.

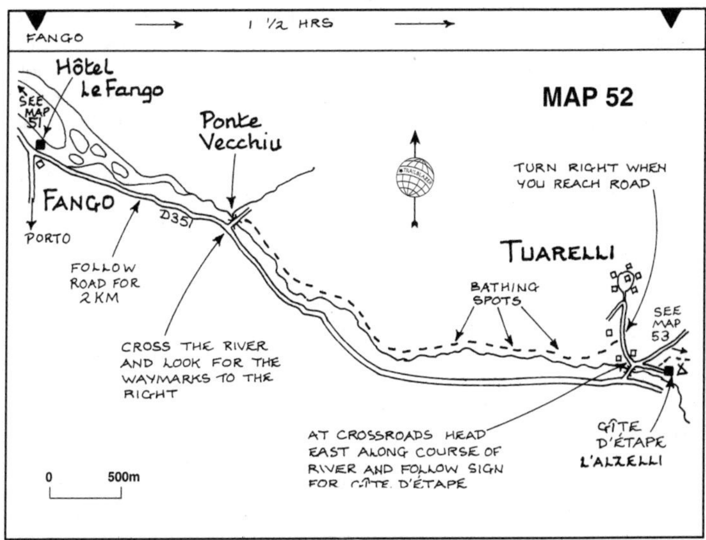

From Fango, another dull 2km trudge along tarmac brings you to **Ponte Vecchiu**, where the Tra Mare e Monti crosses to the right bank of the river via a lovely old stone bridge offering a great view of the *grande barrière* rearing up to the west. The rest of the stage to Tuarelli is an enjoyable amble along the river. Numerous pebble beaches and deep natural pools provide perfect bathing spots.

Around 1½ hours after crossing the bridge you emerge from the maquis onto a tarmac road at **Tuarelli**. The only place to stay and eat here is ***Gîte d'étape 'L'Alzelli'*** (☎ 04.95.62.01.75; open April–Oct), 250m east of the bridge. Slap on the riverbank with a sunny stone terrace and an alfresco dining area, this is a particularly swish gîte with only 24 dorm beds (10€ per head). The gîte has a professional chef and kitchen staff so the meals are consistently good and not all that expensive (half-board costs 30€ per head). Adjacent to it is a small campsite where you can pitch your tent or bivouac for 5.30€, although there isn't much flat ground and the *bloc sanitaire* struggles to cope in peak season.

TUARELLI → BONIFATU [MAP 53, OPPOSITE; MAP 54, p269]

Officially this is the last but one stage of the Tra Mare e Monti but most trekkers double up to reach Calenzana before nightfall – a long haul of around 9-10 hours which you'd do well to break at Bonifatu, where there's an inviting little gîte-restaurant.

The route consists of one long climb to start with, followed by a shorter but steeper descent. Its chief appeal lies in the crossing of the Bocca di Bonassa, where you get your first sight of Calvi and its beautiful hinterland, and the luxuriant ancient oak forest below it – the finest *chêne vert* wood in Corsica.

From Tuarelli the Tra Mare e Monti starts 100m down the lane from the gîte d'étape in the direction of the village. Climbing the west flank of a low hill at first, it crosses the ridge to enter the Margine stream valley, shaded by deciduous trees until its sharp change of direction 30 metres below the pass. Once over the **Bocca di Lucca** (589m), you enter the grandiose **Vallée de la Prezzuna,** which culminates in a wild amphitheatre filled with acres of giant holm oak.

The approach to the second pass of the day, via a succession of wooded gullies, progresses at a mostly level gradient. Gradually, however, the oak forest gives way to huge Laricio pines and the path steepens, gaining ground more rapidly through a series of sweeping switchbacks. The final pull to the ridge takes you clear of the tree line into more rocky terrain.

From the **Bocca di Bonassa** (1153m), the views extend north over the course of the Figarella River to the Golfe de Calvi, east to the immense granite pinnacles of the Cirque de Bonifatu and across the valley towards Calenzana, with all but the final half-hour of the remaining route visible. If you're lucky you might catch a glimpse of one of the golden eagles that nest on the Punta di Bonassa, just to the west.

Make the most of the air up here because for the next hour, as the Tra Mare e Monti loses 600m of altitude, you'll be hemmed in by dense, damp oak forest. Many of the ancient holm oaks lining this stretch, which in places preside

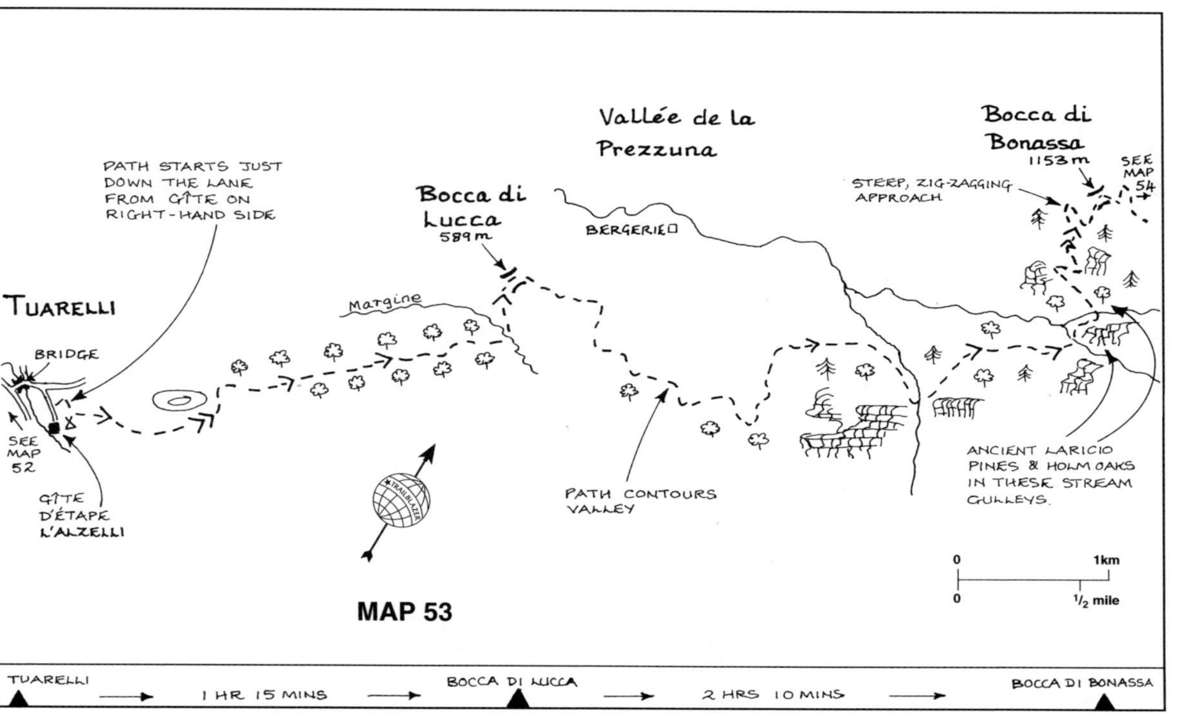
PATH STARTS JUST DOWN THE LANE FROM GÎTE ON RIGHT-HAND SIDE
TUARELLI
BRIDGE
SEE MAP 52
GÎTE D'ÉTAPE L'ALZELLI
Bocca di Lucca
589m
Margine
Vallée de la Prezzuna
BERGERIE
PATH CONTOURS VALLEY
Bocca di Bonassa
1153m
SEE MAP 54
STEEP, ZIG-ZAGGING APPROACH
ANCIENT LARICIO PINES & HOLM OAKS IN THESE STREAM GULLEYS.
TRAILBLAZER
MAP 53
0
1km
0
1/2 mile
TUARELLI
1 HR 15 MINS
BOCCA DI LUCCA
2 HRS 10 MINS
BOCCA DI BONASSA

over glades piled with mossy boulders that wouldn't look out of place in northern Europe, are the oldest and largest left on the island.

They are soon outnumbered by maritime pines as you approach the valley floor, where the D251 from Calvi wriggles into the heart of one of the region's most spectacular valleys. On reaching it, turn left if you're heading for Calenzana, or right for the gîte d'étape at **Bonifatu**.

Benefitting from its prime position at the end of the road, beneath the famous orange crags of the *cirque*, ***Gîte d'étape Auberge de la Forêt*** (☎/📠 04.95.65.09.98; open April–Oct) gets swamped by visitors during the summer, which can detract from both the stupendous scenery and the fragrant Corsican cuisine on offer at the restaurant. Dished up on a small stone terrace overlooking the road, the set menu (16.70€), featuring local specialities such as herb flan and fillet of wild boar, is cooked fresh every day and is a good deal more tempting than most of the meals available at Calenzana. They also do a range of sandwiches, salads and other light snacks, as well as ice creams and Corsican desserts. Accommodation in the gîte is spartan and cramped but adequate. Beds cost 12€, or 27.40€ for half-board (obligatory in peak season). Bivouackers and campers are charged 6€ to pitch on decidedly lumpy ground in the woods behind the restaurant, with access to a shower and toilet block but not self-catering facilities.

Variant route from Bonifatu to Calenzana

Among the many trekkers you'll see holed up at Auberge de la Forêt in Bonifatu will be a contingent of disappointed-looking GR20 dropouts. Having limped to the refuge of Carozzu (see p125), those for whom the first two stages of Corsica's big walk proved too much head down the red-and-white waymarked liaison route to the roadhead, and catch a taxi back to Calvi to nurse their blisters on the beach. If you've plenty of walking left in you and are not enticed by the prospect of a long plod along pistes to Calenzana to complete the Tra Mare e Monti, the path they followed to get here may, if walked in reverse, provide the perfect extension to this route.

Two alternatives are possible. The first is to follow the GR20 *Variante* (see p124) up the **Spasimata Valley** to **Carozzu**. From there you could tackle one of the toughest but most memorable stages of the GR, over the Punta Innominata and Col d'Avartoli to **Refuge d'Ortu di u Piobbu** (see Map 4, p123). Having overnighted there, the remaining leg to Calenzana is nearly all downhill. Don't underestimate this option though; it takes you above 2000 metres amid mountains notorious for fickle weather. Only attempt it if you are fully fit and well equipped (see advice on p28-34).

A less strenuous and difficult route follows the other section of the GR20 *Variante* up the **Melaghia Valley** to the Refuge d'Ortu di Piobbu. Keeping to the valley floor for most of the way, it's well sheltered but a long, relentless climb all the same, with a descent of 1295m awaiting you the next day.

Full descriptions and sketch maps of these routes feature in the section on the GR20, pp122-5.

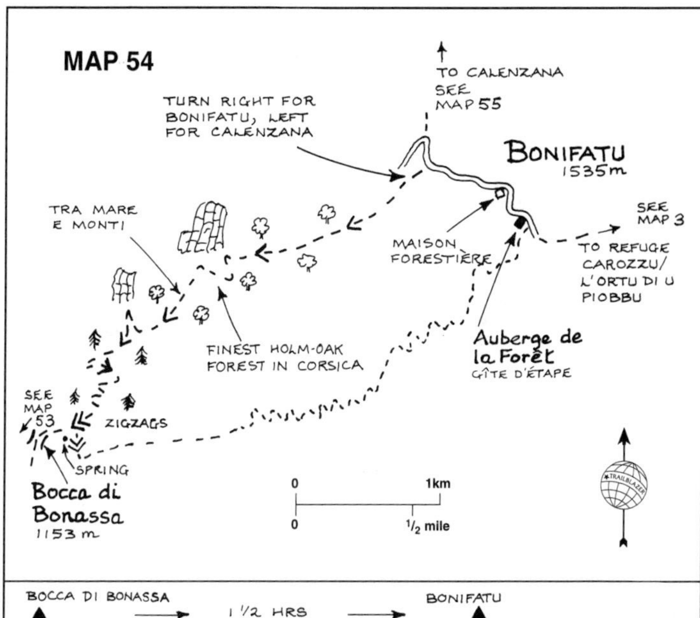

Rather than complete what is admittedly a dull final stage to Calenzana, many trekkers throw in the towel here and head back to Calvi by **taxi** (☎ 04 95.65.30.36). The trip costs 45–55€ depending on the time of day. Alternatively, you can hike to Calenzana via the more challenging route outlined in the box (see opposite) which will give you a taste of the GR20.

BONIFATU → CALENZANA [MAP 55, p270]

Crossing miles of fire-damaged hillside, with little shade or variety the final day of the Tra Mare e Monti is a bit of a march. In hot weather, it's nothing short of an ordeal; either get it behind you early in the day, or rest up at the auberge until temperatures fall in the evening.

The trailhead is one kilometre down the road from Bonifatu, at the bend just beyond where the descent from Bocca di Bonassa hits the tarmac. This first stretch, zigzaging down to the river through tall maquis and then following the left bank to a bridge beneath a weirdly-eroded crag, is actually quite fun. The plod begins at the forestry piste, which climbs gently above the Figarella River to cross what's left of the **Forêt de Sambucu**, devastated by fire a few years back and now entirely replanted.

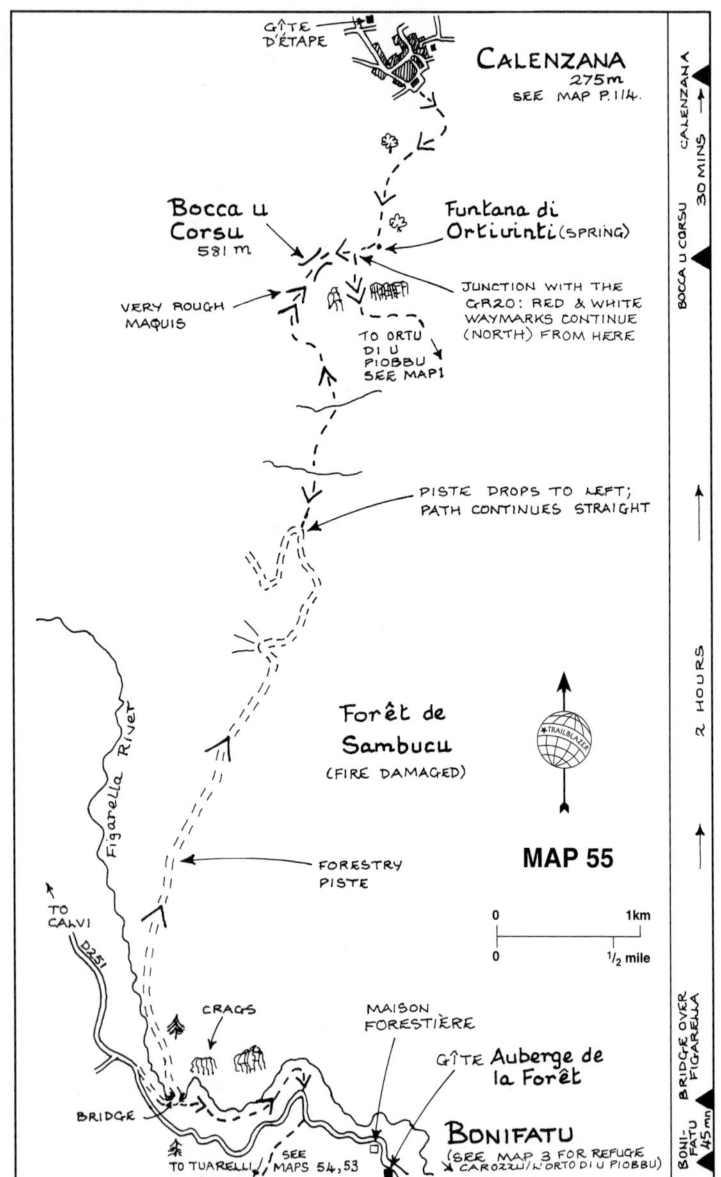
GÎTE D'ÉTAPE
CALENZANA
275m
SEE MAP P.114.
Bocca u Corsu
581 m
Funtana di Ortivinti (SPRING)
VERY ROUGH MAQUIS
JUNCTION WITH THE GR20: RED & WHITE WAYMARKS CONTINUE (NORTH) FROM HERE
TO ORTU DI U PIOBBU SEE MAP1
PISTE DROPS TO LEFT; PATH CONTINUES STRAIGHT
Figarella River
Forêt de Sambucu
(FIRE DAMAGED)
TRAILBLAZER
MAP 55
FORESTRY PISTE
TO CALVI
D251
0
1km
0
1/2 mile
CRAGS
MAISON FORESTIÈRE
GÎTE Auberge de la Forêt
BRIDGE
BONIFATU
(SEE MAP 3 FOR REFUGE CAROZZU/L'ORTO DI U PIOBBU)
TO TUARELLI
SEE MAPS 54, 53
BONI-FATU
45mn
BRIDGE OVER FIGARELLA
2 HOURS
BOCCA U CORSU
30 MINS
CALENZANA

The waymarks steer you the right way at a fork in the track, rounding a spur that overlooks the valley. One kilometre later you part company with the piste and return to the maquis, with the path fording two streams before it starts its climb up to **Bocca u Corsu** (599m), the final stretch of which is through horrendously spiny bushes.

Scratched to bits and footsore, you'll be mighty relieved to see Calenzana nestled at the bottom of the hill below you. The rest of the route, which a short way beyond the pass links up with the GR20 (from where red-and-white waymarks take over) is very easy going. Bivouackers with enough supplies should hunt out the **Funtana di Ortivinti** spring, to the right of the path shortly after the intersection of the two trails, around which are plenty of secluded spots to bed down under old chestnut trees.

A full account of Calenzana appears on pp113-15.

PART 7: MARE A MARE SUD

Overview

After the GR20, the Mare a Mare Sud is southern Corsica's most walked trail, a distinction it fully deserves. Winding from the Golfe de Valinco on the east coast to the Golfe de Porto Vecchio in the west, it takes in the cream of the region's varied landscapes, from the dense chestnut and oak woods of the Rizzanese Valley to the pastureland of the Coscione plateau and the famous pine forest of the Massif de l'Ospédale. Pristine rivers, Pisan chapels and prehistoric ruins punctuate a route that almost always keeps to ancient parish tracks, which makes this a particularly good walk for experiencing village life. Each stage ends at a well-sited *gîte d'étape* in some idyllic hill settlement, where you can breakfast on coffee and fresh croissants in a leafy square – a far cry indeed from the privations of the GR.

The one downside is that the relative accessibility of the village *gîtes* means that hostel beds can be hard to come by from early May until mid-September. Hotels and guesthouses offer an alternative in Aullène, Quenza and Levie, but without an advance reservation you could find yourself having to bivouac or camp illegally in the woods (for more advice on this see p78).

The following account describes the Mare a Mare Sud from west to east, beginning at Burgo, near Propriano, and ending at Porto-Vecchio. Count on five days from start to finish, or four if you hitch the last leg from Ospédale. There's precious little flat walking and quite a few longish climbs along the way, so keep your rucksack as light as possible.

The Mare a Mare Sud and its *variants* are indicated with **orange waymarks** and are very easy to follow throughout. IGN Maps 4254OT and 4254ET cover most of the path except the half-day stretch between Serra di Scapomena and Quenza, which is featured on 4253OT.

The route

PROPRIANO/PRUPRIÀ

Huddled at the end of the spectacular Golfe de Valinco, Propriano, in the south-west corner of the island, is a compact coastal resort, barely larger than some of the car ferries that dock here. For walkers its principal attraction is its proximity to the Mare a Mare Sud trailhead at Burgo, 7km east, as well as its shops, banks and regular bus connections. A couple of mediocre beaches lie beyond the yacht-filled marina and ferry port but, with the imposing backdrop of the Rizzanese Valley beckoning, you'll probably want to be on your way inland as soon as you've stocked up with food and cash.

Orientation and services

The focus of the town is its café-lined ave Napoléon, which runs along the seafront, quai St Érasme, to the recently built ferry port, arrival point for boats from the mainland.

Buses to and from Ajaccio and Porto-Vecchio stop opposite the church, on a hill immediately above the intersection where ave Napoléon meets Propriano's principal shopping street, rue du Général de Gaulle. The quickest route between the two is to follow the steps down from the bus stop.

Three companies run services to Propriano. Eurocorse Voyages (☎ 04 95.76.00.76; 1–4 daily, except Sun in winter) operates the busiest route, along the coast road between Ajaccio and Porto-Vecchio via Sartène, Roccapina and Bonifacio. You can also reach the capital with Balési Évasion (☎ 04.95.70.15.55; July and Aug Mon–Sat daily, or Sept–June Mon and Fri only), who run to and from Porto-Vecchio via a convoluted mountain route passing through Aullène, Quenza, Zonza and Bavella. Propriano is also a port of call for Autocars Ricci's Alta Rocca bus (☎ 04.95.76.25.59), which stops at Levie, Sainte-Lucie-de-Tallano and Sartène en route between the mountain village of Zonza and Ajaccio; they have one departure in each direction daily except Sunday throughout the year.

Timetables can be checked at the **tourist office** (☎ 04 95 76 01 49; July and Aug daily 8am–8pm, June and Sept Mon–Sat 9am–noon and 3–7pm, Oct–May Mon–Fri 9am–noon and 2–6pm), just off ave Napoléon, next to the marina and *capitainerie* (harbourmaster's office). In the same block (on the sea-facing side) are well-maintained public toilets and showers.

You can wash clothes at either of the self-service **launderettes** on the opposite (west) end of ave Napoléon, from where it's a short walk south to the **post office** (one of the region's most popular targets for separatist bombers) on route de Paratella.

Banks and ATMs stand on or around the junction of rue Général de Gaulle and ave Napoléon.

For supplies try the **covered market** next to the *mairie* (near the marina); the largest **supermarket** in town, Coccinelle, lies five minutes' walk up rue Général de Gaulle.

At the well-stocked **Maison de la Presse** near the corner of ave Napoléon and rue du Général de Gaulle you should be able to pick up the full range of IGN maps for the area, as well as FFRP Topoguides.

Where to stay

If you're heading off on the Mare a Mare Sud the two most conveniently situated campsites are ***Camping Tikiti*** (☎ 04 95.76.08.32), 1.5km east of town overlooking the Ajaccio road, and the more pleasant ***Camping Colomba*** (☎ 04.95.76.06.42), 3km down route Baracci beyond the riding centre. There's also a big gîte d'étape in the hamlet of Burgo, 7km east of Propriano at the trailhead (see p275).

Propriano has a huge number of tourist beds, although options at the budget end are very limited. In the town centre, the best deal is at the blue-and-pink two-star ***Hôtel Bellevue*** (☎ 04.95.76.01.86, 🖷 04.95 76.38.94; open year round), overlooking the marina on ave Napoléon; double rooms cost from 44€ to 76€ depending on the season. All have small en suite bathrooms but the front ones can be a little noisy. If it's full try the more modern ***Loft Hôtel*** (☎ 04 95.76.17.48, 🖷 04.95.76.22.04; open mid-April–Sept), 3 rue Capitaine Camille Piétri, where tariffs range from 42.60€ to 57.70€. Otherwise you've a choice between the clean, comfortable but charmless ***Hôtel Claridge*** (☎ 04.95.76.05.54, 🖷 04.95 76.27.77; open March–Oct), tucked away in the streets behind the seafront on rue Bonaparte, whose rates are 48.60–71.40€, and ***Beach Hôtel*** (☎ 04.95.76.17.74, 🖷 04 95.76.06.54; open May–Oct), a large block behind port de Commerce where rooms cost 67–94.40€.

In the three-star price bracket ***Hôtel Le Lido*** (☎ 04.95.76.06.37, 🖷 04.95.76.31.18), overlooking the town beach, west of the centre, is the most appealing choice, with well-shaded rooms opening onto a secluded courtyard. Tariffs for their least expensive

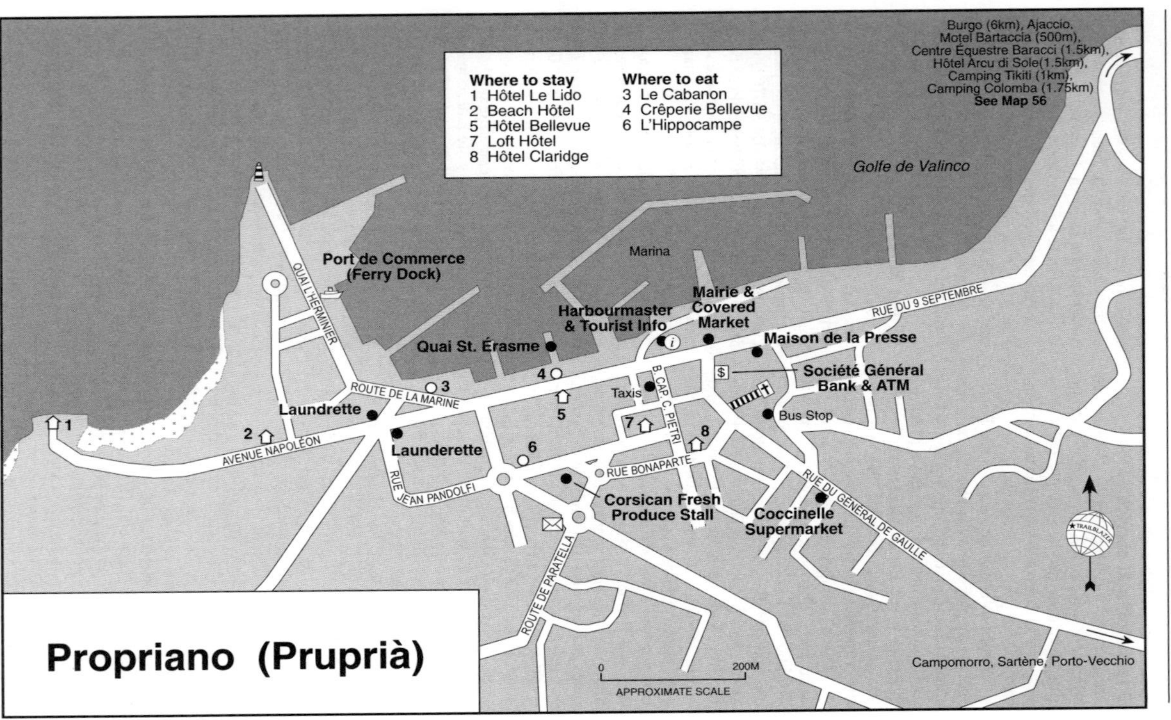
Where to stay
1 Hôtel Le Lido
2 Beach Hôtel
5 Hôtel Bellevue
7 Loft Hôtel
8 Hôtel Claridge
Where to eat
3 Le Cabanon
4 Crêperie Bellevue
6 L'Hippocampe
Burgo (6km), Ajaccio,
Motel Bartaccia (500m),
Centre Équestre Baracci (1.5km),
Hôtel Arcu di Sole(1.5km),
Camping Tikiti (1km),
Camping Colomba (1.75km)
See Map 56
Golfe de Valinco
Marina
Port de Commerce (Ferry Dock)
QUAI L'HERMINIER
Harbourmaster & Tourist Info
Mairie & Covered Market
RUE DU 9 SEPTEMBRE
Maison de la Presse
Quai St. Érasme
Société Général Bank & ATM
ROUTE DE LA MARINE
B. CAP. C. PIETRI
Taxis
Laundrette
Bus Stop
AVENUE NAPOLÉON
Launderette
RUE BONAPARTE
RUE JEAN PANDOLFI
Corsican Fresh Produce Stall
Coccinelle Supermarket
RUE DU GÉNÉRAL DE GAULLE
ROUTE DE PARATELLA
Propriano (Pruprià)
0
200M
APPROXIMATE SCALE
Campomorro, Sartène, Porto-Vecchio

double rooms start at 61€ low season, rising to 114€ in July and August. For the swishest rooms expect to pay between 83.60€ and 182.50€ depending on the time of year.

On the way out of town towards the trailhead at Burgo you pass a string of other hotels, the best value of which is ***Motel Bartaccia*** (☎ 04.95.76.01.50, 🖹 04.95 76.24.92, 🖳 bartaccia@wanadoo.fr; open Easter–mid-Oct), 1km east on the main Ajaccio road, which has fully-equipped self-catering chalets from 41/85.10€ low/high season. One kilometre further on, just beyond the turning for Burgo, the riding centre, ***Centre Équestre Baracci*** (☎ 04.95.76.18.48; open April–Sept), is a good budget choice, with recently refurbished double rooms at 38–47.10€ (includes breakfast). Nearby, the upmarket ***Hôtel Arcu di Sole*** (☎ 04.95.76.05.10, 🖹 04 95.76.13.36) boasts a good-sized pool, flowery garden and attractive rooms but top rates of 105–111€ (or 130–141€ for half-board, obligatory in July–August).

Where to eat Once you've done your shopping, there's precious little to do in Propriano other than pen a few postcards in a café or restaurant. You're spoilt for choice along quai St Érasme, where a long line of sunny terraces make the most of the views over the marina and gulf. While none offers outstanding value, the ***crêperie*** outside Hôtel Bellevue does a brisk trade in inexpensive crêpes and side salads. The pick of the pricier seafood restaurants along this strip is ***Le Cabanon***, just off ave Napoléon on route de la Marine, which does a quality three-course menu fixe (13.70€) that includes fresh fish from the gulf; more elaborate options, such as rays' wing in lemon sauce, feature on their lengthy à la carte selection. If you can live without the Valinco views head for ***L'Hippocampe***, on rue Jean Pandolfi near the post office, whose menus fixes (15.20€ and 30.50€) represent unbeatable value for seafood lovers. Ask for a table on the terrace at the back of the building.

To stock up on quality local produce for the walk ahead, try the stall in the square between L'Hippocampe and the post office which sells *charcuterie* such as wild boar paté, cheeses wine, olives and honey. Prices are on the high side but you get what you pay for.

Getting to the trailhead [Map 56, p277] Burgo, the official start of the Mare a Mare Sud, lies an inconvenient 7km plod east of Propriano. Winding up a broad-bottomed stream valley flanked by green fields, the (non-waymarked) route is not an altogether unpleasant one to walk – at least once you're off the main road. Nevertheless, most hikers try to save time by hitching from the Elf petrol station, 2km east of town on the N196 where the D257 turns inland. No buses run along this road, so you either have to walk all the way or arrange a taxi from Propriano; one can usually be found on rue Camille Pietri, around the corner from the pharmacy on ave Napoléon, or else phone ☎ 04.95.76.11.03. Depending on the time of day, fares range from 15€ to 20.30€.

BURGO → SAINTE-LUCIE-DE-TALLANO/SANTA LUCIA DI TALLA [MAP 57, p279]

The scattering of houses at Burgo (190m) on the western slope of the Fracintu Valley is dominated by the large gîte d'étape, ***U Fracintu*** (☎ 04.95.76.15.05, 🖹 04.95.76.14.31), which sits on a prime site overlooking the woods below and the gulf to the west. It has 60 beds, in two-, four- and six- bed dorms (10.70€ per person), along with a handful of double rooms (35€). Half-board costs 25.90€ if you're in a dorm, or 35€ for those in one of the doubles. All in all,

Mare a Mare Sud *Variant*: via Foce di Verju [see Map 57, p279]
A few metres beyond the point where the path first arrives at a surfaced road, at the hamlet of **Figaniella**, a waymarked *variant* of the Mare a Mare Sud turns left, heading steeply uphill to the hamlet of **Santa Maria**. From there it scales the **Foce di Verju** pass (703m) and drops down the other side in a north-easterly direction to the village of **Loreto-di- Tallano**, where it bends south to rejoin the main route at **Erbajolu**. Although it's well enough waymarked and shaves a good hour off the conventional route, this *variant* bypasses Fozzano and misses one of the highlights of the Mare a Mare Sud, the pass above Altanaria (see below), for which reasons we recommend you ignore it.

this is a better-value option than a hotel room in Propriano, although few hikers setting out on the Mare a Mare stay here.

The trail begins five minutes' walk up the D557 at a hamlet called **San Quircu**: from the gîte you turn left and shortly after pass a ruined house on your right; look for the signpost indicating the start of the path, which drops sharply down the valley side through old *maquis* to cross the Baracci River. Following a short climb up the far bank, the path meets a second river, the Capannajola, which it fords soon after. From here you've a fairly stiff, 45-minute zigzagging ascent through oak forest before the route levels off, emerging at a patch of open maquis; the path then follows the contours of the hillside around to the bottom fringe of Fozzano. The last stretch up to Fozzano from Figaniella follows the road; as you approach the centre, look on the right side for a **spring**, housed in a rather grand arcaded shelter.

Renowned as the setting for *Colomba*, the famous nineteenth-century vendetta novel by Prosper Merimée, **Fozzano** (400m), with its austere buttressed houses clustered together on a granite spur jutting over the valley, epitomizes a region that has always had a reputation for wildness. These days, however, life here is decidedly sedate, revolving around the village shop, the Libre Service Martinetti.

From the village centre orange waymarks thread a route uphill through the old granite houses of the topmost hamlet, where the path heads south from the roadside into the maquis. Climbing steadily across land that has been intensively grazed (and bulldozed in places to create jeep tracks), it rounds the hillside below a craggy hill called Punta di Zibo (951m) and then swings north-east to begin a long, gentle climb to a 700m pass.

This ridge, one of the most memorable viewpoints on the walk, forms the dividing line between the regions of Rizzanese and Alta Rocca. The villages of the latter are scattered across an enormous wooded basin to the north, hemmed in by the granite needles of Bavella and Monte Alcudina. Just below the ridge, a ruined *bergerie* known as **Altanaria** (580m) marks the start of a sharp descent to river level. The path, dropping through dense maquis, is poorly waymarked and occasionally gets confused with secondary goat tracks but if you keep fairly close to the stream and bear right at the fork roughly halfway down, you

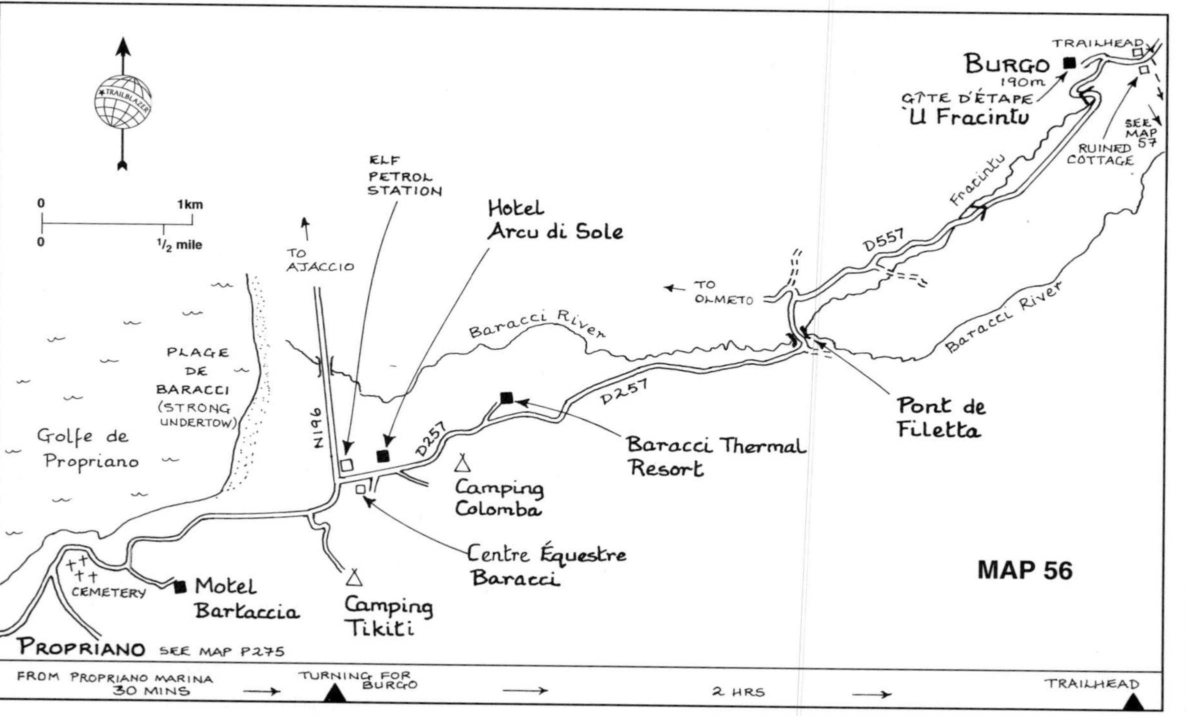

MAP 56
TRAILBLAZER
0
1km
0
1/2 mile
BURGO
190m
GÎTE D'ÉTAPE
'U Fracintu
TRAILHEAD
RUINED COTTAGE
SEE MAP 57
Fracintu
D557
TO OLMETO
Baracci River
Baracci River
Pont de Filetta
D257
D257
Baracci Thermal Resort
ELF PETROL STATION
Hotel Arcu di Sole
TO AJACCIO
N196
PLAGE DE BARACCI (STRONG UNDERTOW)
Golfe de Propriano
Camping Colomba
Centre Équestre Baracci
Camping Tikiti
Motel Bartaccia
CEMETERY
PROPRIANO SEE MAP P275
FROM PROPRIANO MARINA 30 MINS
TURNING FOR BURGO
2 HRS
TRAILHEAD

Vendetta and banditry in Corsica

Vendettas (blood feuds) are common to many traditional Mediterranean societies but in few regions of the world has eye-for-an-eye violence become as pervasive as in Corsica, where jealousy and mutual suspicion have always been defining traits of the island psyche.

References to *la vinditta* date back to the Roman era, but it was during the period of Genoese rule that internecine killing spiralled out of control. At one time in the sixteenth century the murder rate ran at around 900, for a population of only 12,000. Whole villages became locked in states of siege, their windows barricaded, with generations of families incarcerated under threat of death.

All manner of intended or perceived insults could ignite a blood feud: infringement of property rights was a common cause, as was petty theft. In a village in northern Corsica, for example, 36 people died in a dispute over ownership of a chestnut tree, while one of the longest-standing feuds in the south erupted after a donkey wandered into the wrong field.

Once a *vinditta* had kicked off it could take generations to run its course, drawing in ever greater numbers of protagonists. Traditional codes of honour required that blood be avenged with blood, and shame awaited any man and his family who failed to exact retribution. In this way, formerly peaceful, law-abiding individuals were forced to take up arms to uphold clan honour, giving rise to a particularly Corsican kind of hero, the *bandit d'honneur*. To avoid capture by the authorities or reprisal assassination, many men fled to the maquis after committing a vendetta murder, where they hid in remote caves.

Nineteenth-century France saw an extraordinary upsurge in public interest in bandits d'honneur, fuelled by a series of articles on the subject by journalists and wealthy adventurers. Some bandits even became national celebrities, posing for postcards and press calls with their flintlocks and characteristic broad-brimmed felt fedoras.

A spate of best-selling novels followed, the most famous of them Prosper Mérimée's *Colomba*, based on a real-life vendetta that had taken place in the village of Fozzano in the early nineteenth century. Its heroine, a raven-haired, passionate beauty drawn into a vendetta after losing a son in an ambush, was a far cry from the vicious, remorseless gang leader whom the author met in her old age, by which time the brutal reality of Fozzano's feud had been well and truly romanticized.

The last fully-fledged Corsican vendetta officially ended in the 1950s, but the expression *reglements de compte* (literally 'settling of scores') is still frequently used to account for violence on the island. Many commentators regard the protracted bloodshed of the past two decades, in which dozens of murders were perpetrated by opposing factions of armed nationalists and Mafia clans, as essentially a modern manifestation of Corsica's most ingrained problem.

should arrive at a stand of three magnificent old oaks. To avoid the unsightly quarry which the path used to fringe, a new link section leads from here through dense chestnut forest and past a farmhouse to a level track that eventually emerges on the D69, just beyond the hamlet of **Erbajolu**. If, by this stage, you're out of water, turn right here back towards the houses, where you'll find a **spring** on the right (east) side of the road.

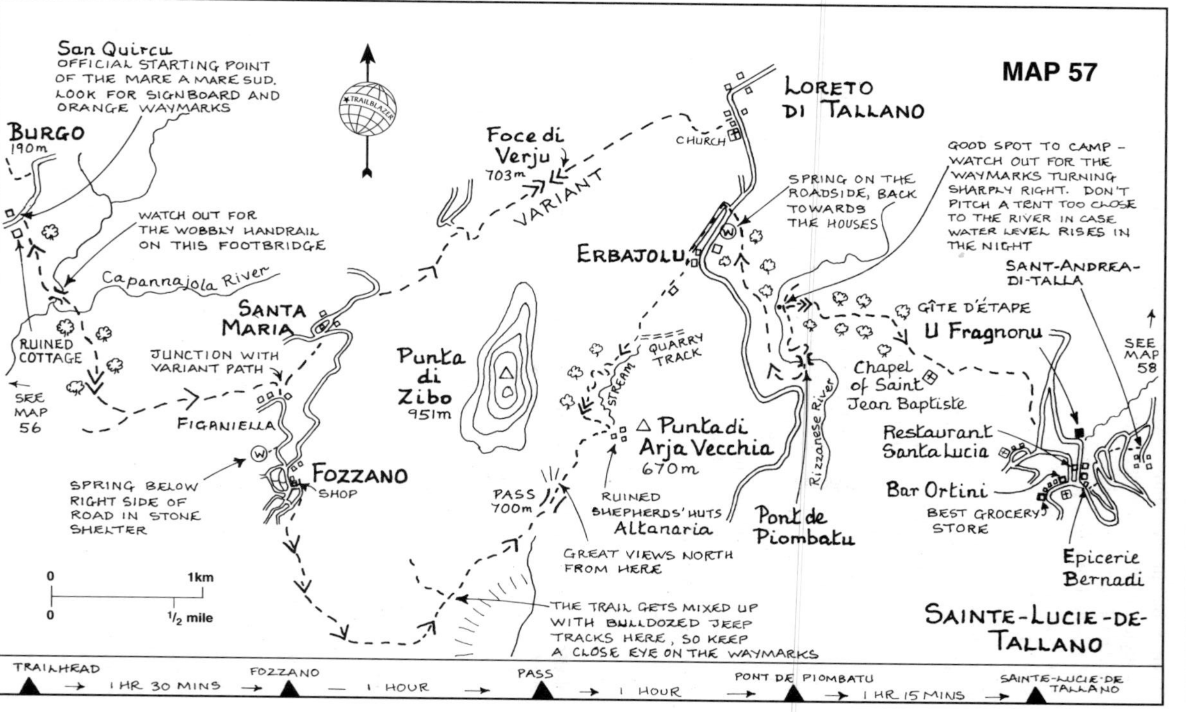
MAP 57
San Quircu
OFFICIAL STARTING POINT OF THE MARE A MARE SUD. LOOK FOR SIGNBOARD AND ORANGE WAYMARKS
TRAILBLAZER
BURGO 190m
WATCH OUT FOR THE WOBBLY HANDRAIL ON THIS FOOTBRIDGE
Capannajola River
RUINED COTTAGE
SEE MAP 56
SANTA MARIA
JUNCTION WITH VARIANT PATH
FIGANIELLA
SPRING BELOW RIGHT SIDE OF ROAD IN STONE SHELTER
FOZZANO
SHOP
Foce di Verju 703m
VARIANT
Punta di Zibo 951m
LORETO DI TALLANO
CHURCH
SPRING ON THE ROADSIDE, BACK TOWARDS THE HOUSES
ERBAJOLU
QUARRY TRACK
STREAM
Punta di Arja Vecchia 670m
RUINED SHEPHERDS' HUTS
Altanaria
PASS 700m
GREAT VIEWS NORTH FROM HERE
THE TRAIL GETS MIXED UP WITH BULLDOZED JEEP TRACKS HERE, SO KEEP A CLOSE EYE ON THE WAYMARKS
Rizzanese River
Pont de Piombatu
GOOD SPOT TO CAMP – WATCH OUT FOR THE WAYMARKS TURNING SHARPLY RIGHT. DON'T PITCH A TENT TOO CLOSE TO THE RIVER IN CASE WATER LEVEL RISES IN THE NIGHT
SANT-ANDREA-DI-TALLA
GÎTE D'ÉTAPE
U Fragnonu
SEE MAP 58
Chapel of Saint Jean Baptiste
Restaurant Santa Lucia
Bar Ortini
BEST GROCERY STORE
Epicerie Bernadi
SAINTE-LUCIE-DE-TALLANO
0 1km
0 1/2 mile
TRAILHEAD → 1 HR 30 MINS → FOZZANO — 1 HOUR → PASS → 1 HOUR → PONT DE PIOMBATU → 1 HR 15 MINS → SAINTE-LUCIE-DE TALLANO

From Erbajolu the Mare a Mare follows an old pathway gently downhill through a mixture of pasture and deciduous woodland to meet the Rizzanese, the Alta Rocca's principal river, which it crosses via a wonderful old stone bridge, the **Pont de Piombatu**. Secluded deep in the forest, this atmospheric spot is not a good one for a swim (the unpredictable currents and white water swirling between the boulders make for dangerous bathing, as signs indicate) but for late starters from Burgo it is the obvious place to camp for the night. Steer clear, however, of the small beach just downstream from the bridge, which can be rapidly submerged in flash floods. A safer spot lies 400m further on: after scaling a bluff the path drops slightly, levels and hugs the river bank until it reaches a spacious, well-sheltered clearing edged by a small beach from which you can bathe safely.

Keep a close eye on the orange waymarks at this point, as the Mare a Mare Sud veers suddenly and without warning to the right (while a well-defined but red-herring route continues upriver). From the Rizzanese, the correct path climbs steeply at first through old oak forest, levelling off after around half an hour, when it meets and then winds in tandem with a forestry *piste*.

After around an hour from the river you arrive at the medieval **Chapel of Saint Jean Baptiste**, one of many small churches erected by the Pisans in the early twelfth century. Only used for around two hundred years, it now stands somewhat forlorn, serving as a cattle shed. The entrance is on the opposite side of the building from the trail.

SAINTE-LUCIE-DE-TALLANO/SANTA LUCIA DI TALLA

Another half an hour along a well-worn mule path brings you to one of the most picturesque and populous villages on the Mare a Mare Sud, Sainte-Lucie-de-Tallano. Ranged around the plane-shaded square, the main attractions for walkers are the two relaxing cafés from whose terraces you can watch the *pétanque* matches and other comings and goings around the *fontaine* and war memorial.

There's no bakery but both of the village shops sell fresh bread, along with samples of the excellent local Fiumicciolli wine, from the vineyards spread across the Rizzanese Valley below. Sainte Lucie's other claim to fame is an extremely rare mineral known as diorite obiculaire ('corsite'), polished fragments of which are proudly displayed in Bar Ortini at the bottom of the square.

Practical information

The village's gîte d'étape, ***U Fragnonu*** (☎ 04.95.78.82.56 or 04.95.82.67; open April–Oct) occupies an immaculately restored old house at the north end of the village, reached via the lane running off the square (look for the signpost for Zoza). Half-board (28.10€ per head) is obligatory but the food – mostly island dishes such as boar stew and chestnut-flour *polenda* – is consistently excellent. The only other place to eat is ***Restaurant Santa Lucia***, at the top of the square, where you can order the usual range of pizzas or choose between two set menus (15€ and 23€). The latter is much the best option, offering Corsican speciality dishes such as local pork in honey, or rabbit in myrtle.

Sainte-Lucie features on Autocars Ricci's **bus** service (☎ 04.95.76.25.59; daily except Sun year round) between Zonza and Ajaccio, via Levie and Sartène.

SAINTE-LUCIE-DE-TALLANO → SERRA DI SCAPOMENA
[MAP 57, p279; MAP 58, p282]

Day two of the Mare a Mare Sud takes you north through the unspoilt deciduous forest of the Rizzanese Valley to the Alta Rocca's most dramatically situated village, Serra di Scapomena. Most of the work on this stage comes towards the end with a long descent to river level from the Col de Tavara, followed by an even longer climb up to the village itself. Although this is in essence a woodland trek, the growing profile of the watershed peaks to the north and dramatic views of shadowy ridges rolling away to the east give a strong sense of the island's topography, particularly towards the end as you ascend to 850m. The stage also features a superb bathing spot.

The trail leaves Sainte-Lucie from the top corner of the square, passing the green-painted **Épicerie Bernadi** on your left. Follow the concrete lane directly in front of you (ie, don't continue along the main road out of the village, the D268). The lane zigzags steeply up to an old stepped mule footpath that picks its way through the topmost cluster of houses in the village (known as **Sant' Andrea di Talla**). The mule path then crosses the road several times before finally swinging north to the hamlet of **Altagène**. On reaching tarmac again, turn right and follow it for around 50m until you see the motorable piste heading straight on towards a bridge (just before a bend in the road).

After gaining ground gently to reach a 1930s stone house, the track narrows to become a proper footpath. The next three-quarters of an hour or so is level, easy walking through exceptionally beautiful oak forest, dotted in spring time with clumps of cyclamen. To your left the valley side sheers steeply down to the Rizzanese and the village of Zoza, visible far below through gaps in the trees.

The short ascent up to the **Col de Tavara** (720m), via a succession of sharp switch backs, begins shortly after two stream crossing and lasts around 20 minutes. The pass, thick with asphodels, is a grassy saddle in a ridge bending south to the peak of Punta di Serradu (1033m). Beyond it the route drops steeply at first through open maquis before heading once again into a lush deciduous forest of oak, *arbutus* (strawberry trees) and, towards the valley floor, old chestnut.

The path rejoins the Rizzanese at a magical river bend where you can sunbathe and swim in deep pools from a small granite-sand beach. An impressive aluminium **footbridge** leads you into a dense birch forest dividing the Rizzanese from one of its tributaries, which you cross via a second, smaller bridge just below the hamlet of **Campu** (400m). Having negotiated a short climb, the path emerges onto the D20.

Turn right here, and follow the road for around 500m until you reach a PNRC signboard pointing left along the waymarked route of a dry-stone wall. This marks the start of the day's longest climb, which ascends through more magnificent beech, oak and chestnut forest via an ancient mule track. Note that 15 minutes up it, the path divides. The right (east) branch keeps to contour level and progresses due east, while the Mare a Mare Sud continues to rise steeply in

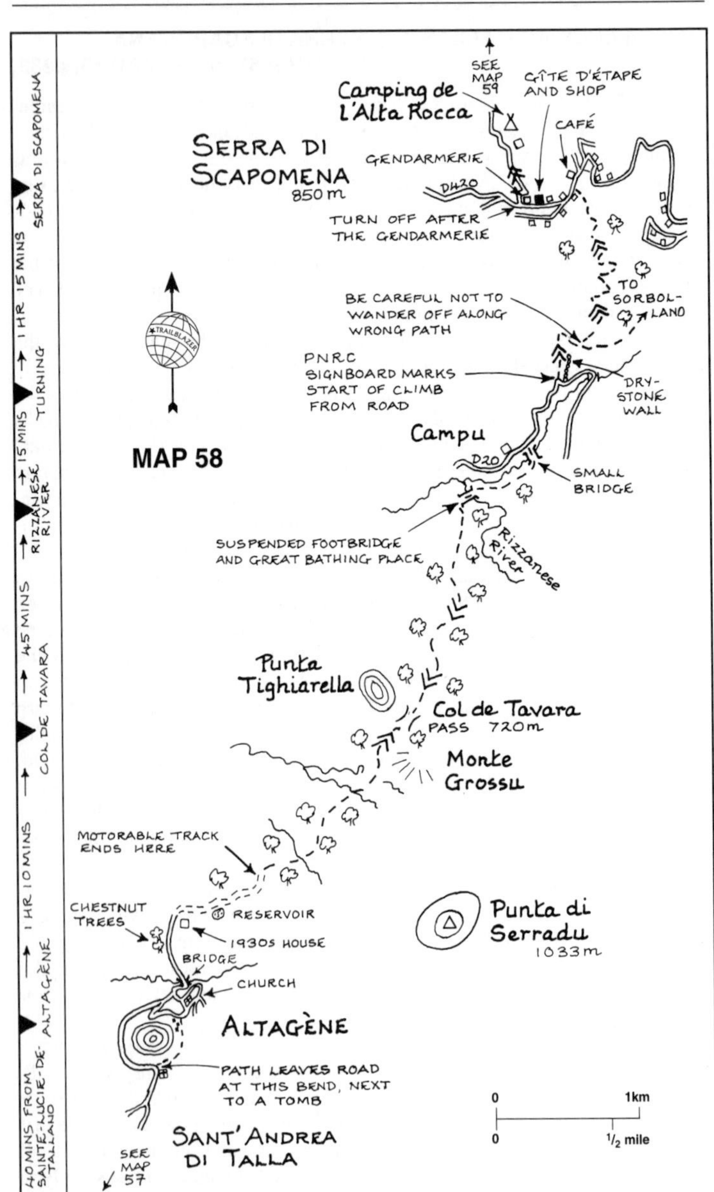

SEE MAP 59
Camping de L'Alta Rocca
GÎTE D'ÉTAPE AND SHOP
CAFÉ
SERRA DI SCAPOMENA
850m
GENDARMERIE
D420
TURN OFF AFTER THE GENDARMERIE
TO SORBOL-LANO
BE CAREFUL NOT TO WANDER OFF ALONG WRONG PATH
PNRC SIGNBOARD MARKS START OF CLIMB FROM ROAD
DRY-STONE WALL
TRAILBLAZER
Campu
MAP 58
D20
SMALL BRIDGE
SUSPENDED FOOTBRIDGE AND GREAT BATHING PLACE
Rizzanese River
Punta Tighiarella
Col de Tavara
PASS 720m
Monte Grossu
MOTORABLE TRACK ENDS HERE
CHESTNUT TREES
RESERVOIR
1930S HOUSE
Punta di Serradu
1033m
BRIDGE
CHURCH
ALTAGÈNE
PATH LEAVES ROAD AT THIS BEND, NEXT TO A TOMB
0
1km
0
1/2 mile
SANT'ANDREA DI TALLA
SEE MAP 57
40MINS FROM SAINTE-LUCIE-DE-TALLANO
ALTAGÈNE → 1HR 10MINS → COL DE TAVARA → 45MINS → RIZZANESE RIVER → 15MINS → TURNING → 1HR 15MINS → SERRA DI SCAPOMENA

a north-easterly direction. If you lose the waymarks at any stage, backtrack to find the correct route or you could end up making an unwelcome diversion to the village of Sorbollano.

SERRA DI SCAPOMENA

Serra di Scapomena appears after what can seem like an endless haul up the crumbling mule track from the river. Perched on a wide ledge high above the Rizzanese valley, its scattering of red-tiled granite houses stare east across a vast sweep of receding ridges. To the north the needles of Bavella dominate the landscape, as they will for most of the remaining route, while the dark wall of the Ospédale massif forms the eastern horizon.

Practical information

One of the best places from which to admire Serra di Scapomena's mesmerizing view is the excellent little ***gîte d'étape*** (☎ 04.95.78.72.43; open April–Oct) on the western edge of the village. To reach it, turn left where the path joins the D420 and follow the road for 500m; the gîte is on the right, above the village **shop**. It's a congenial, well-run little place, with four-bed dorms and a superb balcony that makes the most of the panorama. Unfortunately for hikers on tight budgets, half-board (25.10€) is obligatory, but the Corsican cuisine is copious, fresh and of restaurant standard, which is just as well as there is nowhere else to eat.

Apart from the gîte, the only other accommodation in this area is the excellent ***Hôtel de la Poste*** in the neighbouring village of Aullène, reached via a *variant* route of the Mare a Mare Sud (see the box on p284).

Campers have another steep pull to reach the municipal campsite, ***Camping de l'Alta Rocca*** (☎ 04.95.78.62.01; open mid-June–mid-Sept), on the hillside above the village. To find it, follow the Mare a Mare Sud waymarks past the gîte, turn right after the *gendarmerie*. In early spring or late autumn when it's closed, jump the fence and set up anyway; the spring in the middle of the clearing is always running, although the toilet blocks are locked out of season.

SERRA DI SCAPOMENA → QUENZA [MAP 59, p285]

Day three of the Mare a Mare Sud takes you to the highest point on the route as it skirts the edge of the Coscione plateau and then winds south into the wooded heart of the Alta Rocca. Carpeted in dense forest, the undulating uplands and stream valleys of this depopulated region were once the epicentre of Neolithic Corsica. One of the highlights of the day, if not the entire walk, is the extraordinary prehistoric remains of the Pianu de Levie (see the box on p288), where weirdly-eroded granite outcrops which formerly served as rock shelters and Neolithic fortifications protrude above the tree cover. The hill village of Quenza, with its cafés and picturesque church square, makes an ideal place to pause for lunch.

Leave Serra di Scapomena by the road running north off the D420, a short way beyond the gendarmerie. Fifteen minutes up the lane, after passing the campsite, you reach a fork at a low pass called **Bocca di Paradisu** (969m), where a variant of the Mare a Mare Sud peels left (north-west) towards the village of Aullène.

Once over a dirt piste, the main route more or less follows the contours of the hillside, bending north to approach the **Arja la Foce** pass (1040m), from where you get fine views over the southern slopes of the Coscione

Variant Route: Serra di Scapomena → Aullène → Bocca d'Arja Petrosa

[Map 59, p285]

The reason you might want to follow this variant is to stay at the only hotel in the area, in Aullène, 75 minutes' walk north-west of Serra di Scapomena.

Waymarked in orange like the main route, it starts at the **Bocca di Paradisu** pass, dropping gently via a motorable track along the north-west flank of the **Pianu Sottanu** plateau to cross two streams. After the second, the path makes a short ascent through a wood of old chestnut trees to rejoin the road, 10 minutes' or so from the village centre.

Hôtel de la Poste (☎/📠 04.95.78.61.21; open May–Oct), in an old granite building shaded by a row of lime trees, stands just off the crossroads in the middle of Aullène. It's a well-run, good-value little place that's popular with walkers, so phone ahead to check they've got vacancies before you opt for the variant, or better still book well in advance. The rooms are simple but clean, costing 35€ year-round. Half-board, served in the charming restaurant or roadside terrace on the ground floor, is 31€ per head (and obligatory in August). Wild boar stews are the house speciality, and they also offer wonderful local *charcuterie*. Set menus range from 15.20€ to 21.30€.

The onward path leads off a lane leading north-east from the centre of the village, close to the hotel. Keeping to a level gradient, it winds north-west through dry maquis to rejoin the main route at the Bocca d'Arja Petrosa.

plateau. A gentle descent brings you back to the piste, which the path follows for 200m before branching off to the right (east) at another pass, the **Bocca d'Arja Petrosa** (1014m).

About 15 minutes later you arrive at a renovated bergerie called **Lavu Donacu** (978m), where the route dips to cross a stream. Rising to meet the surfaced road, it then levels off as it approaches the hamlet of **Jallicu**, little more than a riding stables and cluster of bergerie buildings converted into summer accommodation for inhabitants of Quenza.

At 1185m, Jallicu is the highest point on the Mare a Mare Sud. You can stay here at a remote gîte, ***Chez Pierrot*** (☎ 04.95.78.63.21 or 04.95.78.61.09; open year round) which offers dormitory accommodation and definitive Corsican mountain cooking, served in the confines of a traditional stone shepherds' house. In principal, half-board (29.60€) is obligatory but when demand is slack you shouldn't have too much trouble talking Pierrot into offering you a bed-only price. The dorms, which sleep four to eight persons each, are intended primarily for horse trekkers who use the centre as a base for trips onto the Coscione plateau.

From Jallicu it's pretty much downhill all the way to Quenza, via a rocky path that cuts across the wooded slope above the Codi stream. After a 100m stretch on the road you drop more steeply towards the floor of the valley, with the sound of waterfalls crashing below. The Mare a Mare Sud then crosses a tributary of the Codi and follows a lane over a low rise to the edge of the village.

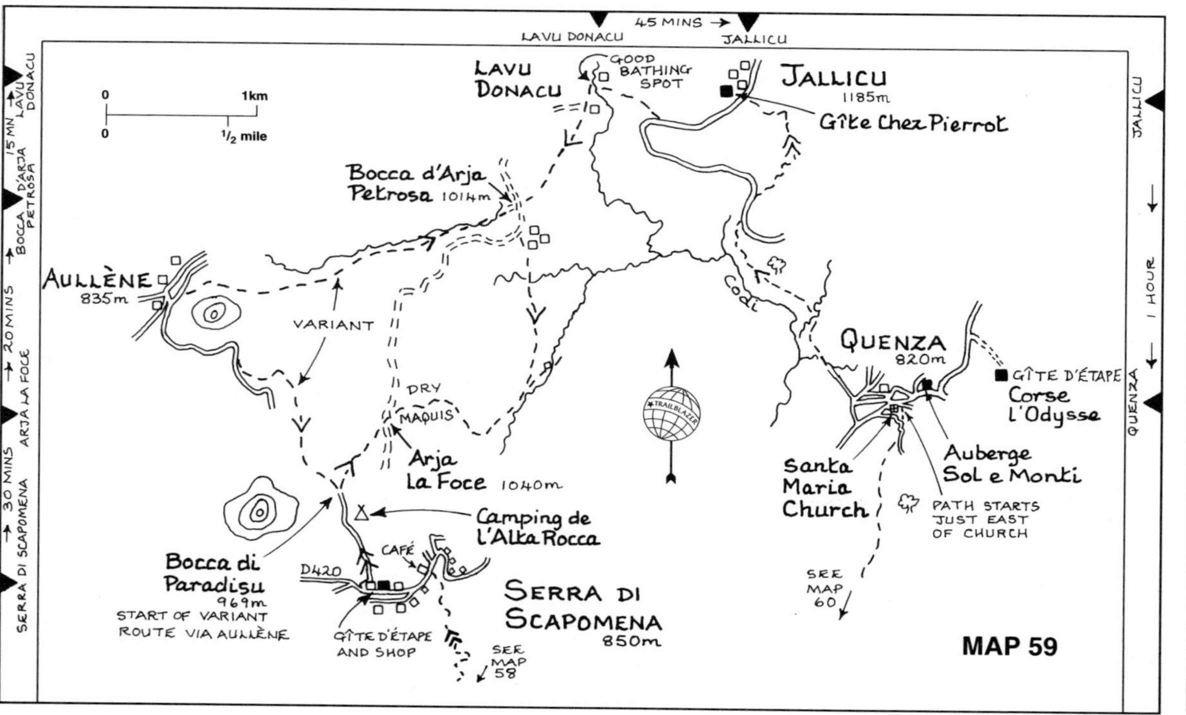
LAVU DONACU
45 MINS →
JALLICU
LAVU
DONACU
GOOD
BATHING
SPOT
JALLICU
1185m
Gîte Chez Pierrot
0
1km
0
1/2 mile
Bocca d'Arja
Petrosa 1014m
AULLÈNE
835m
VARIANT
Codi
QUENZA
820m
GÎTE D'ÉTAPE
Corse
L'Odysse
DRY
MAQUIS
Arja
La Foce 1040m
Santa
Maria
Church
Auberge
Sol e Monti
PATH STARTS
JUST EAST
OF CHURCH
Camping de
L'Alta Rocca
CAFÉ
D420
Bocca di
Paradisu
969m
START OF VARIANT
ROUTE VIA AULLÈNE
GÎTE D'ÉTAPE
AND SHOP
SERRA DI
SCAPOMENA
850m
SEE
MAP
58
SEE
MAP
60
MAP 59
SERRA DI SCAPOMENA
→ 30 MINS
ARJA LA FOCE
→ 20 MINS
BOCCA D'ARJA PETROSA
→ 15 MN
LAVU DONACU
JALLICU
← 1 HOUR ←
QUENZA
TRAILBLAZER

QUENZA

Presiding over the northern edge of the Alta Rocca, Quenza has always earned its living off the barren plateau of Coscione to its north and the vast oak forest that spreads across the deep stream valleys to the south. The village's isolated position, well off the tour-bus trail, mean that it has largely retained its traditional feel. Most visitors are walkers, supplemented by a trickle of tourists in hire cars.

Quenza's pride and joy is its splendid Romanesque church, **Santa Maria**, whose carved granite belfry dominates the square. Erected by the Pisans in the eleventh century, it is among the oldest churches on the island.

Practical information

For accommodation, the cheapest option is the local gîte d'étape, ***Corse l'Odysse*** (☎ 04.95.78.64.05, 🖷 04.95.23.61.91; open April–Oct), where half-board (28.90€ per head) is obligatory. Non-residents may eat in the gîte's restaurant for around 16€. It's 1km north-east of the village; head east from the square and take the first turning left. The piste to the gîte is signposted from the roadside.

The only other place to stay is the pricey and rather formal ***Auberge Sol e Monti*** (☎ 04.95.78.62.53, 🖷 04.95.78.63.88; open mid-May–mid-Oct) on the eastern edge of the village. Once again, half-board (68.40/76€ low/high season) is obligatory, although non-residents are welcome to eat in their gourmet restaurant, which offers set menus of mostly local specialities from 30€ to 42€.

QUENZA → LEVIE [MAP 60, OPPOSITE]

To pick up the trail south to Levie, follow the road running alongside the church and turn immediately right down a path. This comes out shortly afterwards at a lane, which you keep to for around 100m before turning right again down a narrow walled pathway. For the next hour the going is mostly level and easy as the route meanders through fields and pine forest, with occasional views of the Bavella needles rising dramatically over the treetops to the north.

Tall fences lining the piste around the now deserted hamlet of **Campu di Bertu** form the limits of a project to reintroduce a rare species of Mediterranean **deer** to the island. Formerly indigenous, *Cervus elaphus corsicanusi* disappeared from the island in the early 1970s. Around 40 animals now live on the 20-hectare site, run by the park, which aims to produce enough animals to repopulate the forest of the Alta Rocca.

At the southern end of the deer sanctuary, roughly 45 minutes from Quenza, you reach a prominent fork in the trail, where a variant path veers north-west to Sorbollano. A left turn, followed by a short, sharp descent brings you to one of the outstanding beauty spots on the Mare a Mare Sud, where it crosses the Rizzanese river for the third and final time. On the far side of the new footbridge, turn right and cross a small side stream to begin a 20-minute ascent through oak forest. The path flattens out after the junction with another orange-marked variant path from Zonza.

The next stretch, passing through gnarled oak woods and eerie outcrops of granite, leads through the heart of an area which, from the fourth millennium BC until the twelfth century AD, formed one of the island's major population centres. The first tangible evidence of human occupation you come to is the tiny

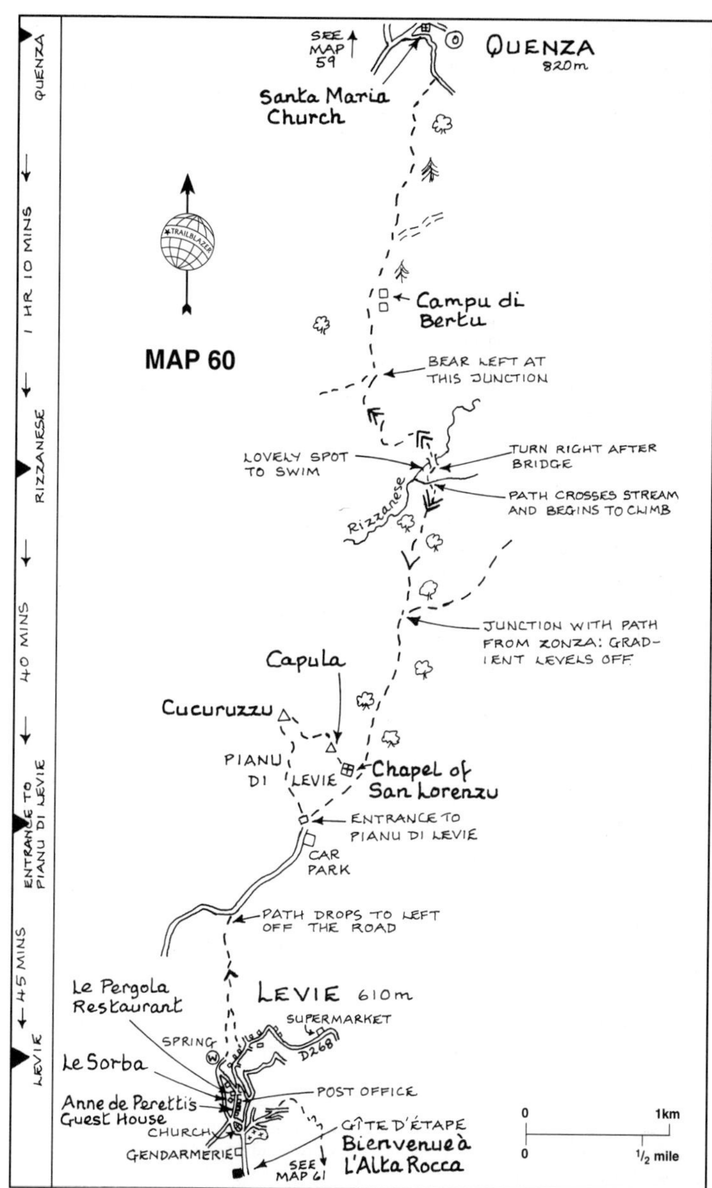
QUENZA
1 HR 10 MINS
RIZZANESE
40 MINS
ENTRANCE TO PIANU DI LEVIE
45 MINS
LEVIE
SEE MAP 59
QUENZA
820m
Santa Maria Church
TRAILBLAZER
MAP 60
Campu di Bertu
BEAR LEFT AT THIS JUNCTION
LOVELY SPOT TO SWIM
TURN RIGHT AFTER BRIDGE
PATH CROSSES STREAM AND BEGINS TO CLIMB
Rizzanese
JUNCTION WITH PATH FROM ZONZA: GRADIENT LEVELS OFF
Capula
Cucuruzzu
PIANU DI LEVIE
Chapel of San Lorenzu
ENTRANCE TO PIANU DI LEVIE
CAR PARK
PATH DROPS TO LEFT OFF THE ROAD
LEVIE 610m
Le Pergola Restaurant
SUPERMARKET
SPRING
D268
Le Sorba
POST OFFICE
Anne de Peretti's Guest House
CHURCH
GENDARMERIE
GÎTE D'ÉTAPE Bienvenue à L'Alta Rocca
SEE MAP 61
0
1km
0
1/2 mile

The Pianu di Levie

The remnants of an ancient settlement scattered over the wooded plateau above Levie – known as the Pianu di Levie – collectively comprise one of the richest prehistoric sites in Mediterranean Europe. Its original inhabitants were cave and rock-shelter-dwelling hunter-gatherers who migrated from northern Italy sometime in the seventh millennium BC. They are believed to have been displaced three thousand years later by Megalithic peoples from Asia Minor, who in turn gave way to a Bronze Age society known as the Torréeans around 1400BC (see p45).

It was the Torréeans who first piled rocks around the tops of granite outcrops across the island to form the circular fortified towers dubbed by archeologists as *casteddu*. The one here at the Pianu di Levie, **Casteddu di Cucuruzzu**, is the most impressive example of its kind left standing. Encircling the top of a chaos of granite boulders, its walls enclose a remarkable complex of chambers and dry-stone shelters thought to have been occupied by artisans and farmers. Tools, weapons and utensils unearthed around the tower (some of which are now displayed in the museum at nearby Levie; see opposite) suggest the structure was of more functional than religious importance, but the site still exudes a decidedly mysterious feel, especially at sunset.

Visits to the Pianu di Levie (April–Oct daily 9am–6pm, or 9am–8pm in July and August) cost 4.30€, which includes a forgettable Walkman tour (in French) and a map. You pay at the entrance hut on the south side of the site and, using the map and numbered waymarkers, walk north from there through atmospheric oak forest to the Casteddu di Cucuruzzu, passing various rock shelters en route. The other main group of monuments at **Capula**, adjacent to the Mare a Mare Sud route, lie another 10- to 15-minutes' walk north-east.

Romanesque **Chapel of San Lorenzu**, which stands just to the right of the path at the top of a glade of asphodels. Built in the thirteenth century, it was the medieval successor to an older Roman church, whose apsidal foundations are still visible nearby. These monuments are relatively modern compared with the prehistoric ruins of **Capula**, centred on the rock outcrop directly opposite the chapel. Officially, these form part of the archaeological site of Pianu di Levie (see the box above), which you have to pay to see at an entrance gate another 10 minutes down the trail. However, no-one is likely to stop you entering the complex here at Capula and working your way around to the more impressive remains of the Casteddu di Cucuruzzu, 15 minutes down a marked path, from where you can leave the site (and pay) at the entrance hut.

If you're bivouacking, note that the clearing beside the Chapel of San Lorenzu is the most convenient place to hole up for the night before Levie, although you'll need enough water to see you through as there is no spring nearby.

Opposite Top: One of the many tempting bays along the Littoral Sartènais route (see pp300-10). **Bottom:** Sorbollano from just outside Serra di Scapomena (see p283). (Photos © David Abram).

The entrance to the archeological site marks the start of a surfaced road which you follow for half a kilometre until the Mare a Mare Sud peels left to begin its descent to Levie, whose fringes you reach 20 minutes later. At a prominent fork in the path, where the old mule track you've been following continues straight downhill, bear right and follow a narrower footpath for 100m; this then dips sharply to join a surfaced road at a spring, just above the main road through the village.

LEVIE/LIVIA

Levie is the largest village in the Alta Rocca and the last dependable source of groceries before Porto-Vecchio, two days' walk to the east. Enclosed by tall granite houses dating from a more populous era, its main thoroughfare, however, is not somewhere you're likely to want to spend much time. Nor is the gîte, on the south edge of the village, particularly congenial. On the plus side, Levie does boast a fair selection of livelier-than-average cafés and a good restaurant.

It also has a well-respected little museum, the **Musée Départemental** (July–Sept daily 10am–6pm, Oct–June Tues–Sat 10am–noon and 2–4.30pm; admission 2.30€), which, when this book was researched, was about to move to new premises below the main street. Alongside a predictable array of pottery shards, tools and stone-age weapons unearthed at prehistoric sites in the Alta Rocca area (including Cucuruzzu and Capula; see opposite), two skeletons are its prize exhibits. The first, that of a now-extinct rat-rabbit, is believed to be the only complete specimen of its kind in the world. The other, known as the Dame de Bonifacio, is a 9000-year-old skeleton of a woman, dug up in southern Corsica. Pointing to evidence of severe chronic injury to her bones, anthropologists have suggested she must have been disabled and thus cared for by members of her family or group – which makes this evidence of one of Europe's oldest known examples of social welfare. The other noteworthy artefact on display is an exquisite ivory crucifix dating from the sixteenth century, gifted to Levie by Pope Sixte Quint (Félix Peretti), whose parents came from here.

Practical information

The gîte d'étape, ***Bienvenue à l'Alta Rocca***, (☎ 04.95.78.46.41; open May–Sept) lies on the far southern side of Levie, near the cemetery and gendarmerie (walk south along the main street and turn downhill at the fountain). The location is none too inspiring and the modern building charmless, but the *gérants* are welcoming enough, and the food is good. A bed in one of its five four-person dorms costs 13€ per night; half-board is 26.60€. The only alternative is a simple but clean room at ***Anne de Peretti's*** small guesthouse (☎ 04.95 78.41.61; open year round), on the east side of the main street; tariffs for double rooms, most with shared showers and toilets, are a bargain at 23–30.40€.

For food, your best bet is the inexpensive ***La Pergola*** restaurant, at the far north end of the main street, which offers an excellent-value 13.70€ set menu of typical Corsican cooking, served on a shady terrace. Less exciting, though cheaper, is the wood-fired pizzeria, ***Le Sorba***, nearby.

Levie's **supermarket,** five minutes' walk beyond the restaurant on the roadside, is small but well stocked with hikers' food, *canastrelli* biscuits and local charcuterie. The **post office** on the main street has an ATM.

From Monday to Saturday, the village is connected by daily **buses** with Ajaccio, Propriano, Sainte-Lucie-de-Tallano and Zonza, run year-round by Autocars Ricci (☎ 04.95.51.08.19 or 04.95.76.25.59).

Opposite: Fire salamander; see p69. (Photo © David Abram).

LEVIE → CARTALAVONU [MAP 61, OPPOSITE]

The fourth stage of the Mare a Mare Sud is a transitionary one, taking you from the deep deciduous forests and river valleys of the island's interior to the high maritime pine woods of Ospédale, from where you get your first glimpse of the sea since day one. Moving from west to east, this also the most strenuous stage on the route. After a fairly leisurely, shaded descent, a long climb from river level via the remote village of Carbini culminates at the Foce Alta pass (1171m), a net gain of over 800m. The pay off is a succession of unforgettable views as you scale the barrier dividing the Alta Rocca from the plains of the east coast. Descending from the crown of the Ospédale massif to the gîte at Cartalavonu towards the end of the day, the whole southern tip of the island is spread out below you, with the lighthouses and brooding mountains of Sardinia visible in the distance.

The path out of Levie begins at the south end of the village, next to the fountain and phone box (cards for which are sold at the post office and little tobacconist further down the main street on the right). Follow the lane down (past the turning for the gîte and gendarmerie) but before you reach the last house look for the waymarks leading left onto a narrow track. Cross a stream and carry on through woods on the opposite side of the valley. Rounding a sharp spur below the D59, this gentle descent passes though some of the finest chestnut, beech and oak forest in the area. Shortly before a steeper drop to the **Fiumicciola River**, you pass a splendid old mill surrounded by terraces of olive trees, which would make a pleasant place to pitch a tent.

From the river bridge, the path, marked by a string of cairns, bears right to begin the hour-long haul up to Carbini. Much of this climb through oak forest follows ancient dry-stone boundary walls. These peter out as you approach the main D59, which the Mare a Mare Sud crosses twice before it arrives at the edge of a broad plateau.

Crossing the outskirts of **Carbini**, you get a good view of the village's famous Romanesque church, **San Giovanni Battista**, erected in the early twelfth century. Both it and the beautifully arcaded, square campanile that now stands nearby were extensively renovated in more recent times. Between the two lie the remains of the Church of San Quilico, which some historians think may have been the original home of the Giovannali sect, whose alleged antics have been raising eyebrows since they were first chronicled over six centuries ago (see the box on p292).

Following the papal massacre of the Giovannalis in 1362, and repeated pirate raids which decimated the population over the following century, Carbini lay deserted until it was resettled in the 1700s by incomers from the Sartène area, to the south. They brought with them their blood feuds, and for most of the modern era the village has been synonymous with the vendetta fought between the Giuseppi and Nicolai families.

Clan violence is now a thing of the past here but you can still see why in the 1970s Dorothy Carrington likened Carbini to 'a despairing village of the

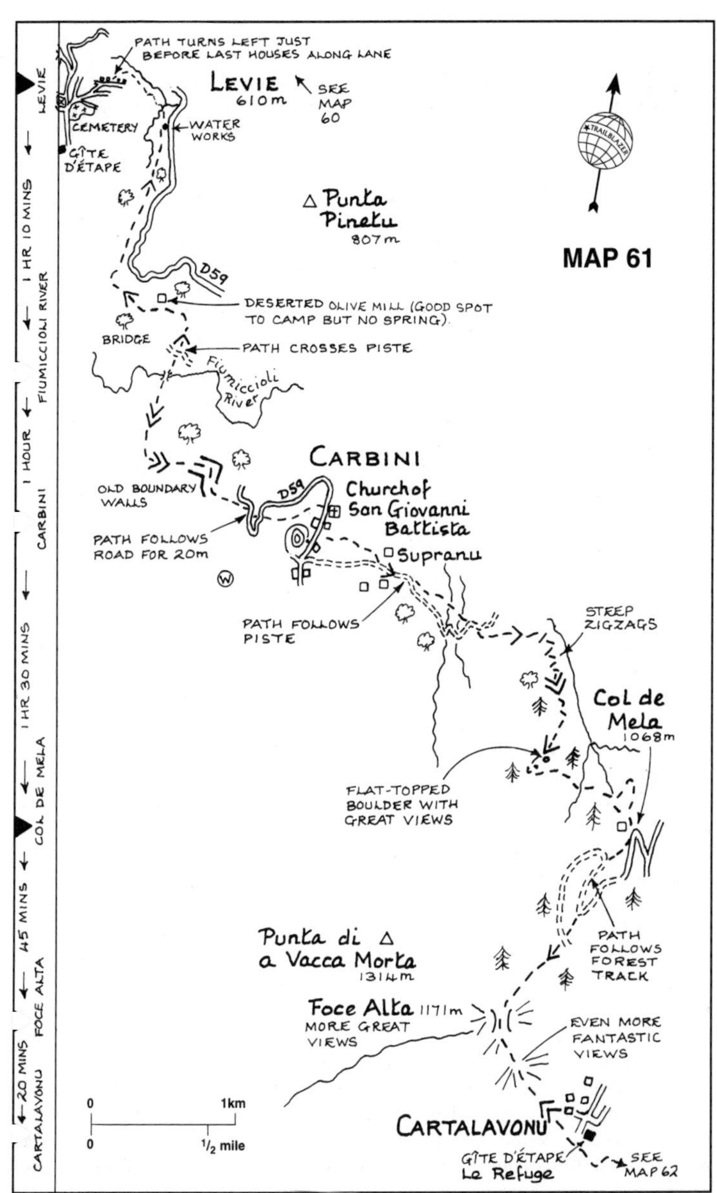
PATH TURNS LEFT JUST BEFORE LAST HOUSES ALONG LANE
LEVIE
610m
SEE MAP 60
CEMETERY
WATER WORKS
GÎTE D'ÉTAPE
Punta Pinetu
807m
MAP 61
D59
DESERTED OLIVE MILL (GOOD SPOT TO CAMP BUT NO SPRING)
BRIDGE
PATH CROSSES PISTE
Fiumicciolì River
CARBINI
OLD BOUNDARY WALLS
D59
Church of San Giovanni Battista
PATH FOLLOWS ROAD FOR 20m
Supranu
PATH FOLLOWS PISTE
STEEP ZIGZAGS
Col de Mela
1068m
FLAT-TOPPED BOULDER WITH GREAT VIEWS
Punta di a Vacca Morta
1314m
PATH FOLLOWS FOREST TRACK
Foce Alta 1171m
MORE GREAT VIEWS
EVEN MORE FANTASTIC VIEWS
CARTALAVONU
GÎTE D'ÉTAPE Le Refuge
SEE MAP 62
0
1km
0
1/2 mile
LEVIE
1 HR 10 MINS
FIUMICCIOLI RIVER
1 HOUR
CARBINI
1 HR 30 MINS
COL DE MELA
45 MINS
FOCE ALTA
20 MINS
CARTALAVONU

The Giovannalis

The Church of San Giovanni Battista at Carbini is infamous as the birthplace of a fourteenth-century religious sect who was said to have conducted bizarre sexual orgies by candlelight here. Originally an heretical off-shoot of the Third Franciscan Order, the Giovannalis formed in the wake of the Black Death, one of several groups who emerged in reaction to the increasing profligacy and decadence of the Catholic church. Early chronicles record that they held all their worldly possessions – including land, money, children and women – in common and that at night they would assemble in the church under cover of darkness to conduct unholy rites, 'adopting the most shameful and disgusting postures they could imagine ... without making distinction between men and women'.

The sect was finally wiped out in 1362 when troops dispatched from Avignon by Pope Urban V hunted down and burned its members to death in a massive pyre on a rock above the village.

Corsicans still talk in hushed tones about the sect's dreadful heresies, but in fact the salacious stories have no historical basis. They were details added two-hundred or so years after the events by a biased cleric. This lurid gloss has obscured the fact that the sect was actually more austere and pious than the prevailing orthodoxy of the day. The pope saw their popularity in Corsica – where the Giovannalis' doctrine of equality and community of possessions had strong parallels in traditional society – as a threat and feared it might weaken the church's grip on the island.

steppe'. Its dwindling population of pensioners doesn't even have the luxury of a shop or bar. For walkers, the only reason to linger is to refill water bottles at the spring – a tap in the wall halfway up the main street below the phone booth.

The onward route from Carbini is indicated off the east side of the street. Climbing first to the hamlet of **Supranu** (upper Carbini) it plunges once more into a cover of mature chestnut trees, briefly following the route of a piste before turning left past a farmhouse and entering the forest proper, where the undergrowth is patrolled by gangs of semi-wild pigs. After crossing two stream gullies full of large boulders, you cross the piste one more time and begin the crux of the climb up the Ospédale massif. The steepest section comprises a long sequence of zigzags, paved with worn old slabs that must have lain here for hundreds, if not thousands, of years.

Maritime pines start to predominate as you progress upwards. You'll know the end of the hardest stretch is near when, around one hour out of Carbini, you pass a large flat-topped granite boulder from which the views encompass the entire Alta Rocca and Rizzanese regions, down to the Golfe de Valinco shimmering in the distance. In fine weather it is possible to trace almost the entire Mare a Mare Sud up to this point. A second, similar boulder lies five minutes further along the trail but doesn't afford such an impressive panorama.

Almost immediately after the boulders the path bends left (east) and levels off as it approaches the **Col de Mela** (1068m), where pine needles form a springy carpet underfoot, overlaid in May by a haze of purple cyclamen. The pass, reached 30 minutes after the viewpoints, is basically a broad saddle dis-satisfyingly hemmed in by trees. For your first glimpse of the Ligurian Sea you'll have to press on another 45 minutes or so south-west, following a route of well waymarked paths and forestry tracks that scale the east flank of Punta di a Vacca Morta (literally 'Dead Cow Peak').

The approach to **Foce Alta** (1171m) is a long, gradual climb through some superb stands of old maritime pine, which open out near the ridge. A gust of cool sea air should greet you as you arrive at the pass proper, which looks south-west across to the summit of Oumo di Cagna (1217m), the highest peak in Corsica's far south, and down to the wildest stretch of the Sartènais shoreline (a trek along which is described on pp300-10).

Just when the sustained, rocky descent from Foce Alta has you thinking the best views are behind you, the ridge falls away to reveal an extraordinary vista of maquis tapering away to the sea. The vision of Sardinia's interior range unfolding to the south provides a fitting culmination to a day of steadily improving scenery. Make the most of it; from here on you'll be in tumbling downhill through miles of dense forest and scratchy scrub.

CARTALAVONU → PORTO-VECCHIO [MAP 62, p294; MAP 63, p295]

A cluster of neatly converted former shepherds' huts scattered around a wooded hollow, the hamlet of **Cartalavonu** centres on the gîte d'étape and restaurant of ***Le Refuge*** (☎ 04.95.70.00.39; open mid-March–Oct), an attractive stone building that does a roaring trade with well-heeled hikers and day-trippers in the summer months, but languishes empty for most of the winter (when it opens only at the weekend). Dorm beds here cost 9.10€, or 24.40€ for half-board. The restaurant is a more serious and pricey affair, with no *menu fixe*; count on around 25€ per head à la carte. House specialities include fragrant charcuterie *maison* and wild-boar terrine. Those roughing it should creep off to the edges of the clearing, where a pile of enormous granite boulders offers minimal shelter. Bivouacking and camping are tolerated but technically forbidden; there's no easily accessible water source and you'll get a frosty response in the bar if you ask to use their toilets.

Half-an-hour's easy walking through pine forest brings you to the larger and busier village of **Ospédale**. Barely a handful of people live here year-round. Most of the cottages straddling the D368 are inherited properties that serve as weekend retreats from the stifling heat of summer down on the plains. Its fine views over the Golfe de Porto-Vecchio ensure the village is also a popular destination for bus parties during the season. For walkers, the main incentive to stop is to savour the views over a coffee from café's terrace at the bend in the main road. The village spring gurgles nearby, under a sign requesting you not to wash clothes or kitchen utensils in the water.

Many walkers call it a day at Ospédale, preferring to hitch rather than walk the rest of the way through the pine forest to Porto-Vecchio. In terms of views and landscape, the most impressive stretches of the Mare a Mare Sud are behind you but the forest ahead has its charms and it can be satisfying to feel the ground

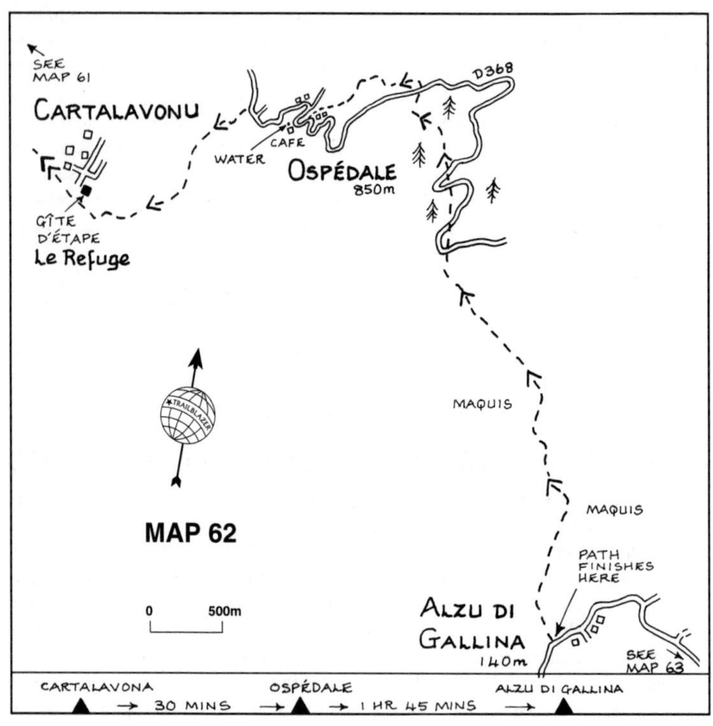

level out for the first time, and to reacquaint yourself with the heady fragrance of the coastal maquis.

The footpath begins again at the third hairpin bend in the village, making its way up a lane between the houses. After a short flat stretch it drops to the right to begin the descent proper. Old-growth pines shade much of the route, which crosses the D368 five times before emerging at an expanse of fire-damaged forest, now overgrown with maquis. The gradient eases off gradually from here on, steepening briefly just before the roadhead, preceded by the appearance of concrete on the piste and a water-pumping station on your right.

Once at **Alzu di Gallina**, the hamlet where the path joins the road, it makes sense to try for a lift as the rest of the route is monotonous and a trial in hot weather. If you decide to walk, keep to the main road until it reaches a crossroads, where you should bear left. Thirty metres later, after crossing a little bridge, you reach a 'T' junction, where a right turn takes you south alongside the Petrosu river, past a turning for the hamlet of **Nota** and thence to another junction, this time with the D159, where you turn left for Porto-Vecchio. On

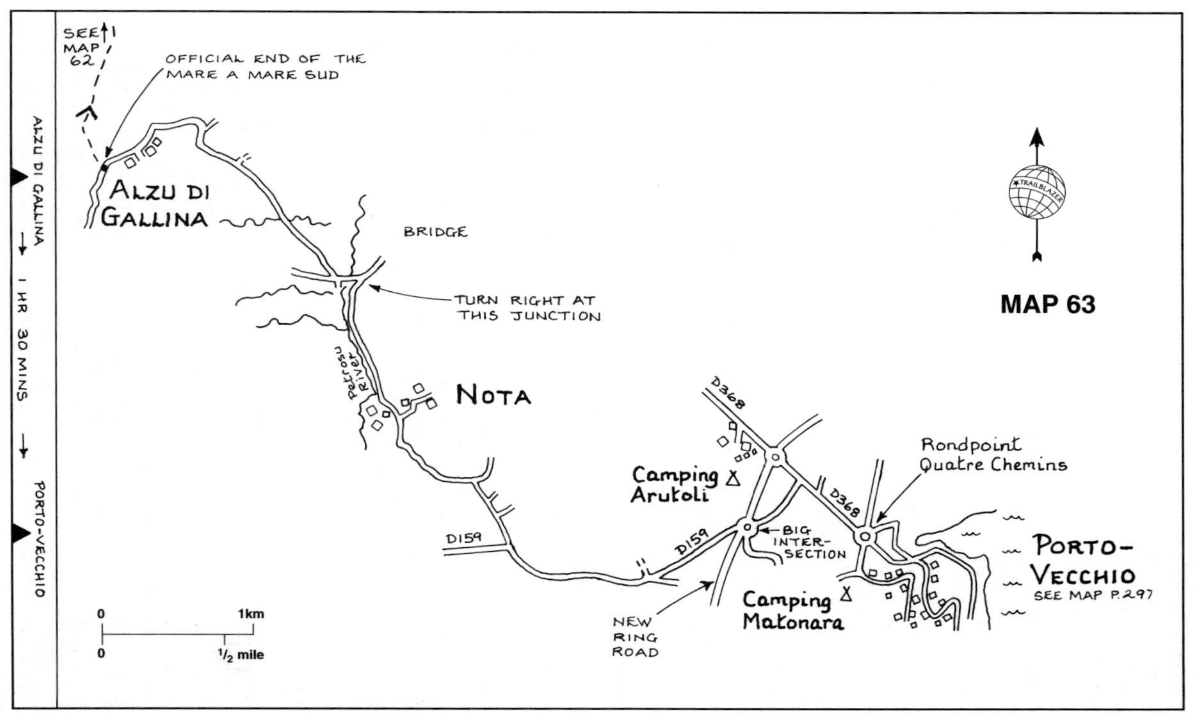
SEE MAP 62
OFFICIAL END OF THE MARE A MARE SUD
ALZU DI GALLINA
BRIDGE
TURN RIGHT AT THIS JUNCTION
MAP 63
TRAILBLAZER
Petrosu River
NOTA
D368
Camping Arutoli
Rondpoint Quatre Chemins
D368
D159
D159
BIG INTER-SECTION
PORTO-VECCHIO
SEE MAP P.297
Camping Matonara
NEW RING ROAD
0
1km
0
1/2 mile
ALZU DI GALLINA
1 HR 30 MINS
PORTO-VECCHIO

reaching the D368, turn right and from there follow the main road as far as a large roundabout (*rondpoint*) called **Quatre Chemins**, opposite a 'Hyper U' supermarket. Ignore the signs for 'Centre Ville' and instead take the fourth exit (south). This passes Porto-Vecchio's most convenient campsite, Camping Matonara (see p298), before continuing uphill to the old town.

PORTO-VECCHIO/PORTO VEGHJU

Porto-Vecchio has been south-west Corsica's principal town since it was founded by the Genoans in the sixteenth century. Controlled from the confines of its crumbling citadel, which still overlooks the gulf from its hilltop vantage point, a flourishing trade in cork and wine originally ensured the town's prosperity, which endured well into the 20th century despite the perennial threats of malaria and pirate raids. Today, with a permanent population of around 10,600, Porto-Vecchio remains a well-heeled town, only nowadays tourism forms the backbone of its economy. Shiploads of visitors, the majority of them wealthy Italians, pour through each summer en route to the famous white-sand-and-turquoise-water beaches to the south. This, however, is where they come to shop and strut their stuff in the evenings. Consequently the narrow lanes of the old town are crammed with designer boutiques and chic souvenir chops – Corsica at its most bijou.

Lumbering out of the hills with a backpack, you'll probably feel underdressed and out of place here. After a laze in the square and an amble around the back lanes of the citadel, most hikers make a beeline for the bus office and head off in search of somewhere more low-key. With hotel rates among the island's highest and the fabled beaches difficult to reach without your own transport for much of the year, this is not the ideal place to rest up.

Orientation and services

Although surrounded by an unprepossessing belt of supermarkets and roundabouts, Porto-Vecchio's heart comprises a quaint, compact grid of late-medieval streets encircled by fragments of Genoan walls and gateways. Its focus – place de la République – is a sunny square which for nine months of the year metamorphoses into one large café terrace, overlooked by the stately Church of Saint Jean Baptiste. Across the square you'll find the helpful **tourist office** (☎ 04 95.70.09.58, 💻 www.accueil-portovecchio.com; July–Aug Mon– Sat 9am–8pm, Sun 9am–1pm; June and Sept Mon–Sat 9am–1pm and 3–6pm; Oct–May Mon–Fri 9am—noon and 2–6pm, Sat 9am–noon). Most of the town's hotels and restaurants lie within five minutes' walk of here. The **post office**, however, stands just outside the citadel, past the mairie on rue Général-Leclerc. It has an ATM as does the Société Générale **bank** nearby; both accept Visa and MasterCard.

Porto-Vecchio's **marina** is not the most picturesque on the island but it's as good a

Figari-Sud-Corse Airport

Southern Corsica's airport, Figari-Sud-Corse (☎ 04.95.71.10.10), lies 20km south-west of Porto-Vecchio. Shuttle buses, run by Transports Rossi (☎ 04.95.71.00.11), operate from mid-June until early September, connecting with flight arrivals and departures. Leaving town, you can pick them up from the marina, opposite the capitainerie. Tickets cost 8.40€.

Taxis charge 38–45.60€ depending on the time of day. The only other option, apart from hitching, is to catch Eurocorse Voyage's Ajaccio bus from Porto-Vecchio and get off at Figari village, which straddles the main road, and walk or hitch the remaining 5km to the airport.

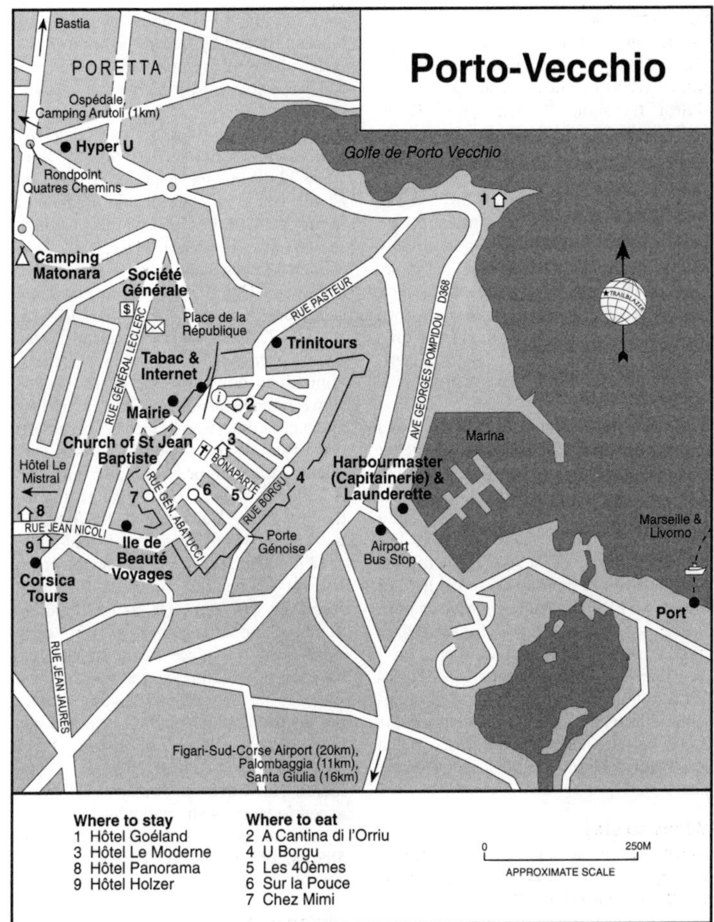

place as any to kill an hour or two, especially in the midday heat. To reach it, walk under the Porte Génoise, the grand old gateway at the south-east corner of the citadel, and follow the road downhill. The main port de commerce, the arrival and departure point for the ferry boats, lies further east.

Buses drop and pick up passengers at several different locations, depending on the route. **Eurocorse Voyage**'s service to and from Ajaccio via Propriano uses the small car park opposite the Trinitours travel agency (☎ 04.95.70.13.83) on rue Pasteur, two minutes' walk north of the citadel. For destinations up the east coast (including Sainte-Lucie-de-Porto-Vecchio, the turn-off for Conca and the GR20 trailhead, Aléria and Bastia), **Rapides Bleues**' bus (☎ 04.95.70.10.36) uses the Corsicatours office at 7 rue Jean-Jaurès. The company serving villages in the Alta Rocca (Zonza, Aullène and Quenza) is **Balési Évasion** (☎ 04.95.70.12.31 or 04.95.70.15.55), which operates from Ile de Beauté Voyages, 13 rue Général de Gaulle. Always check bus times at the relevant office (the timetable is usually displayed in the window), not at the tourist office, which is notoriously unreliable. Fares are usually paid to the driver when you get on. Note, too, that the travel agents will usually look after your luggage if you're leaving town on the next bus; Porto-Vecchio has no official left-luggage facility. The bus to Figari-Sud-Corse Airport leaves from opposite the capitainerie.

For serious provisions **shopping** and outdoor bits and bobs you won't do better than the huge Hyper U supermarket next to rondpoint Quatre Chemins, 20 minutes' walk north of the citadel. A bakery and a pharmacy are in the same complex. The bookshop here stocks a good range of IGN maps but you're more likely to get hold of the latest FFRP Topoguides at Maison de la Presse on rue Pasteur, which also sells a modest range of foreign newspapers.

The only **launderette** in Porto-Vecchio is in the marina, next to the capitainerie. **Internet access** is available at the *tabac* on the north side of place de la République (3€ for 15 minutes, or 9.1€ per hour).

Where to stay

Much the most convenient **campsite**, although a correspondingly busy one, is ***Camping Matonara*** (☎ 04.95.70.37.05; May–Oct), near rondpoint Quatre Chemins, whose terraces are shaded by old cork trees. A less crowded alternative is ***Camping Arutoli*** (☎ 04.95.70.12.73; open May–mid-Sept), 1km up the Ospédale road (the D368) from rondpoint Quatre Chemins and a short way off the end of the Mare a Mare Sud.

In spring and autumn Porto-Vecchio is a prime destination for bus parties of French pensioners, so pressure on rooms is intense even outside peak season; during peak season, every hotel seems to be blocked booked by Italians. Whenever you come, therefore, reserve well in advance and brace yourself for higher-than-average room rates.

A safe mid-price bet is ***Hôtel Panorama***, (☎ 04.95.70.07.96, 🖷 04.95 70.46.78; open June–Sept), at 12 rue Jean Nicoli, where en suite double rooms cost from 45/50.20€ to 48.60./56.20€ low/high season. It's a modest place, but clean enough for a night and there's a friendly bar downstairs. Otherwise try the elegant three-star ***Hôtel Goéland*** (☎ 04.95.70.14.15, 🖷 04.95.72.05.18, 💻 hotel-goeland@wanadoo.fr; open April–Oct), on ave Georges-Pompidou, down on the water's edge between rondpoint Quatre Chemins and the marina; tariffs (which include breakfast) range from 44.20€ to 68€ for a room with shared bathroom, or 82–127.70€ en suite. Alternatively check out the more run-of-the-mill ***Hôtel Holzer*** (☎ 04.95.70.05.93, 🖷 04.95.70.47.80; open March–mid-Nov), at 12 rue Jean-Jaurès, where a double room will set you back 62.30–111€. Rooms at ***Hôtel Le Moderne*** (☎ 04.95.70.06.36, 💻 hotel.moderne@libertysurs.fr; open April–Sept), on place de la République, have recently been revamped and are good value at 38/79€– 65.40/103.40€, depending on the level of comfort required and time of year. ***Hôtel Le Mistral*** (☎ 04 95.70.08.53, 🖷 04.95.70.51.60; open March–Nov), at 5 rue Toussaint-Culioli, is a comfortable, well maintained two-star, with a selection of double rooms from 38€/88.20€ to 53.20€/103.40€ low/high season.

Where to eat

Cheap eats in the citadel are in short supply, to say the least. For a quick snack, try the ***boulangerie*** on place de la République, which does the usual savoury bakes – hot pizza or *brocciu*-and-spinach *bastelles* (pasties), or ***Sur la Pouce***, down the lane leading to Porte Génoise, where you can order from a vast range of filling, inexpensive *paninis* (hot baguettes) from around 3€. Nearby, on the corner of rue

Beaches around Porto-Vecchio

Postcard racks across the island gleam with images of the translucent water and inviting white sands that lie south down the coast from Porto-Vecchio, but for most of the year the best of these beaches are hard to reach without some form of transport. In July and August, however, a shuttle bus (*navette*) runs out to the most developed of them, Palombaggia and Santa Giulia, starting at Camping Matonara and stopping at various points along the road behind the marina. For details ask at the tourist office or campsite reception.

Backed by ranks of distinctive umbrella pines, **Palombaggia** is a long, perfectly white curve dotted with clumps of pink granite. Get there early in the morning to enjoy it before the rush starts. If the crowds become too much walk south to the quieter **Plage d'Asciaghju**, where there's an excellent campsite (☎ 04.95.70.37.87) just 300m behind the beach. **Santa Giulia**, further down the coast, is perhaps the most spectacular, with brilliant turquoise water, but is spoilt by a huge holiday villa complex behind it.

An alternative way to see some of the beautiful coast south of Porto-Vecchio is to take one of the **boat trips**, costing around 53.20€, offered at the marina. The excursions last a full day, taking you down as far as Bonifacio and the Îles Lvezzi marine reserve, with a stop for lunch and a swim at one of the more remote coves along the way. Look for the 'Le Ruscana' sign opposite the capitainerie.

Finally, if you've just finished the GR20 and are considering a spell on the beach, check the box on p203 for suggestions of places closer to Conca.

Bonaparte and rue Borgo, ***Les 40èmes*** is a pleasant backstreet *crêperie* offering a wide choice of sweet and savoury Breton pancakes from 3.80 to 8.40€. To sample the cream of the island's cheeses and charcuterie go to ***A Cantina di l'Orriu***, a Corsican speciality shop just north of place de la République, where you can order servings of particular hams, sausages, pâtés and cheeses, as well as wine by the glass and traditional puddings. At 9.10€ to 12.20€ per dish, prices are on the high side but quality is guaranteed. The shop next door sells the same food to take away as souvenirs.

Of the town's many bona fide restaurants, the best value are those along rue Général Abatucci offering three- or four-course menus fixes. ***Chez Mimi***, at No 5, is an established and dependable favourite, with a particularly strong Corsican menu that includes the delicious Bonifacienne speciality, stuffed aubergine. For optimum views of the gulf, though, take your pick from one of the more overtly touristy places along rue Borgu. ***U Borgu*** is predictably pricey but its delicious wood-baked pizzas are affordable; ask for a table on its rear terrace, from where you can look over the bay and harbour to the salt pans in the distance.

PART 8: LITTORAL SARTÈNAIS

Overview

Corsica has nearly 1000km of pristine coastline but little of it is accessible by easy-to-follow footpaths. An exception is the rugged south-west between Propriano and Bonifacio, known as the Littoral Sartènais (Sartène Coast). The virtually roadless section between Campomoro at the mouth of the Golfe de Valinco and beautiful Roccapina beach in the south is particularly wild, its hinterland of impenetrable *maquis* dotted with standing stones and Neolithic tombs. At the shore, massive outcrops of granite boulders tumble into a perfectly blue sea, edged by a succession of remote coves. Some are too striking to have escaped the attention of the region's yachties but others lie permanently deserted, piled high with sun-bleached driftwood, flotsam and seaweed.

The entire Littoral Sartènais was recently acquired by the French state and accorded special protection. Part of the plan for area was to inaugurate a coast path, and after clearing miles of overgrown hunters' trails and installing waymarkers, the route was opened to the public in 1999. Starting behind Campomoro's famous Genoan watchtower, it wriggles south around the Capu di Senetosa and on to the fishing anchorage of Tizzano. The second stretch winds on from there via two of Corsica's most spectacular beaches to Roccapina, close to the main Ajaccio–Bonifacio road.

With a night at Tizzano, the coast path can be comfortably covered in two days. Do it in three and you'll have more time to laze on the beaches along the way. Camping and bivouacking are technically forbidden (as you're reminded at regular intervals by specially erected panels) but no-one seems to take much notice and in summer, makeshift shelters spring up at several coves. Don't, however, be lulled into a false sense of security. This is a wilderness area and you should be completely self-reliant if you aim to walk through it. First and foremost, take enough water (at least four litres). There's only one source on the route (just beyond Cala di Conca) and the heat can be ferocious from May onwards. By July you'd have to be foolhardy, or immune to the effects of solar radiation, to attempt it at all. Temperatures only become bearable again around late September

Food is available at the small grocery shop in Tizzano, where there are also two restaurants and a café as well as a hotel and campsite, but after that you'll have to wait until you get back to civilization to buy supplies. Most people stock up in Campomoro.

Maintained by a lone Moroccan labourer, the path is waymarked at key points by rusty iron posts and occasional double orange slashes. They're

Torri

If you come across a photograph of the Littoral Sartènais the chances are it will show one of the three ruined Genoan watchtowers (*torri*) that overlook the shore from three strategic headlands: at Campomoro, Capu di Senetosa and Roccapina.

The towers were part of a chain of ninety-one similar structures erected by the Genoans to guard the Corsican coast against pirates. Originating in the Barbary and Moorish states of North Africa, the raiders came in search of plunder and slaves for sale in the bazaars of Algiers. By the time the Genoans took control of the island in the fifteenth century, however, the frequency and ferocity of these attacks had ravaged the population to such an extent that whole villages had been forced to retreat to the safety of the hinterland. This explains why most of Corsica's coastal settlements date from the eighteenth and nineteenth centuries as the pirate threat had subsided by then.

Torri proved a highly cost-effective early-warning system against the raids, allowing villagers time to escape with their valuables to the maquis. Each tower comprised two or three storeys, with a rampart on top. Access was via a ladder, which could be withdrawn through the lowest entrance, usually five metres off the ground. In the event of an attack the guardians of the tower, or *torregiani*, would light a fire to alert both the village and neighbouring watchtowers, who would in turn ignite their fires, and so on until the whole island was warned by a giant ring of flames.

One of the greatest fans of Corsican watchtowers was Horatio Nelson, whose entire fleet was held at bay by one for three days in 1794 during an attack on the French garrison at Saint-Florent. The future admiral was so impressed that he later commissioned a string of torri around the south coast of Britain as defences against Napoléon.

dependable until the Senetosa Tower (Tour de Senetosa) but peter out after that and are rare on the second leg between Tizzano and Roccapina. Save for the very last headland between plage d'Erbaju and Roccapina (featured on IGN Map 4254OT) the entire route is covered on IGN 4154OT.

Finally, bear in mind the advice about low-impact trekking on p79: don't make any fires or leave rubbish, and bury faeces.

The route

CAMPOMORO

Overlooked by a stately old Genoan watchtower, Campomoro, 17km west of Propriano, is strung around a well-sheltered crescent of turquoise water and white sand at the south-westerly tip of the Golfe de Valinco. It's a perfect place to unwind, free from obtrusive development and within easy reach of the unspoilt coast to the south. Things only get hectic here in July and August when the village's two campsites burst at the seams and the beach gets totally overrun with Italian families.

Orientation and services

Unfortunately for walkers Campomoro is inaccessible by public transport. From Propriano you'll either have to catch a taxi (drivers charge a hefty 38–45€ if they think they can get away with it), or hitch: start as far up rue Général de Gaulle as you can be bothered to trudge and catch a ride to the Campomoro turning, 4km out of town, from where it's fairly easy to pick up a lift.

The village's well-stocked **shop** (open mornings only out of season and 8am–9pm in July/Aug) stands just to the right of the place where the road into the village hits the beach. Directly opposite it is the **post office** (Mon–Sat 8am–noon), where you can buy cards for the telephone kiosks nearby. Note that there is no ATM here so bring enough cash with you from Propriano.

Where to stay and eat

Of the two campsites, ***Camping Peretto Les Roseaux*** (☎ 04.95.74.20.52; open May–Sept), 500m beyond the post office up the lane leading inland from the beachfront, has the edge over its rival with more shade and secluded corners. The much larger and more exposed ***Camping Campomoro*** (☎ 04 95.34.56.86; open May–mid-Oct) lies to the left of the road as you enter the village.

Much the most pleasant hotel in the village is ***Hôtel le Ressac*** (☎ 04.95.74.22.25; open mid-April–mid-October), behind the seafront near the chapel. During low season rates here start at 45.60€ for a comfortable, attractively furnished en suite double. In peak season half-board (76€ per head) is obligatory. If it's full try the pricier ***Hôtel Campomoro*** (☎ 04.95.74.20.89), at the other end of the village below the tower, where rooms cost 59.20–80.50€/68.40–88.20€ low/peak season. Both places charge extra for a sea view.

For a cheap meal you can't beat the delicious onion, spinach and *brocciu bastelles* (Corsican pasties) sold at the village shop, along with the usual selection of fresh pastries and breads. Otherwise, you've a choice between the two surprisingly good-value, unpretentious restaurants next to the chapel, ***La Mouette*** and ***Le Goéland***, which both offer *plats du jour* from around 8€, in addition to an à la carte choice of salads, Corsican pasta, and seafood (3.80–14.40€). The cooking is formulaic but the location is great. The two terraces are also perfect spots for an early evening pastis while the locals play *pétanque* on the tiny pitch nearby.

CAMPOMORO → TIZZANO [MAP 64, OPPOSITE; MAP 65, p305]

To reach Tizzano before nightfall, with time to sit out the midday heat on one of the beaches along the way, it's essential to get an early start from Campomoro. The trail begins at the north-western edge of the village. Follow the lane behind the beach, past the last houses and uphill towards the watch-tower (well worth visiting if you haven't already). Continuing over the rise, a clearly defined path drops down the far side through low maquis to the shore-line, where you'll see some of the route's most intriguing rock formations. Twenty minutes later you scale the first of many granite outcrops, through tunnels of old-growth maquis, and crest a second ridge from where the coast opens up to the south.

The route from here on is easy to follow until you reach a tiny beach of coarse orange sand after around 45 minutes; cross it halfway up, looking for the faded orange waymark on a boulder on the opposite side. Traversing a wide stretch of open maquis, with rubbish-strewn pebble coves to your right, the path then forks (bear left) before running over a low rise.

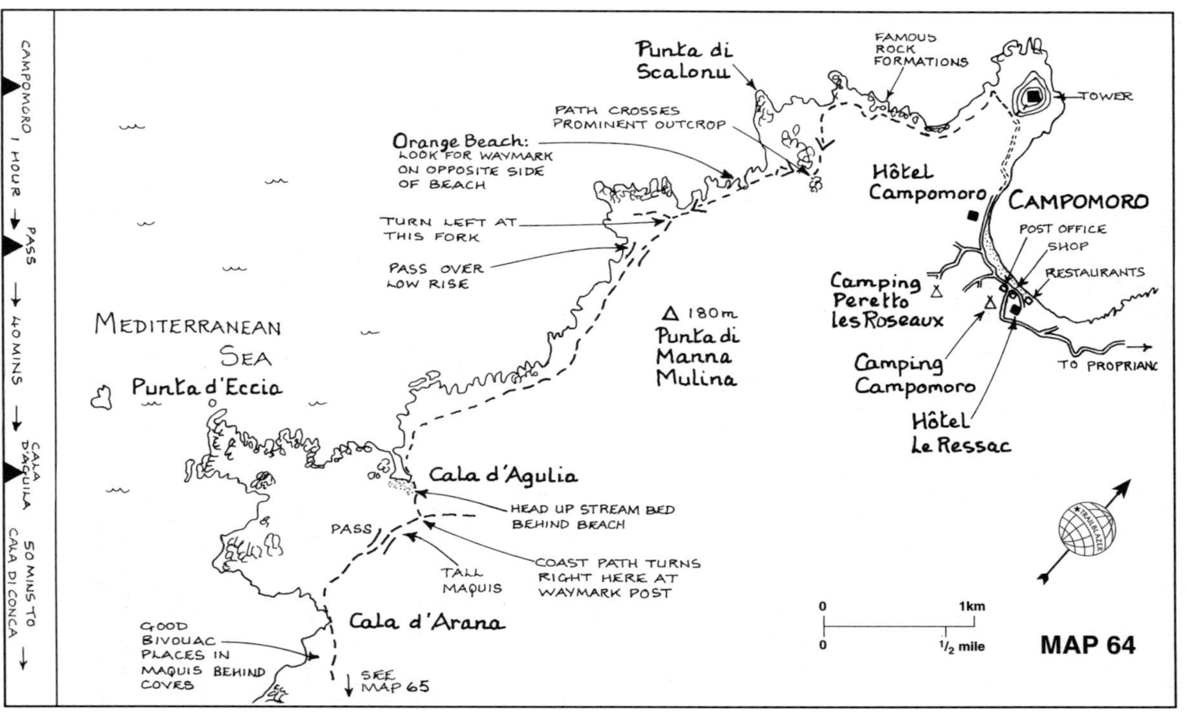
Punta di Scalonu
FAMOUS ROCK FORMATIONS
TOWER
PATH CROSSES PROMINENT OUTCROP
Orange Beach: LOOK FOR WAYMARK ON OPPOSITE SIDE OF BEACH
Hôtel Campomoro
CAMPOMORO
POST OFFICE
SHOP
RESTAURANTS
TURN LEFT AT THIS FORK
PASS OVER LOW RISE
Camping Peretto les Roseaux
Δ 180m Punta di Manna Mulina
MEDITERRANEAN SEA
Punta d'Eccia
Camping Campomoro
TO PROPRIANO
Hôtel Le Ressac
Cala d'Agulia
HEAD UP STREAM BED BEHIND BEACH
PASS
TALL MAQUIS
COAST PATH TURNS RIGHT HERE AT WAYMARK POST
Cala d'Arana
GOOD BIVOUAC PLACES IN MAQUIS BEHIND COVES
SEE MAP 65
0
1km
0
½ mile
MAP 64
TRAILBLAZER
CAMPOMORO
1 HOUR
PASS
40 MINS
CALA D'AGUILA
50 MINS TO CALA DI CONCA

The next 40 minutes is level going as you approach the first major headland, Punta d'Eccia, beyond which lies a hidden bottle-shaped cove known as **Cala d'Agulia**. From the path above, it looks a promising place for a swim but on closer inspection turns out to be dirty. The water here can also get very polluted by the motorboats that routinely moor in the middle of the inlet.

Instead of rounding the headland on the far side of the cove, as you might expect, the path heads inland from Cala d'Agulia along the streambed. Turn right after about five minutes when you come to a waymark post, indicating a gap in dense maquis through which the path, hemmed in by scratchy vegetation, winds uphill along a flood channel. Eventually you arrive at a pass due east of the Punta d'Eccia, from where the Senetosa Tower is visible for the first time.

A steady downhill section then brings you to a bay called **Cala d'Arana**. Hunt around in the maquis behind the coves here and you'll find a group of shelters erected by bivouackers, despite the absence of water (most people who come here do so by boat and bring their own supply).

Continue for another half an hour or so through more dense maquis, with the stark profile of the Senetosa to the south, and you'll arrive at one of the real highlights of this walk, **Cala di Conca**, a small bay of perfect white shell sand enfolded by hills. Accessible by 4WD only and with a dependable spring close at hand the beach can get quite busy during the summer, but even so the translucent water might tempt you to hole up in one of the nooks off the bay (see map opposite).

The **spring**, known locally as Funtana di l'Acula (Eagle Spring), lies at the end of a small side valley, 10 minutes beyond the beach up a path indicated from the main route by a waymark post. The water is a little salty and slow running but in dry weather this is the only source before Tizzano so make the most of it.

Beyond the Cala di Conca the path emerges briefly from the maquis to round the **Capu di Senetosa**, crowned by its distinctive, pale granite watchtower and, lower down, a lighthouse powered by wind turbines. A *piste* runs up the south-west flank of the hill to the lighthouse, with the path turning off where the track makes a sharp left bend; look for a waymark post showing the route. From here, you've 15 minutes through rough maquis before dropping down to pass the beautiful **Cala di Tivella**, another gorgeous bay backed by an orange beach. The tree cover behind makes this a better bivouac spot than the next inlet, a narrow funnel of unbelievably turquoise water called **Cala Longa**.

Once through the rocks and scrub beyond Cala Longa, you soon reach the start of a rutted piste that runs all the way to the hamlet of **Barcaju**, passing a string of hidden coves with fine views across the Golfe de Tizzano. The final stretch, along tarmac, seems to take forever. To round the Cala di Tizzano, the road has to make a swooping detour inland, bypassing a marshy area and then bending south towards the fishing jetty.

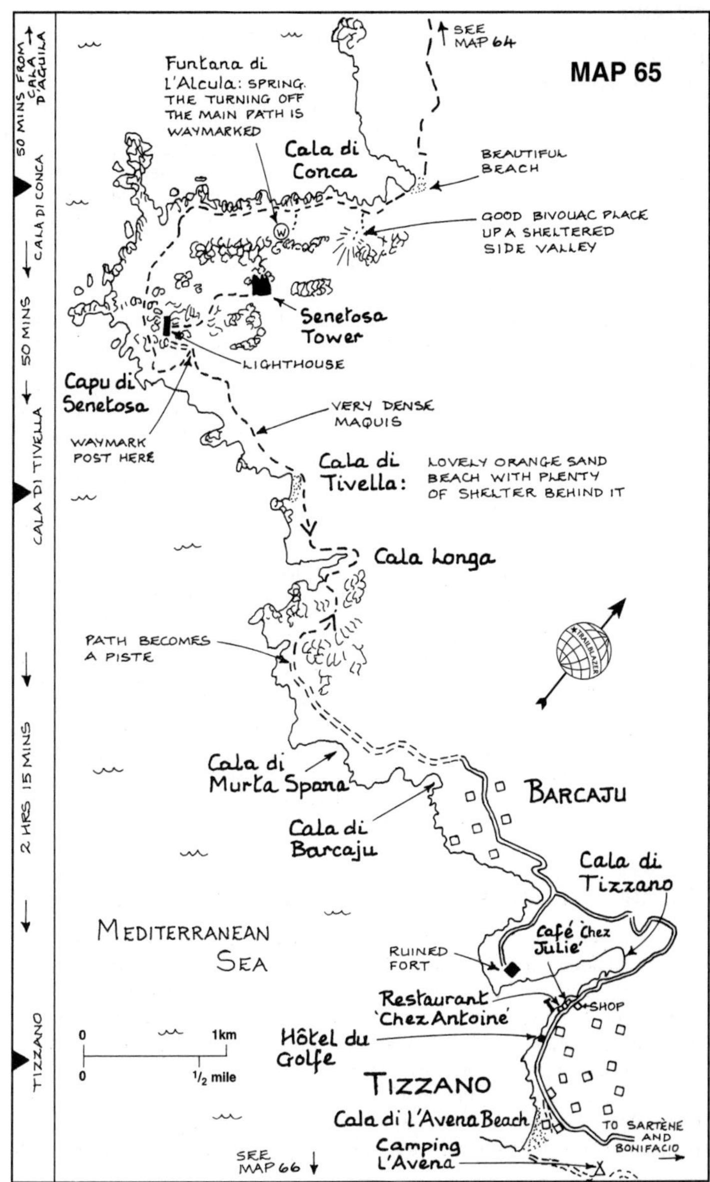
MAP 65
SEE MAP 64
Funtana di L'Alcula: SPRING. THE TURNING OFF THE MAIN PATH IS WAYMARKED
Cala di Conca
BEAUTIFUL BEACH
GOOD BIVOUAC PLACE UP A SHELTERED SIDE VALLEY
Senetosa Tower
LIGHTHOUSE
Capu di Senetosa
WAYMARK POST HERE
VERY DENSE MAQUIS
Cala di Tivella:
LOVELY ORANGE SAND BEACH WITH PLENTY OF SHELTER BEHIND IT
Cala Longa
PATH BECOMES A PISTE
TRAILBLAZER
Cala di Murta Spana
BARCAJU
Cala di Barcaju
Cala di Tizzano
Café 'Chez Julie'
RUINED FORT
MEDITERRANEAN SEA
Restaurant 'Chez Antoine'
SHOP
Hôtel du Golfe
TIZZANO
Cala di L'Avena Beach
Camping L'Avena
TO SARTÈNE AND BONIFACIO
SEE MAP 66
0 1km
0 1/2 mile
50 MINS FROM CALA D'AGUILA
CALA DI CONCA
50 MINS
CALA DI TIVELLA
2 HRS 15 MINS
TIZZANO

TIZZANO

If you weren't footsore by the time you reached the lighthouse, you doubtless will be after the long plod into Tizzano, a village that somehow fails to live up to its dramatic location. Little more than a desultory collection of half-finished second homes scattered over a wind-blown headland, it can appear a bleak, unwelcoming place out of season. From late June onwards, however, Tizzano's handful of permanent residents are overwhelmed by crowds of holidaymakers who come for the spectacular **Cala di l'Avena beach**, on the southern edge of the village. In the evenings they fill the terraces of the two cafés on the headland, which overlook the narrow Cala di Tizzano to a ruined fort on the far side of the bay. Another Genoan anti-piracy effort, the fort stood for 500 years until it was destroyed in WWII by a team of trainee Corsican commandos, led by a maverick British undercover agent called Andrew Croft. Half a century later the locals are bemused as to why their grandfathers needed a Brit to teach them how to blow things up.

Where to stay and eat

Tizzano's one hotel, ***Hôtel du Golfe*** (☎ 04 95.77.14.76; open April–Oct) overlooks the mouth of the bay from the roadside and is situated above its own tiny beach. All the rooms in this modern building have sea views although the tariffs are on the stiff side at 53.30–85.40€, depending on the season. If you intend to stay here, be sure to phone ahead, as plans are afoot to sell the place.

Finding somewhere to bivouac in Tizzano is a problem. The dunes behind the beach seem the obvious choice but turn out to be a de facto public toilet. Nor is there anywhere suitable along the path beyond the village. Either backtrack and look for somewhere at Cala di Murta Spana, just west of Barcaju, or press on to the far side of Capu di Zivia, another half-hour or so south-west. Better still, check in to ***Camping l'Avena*** (☎ 04.95.77.02.18; late-May–Sept), 300m behind the beach. Note that without a tent you'll need some kind of outer cover for your sleeping bag as the valley gets a heavy dew.

Tizzano's cosy shop (May and Sept Mon–Sat 9am–noon; June–Sept daily 8.30am–12.30 and 4–7pm) is the place to stock up on supplies. You'll find it above the harbour, opposite the ***Café Chez Julie***, whose terrace makes an ideal breakfast venue. The shopkeeper brings fresh croissants and pains au chocolat from Sartène each morning.

To sample the wonderful seafood landed at the village's jetty you should splash out on a meal at ***Chez Antoine*** (☎ 04 95.77.07.25), a classy place offering a 20€ set menu served on a lovely covered terrace overlooking the water. It's a cut above most village restaurants, with a strong local following who come here for the grilled snapper, monkfish, ray's wing, lobster and famous bouillabaisse (36.50€ per head).

TIZZANO → ROCCAPINA [MAP 66, OPPOSITE; MAP 67, p309]

The coast path starts again at the far southern end of Cala di l'Avena beach; look for a faded double orange slash on the rocks. This first stretch is a true foretaste of the day ahead: a trudge down a long sandy beach followed by an awkward climb through thick, spiny maquis. Eventually you emerge, scratched to pieces from the vegetation, at a piste which you turn right onto and follow as it bends downhill, seeming to double back towards the village.

From the clearing at the bottom of the hill the onward route through the rocks along the shore is well cairned, leading you through a mass of wind-sculpted granite to an open, bare headland after around 10 minutes. The path

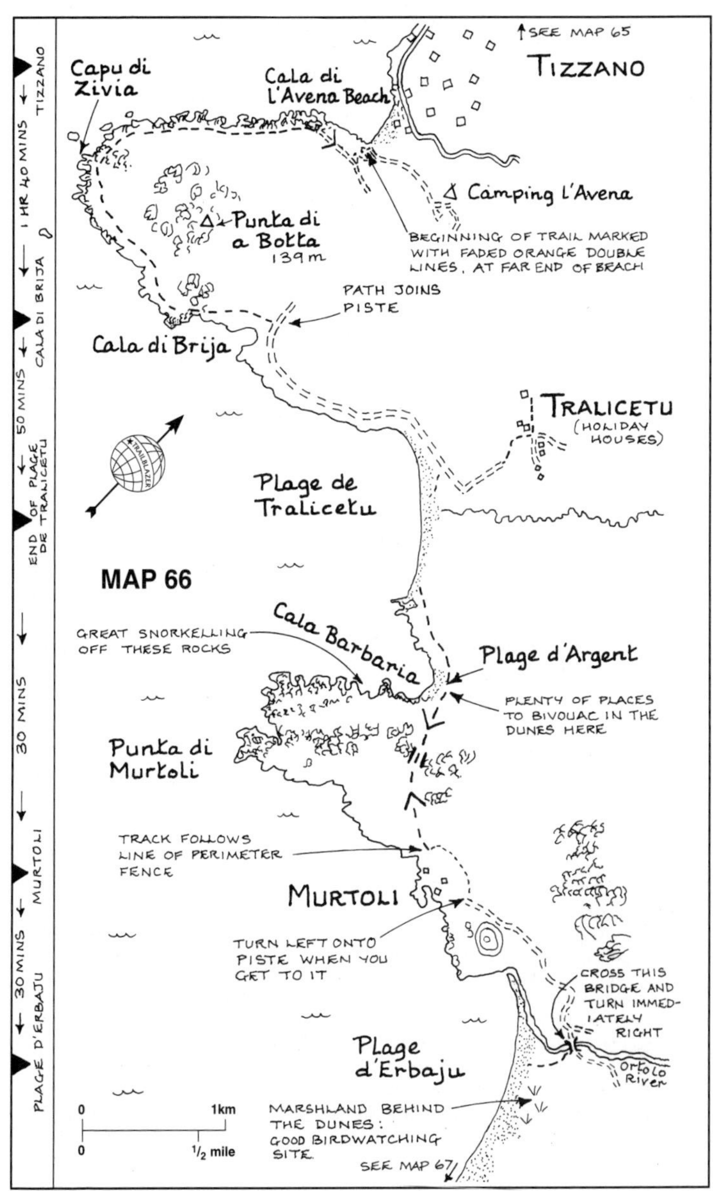

TIZZANO
1 HR 40 MINS
CALA DI BRIJA
50 MINS
END OF PLAGE DE TRALICETU
30 MINS
MURTOLI
30 MINS
PLAGE D'ERBAJU
SEE MAP 65
TIZZANO
Capu di Zivia
Cala di L'Avena Beach
Camping L'Avena
Punta di a Botta 139m
BEGINNING OF TRAIL MARKED WITH FADED ORANGE DOUBLE LINES, AT FAR END OF BEACH
PATH JOINS PISTE
Cala di Brija
TRALICETU (HOLIDAY HOUSES)
Plage de Tralicetu
MAP 66
Cala Barbaria
GREAT SNORKELLING OFF THESE ROCKS
Plage d'Argent
PLENTY OF PLACES TO BIVOUAC IN THE DUNES HERE
Punta di Murtoli
TRACK FOLLOWS LINE OF PERIMETER FENCE
MURTOLI
TURN LEFT ONTO PISTE WHEN YOU GET TO IT
CROSS THIS BRIDGE AND TURN IMMEDIATELY RIGHT
Plage d'Erbaju
Ortolo River
0 1km
0 1/2 mile
MARSHLAND BEHIND THE DUNES: GOOD BIRDWATCHING SITE
SEE MAP 67

sticks close to sea level all the way around **Capu di Zivia**, as dramatic rock formations tower above the path. Once you're around the headland a wonderful view opens up, down to Rocher du Lion (Lion Rock) and its adjacent watchtower, whose dramatic profiles dominate the rest of the day.

Your first glimpse of the awesome **Plage de Tralicetu**, a kilometre-long strip of shining orange sand backed by dunes, comes a little over an hour into the walk as you emerge from the rocks above secluded Cala di Brija. Once at stream level the path meets a rutted piste, which takes you all the way around the hillside to Tralicetu. Don't be tempted to cut down to the track hugging the coast on your right: it peters out before the beach.

Tralicetu is accessible by motor vehicle but remains one of the few beaches in Corsica where you can be sure to have plenty of room to yourself, even in high season. Its most beautiful corner is a cove called **Cala Barbaria**, at the far south-western end, where the aptly-named **Plage d'Argent**, a more sheltered beach of perfect silver sand, is secluded by rocks that are great to snorkel around. Behind it, hollows beneath some of the wind-deformed pines dotted around the higher reaches of the dunes make great bivouac sites, although once again water is a problem.

The path turns inland slightly at the top of the rise dividing Plage d'Argent from Plage de Tralicetu and then heads south-west for the gap in the outcrop atop Punta di Cala Barbaria. Descending through maquis on the other side you get tantalizing glimpses of Erbaju, a beach even more impressive than the previous one. However, to reach it you have to first negotiate one of the few man-made obstacles on this path.

Surrounding the estate of **Murtoli**, whose superbly renovated, buttress-walled tower cottages are visible in the foreground, is a boundary fence which the path follows closely until it reaches a piste and gateway marked 'Proprieté Privé'. At this stage you're technically on private land. To get off it and onto the beach ahead you have to follow the piste inland for around 1km until you reach a bridge across the Ortolo River. There you turn sharply right and follow the line of the field down to the dunes.

Roccapina's hidden treasure

The rocks around the Roccapina watchtower are synonymous with the name of the nineteenth-century bandit Barritonu, who made his hideout here. Local legend has it that this is also where he buried his most famous booty, a hoard of jewels salvaged from the wreck of a P&O liner, *Tasmania*, which ran aground on the nearby Des Moines Rocks in 1887. Barritonu is said to have hidden the gems in a cave, whose precise location he took with him first to prison, and then to his grave. As yet no-one has found a stash of valuables at Roccapina but some credence has been lent to the story by the discovery that among *Tasmania*'s cargo was a consignment of gemstones gifted by India's wealthiest maharajahs to the Queen Empress Victoria on her silver jubilee.

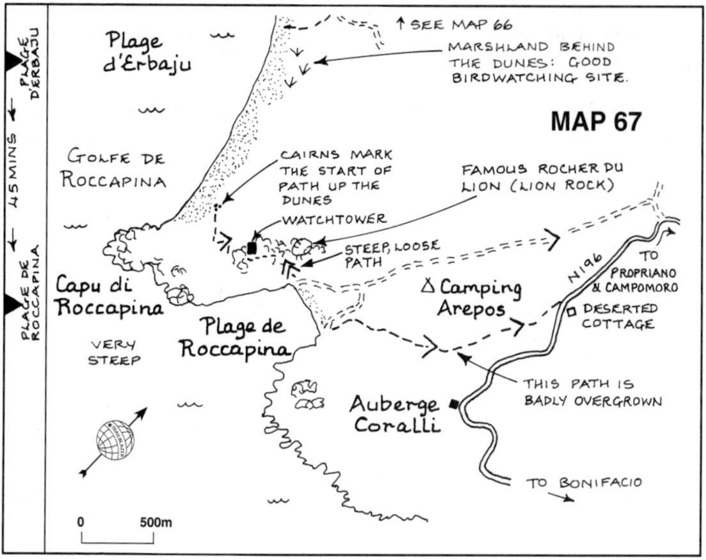

If at any stage you're stopped by an angry-looking landowner or farm manager, smile and politely ask the way to Erbaju beach. The confusion stems from the fact that although you've a right to walk along the coastline here, the only safe way to cross the potentially dangerous mouth of the Ortolo is via the estate's own bridge.

Running the gauntlet of baying hunting hounds and unfriendly farmers seems a small price to pay once you reach **Plage d'Erbaju**, as sublime a stretch of sand as you'll find anywhere in the Mediterranean. Overlooked by the famous Rocher du Lion and its neighbouring tower, with a dramatic amphitheatre of maquis-covered hills as a backdrop, the sand bends south in a graceful arc with not so much as a car park or ice-cream stand behind it. Access is denied to drivers (who'd have to cross the estate land to get here) so for once this is truly a beach you can reach only on foot or by boat.

It takes a good half-hour to plod the two kilometres from one end of Erbaju to the other. Before reaching the headland, however, keep an eye out for the cairns indicating a route through the scrub and dunes on your left to the base of Capu di Roccapina. Soon you'll pick up a clearer path that zigzags up to the ridge and thence north-east to the base of the Genoan tower. From here a very steep and, in places, slippery descent through tall maquis brings you to **Plage de Roccapina**. Visible from the main road and renowned for the weirdly life-like granite lion which presides over it, this beach attracts its fair share of visitors, even early in the season. What it lacks in wildness it more than makes up for in the colour of its sand and water: a stunning combination of pearl white and brilliant turquoise that wouldn't look out of place in the Seychelles.

Fittingly, the official end of this walk is marked by the first view, best enjoyed from the foot of the tower, across the Straits of Bonifacio to Sardinia's mountainous coastline.

ROCCAPINA

Reach Roccapina early enough in the day and you might be able to get away on the last of Eurocorse Voyage's two or three daily Porto-Vecchio–Ajaccio **buses**, which passes through around 3pm; check the exact time with the bus company (☎ 04.95.70.13.83).

The bus stops outside Auberge Coralli on the main road, a good hour's walk from the beach. The most direct (though far from easiest) way there is to follow the path that winds uphill from the car park at the far south-eastern end of the beach, coming out on the N196 1km north of the auberge. The path is totally overgrown in places with particularly spiny maquis but it does save you the 4km walk up the piste past the campsite and then back down the main road (see map, p309).

Auberge Coralli (☎ 04.95.73.45.56; open April–Oct) is the most comfortable – indeed the only – hotel for miles. Unfortunately it only rents out rooms by the week but non-residents are welcome to eat at their popular terrace restaurant, which enjoys fine views over Roccapina bay and serves quality local seafood à la carte, in addition to a 12.20€ *menu fixe*.

For campers and bivouackers, ***Camping Arepos*** (☎ 04.95.77.19.30; open May–September), on the valley floor 500m inland from the beach, is a cheap and cheerful alternative run by the local municipality. Basic supplies are sold at its small shop.

APPENDIX A: FRENCH/CORSICAN GLOSSARY

balisage waymarking
bandit d'honneur outlaw who, by tradition, has been forced into banditry after committing a vendetta murder
bastelle* Corsican pasty, usually filled with spinach and ewe's cheese
belvédère natural balcony or viewpoint
bergerie shepherds' settlement/hut
bocca* pass
brêche gap in a rocky ridge serving as a pass
buvette snack van
cala* beach
camping sauvage wild camping (ie not on a designated campsite)
canastrelli* traditional Corsican biscuits
capitainerie harbour master's office
capu peak*
castagna* chestnut
casteddu* Megalithic castle
châtaigne/iers chestnut/chestnut tree
chiostru* circular stone shelter for storing and drying chestnuts
cirque natural amphitheatre at head of valley
col pass
contrôleur ticket inspector
curé priest
département administrative region
étang lagoon
étape stage (of walk)
farina* (chestnut) flour
fiadone Corsican flan made with chestnuts and honey
flèchage waymarking
foce pass
funtana spring
gardien warden of a refuge
gérant warden of a gîte d'étape
Grande Barriére nickname for the Paglia Orba massif
Grande Randonnée French Trekking Authority's official designation for a special class of long-distance routes, all numbered separately
Hôtel de Ville town hall
lavoir village laundry tank
libre service self service (supermarket)
mairie town hall (mayor's office)
maison forestière forest hut (for use by forestry staff)
maquis* Corsican scrub
maquisard Resistance fighter in World War II
menhir standing stone
mouflon rare Corsican mountain sheep (see p134)
navette shuttle bus
névé patch of eternal snow
ONF French national forestry service
Parc Naturel Régional Corse (PNRC) regional nature park of Corsica (see p63)

* = Corsican word

partage des eaux watershed (see p61)
passarelle (suspendu) (suspension) footbridge
pétanque boules (French bowls)
piste unmade, dirt road
piste forestière forest track
polenda* traditional Corsican dish – a paste made from chestnut flour
polyphony/ies choral singing
pozzi*/pozzines high-altitude streams running through spongy turf banks
Préfet French government's top representative in Corsica
rau* stream
ravin gully
reglement de compte 'settling of scores' – a vendetta term
sac allegé 'lightened bag' – a bag-carrying service offered by some trekking companies
scandule* roof tile
séchoir drying shelter (for chestnuts)
Topoguide French trekking authority (FFRP)'s official route guide, featuring topographical maps
torregiani* wardens of Genoan watchtowers
torri* Genoan watchtowers
trinighellu* Corsica's diminutive train
vendetta/vinditta* feud

* = Corsican word

APPENDIX B: USEFUL WORDS AND PHRASES

As English is not widely spoken or understood in Corsica, you'll almost certainly have to speak French at some stage during your trek. The following list of words and phrases is designed as a practical aid, to help you converse with fellow trekkers, understand directions and weather forecasts, secure accommodation and find what you need in the towns and villages. An additional glossary, explaining the meaning of words and phrases that appear in italics in this book, appears above.

In the following list (m) designates a masculine noun (to be preceded by 'un' or 'le'), (f) a feminine noun (to be used with 'une' or 'la') and (pl) a plural (to be used with 'les').

Basic words and phrases

When addressing people in French always use Monsieur for a man, Madame for a woman and Mademoiselle for a young woman. Bonjour alone is not enough.

Hello/Good morning/Good day	*Bonjour*
Good afternoon	*Bon aprés midi*
Good evening/good night	*Bonsoir/bonne nuit*
Goodbye	*Au revoir*
Hi	*Salut*
Help!	*Au secours!*
How are you?/Fine thanks	*Ça va?/Oui ça va*
Do you speak English?	*Est-ce vous parlez Anglais?*
I don't understand	*Je ne comprends pas*
Excuse me	*Pardon*

How much is this please?	*C'est combien s'il vous plaît?*
Please	*S'il vous plaît*
Thank you	*Merci beaucoup/Tiran graze**
today/tomorrow	*aujourd'hui/demain*
the morning/afternoon/evening	*le matin/l'après-midi/le soir*
open/closed	*ouvert/fermé*
more/less	*plus/moins*
hot/cold	*chaud/froid*

General vocabulary

bank	*banque* (f)	post office	*poste* (f)
stamp	*timbre* (m)	money	*argent* (m)
grocery shop	*épicerie* (f)	supermarket	*supermarché* (m)
bakery	*boulangerie* (f)	tobacconist's	*tabac* (m)
launderette	*laverie automatique* (f)	toilet	*toilettes* (pl)
police	*gendarmes* (pl)	police station	*gendarmerie* (m)
telephone booth	*cabine téléphonique* (f)	phone card	*télecarte*
mobile phone	*portable* (m)	timetable	*horaire* (m)
methylated spirits	*alcool à bruler* (m)	left-luggage office	*consigne* (f)

toilet block (on campsite) *bloc sanitaire* (m)
slide film *pellicule diapositive* (f)
cash dispenser/ATM *distributeur (automatique) de billets* (m)
tourist office *office de tourisme* (m) or *syndicat d'initiative* (m)

Directions and travel

(to the) left	*(à) gauche*	straight on	*tout droit*
(to the) right	*(à) droite*	behind	*derrière*
north	*nord*	in front of	*devant*
south	*sud*	before	*avant*
east	*est*	after	*après*
west	*ouest*	under	*sous*
single ticket	*billet simple*	over	*sur*
return ticket	*billet aller-retour*		
near	*près de*	far	*loin*

Where is . . .? *Où se trouve ....?*
the bus station *la terminal routière* or *gare routière* (f)
the train station *la gare SNCF* (f) the airport *l'aéroport* (m)
the ferry terminal *la gare maritime* (f) the bridge *le pont* (m)
What time does the train/bus leave? *Il part à quelle heure, le train/bus s'il vous plaît?*
What time does the train/bus arrive? *Il arrive à quelle heure, le train/bus s'il vous plaît*
Is this the road to ....? *Est-ce que c'est la route à .... ?*
How many kilometres to .....? *Combien de kilomètres à ....?*

On the trail

trekking	*randonnée* (f)	trekker	*randonneur* (m)/*randonneuse* (f)
footpath	*sentier* (m)	mule track	*chemin muletier* (m)
waymarking	*balisage* (m)	well/badly waymarked	*bien/mal fléché*
stage	*étape* (f)	slope	*pente* (f)
zigzags	*lacets* (pl)	steep	*raide*
descent	*descente* (f)	ascent	*ascension* (f)
map	*carte* (f)	compass	*boussole* (f)
rucksack	*sac à dos* (m)	head-torch	*lampe frontale* (f)
water bottle	*gourde* (f)	corkscrew	*tire bouchon* (m)

shepherds' huts *bergeries* (f)
signboard *panneau* (m)
provisions/re-provisioning *ravitaillement* (m)
slippery *glisseux*
to climb *grimper*
to go up again *remonter*
to follow *suivre* or *longer*
suspension bridge *passarelle suspendue* (f)
pocket knife *couteau de poche* (or *Opinel*)
Is this the Mare a Mare path? *Est-ce que c'est bien le sentier Mare a Mare?*

sleeping bag *sac de couchage* (m)
spring *source* or *fontaine* (f)
It's steep! (colloquial) *Ça grimpe!*
to cross *traverser* or *franchir*
to go down again *redescendre*
to bear or turn (left) *bifurquer (à gauche)*

Landscape

mountain *montagne* (f)
pass *col* (m)/*bocca** (f)
summit *cime* (f)/*sommet* (m)
plateau *plateau* (m)/*pianu** (m)
forest *forêt* (f)
wood *bosquet* (m)
gorge or ravine *défile* (m)
slab *dalle* (f)
rock *rocher* (m)
cliff *falaise* (f)

ridge *crête* (f)
valley *vallée* (f)
river *rivière* (f)
stream *ruisseau* (m)
mountain stream *torrent* (m)
waterfall *cascade* (f)
boulder choke *éboulis* (m)
snow patch *névé* (f)
rocky *rocailleux*

Health

blister *ampoule* (f)
sun cream *crême solaire* (f)
sprained ankle *cheville tordue* (f)
broken leg *jambe cassée*
sore knees *mal aux genoux* (m)
doctor *docteur* (m)
toilet paper *papier hygènique* (m)
tampon *tampon* (m)
It hurts *Ça me fait mal*

plaster *pincement* (m)
sunstroke/sunburn *coup de soleil* (m)
knee *genou* (m)
twisted leg *jambe tordue* (f)
toothache *mal aux dents* (m)
dentist *dentiste* (m)
ear plugs *bouches d'oreille* (f)
condom *préservatif* (m)

Weather

weather *temps* (m)
good weather *beau temps* (m)
rain *pluie* (f)
drizzle *crachin* (m)
snow *neige* (f)
ice *glace* (f)
storm/stormy *orage* (m)/*orageux*
lightning *foudre* (f)
flooding *innondation* (f)

weather forecast *météo* (m)
bad weather *mauvais temps (m)*
wind *vent/venteux*
strong/weak (wind) *fort/faible*
hail *grêle* (f)
fog *brouillard* (m)
mist *brûme* (f)
thunder *tonnerre* (m)

Accommodation (see also pp75-79)

accommodation *hébergement* (m)
hotel *hôtel* (m)
hostel *gîte d'étape* (m)
B&B *chambre d'hôte* (f)
municipal campsite *camping municipal* (m)
bed *lit* (m)
breakfast included *petit déjeuner compris*
warden (refuge) *gardien(ne)*(m/f)

mountain hut *refuge* (m)
dormitory *dortoire* (m)
bivouac area *aire de bivouac* (f)
restaurant/inn *auberge* (f)
campsite *le camping* (m)
one night's stay *nuitée* (f)
half-board *demi-pension* (f)
warden (gîte d'étape) *gérant*

boss/proprietor	*patron(ne)* (m/f)
I'd like to reserve	*Je voudrais reserver ....*
a room for one/two/three people	*une chambre pour un(e)/deux/trois person(ne/s)*
with/without a shower	*avec/sans douche*
with/without washbasin	*avec/sans lavabo*
with separate toilet	*avec WC à l'étage*
en suite	*avec douche-WC dans la chambre*
with a balcony	*avec balcon* (m)
Can I see the room?	*Est-ce que je peux voir la chambre?*
Do you accept credit cards?	*Est-ce vous acceptez les cartes de crédit?*

Eating and drinking

breakfast	*petit déjeuner* (m)	lunch	*déjeuner* (m)/*repas du midi* (m)
dinner	*repas du soir* (m)	snack	*casse croûte* (f)
desssert	*déssert* (m)	bill	*l'addition* (f)
service included	*service compris*	service not included	*service non compris*
set menu	*le menu/menu fixe* (m)	Corsican menu	*menu corse* (m)
menu	*carte* (f)	meal(s) of the day	*plat(s) du jour* (m)
pancake shop	*crêperie* (f)	vegetarian	*végétarien(ne)* (m/f)
biscuits	*biscuits*(pl)	cheese	*fromage* (m)
bread	*pain* (m)	egg	*oeuf* (m)
fish	*poisson* (m)	meat	*viande* (f)
pasta	*les pâtse* (pl)	noodles	*nouille(s)* (f/pl)
salt	*sel* (m)	pepper	*poivre* (m)
vegetables	*légumes* (pl)	sandwich	*sandwich* (m) or *panini* (m)
ewe's cheese	*brocciu*	warm goat's cheese	*chèvre chaud*
cured meat	*charcuterie* (f)	dry sausage	*saucisson sec* (m)
liver sausage	*figatellu*	morel (mushroom)	*morille* (f)
Moroccan stew	*tagine*		
aniseed spirit	*pastis*	local spirit	*eau de vie*
wine	*vin* (m)	jug (of wine)	*pichet* (m)
beer	*bière* (f)	milk	*lait* (m)
tea	*thé* (m)	coffee	*café* (m)

Numerals

1	*un/une*	19	*dix-neuf*	80	*quatre-vingts*
2	*deux*	20	*vingt*	90	*quatre-vingt-dix*
3	*trois*	21	*vingt et un*	95	*quatre-vingt-quinze*
4	*quatre*	22	*vingt-deux*	100	*cent*
5	*cinq*	23	*vingt-trois*	150	*cent-cinquante*
6	*six*	24	*vingt-quatre*	200	*deux cents*
7	*sept*	25	*vingt-cinq*	300	*trois cents*
8	*huit*	26	*vingt-six*	400	*quatre cents*
9	*neuf*	27	*vingt-sept*	500	*cinq cents*
10	*dix*	28	*vingt-huit*	600	*six cents*
11	*onze*	29	*vingt-neuf*	700	*sept cents*
12	*douze*	30	*trente*	800	*huit cents*
13	*treize*	40	*quarante*	900	*neuf cents*
14	*quatorze*	50	*cinquante*	1000	*mille*
15	*quinze*	60	*soixante*	5000	*cinq mille*
16	*seize*	70	*soixante-dix*	1,000,000	*un million*
17	*dix-sept*	71	*soixante et onze*		
18	*dix-huit*	75	*soixante-quinze*		

INDEX

Trekking in the Pyrenees *Douglas Streatfeild-James*
2nd edition, £11.99, Can$27.95 US$18.95
ISBN 1 873756 50 X, 320pp, 95 maps, 55 colour photos
All the main trails along the France-Spain border including the GR10 (France) coast to coast hike and the GR11 (Spain) from Roncesvalles to Andorra, plus many shorter routes. 90 route maps include walking times and places to stay. Expanded to include greater coverage of routes in Spain. *'Readily accessible, well-written and most readable...'* ***John Cleare***

Trekking in the Dolomites *Henry Stedman*
256 pages, 52 trail maps, 13 town plans, 30 colour photos
ISBN 1 873756 34 8, *1st edition,* £11.99, US$17.95
The Dolomites region of northern Italy encompasses some of the most beautiful mountain scenery in Europe. This new guide features selected routes including Alta Via II, a West-East traverse and other trails, plus detailed guides to Cortina, Bolzano, Bressanone and 10 other towns. Also includes full colour flora section and bird identification guide.

West Highland Way *Charlie Loram*
224pp, 48 maps, 10 town plans, 40 colour photos
ISBN 1 873756 54 2, £9.99, Can$22.95, US$16.95 *1st edition*
Scotland's best-known long distance footpath passes through some of the most spectacular scenery in all of Britain. From the outskirts of Glasgow it winds for 95 miles (153km) along the wooded banks of Loch Lomond, across the wilderness of Rannoch Moor, over the mountains above Glencoe to a dramatic finish at the foot of Britain's highest peak – Ben Nevis. Includes Glasgow city guide.

Trekking in the Moroccan Atlas *Richard Knight*
256 pages, 53 maps, 30 colour photos
ISBN 1 873756 35 6, *1st edition,* £11.99, US$17.95
The Atlas mountains in southern Morocco provide one of the most spectacular hiking destinations in Africa. This new guide includes route descriptions and detailed maps for the best Atlas treks in the Toubkal, M'goun, Sirwa and Jbel Sahro regions. Places to stay, walking times and points of interest are all included, plus town guides to Marrakesh and Ouarzazate.

The Inca Trail, Cuzco & Machu Picchu *Richard Danbury*
2nd edition, £10.99, Can$24.95, US$18.95
ISBN 1 873756 64 X, 288pp, 45 maps, 24 colour photos
The Inca Trail from Cuzco to Machu Picchu is South America's most popular hike. This practical guide includes 20 detailed trail maps, plans of eight Inca sites, plus guides to Cuzco and Machu Picchu. *"Danbury's research is thorough...you need this one'.* ***The Sunday Times***

Trekking in Ladakh *Charlie Loram*
288 pages, 70 maps, 24 colour photos
ISBN 1 873756 30 5, *2nd edition,* £10.99, US$18.95
Since Kashmir became off-limits, foreign visitors to India have been coming to this spectacular Himalayan region in ever-increasing numbers. Fully revised and extended 2nd edition of Charlie Loram's practical guide. Includes 70 detailed walking maps, a Leh city guide plus information on getting to Ladakh. *'Extensive...and well researched'.* ***Climber Magazine***

For more trekking guides, rail guides and route guides see overleaf

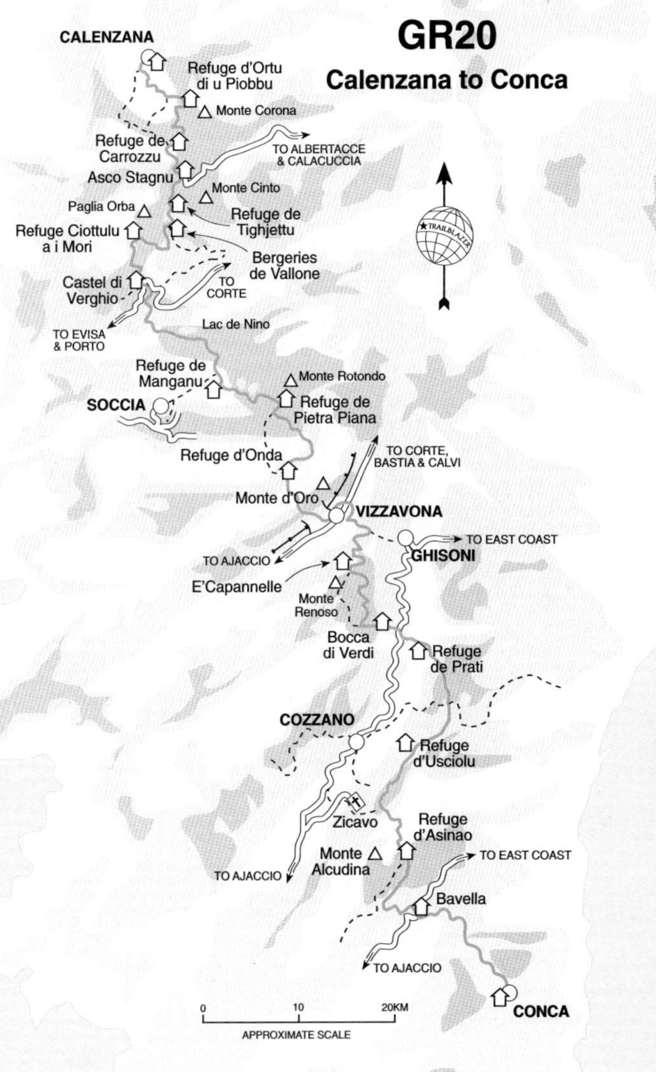
GR20
Calenzana to Conca
CALENZANA
Refuge d'Ortu di u Piobbu
Monte Corona
Refuge de Carrozzu
TO ALBERTACCE & CALACUCCIA
Asco Stagnu
Monte Cinto
Paglia Orba
Refuge de Tighjettu
Refuge Ciottulu a i Mori
Bergeries de Vallone
Castel di Verghio
TO CORTE
TO EVISA & PORTO
Lac de Nino
TRAILBLAZER
Refuge de Manganu
Monte Rotondo
SOCCIA
Refuge de Pietra Piana
Refuge d'Onda
TO CORTE, BASTIA & CALVI
Monte d'Oro
VIZZAVONA
TO EAST COAST
GHISONI
TO AJACCIO
E'Capannelle
Monte Renoso
Bocca di Verdi
Refuge de Prati
COZZANO
Refuge d'Usciolu
Zicavo
Refuge d'Asinao
Monte Alcudina
TO EAST COAST
TO AJACCIO
Bavella
TO AJACCIO
CONCA
0
10
20KM
APPROXIMATE SCALE

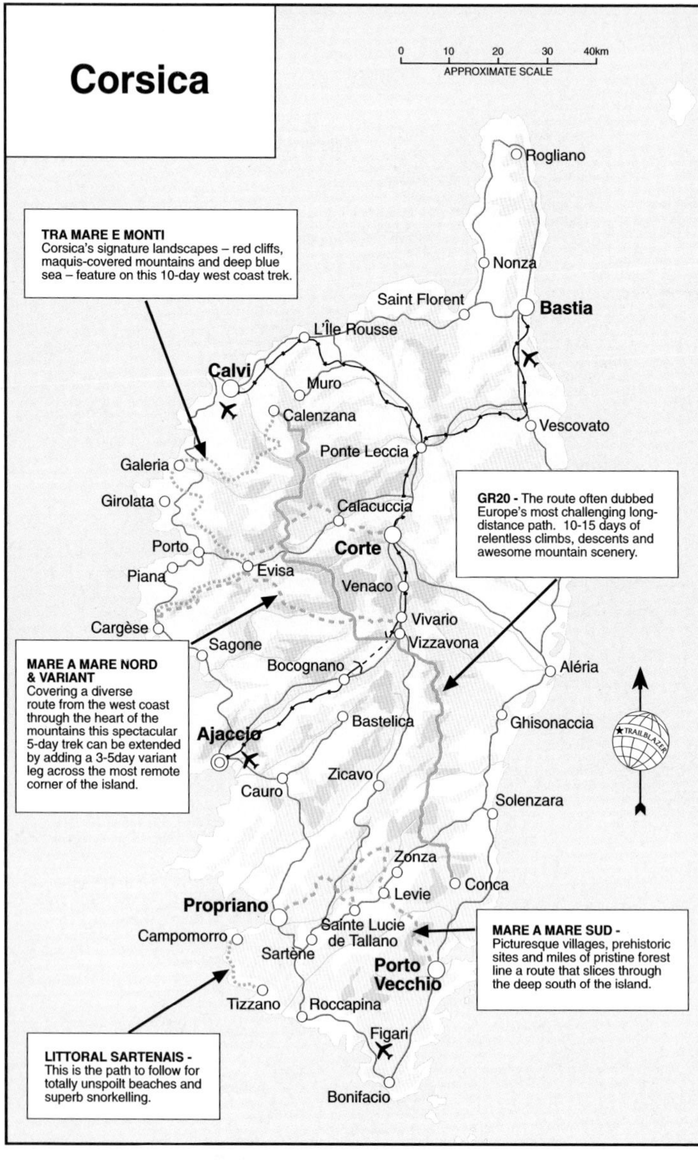
Corsica
0
10
20
30
40km
APPROXIMATE SCALE
TRA MARE E MONTI
Corsica's signature landscapes – red cliffs, maquis-covered mountains and deep blue sea – feature on this 10-day west coast trek.
GR20 - The route often dubbed Europe's most challenging long-distance path. 10-15 days of relentless climbs, descents and awesome mountain scenery.
MARE A MARE NORD & VARIANT
Covering a diverse route from the west coast through the heart of the mountains this spectacular 5-day trek can be extended by adding a 3-5day variant leg across the most remote corner of the island.
MARE A MARE SUD -
Picturesque villages, prehistoric sites and miles of pristine forest line a route that slices through the deep south of the island.
LITTORAL SARTENAIS -
This is the path to follow for totally unspoilt beaches and superb snorkelling.
Rogliano
Nonza
Saint Florent
Bastia
L'Île Rousse
Calvi
Muro
Calenzana
Vescovato
Ponte Leccia
Galeria
Girolata
Calacuccia
Corte
Porto
Piana
Evisa
Venaco
Vivario
Cargèse
Vizzavona
Sagone
Bocognano
Aléria
Ajaccio
Bastelica
Ghisonaccia
TRAILBLAZER
Cauro
Zicavo
Solenzara
Zonza
Conca
Levie
Propriano
Sainte Lucie de Tallano
Campomorro
Sartène
Porto Vecchio
Tizzano
Roccapina
Figari
Bonifacio